TELEVISION IN POLITICS
ITS USES AND INFLUENCE

Television in Politics

ITS USES AND INFLUENCE

by
JAY G. BLUMLER
and DENIS McQUAIL

The University of Chicago Press

Library of Congress Catalog Card Number: 69–12843
The University of Chicago Press, Chicago 60637
Faber and Faber Ltd., London, W.C.1

CONTENTS

v

CONTENTS

ACKNOWLEDGEMENTS

While the authors assume full responsibility for the ensuing text, they appreciate that it would not have seen the light of day without the assistance of many indispensable collaborators.

Miss Alison J. Ewbank, our Research Assistant, played a substantial part in the organization and execution of the several surveys reported in this volume, and she processed masses of data with imagination, meticulous accuracy, and good humour. Our Secretaries—Miss Frances V. Tipple and Miss Celia Parkinson—applied high professional standards and inexhaustible patience to the typing and duplicating of countless tables and chapter drafts. For an excellent public response to the main survey, we are indebted: to the 748 electors of West Leeds and Pudsey who consented to be interviewed on three different occasions in 1964; to the army of 50 interviewers who responded so constructively to our many instructions; and to Mrs. Pamela Rattee, our Fieldwork Supervisor, who marshalled and advised that force with both energy and charm. Our persistent and complex needs for statistical guidance were skilfully met by Mr. R. E. A. Mapes, Director, Nuffield Research Unit in Statistical Sociology, University of Keele; Dr. J. A. John, Department of Mathematics, University of Southampton; and Dr. Robert W. Hiorns, Department of Biomathematics, University of Oxford. For the generous provision of information-processing facilities, we are indebted to Professor G. B. Cook of the Computing Laboratory of the University of Leeds, and to all the members of his staff; and particularly to Mr. B. R. Calvert, Administrative Assistant in charge of the Data Processing Section of the Registrar's Department, who enabled us to use Hollerith machines which were

ACKNOWLEDGEMENTS

not originally intended to serve research purposes. The presentation of some of our material in the form of graphs was made possible by the attractive draughtsmanship of Mr. B. Emmison, University Artist, Department of Photography.

Consultations with many academic colleagues in Leeds and elsewhere enhanced both the precision and the depth of our enquiry. Our heaviest demands were directed at Dr. Mark Abrams, the Chairman of Research Services Ltd., whose wisdom was exceeded only by his generosity. A formative contribution to the design of the investigation resulted from an early discussion with Professor Donald E. Stokes, of the Survey Research Center of the University of Michigan, and with Dr. David E. Butler of Nuffield College, Oxford. Professor Martin Harrison, of the Department of Political Institutions at the University of Keele, may be regarded virtually as a contributor in his own right to this volume, for he has unstintingly conveyed the lessons of his experience of studying election television in many private conversations and in detailed and thoughtful comments on a previous draft of the manuscript. Mr. Brian Emmett, now Head, then Deputy Head, of the Audience Research Department of the BBC, was another source of shrewd advice. We are grateful to him and to Mr. Robert Silvey, former Head of the ARD, for having permitted us to distribute a questionnaire to the members of the BBC Viewing Panel. Other targets of our requests for comments and suggestions, who did not send us away empty-handed, include:

Professor Samuel Becker, Division of Television, Radio, and Film, University of Iowa.

Professor A. H. Birch, Department of Political Studies, University of Hull.

Dr. George Jones, London School of Economics.

Dr. Anthony King, Department of Government, University of Essex.

Professor Peter Nettl, Department of Sociology, University of Pennsylvania.

Professor Richard Rose, Department of Politics, University of Strathclyde.

Professor Percy Tannenbaum, The Annenburg School of Communications, University of Pennsylvania.

We are pleased to acknowledge the encouragement which

ACKNOWLEDGEMENTS

we received when analysing our results from Professor Morris Janowitz of the University of Chicago. The completed manuscript also benefited greatly from an attentive reading by Professor Paul F. Lazarsfeld, of the University of Columbia, and from his imaginative approach to the interpretation of sociological evidence.

Survey research is expensive, and we are deeply grateful to Granada Television for having made this investigation financially possible, and in particular to Sir Gerald Barry for the expression of a sustained interest in this study. For meeting the costs incurred in re-interviewing certain voters who had participated in an earlier election study in 1959, we are obliged to the Institute of Electoral Research. We were helped, too, by the continuing support of a university steering committee, which was set up to guide our endeavours, and by its forbearance with the sometimes laborious pace of our work. Of its members, Professor E. Grebenik, Head of the Department of Social Studies, and Mr. Derek J. G. Holroyde, Director of the University Television Service, were inevitably most familiar with our aims and anxieties.

Finally, we owe a very special debt to the late Dr. Joseph Trenaman, the first Granada Television Research Fellow. Many of our techniques for measuring communications effects derived from his pioneering enquiries; in addition we were conscious of the exacting standards of academic integrity and achievement which he set. We should be more than content if this volume were deemed a worthy successor to *Television and the Political Image*.

JAY G. BLUMLER
DENIS McQUAIL

FOREWORD TO THE
AMERICAN EDITION

ELECTIONS AND
BROADCASTING IN BRITAIN

This book presents the results of a British investigation of the
role of television in a modern election campaign. It is
shaped by two equally central concerns. First, how do voters
wish to *use* political programmes when following a campaign?
Second, how does televised propaganda *influence* their political
outlook?

The first question has been approached from several angles in
this study. It examines viewers' reasons for watching and avoiding political programmes. It charts their preferences about the
format of political broadcasts. And it connects those preferences
with voters' attitudes towards election campaigning itself. The
second question involves an analysis of the impact of a television
campaign on information levels, voting intentions, attitudes
towards the competing parties, images of the rival leaders, and
awareness of current issues. These two main bodies of evidence
are not considered in isolation from each other, however, for the
entire study rests on a hypothesis which links them together. Its
crux is the assumption that influence depends on motivation.
That is, we supposed that the effects of election television on a
voter's political thinking depend on the motivations that have
encouraged him to follow a campaign.

In order to test this assumption, approximately 750 electors, who resided in two parliamentary constituencies in Yorkshire, were interviewed on three different occasions during the British General Election of 1964. But before turning to the evidence they provided, American readers may welcome a chance to orient themselves to certain features of the British scene. This foreword aims to answer three questions that might be asked about the context of our study. First, how are General Elections conducted in Britain? Second, around what parties, leaders, and issues was the British General Election of 1964 fought? Third, how is political broadcasting arranged in Britain?[1]

The system of parliamentary elections in Britain

An American observer of a British General Election would inevitably notice several striking differences from the conduct of a presidential election in the United States. Instead of the American pattern of a prolonged, diffuse, and colorful period of electioneering, a British campaign is short, uniform, and rather subdued – lacking, for example, the excitement generated by primary elections and nominating conventions. In Britain the personal fortunes of the top political leaders are not so directly at the mercy of the voters as they are in the United States. They invariably hold 'safe seats' in the House of Commons (ones they can count on winning), and even the leader of the defeated party normally continues to serve in an official and paid capacity as Leader of the Opposition in Parliament. Campaign platforms are not revealed until the date of the election is known, and then a concentrated struggle is waged by the dominant parties, each of which presents a more or less united front to the electorate from one end of the country to the other.

The basic facts about British election procedures can be briefly summarized. During a General Election only the 630 seats in the House of Commons are contested. Of course the House of Commons is far more powerful than the House of

---

[1] The following writings may be recommended to those readers who wish to consult a fuller treatment of these matters: Leonard, R. L., *Elections in Britain*, D. Van Nostrand Co., Ltd., Princeton, N.J., 1968; Butler, D. E. and King, Anthony, *The British General Election of 1964*, Macmillan & Co., Ltd., New York, 1965; and Becker, Samuel, L., 'Politics and Broadcasting in Britain', *Quarterly Journal of Speech*, Vol. LIII, No. 1, 1967, pp. 34–43.

Lords (the second chamber of the British legislature), membership of which is not achieved by election. Neither is any member of the British executive directly elected. The leader of that political party which wins a majority of the seats in the House of Commons becomes the Prime Minister, and he forms a government largely from members of his party in the House. In the post-war period Labor administrations resulted from the elections of 1945 and 1950 and Conservative administrations from the elections of 1951, 1955, and 1959.

At a General Election all subjects over the age of 21 – except peers, felons, and the insane – are eligible to vote. Since registration procedures are simple and effortless (the head of each household is merely required annually to complete a form, giving details of all eligible voters living at his address), a high turnout at the polls is customary (77·1 per cent in 1964). The 630 seats at stake in an election are based on single-member constituencies, the territorial boundaries of which are occasionally re-drawn to ensure that they cater for approximately equal-sized electorates. The sample members of our survey were drawn from the constituencies of West Leeds (one of six seats in the city of Leeds) and Pudsey (a semi-rural, semi-urban area just outside Leeds). Most constituencies are fought by two or three contenders, depending on whether the Conservative and Labor candidates are joined by a Liberal – although a few seats may also attract Communist, Welsh and Scottish Nationalist, or other independent candidates. The individual who receives the largest number of votes is returned as his constituency's Member of Parliament. In 1964 three candidates stood in both West Leeds and Pudsey (Conservative, Labor, and Liberal), and Labor was victorious in the former seat while the Conservatives won the latter.

Perhaps four important features of British electoral practises should be borne in mind by readers of this book. First, the timing of a General Election is quite irregular – in contrast to the fixed four-year duration of a presidential term. The interval between two British elections must not exceed five years, but provided the incumbent administration retains the confidence of a majority in the House of Commons, it may call an election whenever it wishes. Guided by opinion poll findings, a government will aim nowadays to stage an election at the height of its

FOREWORD TO THE AMERICAN EDITION

popularity. The 1964 election came right at the end of the Conservatives' five-year spell of office, however, because, after having met a series of political reverses from 1961 to 1963, the government needed all the time that the system allowed to try to recover its lost ground. In fact when the 1964 campaign began, the opinion polls showed the Conservative and Labor Parties to be on more or less equal terms.

Second, a British campaign is a highly concentrated affair—in contrast to the straggling and protracted events of a presidential election. Officially it consists of only 17 days (excluding Sundays and holidays) between the formal dissolution of Parliament and Polling Day. Although in recent years the major parties have tended to mount between-election advertising campaigns on posters and in the press, the main vote-winning efforts are still confined to the period of the official campaign, when a barrage of media coverage supplements the parties' own activities. Uncertainty about the timing of an election favors this approach, for no party wishes to risk shooting its bolt (and emptying its treasury) at an electorally insignificant time. In addition, the parties are allocated a generous quota of broadcasting time for use in an official campaign—in contrast to the much more scattered transmissions of party broadcasts in out-of-election periods. During the 17 days of the 1964 campaign, for example, the three main parties put out a total of 13 television broadcasts and 18 radio broadcasts between them. Of course such a short campaign eases the lot of would-be investigators of the impact of election television. It is feasible to ask respondents about political materials they have received during the $2\frac{1}{2}$-week period of an official campaign, and the influence of extraneous events on their attitudes is likely to be kept to a minimum.

Third, the British political system discourages a tendency to vote for an individual as such. Formally, British electors do vote for an individual—their Member of Parliament. But he is not obliged to reside in the constituency he represents, and once he enters Parliament, his scope to act as a local spokesman is severely limited by the subordination of legislative behaviour to a regime of strict party discipline. Therefore, he is mainly perceived as a representative of his party, and in fact most votes are cast for a party, not for its candidate. (It has been calculated that the purely personal following of the most popular candidate

xiv

is not worth more than 500 votes.) This explains the inclusion in our questionnaires of many attitude items about the parties as such and the use of only one question about the individuals who actually stood as candidates in West Leeds and Pudsey.

At the other end of the pyramid of political authority the British voters do not choose a Prime Minister (as Americans elect their President), though through their votes they have an indirect say in whom he shall be. This means that his proven vote-getting power is less important to a would-be Prime Minister than to a presidential aspirant. Instead political advancement depends very much on an individual's standing with his parliamentary colleagues. Some observers believe, however, that the arrival of television on the political scene has helped to change this situation. They consider that the office of the Prime Minister is steadily evolving towards the presidential model, and that television enables a confident user of the medium to base his authority on a favorable public image. It is also suggested that in general television is strengthening the influence of personality factors in British politics. Certain aspects of our study are relevant to these issues. For example, we tapped viewers' own opinions about the leader qualities that television can reveal. We plotted the changes that took place during the campaign in our respondents' attitudes towards each of the three main party spokesmen. And we examined the independent contribution of exposure to political programmes to these developing leader images.

Finally, a British General Election is largely a national rather than a local exercise. It invariably occurs at a different time from purely local elections for town and county councils, and the boundaries of most parliamentary constituencies do not coincide with those of any other governmental unit. Most of the major media of political communication, including the morning and Sunday papers and the British Broadcasting Corporation, blanket the nation as a whole, and even the more regionally oriented commercial television companies cater for very large territorial areas. Naturally at election time the constituency parties mount a local campaign, the principal components of which are public meetings, canvassing, and the delivery to every household of an election address (a promotional leaflet). But the chief point of this local effort is to enable the party workers to locate their supporters and get them to the polls. The main onslaught on their opinions and attitudes is launched through the national media, which direct the attention of electors largely to events on the national scene. All this lends support to the view that a British election is by and large a time when civic judgements are registered about the overall competence of the rival parties to govern. Thus, the concentration in this study on national propaganda, and on national issues, leaders and party symbols, is not simply a consequence of our interest in television. It arises from certain enduring features of the British electoral system.

The actors in the 1964 election

Throughout 1964 the impending General Election was keenly awaited. As the Conservatives overhauled Labor's opinion poll lead, it seemed that the verdict could swing just as easily one way as the other. The leaders of both major parties had been chosen as recently as 1963, and it was still not clear how they would shape up to each other in a tough campaign. And several new themes were being introduced into the political argument as by-products of the recent emergence of both parties from something like a crisis of identification.

The stage for the 1964 encounter was set by the domination of British politics ever since the 1920s by two large and fairly evenly balanced parties. Although the differences between the Conservative and Labor Parties resemble those which divide Republicans and Democrats in the United States, the parallel is by no means exact. In both countries the major parties are based on coalitions of diverse elements, with one party grouping tending to adopt a more radical and the other a more conservative stance on many issues. But the ties that bind the American coalitions are generally much looser than their British equivalents. Regional and local differences inside the parties, for example, are far less noticeable in Britain than in the United States.

Class is an important determinant of voting behavior in both political systems, but in Britain party alignments have polarized along class lines more sharply than anywhere else in the English-speaking world. Even in Britain, however, the association between voting and class is imperfect. Although the Labor Party is formally tied to certain working-class organisations (affiliated trade unions and co-operative societies), and although it draws most of its electoral support from working-class sources (about 85 per cent of its voting strength), class-determined voting is paradoxically more common among non-manual than among manual workers. Whereas up to four-fifths of the former tend to support the Conservatives, only about two-thirds of the latter usually vote for Labor.

In the past active political workers have tended to assume that in Britain (unlike the United States) party cleavages were firmly rooted in ideological differences. Labor supporters felt identified with a democratic socialist party, which aimed to advance the interests of the working class, stood for generous social welfare provisions, and sought to extend state planning and public ownership of industry. Conservative activists imagined themselves to be less doctrinaire than Labor stalwarts and claimed that their party embodied the interests of the nation as a whole in contrast to Labor's more narrow working-class basis. Nevertheless, Conservatism was supposed to stand for private enterprise, individual freedom, and the sustaining of a major role for Britain as a great power in the world. This ideologically colored picture of British party differences was inevitably selective and conveniently ignored certain facts of political life. From 1950 onwards, for example, nationalization projects had received merely a few lines in Labor's election manifestoes. And throughout the 1950s the Conservatives had based their electoral appeal on a claim to have achieved a steadily rising standard of living for the ordinary man in the street. But in the 1960s the ideological contrast between the major parties became even less applicable to the political situa-tion—as the battle lines that were drawn up for the 1964 election clearly showed.

The year 1964 was equally crucial to both parties. Labor had been out of office for 13 years, following three successive defeats at the polls in 1951, 1955, and 1959. On each of these occasions the Conservatives had increased their lead, and after 1959 the future of the Labor Party itself had become a matter for gloomy speculation. It appeared that a modest degree of economic success was sufficient to sustain the Conservative grip on power, and inside Labor's ranks a spirited and bitter inquest was held, in which rival leaders nearly tore the party apart in disputes over public ownership and nuclear disarmament.

As it happened, it only required the development of an economic crisis in 1961–2 to improve Labor's prospects dramatically. And as the wheel of political fortune turned, the Conservative Party had to face a severe challenge of its own. Not only was its long-standing claim to competence in the management of economic affairs undermined. In addition, a growing number of journalists and academic writers stressed the need for radical measures, if Britain was to compete effectively in world markets and surmount her chronic economic weaknesses. Judged in this light, the administration of Harold Macmillan (the Conservative Prime Minister of the time) was tarred with the brush of complacency.

Then early in 1963 the Leader of the Labor Party, Hugh Gaitskell, died suddenly, and Harold Wilson was elected by the Labor Members of Parliament to fill his place. Mr. Wilson soon developed a propaganda line which united the previously warring factions of his party at the same time that it offered a way out of Britain's economic plight. This presented Labor as a party which would give high priority to economic growth, modernization of industrial methods and structures, and the promotion of a science and technology based industrial advance. Meanwhile, the Conservative administration continued to flounder, until in October, 1963, Mr. Macmillan resigned at last in favor of Sir Alec Douglas-Home.

In the year that was left before an election had to be held, economic conditions eased at home (although there was no sign of an improvement in the balance of payments), and the Conservatives gradually edged back to parity with Labor in the opinion polls. Thus, many party guns were primed to fight an election campaign over the state of the British economy. Would the electorate accept Labor's charge that the Conservatives had neglected the underlying health of the economy? Alternatively, would the voters put their faith once again in the Conservatives' claimed ability to maintain and improve popular living standards? Naturally other questions figured in the election as well: pension levels, housing targets, educational standards, unemployment benefits, etc. And, as a former Foreign Secretary,

FOREWORD TO THE AMERICAN EDITION

Sir Alec Douglas-Home injected foreign and defense issues into the campaign, claiming that Britain's continued participation in the highest counsels of world statesmanship depended on her retention of an independent nuclear deterrent. Nevertheless, more propaganda was devoted in the 1964 campaign to economic issues than to any other topic, and certain instruments in our questionnaires were designed to test electors' reactions to the rival parties' arguments about the economy.

The limelight was not monopolized entirely by the major parties in 1964, for the Liberal Party was enjoying a modest revival at that time. This was a remnant of the great nineteenth-century reforming party, which in the inter-war period had been displaced by Labor as the second main party in the land. Since the end of the Second World War, it had occupied an uneasy position in the state, at times a recipient of disgruntled protest votes, at other times appearing as a fresh wind in British politics. The Liberals had won only six seats in the 1959 election, but their hopes of gaining a new lease of political life in 1964 were not just flights of fantasy. They were founded on a run of good results in by-election contests; on the possible appeal of a third party to undecided voters who were disenchanted with the Conservative record but doubtful about Labor's reliability; and on the chance that, with popular support for the major parties equally divided, the Liberals might well hold a balance of power in the House of Commons after the election. The Liberal Party also put up many more candidates in the 1964 election than in 1959 (365 compared with 216), and this entitled it to the use of a bigger share of broadcasting time than it had received at any previous election. This accounts in turn for our decision to examine voters' responses to the presentation of the Liberal case on television during the 1964 campaign.

Finally, the 1964 election generated much interest in the ability of the three different party leaders to wage a modern campaign. Some of this centred on the sharply opposed personalities of the Labor and Conservative Leaders. Harold Wilson was a Yorkshireman who presented himself as a self-made man of the people. Despite an Oxford education and his training as an economist, his origins were working or lower middle class, and he aimed to be accepted as a practical and straightforward leader with substantial reserves of common sense and strength.

His own record as a left-wing rebel during the 1950s had not prevented him from uniting all factions in the Labor Party under his banner, and he quickly developed a reputation for political shrewdness.

Sir Alec Douglas-Home (since succeeded as Conservative Leader by Edward Heath) had surrendered a hereditary earldom to become eligible for the Premiership. His path to the top was probably smoothed by the fact that he seemed a less controversial figure than either of his Conservative rivals, Mr. R. A. Butler and Mr. Quintin Hogg. But Sir Alec's aristocratic background seemed to set him apart from certain newer men in the Conservative Party, who had risen by sheer ability, and hindered his attempts to establish a measure of rapport with the general public. Although many colleagues are said to have respected his integrity and amiability, Sir Alec certainly seemed less at ease with modern communications methods and media than did his Labor opponent.

The Liberal Leader, Jo Grimond (since succeeded by Jeremy Thorpe), was regarded by some observers as his party's greatest asset. He had carried the Liberal flag for nine years and was highly respected by attentive followers of politics. Despite an upper middle class background, he was less easy to place in class terms than the other two leaders. His views were expressed in a progressive idiom, seemingly free from platitudes and dogma, and on a number of issues—of which the Common Market is an outstanding example—he presented policies which the two larger parties subsequently borrowed for themselves. Mr. Grimond seemed able to preserve a perpetually youthful appearance, and his attractive personality may have helped to keep his party's fortunes alive in the late 1950s and early 1960s. Despite these qualities, however, it was not clear how much notice the ordinary voter would pay to a man whose party could not conceivably win an election.

This study was designed to examine the role of election television and not to explain an election result. But it may be noted here that the 1964 election produced a narrow Labor victory, Mr. Wilson's party having won 317 seats in the House of Commons, compared with 303 Conservative and nine Liberal seats. The government proceeded with a heavy programme of new legislation and after 18 months went to the country again in order to acquire a fresh mandate and a more viable parliamentary majority. This it obtained in March 1966, but at the time of writing the government's popularity is at a low ebb, largely because those fundamental economic problems, which had provided the central focus of the 1964 campaign, have persisted without relief.

Political broadcasting in Britain[2]

The distinctive flavor of British political broadcasting reflects a blend of uninhibited vigor and firm control – or, as some would put it, of freedom and paternalism. Since this is an unstable compound, the past decade has witnessed a continual evolution of the pattern of political programming in response to pressures from many sources. The supporters of control have included, first, those who fear that the flow of political information to the electorate may diminish to a mere trickle if certain protective arrangements are removed; second, the major political parties which enjoy the benefits at present of untrammelled access to huge audiences via television; and third, those believers in fair play who consider that the norms of political balance and impartiality must ultimately be upheld by legal sanctions. The fighters for more freedom have included, first, those broadcasters who believe that audience interests and tastes should govern the amount and style of political coverage; second, those who fear the degeneration of seemingly sensible rules into petty restrictions; and third, those who regard television journalism as a searching and probing instrument which can raise issues that the parties prefer to ignore and hold politicians to account for their decisions and policies before the viewing public.

[2] This section deals mainly with arrangements for the presentation of politics on British television. Many of the same provisions also apply to radio, a medium which plays little part in an election campaign, however, because usually only small audiences are available for evening listening. The press is subject to much less public control than are the electronic media, and in the past controversy about its political role has centred mainly on the pro-Conservative leanings of the majority of British newspapers. Some of the heat has gone out of this debate in recent years, however, largely because the influence of partisanship on the reporting of political events has declined and editorial views (especially in the quality press) have tended to become more flexible and less predictable.

FOREWORD TO THE AMERICAN EDITION

It is little wonder that the place of television in the 1964 election proved at least as controversial as its more obviously political issues. Details of TV and radio coverage of that campaign (and of our sample members' exposure to the various programmes) appear in Chapter 3 below, and the main bones of contention about the organization of election television are outlined in the opening pages of Chapter 5. Our survey elicited viewers' opinions about some of the questions that figured in the controversy of that time, and it may help non-British readers to understand what was at stake if we note here the salient features of British arrrangements for political broadcasting.

In Britain radio broadcasting originates from an independent public body, the British Broadcasting Corporation (BBC), which is ultimately responsible to Parliament through a government minister, the Postmaster General. Television programmes are provided by two authorities: the BBC, which transmits material on two different channels; and a commercial network (ITV), with one channel only, the operations of which are strictly controlled by another public agency, known as the Independent Television Authority (ITA). The ITA leases broadcasting franchises to 15 regionally-based commercial television companies, which produce the actual programmes. Apart from certain differences in constitution and systems of control, the BBC and ITV are differentiated by their methods of finance. Whereas the BBC is supported by revenue from a license that every radio or television set-owner must purchase, the commercial television companies recover their operating costs and draw their profits from the sale of advertising time, which is available between programmes or during 'natural breaks' within programmes.

A crucial difference from American arrangements for political broadcasting arises from the fact that the British parties may not purchase time slots from either network. This helps to hold down the costs of campaigning and also to differentiate a political talk from an advertising commercial. In Britain political materials may be broadcast in one of two different outlets: in programmes that are prepared by the parties themselves; and in programmes that are originated by the broadcasters in their role as newsmen and political commentators.[3]

[3] Provision is also made for the occasional transmission of so-called

Much of the controversy about election broadcasting has reflected an apparent struggle for power between these two elements, revolving around the amount of time that the former should occupy and the amount of freedom that the latter should be permitted to exercise.

The parties' own programmes are called party political broadcasts (PPBs) when transmitted in out-of-election periods and party election broadcasts (PEBs) when scheduled during an official campaign. Usually lasting ten or 15 minutes, they are periodically allocated on a quota basis by an unofficial committee, which includes representatives of the three main parties, the BBC, and the ITA, and which fixes details—usually after a certain amount of haggling—of timing, duration, and number. Any single party's quota (there is no element of interparty confrontation in these programmes) is usually proportional to its representation in the House of Commons, or, at election time, to the number of seats it has decided to fight. The between-election allocation works out at about one telecast every ten weeks for each of the major parties and approximately two per year for the Liberals. During the 1964 campaign a 5:5:3 ratio governed the allocation of PEBs. Whereas the Conservative and Labor Parties had five PEBs each, the Liberals received three and the minor parties none. [4]

To the recognized parties the value of this quota is accentuated by another distinctive feature of British political broadcasting: PPBs and PEBs are invariably beamed *simultaneously* on all available television channels at peak viewing periods. The national coverage of the broadcasting organisations also guarantees their reception in every part of the country. With all possible competition from other programmes thus eliminated, PPBs and PEBs are seen by very large and heterogeneous audiences. Each of the 1964 election programmes, for example, was viewed by well over a quarter of the voting public. One writer has calculated that at commercial rates the free time put

ministerial broadcasts, in which non-controversial government statements are presented to the public. Of course these play no part in an election campaign.

[4] A minor party will receive broadcasting time only if it puts up a minimum of 50 parliamentary candidates (or, in the case of a regional party, if it fights an equivalent proportion of the seats in its area).

at the disposal of the political parties before and during the 1964 campaign was worth £3,000,000.[5]

Outside the parties' own broadcasts, political issues are occasionally ventilated and politicians often appear in the news bulletins and current affairs programmes that the broadcasting authorities themselves produce. At the time of writing, apart from many purely news programmes (ranging from 15 to 30 minutes in length), there are four main nationally networked current affairs programmes on television. The BBC puts out a 30-minute edition of *24 Hours* five nights a week (although this was not available in 1964, having been screened for the first time in late 1965) and a weekly 50-minute edition of *Panorama*. ITV schedules *This Week* for 25 minutes weekly and *World in Action* for 30 minutes weekly. In addition, longer political documentaries are mounted very occasionally. For several years before the 1964 election the BBC also transmitted a weekly half-hour programme of exclusively political comment, called *Gallery*, but this was taken off the air in 1965. The political tone of these programmes is set by a corps of able and well-known reporters, such as Robin Day, George Ffitch, Kenneth Harris, Robert Mackenzie, and James Mossman. These men have fashioned the political interview into a powerful tool for probing the character and intentions of politicians. In fact the art of delivering hard-hitting questions which are within the rules of the game has been taken a long way in Britain. One observer of political broadcasting on both sides of the Atlantic has commented that:

> . . . BBC and ITA interviewers are extremely aggressive, even hostile to almost any politician being interviewed, even if the latter is a prime minister or shadow prime minister. There is nothing on American radio or television to compare with the sharp questioning to which British politicians are subjected on the air.[6]

This may help to explain the politicians' determination to cling to their own block of broadcasting time in the form of PPBs and PEBs.

Of course most of the legal controls apply to the non-party

[5] Rose, Richard, *Influencing Voters; A Study of Campaign Rationality*, Faber and Faber Ltd., London, 1967, pp. 204–5.

[6] Becker, Samuel L., op. cit.

sphere of political programming. They stipulate that the broadcasting authorities should not put forward editorial opinions of their own; that they should not spend money to promote the election of any candidate for public office; and that an impartial balance should be preserved in presenting the views of the rival parties.

The kind of political balance which the British broadcasters are expected to maintain differs in several ways from that which is enshrined in the famous equal time clause of Section 315 of the American Federal Communications Act. Whereas newscasts, interviews, and documentaries are specifically exempted from the latter, they fall within the province of British legal and policy requirements.[7] Otherwise, the British notion of party balance is at once more flexible and more strict than the American interpretation. Its greater flexibility arises from the fact that it is unnecessary to make time available to all and sundry, even the most unorthodox of minor parties, whenever the spokesman of a particular party has appeared on the air. During an election campaign, for example, the criterion of balance is satisfied by ensuring that the various parties receive the same share of time on news and current affairs programmes that governs their quota of PEBs. The British concept of balance is more strict than the American, however, in regarding a mere *offer* of time to the contending parties as insufficient. They must actually participate, and this sometimes enables one party to stop the others from airing their views on a certain topic by refusing to supply a spokesman of its own to appear in a current affairs programme. This power of veto has recently been weakened, however, by the acceptance of a ruling that it is unnecessary for every single programme to be balanced in party terms. It is now good enough for a series of programmes as a whole to achieve a balance.

It is striking to recall that there was once a time when the news and current affairs programmes virtually shut up shop between the dissolution of Parliament and Polling Day. The campaign was represented on radio and television only by the

[7] The boundary line between law and policy is difficult to draw in these matters, especially since very few cases have ever reached the British courts. In practise, 'the law' tends to be defined by the legal advisors of the Postmaster General, the BBC, and the ITA.

parties' own election broadcasts. In 1955, for example, all the regular current affairs programmes went off the air for the duration of the campaign, and the news bulletins studiously refrained from even mentioning the election! This remarkable situation reflected the timidity and exaggerated sense of fairness of certain broadcasters who did not wish to be accused of having had any influence at all on how the voters had cast their ballots. It was also sustained by a very narrow interpretation of the legal requirement that radio and television should not advance the cause of any candidate.

In time a more positive view of television's independent contribution to a campaign prevailed. This reached something like a high-water mark during the 1964 election and is described in Chapter 3 below. One source of the change was unremitting pressure from television journalists, who found their enforced silence at election time frustrating and professionally insulting. Although the politicians engaged in a few rear-guard skirmishes, they were usually prepared to renounce the most anomalous restrictions, so long as their own preserve of party broadcasting time remained inviolate. The move to freedom was also eased by a more liberal interpretation of the law. The courts eventually ruled, for example, that if the broadcasters' dominant motive was to inform the public and not to promote an individual's candidacy, it was permissible to screen an election speech or a political interview, provided that the politician's own constituency was not mentioned.

In the event, both television networks were unprecedentedly active in the 1964 campaign. Among the election materials they produced, it is useful to distinguish between the news bulletins and the other programmes. In the news field both the BBC and ITV put out two evening broadcasts (at approximately 6.00 and 9.00 p.m.), which lasted about 15 minutes each, plus a longer late news programme (at about 11.00 p.m.), which was devoted exclusively to campaign speeches and events. Even the regular news programmes contained a heavy diet of election matter–an average of about 40 per cent according to one count.[8]

The other programmes provided by the BBC and ITV were varied in format and included attempts to follow election trends,

[8] Harrison, Martin, 'Television and Radio', Ch. X in Butler, D. E. and King, Anthony, op. cit., p. 168.

to highlight the key issues, and to help the viewer to assess the rival claims of the three main parties for himself. A brief guide to the main programmes that were presented during the 1964 campaign follows:

Election Forum

This series of three BBC programmes was transmitted on both radio and television in the week immediately before the start of the official campaign. The three party leaders appeared separately in successive editions to answer viewers' questions that were put to them by prominent television reporters. The programmes provided an opportunity for viewers to weigh up the contenders under identical conditions and were about as near as television got to staging leader debates in 1964.

Election Gallery

This series of seven programmes was a campaign version of the BBC's then regular programme of political comment. It relied on a magazine format and combined news, film reports, discussion, and political interviews.

Question Time

This series of three BBC programmes was broadcast in different versions in each of several regions of the country. Its format involved the posing of questions by local journalists to local spokesmen of the three main parties.

This Week

This was a campaign version of one of ITV's regular weekly current affairs programmes. Each of the four editions was devoted to a detailed examination of a major issue of the election, including housing, public ownership, immigration, and the standard of living. In the first edition a debate was arranged between spokesmen of the major parties, but thereafter the parties declined to confront each other in this way.

FOREWORD TO THE AMERICAN EDITION

Election Marathon

   This was an ambitious series of afternoon programmes produced by Granada TV, Ltd., the commercial company which catered at the time for the northern area in which this study took place. Candidates standing in all the constituencies of the region were invited to deliver brief statements of their aims and policies. For any single candidate to appear, however, each of his opponents had to take part as well.

PART I

APPROACHING THE PROBLEMS

CHAPTER I

THE AIMS OF THE ENQUIRY

The aims of this, the second major investigation of the impact of election television to be undertaken by the Television Research Unit at the University of Leeds, need to be considered in a broader context of uncertainty and controversy about the place of mass communications in British politics. The use of the most pervasive, most trusted, and (as many suppose) the most potent of the mass media is beset by many doubts. We are unsure about the degree of freedom that politicians should have to present unadulterated party propaganda to a virtually captive audience on television, and about the freedom given to journalists and producers to direct public attention to whatever issues *they* deem important. Pressure mounts for the relaxation of various controls, but the arguments used in support of change are based more often on speculation and personal impression than on evidence. Although a tradition of conferring a social purpose on broadcasting is as old in this country as broadcasting itself, there is reluctance to define a specifically democratic objective for political television and vagueness about what it might really contribute to citizenship. Meanwhile, those who jib at the present arrangements encounter considerable unwillingness to disturb a *status quo* that can evidently be managed at least tolerably well by the politicians and broadcasters. Such feelings as these are unlikely to be swept aside by factual evidence collected from viewer surveys, but at two important points at least such an enquiry can contribute relevantly to the continuing debate.

Those matters that cannot be resolved simply by reference to principle, ideology, or value preferences concern, first, public attitudes to political communication, and second, the measured impact of television on political opinions. In the first case, there is much confusion about what the electorate actually wants in the nature of political materials from the mass media, about the uses that voters make of what is available, and about the motives and preferences which govern those uses. Broadcasters and politicians are uncertain about the volume and type of coverage that would prove most acceptable to the public and about the lines of policy that would reconcile viewer interests and social purposes most satisfactorily. Only an enquiry into viewers' motives and preferences could help to dispel such doubts as these.

There are also grounds for uncertainty about the impact of viewing on the political outlook of electors. It is true that this had already been the subject of an earlier study, which was carried out by the Television Research Unit during the General Election of 1959 and reported in *Television and the Political Image*.[1] Before that volume appeared, exaggerated notions of the power of televised persuasion had tended to prevail, and its main function, therefore, was to explode the myth of this medium's irresistible potency. The findings of Trenaman and McQuail showed that election television fulfilled an educational role, for increasing exposure to the 1959 campaign had accompanied the acquisition by voters of increasingly accurate information about party policies. There was no evidence to show, however, that the viewing of party broadcasts had affected voting or the attitudes of electors to the Labour and Conservative Parties. Despite a marked improvement in attitudes towards the Conservative Party during the campaign, no form of exposure to political materials in any mass medium had been associated with that development. In fact the lack of any connection between campaign exposure and attitude change was so striking that Trenaman and McQuail even referred to the presence in voters' minds of something like a 'barrier between sources of communication and movements of attitude in the political field at the General Election.'[2] Perhaps it is not surprising that shortly afterwards the academic community began to refer to political television as a negligible

---

[1] Trenaman, J. and McQuail, Denis, *Television and the Political Image*, Methuen, London, 1961.
[2] Ibid., p. 192.

4

rather than a powerful force and that a doctrine of what might be termed the political impotence of television was born. As Professor A. H. Birch expressed it, 'The evidence suggests that the mass media of communication have no direct effect on ... [political] attitudes.'[3] And as Martin Harrison put the prevailing view, 'Television ... may inform or reinforce attitudes, but it rarely converts.'[4]

Despite this consensus, three different sets of considerations encouraged us to re-open the question of television's political significance. We were influenced, first, by doubts about the validity of generalizations drawn from the results of only one survey. It seemed premature to dismiss the persuasive potential

[3] Birch, A. H., *Representative and Responsible Government*, Allen and Unwin, London, 1964, p. 186.

[4] Cf. 'Television and Radio', Ch. X, in Butler, D. E. and King, Anthony, *The British General Election of 1964*, Macmillan, London, 1965, p. 156. This conclusion was consistent with the findings of several investigations of American election campaigns. It was also supported by the following conclusion which Joseph Klapper drew from his authoritative review of a large number of studies of communications effects: 'The tendency of mass communication to reinforce rather than convert has ... been documented by various ... studies, and in reference to communications on political and non-political topics.' (Cf. Klapper, Joseph, *The Effects of Mass Communication*, The Free Press, Glencoe, Illinois, 1960, p. 17.)

For example, the authors of a study of the presidential election of 1948 reported that, although exposure to campaign materials in the mass media had helped to increase political interest and to generate an understanding of the policy positions of candidates, it had not discernibly influenced the voting intentions of the electorate. That part of their sample (amounting to a tenth), whose members were converted during the campaign from support of one party to a decision to vote for another party, consisted in the main of those individuals who had been *least* exposed to party propaganda on the radio and in the press. Not only were the most highly exposed respondents least likely to have changed; they had also tended to consume campaign materials selectively, paying most attention to messages emanating from the party they initially favoured. The authors concluded, therefore, that during an election campaign, exposure to the mass media 'crystallizes and reinforces more than it converts'. (Cf. Berelson, Bernard, Lazarsfeld, Paul F. and McPhee, William N., *Voting: A Study of Opinion Formation in an Election Campaign*, University of Chicago Press, Chicago, 1954, p. 248.) That part of their data, however, which referred to selective exposure among highly partisan voters, has subsequently been critically re-examined in Sears, David O. and Freedman, Jonathan L., 'Selective Exposure to Information: A Critical Review', *Public Opinion Quarterly*, Vol. XXXI, No. 2, 1967, pp. 194–213.

of television on the basis of a single study carried out in the circumstances of a particular election campaign. Until the findings of Trenaman and McQuail had been confirmed under different conditions, nobody could be sure that one myth about political television had not been displaced by its uncritically accepted antithesis. A second argument arose from the lack of any attention to the Liberal Party in the election study of 1959. Given the electoral situation and the rules that govern political broadcasting in this country, it was possible that a third party had most to gain from its access to television during an election campaign. Until 1964, however, no evidence was available for testing this assertion. But, third, this enquiry would not have been launched had we not wished to try out an entirely new approach to the study of political broadcasting. Its point of departure was the expectation that in the persuasive process sheer amount of exposure to television might matter less than the precise motives, and the different degrees of motivation, underlying the reception by viewers of political materials.

The enquiry which was planned in 1964, then, enabled us both to re-examine previous findings in the circumstances of a different election and to raise a number of new questions. In particular it was intended to combine in one study two areas of empirical enquiry, sometimes explored in isolation, which we suspected were intimately related to each other—namely the gratifications sought by viewers from following an election on television and the political effects that might ensue from such exposure. The additional paragraphs below spell out these aims, and the implications of our approach to audience motivation, in greater detail.

A different election

As the General Election of 1964 approached, there were a number of indications, arising both from the prevailing climate of political opinion, and from the parties' increasing concern to use the mass media effectively, that it might prove significantly different from its predecessor. Seen in retrospect, the General Election of 1959 seemed to mark the end of a decade of relative political stability, and between 1959 and 1964 certain portents of more fundamental change began to emerge on the political scene. One has been described as a 'profound sea-change in articulate opinion'.[5] Complacent confidence in Britain's economic and political future was eroded by a wide-ranging critique of traditional practices, long-established institutional arrangements, and the government's management of the economy. It was not clear how far this mood of disenchantment penetrated beyond journalistic and academic circles into the ranks of ordinary citizens, but the major parties reacted to the new climate as if a disposition to innovate was expected of them. The Conservative Party played down its former role as the heir of a continuous national tradition and presented itself, at least intermittently, as a modernizing party instead. Labour, too, sought to shed its predominantly working-class image and to become accepted as a party of the whole nation which could revive the flagging economy and place it on more secure foundations. We reasoned that in such a state of flux some voters might apply different standards in judging the competing parties than they had used in the 1950s and might turn in particular to the mass media during the 1964 campaign for their new impressions.

Certainly both major parties were responding at this very time with increasing sensitivity to the availability of sophisticated publicity techniques. Whatever the academics might say about the marginal impact of persuasive campaigns, the politicians behaved as if the mass media mattered and used them avidly in order to project their parties' refurbished images to the public. This was part of a 'major change . . . in the conduct of election campaigns', occupying some 15 years, which Richard Rose has documented elsewhere. But some of its most important developments, including the decision of the Labour Party in 1961 to seek help for the first time from experts in media techniques, occurred between the elections of 1959 and 1964. Consequently, the latter 'was in duration, expense, and expertise the biggest propaganda campaign in twentieth-century British politics.'[6]

We wished to ascertain, then, whether, in these new

[5] Butler, D. E. and King, Anthony, op. cit., p. 30.
[6] Rose, Richard, *Influencing Voters: A Study of Campaign Rationality*, Faber and Faber, London, 1967, Ch. 1.

circumstances, television would prove to be a more influential campaign force in 1964 than it had been in 1959.[7]

Television and third-party campaigning – the Liberals

Our investigation of the campaign fortunes of the Liberal Party did not amount merely to an effort to tidy up a marginal detail. It was known that television would pay considerably more attention to the Liberal Party in 1964 than it had in 1959, when its quota of election broadcasts amounted to only 25 per cent of the time given to each of the major parties. The new 5:5:3 ratio not only increased its share to 60 per cent of the time available to the other parties for overt electioneering; it would also guide the producers of regular news and current affairs programmes when deciding how to balance *their* coverage of the various contenders. Politically too, as by-elections and opinion poll trends showed, the third party had become more significant than it had been in the 1950s, and although the Liberal revival did not proceed evenly, by 1964 the national Liberal vote had doubled in comparison with 1959. The decision to include the Liberal Party in this study was influenced mainly, however, by an interest in its position as a political minority that enjoys greater access to a powerful mass medium during an election campaign than it usually has at other times.

The significance of this is traceable to the scarcity of broadcasting time, which obliges all democratic states to regulate the use that competing parties and candidates make of television and radio for propaganda purposes. A wide range of arrangements has been adopted in different states. At one extreme there can be a near-monopoly of political broadcasting by the ruling party, and at the other a situation in which the appearance of any single party on television entitles any other party, however small, to claim an equal amount of time in which to present its case to the electorate (as specified in the

[7] Relevant too was evidence that the planned coverage of the 1964 campaign by the television authorities would be more vigorous and comprehensive than at any previous election. For a comparison of the 1959 and 1964 campaigns in terms of the availability of various programmes and how the two samples examined in those years were exposed to them, see Ch. 3 below.

THE AIMS OF THE ENQUIRY

United States by Section 315 of the Federal Communications Act).

The formal equality of American election law is distorted in practice by the need for a political party to pay at commercial rates for any time it uses. Nevertheless, before Kennedy and Nixon could take part in the 'Great Debates' of 1960, Congress had temporarily to repeal Section 315. This instituted, at least so far as the presidential candidates were concerned, a third possible arrangement: a duopoly in which only the two majority or near-majority parties may reach the electorate through the most important medium of modern communications. All this underlines a dilemma in democratic theory and practice. If minorities are prevented from expressing their views on radio and television, important impulses of political criticism may be stifled at source. But if they are accorded the same broadcasting facilities as those enjoyed by parties that have a real chance of winning power, the time they consume can be out of all proportion to their political relevance or to the interest of audience members in hearing their ideas.

A possible response to this dilemma is provided by a fourth type of arrangement, which Britain operates. Broadcasting time is not bought and sold, but is allocated to the various parties in agreements arrived at between representatives of the broadcasting authorities, the Government, and the Opposition. According to the terms of the agreement which was reached in 1964, tiny parties without any parliamentary representation— such as the Communists and the Welsh and Scottish Nationalists—presented no broadcasts.[8] But duopoly did not prevail, since a third party (the Liberals) received a relatively generous quota of three 15-minute election broadcasts on television (compared with five each for the Conservative and Labour Parties) and equivalent shares on radio.

This created an opportunity to examine the actual effect of the rules that govern campaign broadcasting on the electoral appeal of a minority party. Two broad possibilities occurred

---

[8] During the 1966 campaign, party broadcasts were again divided among the Labour, Conservative, and Liberal Parties in a ratio of 5:5:3. But in addition the Communists received a five-minute election broadcast, and the Welsh and Scottish Nationalists were given five minutes each for separate transmissions to their respective areas.

to us. One was that the *status quo* was too deeply entrenched for the Liberals to gain significantly from their access to broadcasting. (After all, throughout their voting lives most electors have supported one or the other of the major parties, which would also continue to receive voluminous publicity in the mass media.) Alternatively, the Liberal Party's quota of election broadcasts might help it to counteract the many disadvantages under which it labours in the British political system.[9]

In comparison to the resources of the major parties, for example, the Liberals have much less extensive organization, less money, no press backing, and few opportunities to make news headlines. Consequently, 'The radio and TV programmes assigned to the parties were the only nationwide electoral propaganda resource of Liberal headquarters',[10] by skilful use of which the Liberals might hope to gain some ground. If, in addition, it is assumed that the limited appeal of the Liberal Party is due partly to unfamiliarity with its policies or personnel, relatively widespread coverage of its activities on television and radio during a campaign could prove favourable. And finally, if opinions about the Liberal Party are anchored less firmly in underlying social attitudes and relationships than are convictions about the major parties, they might be modified more readily by televised persuasion. It was hoped, then, that by incorporating attitudes towards the Liberal Party and its Leader into this study, the consequences of enabling a third party to put its case to the electorate on television would be clarified.

The pivot of the survey – the uses-and-gratifications approach

Perhaps the central aim of this investigation, however, was to find out why people watch or avoid party broadcasts; what

---

[9] According to J. D. Lees, '. . . the British political system possesses a series of built-in obstacles to the effective growth of third parties', including the persistence of partisan attachment by citizens of voting age, the low level of awareness on the part of voters, the tendency to re-elect incumbents, the high percentage of safe seats, and the customary dominance of the mass media by the major parties. ('Aspects of Third-Party Campaigning in the 1964 General Election', *Parliamentary Affairs*, Vol. XIX, No. 1, 1965–6, pp. 83–90.) [10] Rose, Richard, op. cit., p. 92.

uses they wish to make of them; and what their preferences are between alternative ways of presenting politicians on television. In the language of the sociology of mass communications we intended to apply 'the uses-and-gratifications approach' to the study of election television. In fact this approach supplied the pivotal organizing principles of the research design of the 1964 survey, and it marked the methodological sense in which, despite many common features, it differed from the 1959 enquiry.

But this change of perspective followed naturally from reflection upon some of Trenaman and McQuail's more intriguing findings. If voters are not perceptibly influenced in their political outlook by exposure to a television campaign, why do they follow it at all? What do they hope to get out of it, if not material on the basis of which they can judge the competence of parties and leaders to govern? And does an individual's motivation for following a campaign have any effect upon his susceptibility to persuasion? If so, perhaps the lack of association between campaign exposure and attitude change, reported by Trenaman and McQuail in 1959, was due to their failure to distinguish between informants according to their various reasons for watching election broadcasts.

In adopting the uses-and-gratifications approach we were also influenced by the favour that it had won lately among students of mass communications, especially in the United States.[11] One reason for its popularity is that it helps to counteract the plausible but often misleading assumption of the passivity of the mass media audience. By emphasizing the gratifications that people derive from consumption of media materials, and the uses to which they put them in the circumstances of their own lives, this approach draws attention

[11] The first important plea on behalf of the uses-and-gratifications orientation appeared in 'Mass Communications Research and the Study of Culture: an Editorial Note on a Possible Future for this Journal' by Elihu Katz in *Studies in Public Communication*, No. 2, 1959, pp. 1–6. In addition its adoption has been recommended in such writings as: Klapper, Joseph, 'Mass Communication Research: An Old Road Resurveyed', *Public Opinion Quarterly*, Vol. XXVII, No. 4, 1963, pp. 515–27; Halloran, J. D., *The Effects of Mass Communication: with Special Reference to Television*, Leicester University Press, Leicester, 1964; and Blumler, J. G., 'British Television: The Outlines of a Research Strategy', *The British Journal of Sociology*, Vol. XV, No. 3, 1964, pp. 223–33.

to the significance of what the audience member contributes to the interaction between him and a mass medium. Typical of this outlook is the following passage, which has been taken from a recently published American work on the place of television in children's lives:

> In a sense the term 'effect' is misleading because it suggests that television 'does something' to children. The connotation is that television is the actor; the children are acted upon. Children are sitting victims; television bites them.
> Nothing can be farther from the fact.
> It is the children who are most active in this relationship. It is they who use television, rather than television that uses them.[12]

Application of the uses-and-gratifications approach to the study of political communication, though often recommended, has never been tried. For example, after summarizing the results of many research studies of the impact of the Kennedy–Nixon debates, two outstanding social scientists felt obliged to complain that despite 'current concern in communication research with the "uses" to which people put the media', very little attention had been 'given . . . to the ways in which the debates as a form were perceived.'[13] Perhaps without a body of previous research findings to draw upon from this orientation, investigators were unsure precisely what motives for following a campaign should be studied and how best to detect them. Much of our own work along these lines was certainly exploratory in character. Looking back on its results, we would not maintain now that all our procedures proved entirely satisfactory. It is by the extent of our advance into an important field, and by the opportunities created for other research workers to develop and improve upon our methods, that we should wish our labours to be judged.

One danger of looking at mass communications in this way is that it might yield only a rather obvious list of the gratifications that people seek from political broadcasts without adding

[12] Schramm, Wilbur, Lyle, Jack and Parker, Edwin B., *Television in the Lives of Our Children*, Stanford University Press, Stanford, California, 1961, p. 1.
[13] Katz, Elihu, and Feldman, Jacob J., 'The Debates in the Light of Research: A Survey of Surveys', Ch. 11 in Kraus, Sidney (Ed.), *The Great Debates*, Indiana University Press, Bloomington, Indiana, 1962, p. 216.

greatly to our understanding of their significance. To avoid this danger it was necessary to specify exactly what we hoped to establish by studying the attitudes of viewers to election television.

A major aim was to determine how (if at all) the persuasiveness of a political message depends on an individual's motivation for receiving it. For example, does the inattention of an uninterested viewer inure him against televised political appeals, or does it heighten his susceptibility by relaxing his guard? Pending a fuller examination of these questions, it is sufficient to state here that we expected a division of the members of a sample, according to their different motives for following election broadcasts, either to disclose previously undetected relationships between attitude change and campaign exposure, or to strengthen faint ones appreciably.

The role of the mass media in democratic politics

Our other objectives have already been introduced in the opening pages of this chapter. They can be elaborated by raising a series of questions about the attempts of politicians to persuade and inform the electorate through the mass media. We think that these questions are important and largely without satisfactory answers at present. The uses-and-gratifications approach should help to illuminate them.

Why do people accept political information and propaganda in the mass media? Are electors, as is often supposed, merely interested in confirming positions and attitudes that they already hold? How important are emotional gratifications, such as the excitement of following the rival contenders for the prizes of power? Behind such questions lies an issue which is central to our expectations of political democracy itself. Is there a rational foundation to the efforts of voters to follow the campaigning activities of political parties and leaders? From much survey evidence about the non-rational sources of party preferences, it has sometimes been concluded that the notion of a rational voter is a myth propagated by an out-of-date political theory.[14] If, however, the interest of citizens in

[14] See the analysis of the expectation that the citizen should exercise rational judgement in coming to a voting decision provided in Berelson,

propaganda is merely frivolous, why, in their choice of a campaigning strategy, should politicians be expected to rely on reasoned appeals when their ends might be achieved more successfully by other means? It seems legitimate to expect politicians to discuss public issues honestly and responsibly only if they can count on a serious reception by their audience of what they have to say.

Another set of questions arises from voters' perceptions of the persuasive process in democratic politics. How sensitive are they to the manipulative aim of election propaganda–and how aware of the modern techniques that politicians have adopted when trying to influence public opinion? How prevalent is a sceptical reaction to campaigning politicians, and does this affect the reception of election television in any way? Is broadcasting compromised by its association with the political persuaders, or can it be used to combat sceptical attitudes during a campaign? There are many different ways in which television can be used as an instrument of political communication, and some may be healthier than others for democracy in the long run, especially if they help to strengthen the credibility of political argument.

Some of these questions bear on the still undecided debate that has gone on throughout the 1960s about the organization and regulation of political broadcasting. By concentrating on viewer attitudes, we hoped that some account would be taken of what voters really want from election television before the issue was finally settled. Precisely because it is consumer-oriented, the results of a uses-and-gratifications approach can have policy implications. And because decisions about political broadcasting are usually taken after more or less secret negotiations between the interested parties, the elementary sense in which broadcasting exists to serve the needs of its audience is very easily forgotten. The debate about television in politics has been dominated in the past by the voices of the politicians, journalists, and broadcasters, and it seemed important to give a hearing to the voice of the user as well.

Bernard, Lazarsfeld, Paul F., and McPhee, William N., op. cit., pp. 309–11, where the conclusion is reached that 'a sense of fitness is a more striking feature of political preference than reason and calculation'.

Chapter 2

THE DESIGN OF THE ENQUIRY

The outcome of any survey is determined very much by what is put into it at the planning stage, when priorities are sifted and expectations formed, and when a commitment is made to a particular set of methods. The aim of this chapter is to outline the main features of the design which shaped our investigation, to make explicit some of its methodological assumptions, and to provide the reader with a critical basis for understanding the evidence which is presented in the remainder of this book. A summary is also provided of the different kinds of information sought during the several stages of the research.

Why study an election campaign?

The various aims which shaped our investigation of the influence of television during the 1964 election have already been described. The decision to undertake a second study of the pressures exerted on public opinion in the special circumstances of a campaign calls for some methodological comment, however, since it has been forcibly argued that an examination of an inter-election period would reveal more about the enduring influences which mould political attitudes. The forerunner to this enquiry has been criticized on these very grounds:

> It is the long-term, rather than the short-term, question that is important from our point of view. Although the study referred to provides us with useful information, it would be far more useful to know what impact television has on political attitudes and voting patterns over a 200-week period, and to be able to assess the role

played by television in the shaping of party images which for the most part appear to be carried intact through the campaign. It is the impact over the years that needs to be considered.[1]

There is no doubt that the results of a long-term study would have great intrinsic interest—if a suitably sound one could be designed. It may be significant, however, that none of the experts in the field of mass communications research has been able to recommend a body of methods which could be used with confidence in an attempt to plot the political impact of the mass media over a period of several years.[2] Meanwhile, the advantages of a campaign situation to the research worker retain their appeal. Deliberate efforts are made to persuade people to adopt one of several possible courses of action, and, because they are concentrated within a limited period, it is feasible to isolate them and to study their influence intensively. All electors are under some pressure to come to a voting decision, and measures of attitude change can be validated against the outcome of these decisions. The methodological difficulties which attend the assessment of long-term developments are minimized, since fewer variables need to be considered, and changes due to the passage of time itself can be disregarded. These arguments carried much weight once the formulation of our new hypotheses had shown that in any case another election survey could break fresh ground in relation to the work that had been done in 1959.

Furthermore, even though in recent General Elections the campaign has not caused any last-minute reversal of pre-election trends, the degree of change it can provoke is not slight. Of the members of the sample surveyed in 1959, 27 per cent were not consistent supporters of a party during the course of the campaign. An identical proportion of the sample studied in 1964 fell into this category. The available evidence does not suggest that there is a great deal of difference between this figure and that for change in party allegiance between the

[1] Halloran, J. D., op. cit., p. 13.
[2] At the time of writing, the results of an investigation by Dr. David Butler and Professor Donald Stokes on political attitude change in the British electorate between 1963 and 1966 had not yet appeared. That study, however, was not in the main designed to examine the long-term influence of the mass media.

elections of 1959 and 1964 when the same standards of measurement are applied (i.e. when a reported vote at a previous election is compared with a statement of voting intention at the outset of the subsequent campaign). Leaving out of account those who were too young to vote in 1959, the proportion of the sample interviewed in 1964 whose vote intention differed from their reported vote for 1959 was 30 per cent. We know from the present study that voting intentions were more stable during the $2\frac{1}{2}$ months preceding the 1964 campaign than they were during the $2\frac{1}{2}$-week campaign itself.[3] And we have estimated from another source that approximately two-fifths of the net change in public attitudes towards the major parties which occurred between the elections of 1959 and 1964 could be accounted for by the period of the latter campaign.[4] In addition to these signs that campaign change is not negligible, it can be argued that an election may witness the birth of new issues and the propagation of public images, which can commit politicians for their term of office or opposition and set the lines of the post-election debate.

The use of a panel

Our intention was to measure political change over a designated period of time, and to relate any shifts detected to

[3] Eighty-three per cent of the sample continued, in mid-September 1964, to support the party chosen in June; the comparable figure for the period of the campaign itself was 73 per cent.

[4] Inevitably this estimate is approximate. A measure of inter-election change was made possible by interviews after Polling Day 1964 with the surviving members of the sample originally contacted in 1959 by Trenaman and McQuail. These interviews were planned and executed in collaboration with Professor A. H. Birch and Dr. Robert Benewick of the Department of Political Studies of the University of Hull. It was found that from a period just after Polling Day 1959 to a period just after Polling Day 1964 the respondents in this inter-election panel experienced an average shift in partisanship score towards Labour of 1·98. Between a pre-campaign and a post-election interview in 1964, the members of our freshly drawn sample experienced an average shift in partisanship score towards Labour of 0·86. If all the elements here were fully comparable, the latter would represent 43 per cent of the former. The inter-election panel was older than the 1964 sample, however, and certain individual items in the 1959 measure of partisanship differed from those used in 1964 (though not their total number). The partisanship score is described on pp. 21–24 below.

usage of relevant persuasive materials, while taking account of voters' interest in, and attitudes towards, the persuasive process itself. To achieve these aims, we recruited a panel of electors and interviewed the identical respondents on three occasions. The decisive considerations affecting the choice of this design were (a) the need to pinpoint the actual individuals who had changed, and (b) our wish to obtain measures of respondents' interest in political television at a pre-campaign stage, which could subsequently be related to their actual behaviour during the campaign. The panel design offers the most accurate method of locating individual changers, since a statement of attitude or allegiance relating to one point in time can be compared with a similar statement made later by the same person. This approach enabled us both to test the predictive power of our measures of interest in political materials in the mass media, and to match up a reported pattern of exposure precisely with a known degree and type of opinion change.

Two potential sources of bias in a panel design must, however, be borne in mind. First, repeated interviewing may have a conditioning effect, and second, sample representativeness may deteriorate through a gradual falling off of panel membership. The process of interviewing inevitably has some effect on respondents, which can be eliminated entirely only by the use of indirect or observational methods (inappropriate to a study of political attitudes). This danger could be minimized by separately drawing two different random samples from the same population before and after the campaign, and measuring change by comparing the replies obtained from both samples. But this method cannot locate the particular individuals who have actually changed. A larger sample must also be drawn to reach the same level of confidence in one's measurement of degree of change that can be achieved by a panel.[5] The authors of the earliest panel study of an election campaign actually tested whether repeated interviewing had influenced their respondents by comparing their opinions with those found in a control panel whose members had been contacted only

[5] Cf. Hovland, C. I., Lumsdaine, A. A. and Sheffield, F. D., *Experiments on Mass Communications*, John Wiley and Sons, Inc., New York, 1965, pp. 318–23.

once. The results were reassuring and suggested that the views of the panel members had not been affected.[6]

The effects of panel 'mortality' over time are more easy to assess, since we know something about the characteristics of those who dropped out at each stage of the survey. In our sample, 85 per cent of the 1,072 individuals whose names appeared in the initially drawn list were interviewed successfully in the first round; 86 per cent of that group were interviewed on the second occasion; and 96 per cent of the remainder were interviewed yet again at the third and final stage. The findings which are presented in this book are based on the replies of the 748 respondents (70 per cent of the originally drawn list) who missed no interviews. One result of the process of attrition was an over-representation of Labour supporters, but since much of the analysis turns on trends in sub-groups, this has not interfered with the major objects of the enquiry. It was remarkable to find that there was very little difference between full panel members and those who were lost to the sample in terms of level of interest in politics and related matters. For example, 38 per cent of the 160 respondents who fell out between the first and third interviews were classified as 'strong' in their motivation for following the forthcoming campaign on television, compared with 41 per cent of the loyal panel members. Twenty-five per cent of the drop-outs professed 'not much' interest in the election compared with 23 per cent of the panel. Altogether the composition of the sample seemed to be little affected by panel mortality.[7]

The choice of locale for the study

The survey was carried out, as in 1959, in the two Yorkshire constituencies of Pudsey and West Leeds (some of the social characteristics of which are described in *Television and the Political Image*).[8] The choice of these areas was governed partly

[6] Lazarsfeld, Paul F., Berelson, Bernard, and Gaudet, Hazel, *The People's Choice: How the Voter Makes up his Mind in a Presidential Campaign*, Columbia University Press, New York, 1944, pp. 3 and 159.

[7] Appendix A presents information concerning the sampling method that was adopted, the results of the fieldwork, and tabular details of the representativeness of the panel.

[8] Trenaman, J., and McQuail, Denis, op. cit., pp. 18–19.

19

by a wish to re-examine the conclusions of the previous study in the same circumstances, and partly by the reasons responsible for their selection five years earlier–which still held good. The latter included: lack of a marked disparity in degree of constituency support between the major parties in the past; the presence of a mixture of urban, suburban and rural development; and the near equivalence of the economic status of the area to the national average. It was relevant, too, that between them Pudsey and West Leeds had showed in 1959 approximately the same party division of the vote as had been recorded

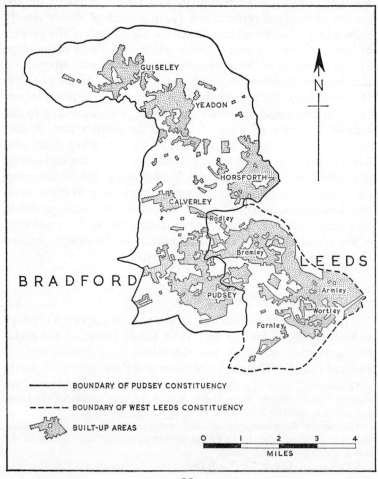

in the country at large. Since we were particularly interested in the fortunes of the Liberal Party, the fact that candidates from all three main parties would be standing in both constituencies was taken into account. Considerations of administrative convenience undoubtedly played an important part, for timing and speed were essential to the success of the field-work demanded for the investigation. In addition, constituency accessibility helped to hold down the level of total cost.

Although it may be argued that the findings of this survey could be purely local in application, we have no evidence of an effect on our results of an important local factor. It would certainly be difficult to trace a direct connection between local circumstances and the major findings which appear below concerning the nature of political change during the 1964 campaign and its association with exposure to the mass media. The expense of a national survey would have been prohibitive, but since our primary aim was not to portray the state of national opinion as such, but to trace relations between certain designated variables, almost any region served by national television programmes might have provided an equally suitable base for this enquiry.[9]

The measurement of attitudes towards the political parties

An election campaign can stimulate many more adjustments of view than are revealed by shifts in party allegiance or expressions of voting uncertainty, and it was such finer shades of change that we wished to chart. Our needs were further complicated by the importance to our study of the Liberal Party, which would be bound to have only a minority following in the sample. A form of questioning was required, therefore, which would yield an attitude score, capable of expressing numerically the *degree* of favour in which each party was held before and after the campaign.

The devising of an attitude scale to meet these requirements presented some intriguing problems. It is well known that

[9] It was found in 1959 that there were no statistical objections to treating the Pudsey and West Leeds respondents as if they were members of one sample. In presenting the findings below distinctions of constituency have usually been ignored.

21

political attitudes are relatively complex, and that an individual voter may hold seemingly contradictory views about his chosen party, approving it in some respects while rating the opposition party more highly in others. Most methods of attitude measurement require the interviewee to respond in some way to statements made about the object of enquiry. When tapping reactions to political parties, however, a major difficulty arises from the changing nature of their public face. This makes it difficult to ensure that the statements being posed reflect the most important features of the parties as they are perceived by the electorate at the time of the interview. It is also important to try, when measuring attitudes, to hinge the items on salient points—on those, that is, which matter to the people whose views are being sought. A person is more likely to criticize his own party on traits he deems unimportant than on those about which he feels strongly; and to this extent questions about unimportant matters are less likely to reveal his political orientation. This generates a temptation to spread the net of attitude items as widely as possible to make sure that all important points have been covered—which is an unsatisfactory solution in any circumstance and particularly in our case, where a single concise attitude scale, which could apply equally well to all three main parties, was wanted. In an already long interview we could not afford the time to ask more questions than were strictly necessary, but we also could not afford to be unsure about the areas in which salient judgements of the political parties were being made. The attitude scales which had been devised for use in the 1959 election study—and which were of proven validity and reliability—were available, but they referred to a different political situation and could not be applied again without considerable risk. In addition, they had not been intended for use in rating the Liberal Party.

The methods which were adopted in 1959 did, however, set a precedent which could be usefully followed again. A list of 25 descriptive statements was drawn up, consisting partly of items used at the previous election, and partly of new ones believed to reflect current trends of opinion. When compiling the latter, guidance was sought from an inspection of spontaneously given opinions about the British political parties which had been collected by two other investigators in 1963.[10] The full list of 25 items was then presented to a sample of electors for endorsement five months before the 1964 campaign opened, and a factor analysis of their replies was carried out. The results helped us to choose the following nine statements as coming closest to fulfilling all our requirements:[11]

Out for the nation as a whole.
Out to raise the standard of living for the ordinary man in the street.
Is disunited and badly organized.
Would weaken Britain's voice in world affairs.
Would get the economy moving.
Has a good team of leaders.
Has no clear policy.
Would know how to run the country well.
Don't keep to their promises.

The participants in the main survey were asked to say which of these statements were true and which not true of the Conservative, Labour and Liberal Parties in turn. An individual's attitude score was calculated by allocating a $+ 1$ to any favourable statement applied to a party and a $- 1$ to any unfavourable statement. The standing of each party in the eyes of our respondents could thus be expressed by a score which ranged from $+ 5$, at the most favourable, to $- 4$ at the most critical, end of the scale. Because of the mutually opposed positions of the Labour and Conservative Parties, it was also convenient for many purposes to express the position of each elector *vis-à-vis* the two major parties by means of a single 'partisanship score'. This was derived by subtracting the Labour Party attitude score from the Conservative Party attitude score, thus giving a possible range of $+ 9$ (at the extreme pro-Conservative pole) to $- 9$ (extremely pro-Labour). The main advantages of these scoring procedures

[10] We are grateful to Dr. Butler and Professor Stokes for making available some of the results of their current enquiry into the structure and change of political attitudes in this country.

[11] Appendix B presents the full list of the original 25 items, the results of the factor analysis, and an account of the procedures and criteria which were applied when choosing, on the basis of those results, the nine statements that were eventually incorporated into our party attitude scales.

were, first, that they enabled us to compare individuals and groups for the relative strength of their feelings about each party, and, second, that change over the course of the campaign could be measured sensitively by comparing the scores derived separately from the pre-campaign and post-election interviews.

The validity of these measures is established by the detection of a close relationship between the attitude scores and the voting intentions and reported votes of the respondents. For example, a pro-Liberal Party attitude score was obtained from 81 per cent of those intending to vote Liberal before the opening of the campaign and from 90 per cent of the Liberal voters. A pro-Labour partisanship score was recorded by 87 per cent of the Labour supporters in September and by 98 per cent of those who actually voted Labour. A pro-Conservative partisanship score was registered by 91 per cent of those who supported the Conservative Party at the pre-campaign interview and by 92 per cent of those who voted for it.

The measurement of attitudes towards the party leaders

Similar problems were encountered in trying to measure changes in the public's impressions of the three party leaders, and a solution along similar lines was devised. In comparison with the 1959 study, however, we wished to break new ground by specifically examining respondents' ratings of leaders for the possession of qualities that might be revealed by television appearances. We also wanted to explore the interrelationships between (*a*) the characteristics which viewers actually attributed to the three leaders, (*b*) the traits they believed to come over most clearly on television, and (*c*) those they deemed most important for a politician to have. Part of an exploratory survey was devoted to a probing of electors' opinions about these matters by asking a series of questions which were intended to stimulate references to leader qualities in these various contexts.

The mode of questioning followed in the main survey was based largely on the results of this early enquiry. A list of 12 qualities was drawn up and expressed in the questionnaire in the form of opposed pairs of adjectival descriptions as follows:

Persuasive speaker	Unpersuasive speaker
Weak	Strong
Likeable	Disagreeable
Inspiring leader	Uninspiring leader
Unsure of himself	Confident
Able	Incompetent
Insincere	Sincere
Conceited	Unassuming
Fair	Unfair
Hard-working	Lazy
Straightforward	Two-faced
Kindly	Inhumane

The respondents were asked to rate each leader for each quality on the list by placing him on a graded seven-point scale somewhere between the two extremes. This device is known as a semantic differential scale, has been used widely in attitude surveys, and is described more fully in Chapter 12. It facilitated the adoption of various scoring methods, use of which depended on the purpose of the analysis. On any single seven-point scale a respondent's rating of a particular leader was represented numerically by scores ranging between $+3$ (which stood for a highly favourable judgement, such as 'very sincere') and -3 (which reflected a highly unfavourable judgement – e.g. 'very insincere'). Although there was insufficient time before the main survey was launched to analyse the underlying structure of leader attitudes as disclosed by this instrument, factor analyses were applied to the data collected in the pre-campaign and post-election interviews. The results enabled us to group certain qualities on the list as belonging with each other in the sense that ratings of a leader on one of them tended to be associated closely with assessments on the others. Consequently, some composite scores were calculated for ratings of leaders on *groups* of qualities. These were used in turn (*a*) to measure the changes that had occurred during the campaign in the attitudes of the respondents towards Sir Alec Douglas-Home, Mr. Wilson, and Mr. Grimond and (*b*) to relate the most important shifts to patterns of exposure to the various sources of the campaign.

THE DESIGN OF THE ENQUIRY

The measurement of exposure to the campaign

In order to gauge the impact of the campaign on political attitudes, it was necessary to obtain as precise a record as possible of each individual's exposure to the different sources of influence. The only feasible way of collecting such information was by means of interview after the event. The main alternative – that of asking panel members to keep some diary of their communications behaviour during the campaign – could have influenced what they had seen and heard and heightened self-consciousness about their opinions. We preferred to run the risk of some error in recall, which we hoped to counteract by providing descriptions of certain campaign materials. Such aids to recall were especially important in the case of television, since we wished in the analysis to distinguish between the impact of the different types of programmes that had been broadcast.[12] The questions about campaign exposure, which were included in the post-election interview, covered all the following communications sources:[13]

1. Party election broadcasts on television.
2. Television news:
    (a) Evening news (approximately 6.00 p.m. and 9.00 p.m.).
    (b) Special late election news.
3. *Election Forum* on television.
4. Other political programmes on television:
    (a) *Election Gallery.*
    (b) *This Week.*
    (c) *Election Marathon.*
    (d) *Question Time.*
    (e) *Look North.*
5. Political programmes on radio:
    (a) Party election broadcasts.
    (b) The news (7.00 p.m., 10.00 p.m., and election round-up after 10.00 p.m.).
    (c) *Question Time.*

[12] For example, descriptions of each of the 13 party election broadcasts on television were issued to the interviewers, listing the principal speakers and the most striking visuals that had been presented.

[13] An account of how the panel members were exposed to each of the main sources of the campaign is provided in Chapter 3 below.

6. Newspapers–reading reports of election speeches (frequency and amount).
7. Participation in the local campaign:
    (a) Being canvassed.
    (b) Reading election addresses.
    (c) Attending meetings.
    (d) Knowledge of local candidates.
8. Inter-personal contact and discussion.

From the replies to the questions a series of scores was calculated for each respondent which expressed the degree of his exposure to each of the main sources of the campaign (those numbered 1–7 in the above list). For example, the range of scores for exposure to party election broadcasts on television was 0–13, since 13 such programmes had been transmitted. Full details of the scores, and of the methods by which they were derived are provided in Appendix C. In assessing the impact of election communications, the resulting indices of exposure to the campaign were each correlated in turn with each of our measured campaign 'effects'. (In addition to changes in attitudes to the political parties and their leaders, those effects included changes in levels of information about party policies and altered assessments of the importance of various campaign issues.)[14] In certain cases, where several influences had apparently overlapped in their effect, regression analyses were carried out to help to estimate the relative importance of each contribution and how they had worked together.

A quantitative basis for measuring the impact of a campaign

Implicit in our research design is the expectation that influence from the campaign can be inferred when we find a positive and progressive association between our measures of change and one or more of our measures of exposure. This is a

[14] The measurement of (a) the respondents' knowledge of party policies and (b) the salience to them of various issues was relatively straightforward and followed the methods originally devised for use in the 1959 study (cf. Trenaman, J. and McQuail, Denis, op. cit., Ch. IX). Details of the particular items that were incorporated in the corresponding instruments in 1964 are presented in Chapters 9 and 10 below.

rigorous test to apply to a hypothesis where not only the selection, but also the subsequent measurement, of the variables involved is difficult. Nevertheless, we believe that any findings which pass such a test should enjoy a unique authority, and so the attendant risks are in a sense justified. The negative results of many studies of communications campaigns in the past have, it is true, raised doubts about the validity of the assumption of a one-to-one relationship between exposure to persuasive materials and opinion or attitude change. In the case of an election campaign there may be doubt as to whether change is induced by a gradual wearing down under a persuasive flood or whether it is some dramatic incident or momentary revelation which causes a once-and-for-all adjustment of viewpoint. It is at least conceivable that a relatively brief exposure to an effective message could be as powerful in changing opinion as a prolonged dose. In addition, a purely quantitative test of influence may be criticized for ignoring qualitative aspects of communications behaviour–in the case of television viewing, for example, the degree of attention that is paid to political programmes and the extent to which they are liked or disliked.

Against the first objection it can be maintained that the more of a campaign which an individual receives, the greater are his chances of being exposed to the crucial or most revealing moments in the appearances of politicians and in the presentation of political arguments. To the second criticism our design has a built-in defence. Many of the advantages of the 'uses-and-gratifications approach' to communications research derive precisely from its introduction of a qualitative dimension. Care was taken to measure the general disposition of respondents towards politics and political campaigning, and the emerging parameters were used as divisors of the sample to see how, if at all, they had affected susceptibility to influence. In the event, certain findings upheld the validity of the assumption of a direct and linear relationship between campaign influences and political attitude change. The results also showed that by holding constant some relevant audience attitudes towards political persuasion itself, we could identify or strengthen direct and independent relationships between the degree of exposure to the campaign and the degree of change.

28

THE DESIGN OF THE ENQUIRY

The assessment of attitudes to the persuasive process

Part II of this book is devoted to a detailed consideration of the gratifications sought from political materials by our respondents and of their attitudes towards political television and certain features of election campaigning. This material was derived from a series of items which varied in their focus of enquiry. Substantial points of design and method are discussed in the chapters where the evidence itself is presented. Meanwhile, it may help in appreciating the overall scope of this aspect of the study to have a summary list of the main areas of questioning. The following is intended to serve this purpose:

1. Degree of expressed interest in the forthcoming campaign.
2. Perceptions of the nature of election campaigning.
3. Views about the attention deserved by campaigning politicians.
4. Degree of trust in political promises and other campaign claims.
5. Reactions to the attacks of politicians on each other.
6. Level of satisfaction with the amount of attention normally paid to politics on television.
7. Reasons for watching party broadcasts.
8. Reasons for watching the broadcasts of an opposing party.
9. Reasons for avoiding party broadcasts.
10. Type of political motivation for watching party broadcasts.
11. Overall strength of motivation for watching party broadcasts.
12. Preferences between the different forms that political programmes can take.
13. Judgements about the revelatory power of political television.
14. Retrospective judgements about the coverage of the campaign on television.
15. Inter-media preferences for following politics (press, radio, television).

The stages of the investigation

As many as five separate stages of interviewing were involved in this study, extending over a nine-month period. In addition to the three rounds of interviewing with members of the main panel, two preliminary surveys were conducted, mainly in order to explore audience attitudes towards the persuasive process and to devise and check measures of those attitudes, but also to collect information intended to guide the construction of political attitude scales. To clarify subsequent references to the various stages of the enquiry, the following outline is provided:

1. *First exploratory survey*

A randomly chosen sample of 119 names was drawn from the electoral registers of three socially diverse polling districts in Leeds. Seventy-nine of these individuals were interviewed in late January and early February 1964, within a period of up to five days following the transmission of a Labour Party political broadcast, which was used as a peg for the posing of questions about respondents' reasons for watching and avoiding such programmes. In order to tap spontaneous expressions of view about political broadcasting and campaigning, many of the questions in the interview schedule (which required between 45 and 60 minutes to complete) were open-ended. The replies were treated as a source of raw material for the design of many of the forced-choice items that were incorporated into subsequent questionnaires.

2. *Second exploratory survey*

A quota sample of 209 electors was interviewed in April 1964 in the vicinity of Leeds. Again the interviews were timed to follow a political broadcast (delivered on this occasion by the Conservative Party), and various forced-choice questions, constructed from material collected in the first survey, were tried out. Otherwise, the main purpose of the survey was to administer 25 statements descriptive of the political parties, responses to which were subsequently factor analysed to assist in the selection of a smaller number of items for use in party attitude scales.

3. *Main survey—initial round*

Between June 19th and June 28th, 1964, 908 of a sample of 1,072 electors, drawn from the registers of Pudsey and West Leeds, were interviewed. This was the longest of the three panel interviews and was used mainly to collect classificatory information about the members of the sample. This included most of the questions about interest in politics, attitudes to campaigning, and assessments of television as a political medium, as well as all the necessary demographic particulars. In addition, questions were included about vote intentions and attitudes to the party leaders.

4. *Main survey—pre-campaign round*

Between September 12th and September 20th, 783 of the 908 individuals who had been contacted in June were re-interviewed. The last interviews were held just before the opening of the official election campaign. The main purpose of the questionnaire was to obtain an advance measure of those opinions and perceptions which might be affected by the campaign. Consequently, questions were administered about voting intentions, attitudes to the three parties and their leaders, the importance of campaign issues, and the party origins of various policy measures. In addition, a few questions were asked about the last pre-campaign political broadcast, which had been transmitted by the Labour Party just before this round of interviewing began.

5. *Main survey—post-election round*
Between October 16th and October 25th, interviews were completed with 748 of the 783 individuals who had been seen in the previous round. The same questions that the respondents had been asked in September about party policies, issues, and party and party leader attitudes were administered again to provide a basis for measuring change over the course of the campaign. There was also a question about whether and how the electors had voted. Many detailed questions were posed about their exposure to each of the main sources of the campaign, and a retrospective judgement of the coverage of the election by television was sought.

CHAPTER 3

THE CHANGING ROLE OF
ELECTION TELEVISION

Much of this study is devoted to the responses of voters to the election campaign of 1964 on television and elsewhere: how they looked forward to it, what they wished to get out of it, how they felt about it afterwards, and whether it had affected their political outlook in any way. Before examining this evidence, however, it is appropriate to consider the nature of the 1964 campaign itself and especially the contribution of television to it. What were the main elements in the campaign? How did they reach the members of our sample? How did this differ from the pattern of exposure recorded by electors who resided in the same constituencies in 1959? And, thinking particularly of television, were there any significant changes in the importance and character of its campaign role?

The major channels of election communication include the local campaign (e.g. public meetings, election addresses and canvassing), the press, radio, and television. In the case of broadcasting a further distinction can be drawn between programmes produced by the parties themselves (party election broadcasts) and those prepared independently by the television authorities (news bulletins, current affairs programmes, and any special programmes about the election). In 1959 Trenaman and McQuail recorded the exposure of their respondents to each of these campaign sources in some detail. In 1964, we used identically worded questions wherever possible to establish which parts of the campaign had reached our sample members —facilitating thereby a direct comparison between the two elections. The main determinant of the differences that emerged from this analysis appeared to be change in the availability to the public of certain election materials.

In their discussion of local campaigning, for example, Trenaman and McQuail showed that such activity had remained surprisingly buoyant throughout the 1950s in this country. Records compiled from constituency surveys in four successive elections (1950, 1951, 1955, and 1959) indicated that the increasing reliance of the electorate on television had not diminished the volume of local campaigning. In exposure to election addresses there was even a steady rise from 1950, when 40 per cent of a Greenwich sample claimed to have read at least one, to 1959, when 69 per cent of the Pudsey/West Leeds respondents recalled consulting one.[1] The information we collected in 1964, however, disclosed a slight decline in the importance of the local campaign. Table 3.1 compares electoral exposure to several indices of the local campaign in 1964 with the equivalent records of 1959. The figures show that only three-eighths of the 1964 respondents reported a call by a canvasser, compared with a half of the 1959 sample, and that the proportion attending local meetings had fallen by a half.

Table 3.1. LEVELS OF EXPOSURE TO THE LOCAL CAMPAIGN WERE LOWER IN 1964 THAN IN 1959

	1959 %	*1964* %
Election addresses		
(at least one copy read by electors)	69	64
Attended a meeting	11	5
Knew of a call by a canvasser	49	37
Knew the name of at least one candidate	91	91
N =	661	748

These changes may have resulted either from a loss of interest among electors in the local activities of the parties or from a reduction in the scale of those activities themselves–e.g. the holding of fewer local meetings by constituency organizations and the adoption of less intensive canvassing procedures. We have no objective means of determining which factor was more important, but we suspect that the latter was largely responsible. Describing the local campaign in one of our constituencies

[1] Trenaman, J. and McQuail, Denis, op. cit., p. 81.

(West Leeds), two informed obervers concluded that, 'All in all the impression was of a campaign reluctantly fought for fighting's sake, over the heads of the electorate, with little confidence in the effectiveness of efforts made.' Although, they said, the Conservative candidate believed in the value of canvassing, the Labour candidate sent some of his workers into more marginal constituencies nearby; both major parties relied little on public meetings; and the local Liberal effort was only sporadically active.[2] Even if television does not directly undermine electoral interest in the local campaign, then, it is possible that some party workers regard local activities as less vital in the television age than they used to be–particularly if their constituency is not marginal.

Of the various mass media from which electors may obtain political information and impressions, radio had already receded by 1959 to a merely peripheral position. Nevertheless, it had evidently declined still further by 1964. Despite nearly universal ownership of radio sets (possessed by 95 per cent of our informants), only ten per cent of the 1964 sample recalled hearing a party political broadcast on sound radio–compared with a figure of 16 per cent for the sample contacted at the previous election. Since over a half of those who heard a party broadcast on the radio also saw at least one on television, only four per cent of the whole sample depended solely on sound for its access to party propaganda, compared with ten per cent in 1959.

If a person's home is equipped with both television and radio, then, he tends to rely almost entirely on the former for election coverage. But if he does not have a TV set, and radio provides his only broadcasting link to the campaign, he is likely now to be the sort of person who isolates himself generally from civic affairs. Thirty-four per cent of our respondents without television sets (24 of the 71 non-owners in the sample) were not reached by any form of election broadcasting during the 1964 campaign, compared with only six per cent of the television owners. This may be a function of their above-average age, for two-fifths of the individuals without television were over 65 years old.

[2] Nettl, Peter and Hill, Dilys, 'Leeds West' in Ch. XV, 'Four Constituency Campaigns', of Butler, D. E. and King, Anthony, op. cit., pp. 277–86.

ELECTION TELEVISION

An interesting sign of the development of this isolation over the years emerged from the results of a separate inter-election panel survey. This involved an attempt after Polling Day in 1964 to locate and re-interview the surviving members of Trenaman and McQuail's sample of 1959. Three hundred and ninety individuals were contacted, of whom 81 (or 21 per cent) did not have a television set in 1959. By 1964, however, 46 had acquired one, the proportion without TV falling, then, to ten per cent (39 cases). When trends in party broadcast viewing from 1959 to 1964 were compared for owners and non-owners, respectively, a marked difference emerged. Whereas the number of party broadcasts seen by the TV owners increased substantially between the two elections, comparable exposure among the non-owners was cut in half. The actual figures are shown in Table 3.2. They suggest that by 1964 the non-TV group constituted a hard core of individuals who were either (*a*) staunchly uninterested in television, or (*b*) staunchly uninterested in politics, or (*c*) so cut off from social contacts that they had few opportunities to watch election television in the homes of friends and relations.

Table 3.2. THOSE WITH TELEVISION SAW MORE PARTY ELECTION BROADCASTS IN 1964 THAN IN 1959, BUT THOSE WITHOUT IT SAW FEWER

Average number of party broadcasts seen by the surviving members of the 1959 sample in:	TV owners	Non-owners
1959	3·9	0·5
1964	5·1	0·2

The outstanding political media, then, are television and the press, and it seems clear, when they are compared, that during the General Election of 1964 television came into its own at last as the most important means of political communication in this country. It had already been said in 1959 to have displaced radio as a partner of the press – 'equal to the latter in penetration if not in volume of output.'[3] It was not that the voters relied any less on the press for election news in 1964 than they had in 1959. Forty-six per cent of our sample claimed

[3] Trenaman, J. and McQuail, Denis, op. cit., p. 81.

35

to have read reports of election speeches in their newspapers 'fairly regularly', for example, compared with 42 per cent of the equivalent sample in 1959.[4] But, as a result of two main developments, television acquired greater prominence in 1964 than it had assumed at any previous election. One factor was an increase in the size of the audience for televised party broadcasts during the 1964 election. The other was a combination of changes in the way that television was used, which amounted to a less restricted and more varied coverage of the campaign, and which also increased the exposure of viewers to the various non-party election programmes.

Table 3.3. OVER THREE SUCCESSIVE ELECTIONS
THERE WAS A STEADY INCREASE IN THE VIEWING OF
PARTY ELECTION BROADCASTS

	National figures		Figures from constituency samples†		
	Extent of set ownership %	Average audience* size for party broadcasts (TV) %	TV set ownership in sample %	Saw at least one TV party broadcast %	Average no. of TV party broadcasts seen
1955	38	14	40	38	1 plus
1959	75	22	76	57	3·1
1964	90	30	91	74	4·5

* Expressed as percentages of the total adult population of the United Kingdom.
† Bristol Northeast in 1955; Pudsey and West Leeds in 1959 and 1964.

Documentation of the growth in audience access to televised propaganda between 1955 and 1964 is presented in Table 3.3. Only a seventh of the population watched a typical party election broadcast in 1955, compared with a fifth in 1959 and three-tenths in 1964. Information provided by a series of

[4] Here is the full comparison of respondents' estimates of their readership of election speeches in the press for 1959 and 1964:

	1959 %	1964 %
Fairly regularly	42	46
Occasionally	27	18
None	31	35
	100	99
N =	661	748

constituency surveys suggests that the proportion of electors viewing at least one party election broadcast increased from two-fifths in 1955 to over a half in 1959 and nearly three-quarters in 1964. Consequently, the average number of party broadcasts seen by the respondents who were contacted in these studies also went up at each election–from about one during the 1955 campaign to three in 1959 and to between four and five in 1964.

This steady rise is attributable in turn to two influences, each of which affected the availability of party broadcasts to the electorate. One was the continuing diffusion of set owner-ship to more households. In 1964 nine-tenths of the households of the nation possessed a television set compared with only three-quarters in 1959. The Audience Research Department of the BBC has estimated that this accounts for about a half of the increase in national exposure to televised party broadcasts between those two election years. Most of the rest of the increase was due to a change in the timing of election broadcasts, which were transmitted at a peak hour of 9.30 p.m. in 1964 instead of 10.00 p.m. as in 1959.[5]

In the long run, however, the increased size of the average party broadcast audience was probably less significant than the provision of a more varied menu of political television in 1964 than had been available in 1959. A summary of how the various non-party political programmes reached the members of our 1959 and 1964 samples is presented in Table 3.4. It is fair to say that before 1964 party broadcasts virtually dominated election television, for the news coverage of cam-paigning was limited, and only a few independently produced political programmes were transmitted. Of the latter, the most important in 1959 were *Hustings* (BBC) and in the north *Election Marathon* (Granada). The former–a series of programmes in which regional politicians answered questions put by electors in a studio audience–was continued in 1964 under the title of *Question Time*. But three editions appeared in each region (instead of two as in 1959), and at the insistence of the political parties, the questions were taken from journalists instead of ordinary voters. A few more viewers saw at least

[5] 'The 1964 General Election', Audience Research Department, British Broadcasting Corporation, 1964, LR/64/1950, p. 6.

one of these programmes in 1964 than was the case in 1959. In *Marathon* the candidates of a large number of northern seats addressed viewers for short periods, constituency by constituency. This format was also repeated in 1964, but at a time much less likely to attract viewers (3.00 p.m. instead of 5.00 and 11.00 p.m. in 1959) with a consequent sharp fall in claimed viewing of this programme.

Table 3.4. ELECTORS SAW MORE OF THE CAMPAIGN THROUGH NON-PARTY POLITICAL PROGRAMMES ON TV IN 1964 THAN THEY HAD IN 1959

	1959 %	*1964* %
News bulletins with election news seen at least 3/4 evenings per week	33	64*
Question Time (known as *Hustings* in 1959)–at least one seen	22	27
Election Marathon–at least one seen	22	6
This Week–at least one of three editions seen	Not screened	36
Election Gallery–at least one of six editions seen	Not screened	32
Election Forum–at least one of three editions seen	Not screened	46†

* In 1959 an appreciable amount of election news was presented only in late bulletins, transmitted usually at 10.15 p.m. by the BBC and at 10.50 p.m. by ITN. Trenaman and McQuail enquired, therefore, only about exposure to those bulletins. In 1964, however, both services presented election news in their main bulletins (at 8.55 p.m. by ITN and 9.15 by BBC), and we asked separately about both the main bulletins and the special late-night election programmes. The figure for 1964 of 64 per cent applies to those individuals who saw one or the other of these main or late bulletins at least three or four nights a week. Twenty-two per cent of the 1964 sample claimed to have seen a special late-night election news programme at least three evenings a week.

† Unlike the figures for exposure to the other campaign programmes, our sample's claimed viewing of *Forum* considerably exceeded the audience estimates provided by the BBC and TAM. According to the former, for example, only 17 per cent of the adult population would have seen Sir Alec Douglas-Home's *Forum* compared with 36 per cent of the members of our sample. This discrepancy probably arose from difficulties peculiar to *Election Forum*. It was the least recent of the various programmes about which the respondents were asked and probably the most difficult for them to recognize and to distinguish from other appearances of the party leaders on television.

ELECTION TELEVISION

The pattern of election television was altered in 1964 mainly by three important developments. First, in the week between announcement of the dissolution of Parliament and the opening of the official campaign, the BBC introduced an entirely new kind of programme: *Election Forum*. On each of three successive evenings a panel of interviewers put questions that had been sent in by viewers to the leaders of the Liberal, Labour, and Conservative Parties, respectively. Although the interviewers were confined in the main to the formulations employed by viewers, some pointed supplementary questions were also allowed. This innovation seemed to symbolize the new approach to election television that was adopted in 1964–particularly a determination not to let the politicians have everything their own way. For it was as if, in addition to putting a prepared case in their party broadcasts, it was thought right that they should be required to deal with the problems which most worried the electors. As one commentator noted, this 'provided a rare opportunity to explore issues which the parties preferred to neglect.'[6] And it 'confronted the party leaders with some refreshing examples of how political controversy strikes the rather sceptical man in the street.'[7] Claimed *Forum* viewing by our own respondents proved unreliable, but according to the BBC 17·4 per cent of the national population saw Sir Alec Douglas-Home's *Forum*, 18·5 per cent saw that of Harold Wilson, and 12·1 per cent that of Jo Grimond.[8]

Second, the regular current affairs programmes of political comment and discussion, which had been taken off the air during the 1959 campaign, were allowed to 'stay in business' in 1964, and both *This Week* and *Gallery* covered the election. By devoting the whole of four weekly editions to single issues of the campaign (housing, steel nationalization, immigration, and the economy), the former managed to avoid some of the

[6] Harrison, Martin in Butler, D. E. and King, Anthony, op. cit., p. 162.

[7] Blumler, J. G., 'Campaign on Television', *Socialist Commentary*, November 1964, pp. 8–9.

[8] 'The General Election of 1964', op. cit., p. 7. The percentages provided by the BBC apply to the population aged five years and older. They have been adjusted upwards in the text above, by means of a formula suggested by the BBC Audience Research Department, to refer to the population of voting age only.

39

tendencies to superficiality in television journalism. Six special editions of the latter were transmitted at a relatively popular time (7.30 p.m. instead of *Gallery*'s usual late-night slot), and much background information, reportage of the progress of the campaign, and discussion of its issues was provided. The significance of the continuation of these programmes was that they helped to put the claims and arguments of the politicians in an informed and critical context. Both *This Week* and *Election Gallery* reached about a third of our respondents with at least one edition, respectively.

Third, coverage of the campaign in the news bulletins proved fuller and more adventurous than at any previous election. In 1955, in order to preclude the possibility that any votes might be influenced, the television newcasts ignored the campaign entirely. This ban was lifted in 1959, but most of the coverage of the campaign was relegated to later bulletins (scheduled at 10.15 p.m. by the BBC and at 10.50 by ITN), and many inhibitions in treatment were still apparent. In 1964 both services devoted considerably more time to the election news. In addition to its special late-night election news programme (*Election Extra*), the BBC covered the campaign in its main news bulletins at 9.15 p.m. as well. The main ITN news bulletin at 8.55 p.m. also included election items, and its special late-night programme (*Election '64*) was extended from an average of about ten minutes in 1959 to 20–25 minutes in 1964. Another difference was the availability in 1964 of outside broadcast cameras which occasionally transmitted live shots of campaign events as they occurred. In addition, the practice of questioning politicians about their statements and policies was followed more extensively in 1964 than in 1959. This was partly an outcome of the dramatic growth in the intervening period of political interviewing as a prominent feature of much current affairs television. But it was also facilitated by the agreement of the political parties to permit the televising of their daily press conferences. The content of those conferences was often a convenient source of material that news interviewers could draw upon when framing their own questions for presentation afterwards to the party spokesmen who had handled them. In 1964, then, election news coverage was considerably less circumscribed than it had been at any previous campaign, and Table 3.4 above suggests that it reached many more electors.

These developments were not so radical as some broadcasters and journalists had hoped. With the exception of one encounter, there were no direct confrontations at national level between rival party spokesmen on television during the 1964 campaign, and as usual both major party headquarters managed at one time or another to veto the airing of some topic it preferred not to discuss or the appearance of some speaker whom it deemed unrepresentative. Taken together, however, the various changes and innovations which were effected in 1964 marked a watershed in election broadcasting in Britain. The change was not just a quantitative tipping of the balance of television coverage away from the earlier preponderance of party broadcasts. In addition, there had been a change in the function of television during an election campaign. It had previously provided a platform, from which the politicians addressed their prepared messages to the public, and of course the party broadcasts continued in 1964 to fulfil that role. But now television had also become a window, through which the elector could observe the activities of the politicians and the independent reactions of informed individuals to the policies and claims of party spokesmen.[9]

[9] Compared with 1964 the role of television in the 1966 campaign was characterized by few new departures. It mainly furthered the various developments that had been pioneered at the previous election. Since party broadcasts were scheduled earlier (at 9.10 p.m. just after the main news), the average size of the audience for these programmes increased again. The total number of election broadcasts, and their distribution among the three main parties, remained as in 1964, but eight of the 13 programmes were shortened from 15 to ten minutes in length. *Election Forum, Question Time,* and *Election Marathon* were transmitted again with only minor changes. (The last-named went out in mid-afternoon only but more interchange was encouraged between the various candidates of given constituencies.) Among the national current affairs programmes, *Panorama* joined the ranks of those that stayed on the air during the campaign, devoting each of its editions, as did *This Week,* to a single election issue. There was no BBC *Election Gallery* but a *Campaign Report* was presented nightly in the relatively new current affairs programme known as *24 Hours.* Perhaps the main difference between 1966 and 1964 arose from the willingness of leading politicians to debate the issues face to face with each other on television. Altogether ten such mini-confrontations were arranged on the national current affairs programmes during the 1966 campaign.

The change seemed indirectly to have affected even the party broadcasts themselves. At times they appeared to be trying to compete with the non-party political programmes in liveliness or in the projection of an impression of authenticity. Long straight talks to camera became the exception instead of the rule, and much film was devoted (especially by the Conservative Party) to the illustration of party points. Efforts were made to devise formats suggestive of the independence that other programmes enjoyed–notably in the first Liberal broadcast in which three party spokesmen answered questions put by members of an audience filmed in a hall, and in the fourth Labour broadcast in which four party leaders dealt with questions taken from a 'coffee meeting' of neighbours in the home of a north London housewife.[10]

The new ethos of election broadcasting also tended to put the supporters of party broadcasts more on the defensive than they had ever been before. Various critics complained that the party programmes had been too numerous or too long, or that they were not entitled to a privileged hold on all available channels. By 1964, then, the organization of television politics itself had become an important subject of debate. This was partly an inevitable outcome of the scarcity of television channels and partly an expression of a natural conflict of interests between politicians, broadcasters, and viewers. But it also reflected a recognition on all sides that television had become the most important medium of political communication to the public.

One sign of the enhanced standing of television emerged from the replies of our respondents when they were asked to assess the relative merits of the newspapers, radio, and television as sources of political news. Table 3.5 shows that television was rated as the best medium in five out of six respects–as most up-to-date, impartial, and trustworthy, and as most helpful in weighing up political leaders and in following

---

[10] Something of a reaction against these methods set in after the election. It was felt by some politicians that they had been overdone, and possibly for this reason illustrative material on film played a more subdued part in the party broadcasts of the 1966 campaign. There were more straight talks to camera–but not necessarily by just one speaker for a whole programme.

ELECTION TELEVISION

political issues–while the press was preferred only for its ability to provide a more full account of political events. This pattern of findings echoes a conclusion, drawn recently by two American investigators from the results of a California survey, that 'the sins of newspapers are in commission . . . while the sins of television are in omission.'[11] For, according to our respondents, the performance of the press was least satisfactory for 'trustworthiness' and 'impartiality', and the greatest weakness of television was its scanty coverage. It is not surprising that the voters overwhelmingly nominated television when asked which medium was best for helping them to weigh up political leaders. Perhaps the degree of public reliance on television is best indicated by the fact that a half of the sample also found it most helpful in enabling them to understand political issues–compared with only a quarter who preferred the press in this respect. We have no evidence to show how

Table 3.5. POPULAR RATINGS OF THE MASS MEDIA AS SOURCES OF POLITICAL NEWS

	Most helpful for weighing up political leaders	Most helpful for understanding political issues	Most up-to-date	Most impartial	Most trustworthy	Most full account of political events
	%	%	%	%	%	%
TV	61	50	46	45	44	34
Press	19	28	31	18	17	50
Radio	6	10	16	18	20	8
Joint mentions	2	2	3	5	6	2
Don't know	12	11	5	13	13	6
	100	101	101	99	100	100

N = 748 informants

[11] Carter, Richard F. and Greenberg, Bradley S., 'Newspapers or Television: Which Do You Believe?', *Journalism Quarterly*, Vol. XLII, No. 1, 1965, pp. 29–34.

these opinions have developed over time, but in the United States there has been a small but steady increase in dependence on television for following current affairs since 1959. Whereas 51 per cent of the members of a national sample mentioned television when asked in that year to name the main source of their news about what was going on in the world, by 1964 the equivalent proportion had increased to 58 per cent.[12]

The preference of an individual for television or the press as a source of political news is a function in part of his demographic traits. The first four sets of bars in Figure 3.1 illustrate the influence of a number of these characteristics on the sample's ratings of the various media for helpfulness in understanding political issues. They reveal that television was most favoured for this purpose by women, rather than men, by skilled manual workers, in contrast to both the non-manual and the non-skilled workers, and by the less educated respondents. Television was least popular with those electors who had reached retiring age and with the highly educated, and reliance on the press was greater among those who had left school at the age of 16 than in any other group represented in the figure.[13]

The role of age and education is complicated by the fact that the young tend to be better educated than their elders. In our sample, for example, 30 per cent of the 21–29 age-group had stayed on at school until at least the age of 16, compared with only five per cent of the 66 + age-group. But when the influence of education on media ratings was examined by controlling for age, it proved even stronger than the figure suggests. Similarly, when the effect of age was inspected with

[12] 'The Public's View of Television and Other Media, 1959–1964', Elmo Roper and Associates, Television Information Office, New York, N.Y., 1965, p. 2.

[13] This demographic pattern is consistent with evidence presented in Carter, Richard F. and Greenberg, Bradley S., op. cit; Westley, Bruce H. and Severin, Werner J., 'Some Correlates of Media Credibility', *Journalism Quarterly*, Vol. XLI, No. 3, 1964, pp. 325–35; and Greenberg, Bradley S., 'Media Use and Believability: Some Multiple Correlates', *Journalism Quarterly*, Vol. XLIII, No. 4, 1966, pp. 665–70. These American studies rely on somewhat different criteria of media preference, and they do not provide data about the role of occupation. But they disclose a clear tendency for women and less-educated respondents to prefer television to the press for current affairs coverage.

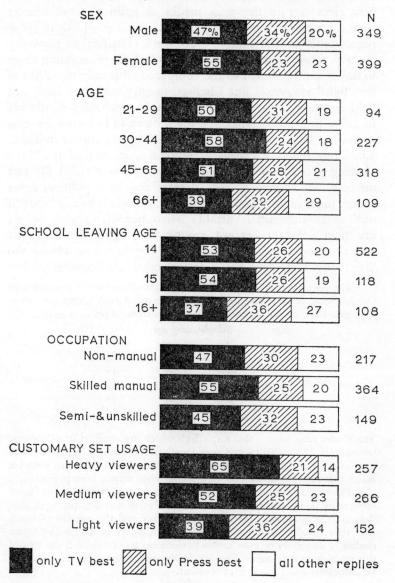

Figure 3.1. CONFIDENCE IN TV AS AN AID TO THE
UNDERSTANDING OF POLITICAL ISSUES VARIED WITH
AMOUNT OF NORMAL SET USE AND, TO A LESSER EXTENT,
WITH SEX, AGE, EDUCATION AND OCCUPATION

SEX

	only TV best	only Press best	all other replies	N
Male	47%	34%	20%	349
Female	55	23	23	399

AGE

21-29	50	31	19	94
30-44	58	24	18	227
45-65	51	28	21	318
66+	39	32	29	109

SCHOOL LEAVING AGE

14	53	26	20	522
15	54	26	19	118
16+	37	36	27	108

OCCUPATION

Non-manual	47	30	23	217
Skilled manual	55	25	20	364
Semi-&unskilled	45	32	23	149

CUSTOMARY SET USAGE

Heavy viewers	65	21	14	257
Medium viewers	52	25	23	266
Light viewers	39	36	24	152

only TV best   only Press best   all other replies

control for education the portrayed relationship was strengthened.[14]

According to the last set of bars in Figure 3.1, however, customary TV set usage is even more important in determining how electors rate the mass media as political news sources than are any of their demographic traits. Two-thirds of those respondents in the sample who were classified as normally 'heavy' viewers found television most helpful in enabling them to understand political issues, compared with only two-fifths of the 'light' viewers.[15] But when customary set usage itself was held constant, most of the demographic variables continued to affect the ratings, although the pattern of influence became somewhat more complex. The detailed figures appear in Table 3.6. They reflect a consistent tendency, in each of the three viewing groups into which the sample was divided for this analysis, for women to regard television as a political news source more highly than do men. Occupation is nearly 'washed out' as an influential variable when normal viewing habits are held constant (except among the 'light' viewers). But education continues to be important (again except among the 'light' viewers). And the oldest electors are consistently less

[14] The interaction of age and education on media ratings is illustrated by the following table. This gives the percentages of each group who cited television alone as best for helping them to understand political issues.

Age	School-leaving age		
	14	15	16 +
	%	%	%
21–29	100*	48	46
30–44	60	69	39
45–65	51	47	32
66+	41	25*	—*

* Very low N.

The reader may assume that any effects which are ascribed in subsequent passages in this work to age or education are genuine. Controls have invariably been applied in examining the data, although the rather complex tables that result from such an analysis have not usually been presented.

[15] The sample members were classified as 'heavy', 'medium', or 'light' viewers by taking account both of the number of evenings per week that they claimed on average to engage in viewing and the number of hours that they usually viewed on a typical evening. None of the American studies of correlates of mass media preferences has considered the role of this variable or determined how far demographic particulars continued to be influential when it was held constant.

impressed with television as a political medium than are the members of any other age group.

Table 3.6. PROPORTIONS REGARDING TELEVISION AS MOST HELPFUL FOR UNDERSTANDING POLITICAL ISSUES BY CUSTOMARY SET USAGE AND DEMOGRAPHIC PARTICULARS

		Heavy viewers %	Medium viewers %	Light viewers %
Sex	Male	61	52	35
	Female	70	57	47
Occupation	Non-manual	68	55	33
	Skilled manual	69	54	46
	Semi-skilled and unskilled	63	51	30
School-leaving age	14	67	58	42
	15	73	53	50
	16 +	47	44	46
Age	21–29	71	47	39
	30–44	67	61	44
	45–65	68	54	37
	66 +	62	48	36

In spite of all these differences, however, no group contains a majority of individuals who think that the press is more helpful than television in enabling them to understand political issues. The differences between groups apply only to the size of the majority that regarded television as superior. What, then, do voters look for when they follow an election by means of this preferred medium? Why do they watch–and perhaps avoid–party broadcasts? Which forms of television politics do they prefer, and how do they feel about some of the novel programme types that have been tried out or proposed? These and many other related questions are discussed in the next Part of this volume, which presents the evidence we have collected about the attitudes of electors to political television.

PART II

A CONSUMER'S VIEW OF POLITICAL TELEVISION

CHAPTER 4

WHY DO PEOPLE WATCH
POLITICAL PROGRAMMES?

Some problems and paradoxes

Before this investigation was undertaken, mass media research had paid little attention to the appeal of politics on tele-vision. Although a large quantity of television propaganda enters many homes, both during an election and in out-of-election periods, its psychological meaning is obscure. (By any standards, the average number of 4·5 party election broadcasts seen by each member of our sample during the 1964 campaign is a high figure.) The problem which this poses is divisible into two main questions. First, how much political viewing should be dis-counted as lacking in political significance and due to such extraneous factors as the habitual and unselective nature of set usage, allied to the monopoly hold of party broadcasts on all channels when they are transmitted? Second, in so far as people watch party broadcasts for any positive reason at all, what par-ticular interests are they seeking to gratify?

So far as the first question is concerned, it can hardly be doubted that some acceptance of political television is unselec-tive, while some is positively motivated, but we do not know what proportion to assign to either category. When they looked into this matter in 1959, Trenaman and McQuail estimated that about three-fifths of the audience for party broadcasts con-sisted of 'voluntary' viewers, but their measure was indirect, and, on the face of it, their calculations seem rather generous.[1]

---

[1] The authors counted a party broadcast viewer as 'voluntary' if he 'had shown a recognizable interest in political news before the election' by viewing *Tonight*, reading most of a paper like the *Yorkshire Evening Post*,

The provision of a realistic estimate of the extent of unselective political viewing could be crucial, if only in order to judge how the size of the audience would be affected, should party broadcasts ever be transmitted on one channel only.

Even among those who have deliberately chosen to watch a party broadcast, it is not clear what motives are involved and how far they spring from a genuine interest in politics. The difficulties may be introduced by considering a model of rational political behaviour, which an American economist, Anthony Downs, has put forward. According to Downs, a rational *homo politicus* would cast his vote for that party which is likely to benefit him most. This would seem to require an effort to gather information from various sources – including party propaganda – about the measures which the competing parties would adopt if elected.[2] But the validity of this model of political information-seeking is vulnerable to two fundamental objections; and we shall see that, once their cogency is admitted, the provision of an alternative explanation of the readiness of voters to follow politics in the mass media becomes very difficult.

First, numerous surveys suggest that Downs' model applies at the most only to a small minority of the electorate. The individuals who make up their minds how to vote during a campaign amount usually to no more than a fifth of those who eventually go to the polls,[3] and some of the undecided electors actually receive less political information than is absorbed by the more firmly committed voters. Consequently, some scholars have interpreted political information-seeking as an expression mainly of a desire for reinforcement: most people, it is said, accept political materials in order to confirm and strengthen their already established loyalties and beliefs. But no attempt has ever been made to determine exactly how many voters are influenced by this motive, and its supposed dominance is difficult to reconcile with the bi-partisan character of the party broadcast audience in Britain. Table 4.1 illustrates the readiness of the

and hearing the morning news on the radio at least three times a week. (Trenaman, J. and McQuail, Denis, op. cit., p. 86.)

[2] Downs, Anthony, *An Economic Theory of Democracy*, Harper and Row, New York, 1957, Ch. 3.

[3] In our sample, for example, 124, or 18·3 per cent, of the 676 respondents who voted on Polling Day either supported a different party (64) or were 'don't knows' or did not intend to vote (60) at the start of the campaign.

supporters of one party to view programmes put out by their opponents during the General Election of 1964. It can be seen that, although the Conservative and Labour voters watched more of their own broadcasts on the average than those which had been put out by any other single party, they also received more television propaganda from the other two parties combined than from their own party.

Table 4.1. PARTY DIRECTION OF ELECTION BROADCAST VIEWING BY 1964 VOTE

Party originating the broadcasts	Average number of party broadcasts seen by:		
	Conservative voters	Labour voters	Liberal voters
Conservative	1·8	1·8	1·9
Labour	1·4	2·2	1·6
Liberal	0·9	1·1	1·2
N =	246	321	86

The second objection to the model of exposure to political materials as rational and related to electoral choice has been advanced by Downs himself. He argues that a rational man would expend no more effort in obtaining information than its acquisition is worth to him; and this leads to the striking conclusion that it is rarely worthwhile for anyone to seek political information. Highly committed voters, he says, have no need for materials which are unlikely to modify their party allegiances, while to the more apathetic mass of the electorate, politics are insufficiently important to justify the trouble involved in finding out what policy measures have been proposed and trying to assess them.[4]

The force of the latter point is strengthened by what we know about the low salience of politics to the average man. As Richard Rose has put it, 'Many Englishmen maintain a shallow intermittent participation in politics . . . '.[5] Mark Abrams has reported that only 15 per cent of the members of a sample who were contacted in an out-of-election period described themselves as 'very interested' in politics.[6] And when the Independent

[4] Downs, Anthony, op. cit., Ch. 13.

[5] Rose, Richard, *Politics in England*, Faber and Faber, London, 1965, p. 93.

[6] Abrams, Mark, 'Social Trends and Electoral Behaviour', *The British Journal of Sociology*, Vol. XIII, No. 3, 1963, pp. 228–42.

Television Authority recently commissioned a survey of public attitudes towards news and current affairs broadcasting, it was found that politics was less popular as a subject of documentary programmes than any of nine other topic areas.[7]

In fact some political scientists tend to portray the masses as so engrossed in their personal affairs that the world of politics appears remote and alien to them. The average man is said to be impressed less with the impact of politics on his everyday concerns than with the divorce between his immediate interests and the affairs of state. The remarks of Robert Dahl illustrate this type of analysis:

> Typically, as a source of direct gratifications, political activity will appear to *homo civicus* as less attractive than a host of other activities; and, as a strategy to achieve his gratifications indirectly, political action will seem considerably less efficient than working at his job, earning more money, taking out insurance, joining clubs, planning a vacation, moving to another neighbourhood or city, or coping with an uncertain future in manifold other ways . . . At the focus of most men's lives are primary activities involving food, sex, love, family, play, shelter, comfort, friendship, social esteem, and the like. Activities like these—not politics—are the primary concerns of most men and women.[8]

These observations bring us directly up against the paradox of high exposure to political communications without any convincing psychological basis. Must we accept that from a political point of view the media behaviour of most people is irrational? Or, so far as party broadcasts are concerned, is it largely casual and motiveless—due mainly to the peculiar organization of political television in Britain? Alternatively, should we agree with Morris Rosenberg that 'politics has deteriorated in meaning for many people to the level of a spectacle like a baseball game or a film'[9] and is often followed in that spirit? Or is there, after all, a serious kernel of interest in the absorption of the average elector in mass media coverage of an election campaign?

[7] 'Report on a Survey of Attitudes towards News, Current Affairs, and Documentary Programmes on Television', prepared for the Independent Television Authority by Sales Research Services, Ltd., London, 1966.

[8] Dahl, Robert, *Who Governs?*, Yale University Press, New Haven, 1961, pp. 224 and 279.

[9] Rosenberg, Morris, 'The Meaning of Politics in Mass Society', *Public Opinion Quarterly*, Vol. XV, No. 1, 1951, pp. 5–15.

In short, if most viewers are not seeking guidance how to vote, what *are* they looking for from political television? In the words of Katz and Feldman, is it 'entertainment or education or politics or what?'[10]

It is towards answering these questions that the following analysis is directed. Since it is political apathy, and what one experienced observer has called the 'inbuilt hostility to party election and party political broadcasting',[11] which raise the most severe doubts about the meaning of the high degree of political exposure, we will deal first with what people dislike about party broadcasts. Then we shall try to penetrate some of the uncertainty about unselective viewing which the organization of political broadcasting has caused. Finally, we shall examine some of the positive motives that may be involved in political viewing.

Reasons for avoiding party broadcasts

A relatively straightforward approach was adopted in assessing the nature and strength of negative feelings about viewing political programmes. A process of exploratory interviewing, designed to obtain spontaneous expressions of view in preliminary enquiries, was followed by the administration of a number of more structured items to the individuals who took part in the initial and pre-campaign rounds of the main survey. Table 4.2 presents the results of a question which required people to respond to a list of nine reasons 'for avoiding party broadcasts'. The sample members were asked, in September 1964, to indicate those 'reasons that might occasionally put you off watching party election broadcasts during the campaign'. (It was made clear that none, one, or more than one could apply.) The response shows that a mild dislike of broadcast propaganda is quite common. Only 22 per cent of the owners of television sets failed to endorse at least one of the reasons for avoiding election broadcasts.

[10] Katz, Elihu and Feldman, Jacob J., in Kraus, Sidney, op. cit., p. 216.
[11] Wyndham-Goldie, Grace, in an address delivered at a meeting on 'Television and Politics', which was arranged on November 26, 1964, by the Society of Film and Television Arts, and reprinted in the *Journal of the Society of Film and Television Arts*, No. 19, Spring 1965, pp. 2–3.

Table 4.2. Reasons for avoiding party election
broadcasts*

		%
1.	Because my mind is already made up	37
2.	Because you can't always trust what politicians tell you on television	35
3.	Because I am not much interested in politics	26
4.	Because they hardly ever have anything new to say	24
5.	Because I prefer to relax when watching television	23
6.	Because some speakers talk over one's head	20
7.	Because some speakers talk down to the audience	16
8.	Because I dislike being 'got at' by politicians	14
9.	Because politics should not intrude into the home and family affairs	9
	N =	677 TV set owners

* Respondents could endorse more than one reason.

Not surprisingly, 'because my mind is already made up' was the most heavily endorsed item, but the position of several others is more interesting. Few viewers seem to regard political television as an unwelcome intrusion into the domestic hearth (item 9). And although a quarter of the sample were conscious of a conflict between party broadcasting and their desire to relax when watching television (item 5), perhaps it is more notable that a large majority did not consider this a sufficient ground for resenting the screening of controversial material.

What, then, are the most important sources of hostility to party broadcasting? If we discount a general lack of interest in politics (which, like a mind that is already made up, campaigning politicians can do little to combat), two points stand out as accounting for much of the dislike of political television. These are a mistrust of party propaganda on the ground of its unreliability (item 2) and a feeling of boredom with its staleness (item 4). These sources of opposition, which our respondents have singled out, seem to derive from attitudes towards propaganda as such, rather than from the viewing situation, or from the manner of politicians when they address the electorate on television (items 6 and 7). Political arguments and claims are regarded in advance as untrustworthy and old hat. But does the prevalence of scepticism and an expectation of boredom in much of the party broadcast audience mean that it is composed largely of people who are indifferent to what is said, and who are just waiting for the next programme on the schedule?

The unselective viewer's tolerance of party broadcasts

The difficulties involved in estimating the size of the involuntary portion of the party broadcast audience are formidable—perhaps insurmountable in any rigorous sense. The notion of an unselective viewer calls for some definition in advance. We are concerned with the person who watches a party broadcast primarily because of inertia or because there is no alternative available on another channel. We would expect a positive political interest to play no part in his decision to view. It would be occasioned instead by circumstance, and the experience would have little intrinsic appeal. The location of such people can only be achieved indirectly; and even if we could experiment with the transmission of party broadcasts under different conditions, in order to establish exactly who enters and leaves the audience in response to different alternatives, we would probably find the movement influenced by the *character* of the alternative and not simply its *availability*. That is, *Coronation Street* would probably deplete the party broadcast audience far more drastically than, say, a symphony concert.

Our estimate derived from the viewer's own freely proffered explanation of his presence in the audience, and it depended on whether or not he gave a political account of this. Respondents were interviewed from one to seven days following the transmission of a party political broadcast, to which their attention was drawn by showing them the pages of the *Radio Times* and the *TV Times* for the date concerned. As an additional aid to recall, the interviewees were asked whether they had seen any of the programmes that had immediately preceded and followed the party broadcast on both channels. Those who remembered having seen the party broadcast were asked a matter-of-fact question that would not suggest any particular reason for having viewed it: 'How did it come about that you watched that programme?'. Non-viewers were asked, 'Did you mind not watching that programme?', and 'Why was that?'.

These items were administered to three different samples

(comprising 79, 209, and 748 respondents, respectively) following the Labour broadcast of January 29, 1964, the Conservative broadcast of April 6, 1964, and the Labour broadcast of September 11, 1964.[12] When the reasons given by those viewers who claimed to have seen one of these programmes were analysed, a distinction emerged between two types of replies. One set of answers referred at some point to the individual's interest in politics, and the other group consisted of completely non-political replies. Some examples of statements provided by the politically interested viewers follow:

> The TV was already on, and I continued watching. I've been interested in politics all my life, and I wanted to hear what they had to say. A lot of changes have occurred in my life, due partly to the Labour Party.

> We already had the television on, but we are interested in the way politics is going. You want to know what's going on and what changes Labour might make if they should become the government.

> I've watched them all to get their different views—Labour, Conservative, and Liberal. I want to see what they're prepared to do. It's instructive. It's the only way they can reach me—by TV. I can't get out to meetings.

> I saw it in the *Radio Times* and decided to watch it. There was nothing else on the other programme so my wife couldn't argue about it. I nearly always watch the political programmes and I like to hear what the politicians have to say. I like to know what

[12] The figures below show how many respondents claimed to have seen the broadcast concerned, in comparison with the BBC's estimate of the proportion of the adult population in the North who had viewed it. It can be seen that claimed viewing diverged markedly from the BBC estimate only in the case of the April survey. The figures correspond most closely for the members of our main sample when they were interviewed in September 1964.

Month of survey	Extent of claimed viewing in sample	BBC estimate of Northern viewing (corrected to apply to adults aged 21 and over)
	%	%
February 1964	33	26
April 1964	43	26
September 1964	26	25

the current ideas are, and I think it's interesting to see the different politicians talking.

Individuals who might be regarded as unselective viewers of a party broadcast replied, however, in the following ways:

I was just in the room sewing, and father was in control of the set.

I watched it because it was on both programmes. If we hadn't watched it, we would have just switched it off—so we left it on as it was but were not very interested.

Force of habit. It never gets switched off. I was waiting for Frank Sinatra, Jr.

The television was on. No one else told me to watch it. I was just bored and liked the sound of voices. It keeps me company.

I was visiting friends who were watching the programme.

A similar distinction separated two groups of individuals who had failed to see the party broadcasts—those who regretted this and those who did not. The former consisted of individuals who, when asked, 'Did you mind not watching that programme?', said:

Yes. I like to hear their ideas, although whether or not they carry them out remains to be seen.

Yes. I wanted to see it because I lean towards Labour.

Yes. I like to actually hear them.

But respondents who did not mind missing a party broadcast were inclined to say that:

It didn't bother me. I don't understand a lot about politics.

I don't like those party political things at all. They're all the same. They're buttering themselves up all the time. They're all goody-goody, saying how good they are and how bad the others are. What they will do and the others won't—that sort of thing. It annoys me.

I wasn't in that night, but I wouldn't have watched it anyway.

I'm not interested in politics. I prefer to relax when I'm watching television. I like to be entertained. Anyway, they always say much the same sort of thing.

No. They never seem to get anywhere in these programmes. They

59

start off about one thing and finish up on something else. Fighting to outdo the others.

No. They are always promising something–the parties fighting against each other to keep in power. Their promises are given but never fulfilled.

Most of the respondents could be assigned, then, to one of four categories. When, for example, two judges were asked to undertake such a classification of the members of the main sample, they agreed on the placing of 84 per cent of the cases. Table 4.3 shows how the classified replies were distributed on each of the three occasions that this method of interviewing was adopted. It can be seen, first, that only a few non-viewers regretted missing the party broadcasts concerned. Second, the politically interested viewers of a party broadcast amounted on each occasion to a considerable part of the total audience. And third, the size of this political element fluctuated: it was apparently much smaller in February 1964 than in April or September of the same year.

Table 4.3. Respondents' reactions to viewing and missing selected party political broadcasts

Month of survey	Proportions of non-viewers who regretted missing the broadcast* %	Proportions of viewers who gave political reasons for having seen the broadcast† %
February 1964	17	38
April 1964	18	50
September 1964	14	53

* These percentages were calculated on the following total numbers of classified non-viewers: 47 (February), 106 (April), and 401 (September).

† These percentages were calculated on the following total numbers of classified viewers: 26 (February), 74 (April), and 167 (September).

Such fluctuations may reflect differences in the prevailing political climate. A viewer is more likely to be aware of a political reason for watching a party broadcast when an election is imminent than at any other time. And the high level of 'voluntary' viewing which was recorded in April 1964 may have been due to the exceptional degree of uncertainty by which Conservative plans and fortunes were affected at that time. There had been much press comment about the need for an early announcement of the date of the forthcoming General Election, and it was publicized in advance that the then Prime Minister, Sir Alec Douglas-Home, would appear in the programme of April 6th. This could help to explain the fact that an unusually large number of Conservative viewers of that broadcast (69 per cent) gave political reasons for having watched it. In fact party allegiance invariably affected responses to our questions. On each occasion political explanations for having seen a party broadcast were greater among supporters than among opponents of the transmitting party. Even among the latter, however, the proportion of 'voluntary' viewers never fell below 30 per cent.[13]

This analysis suggests that the politically interested portion of the party broadcast audience rarely rises above a ceiling of about a half of those who are tuned in–a figure which tends to be reached just before and during an election campaign and possibly at other times of intense political excitement. Trenaman and McQuail's estimate of the level of 'voluntary' viewing of party broadcasts (a figure of 60 per cent within a range of 50–70 per cent) probably erred on the high side. In a 'normal' inter-campaign period the 'voluntary' viewers might amount to only about three-eighths of the audience.[14]

The meaning of unselective viewing was probed further by an analysis which concentrated on the *political information* at the

[13] The effect of party support on viewers' references to political reasons for having watched a party broadcast is shown by the following figures:

	Proportions of viewers who gave political reasons for having seen the broadcast	
	Conservative supporters %	Labour supporters %
Labour broadcast of January 29, 1964	30	45
Conservative broadcast of April 6, 1964	69	48
Labour broadcast of September 11, 1964	54	55

[14] It may be doubted whether the political climate was entirely 'normal' at any time during 1964, for speculation about the forthcoming election was rife throughout the year from January to October. If this influenced the response, the politically interested section of the party broadcast audience might at other times prove even smaller than the estimate of three-eighths given in the text.

disposal of those who mentioned no political reason for having seen a party broadcast and on the degree of their *interest in following the forthcoming election camapign.* The unselective viewers in the September sample (which was sufficiently large for sub-groups to be compared) were contrasted in these respects with two other groups: all the politically interested respondents (including both those who gave a political reason for having seen the September party broadcast and those who regretted having missed it);[15] and all the non-viewers of the party broadcast who had not minded missing it.

Figure 4.1. REACTIONS TO THE LABOUR BROADCAST OF SEPTEMBER 11, 1964, BY LEVEL OF POLITICAL INFORMATION

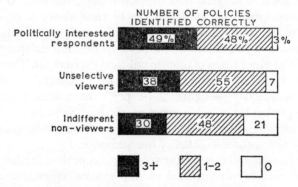

Significant at P = ·001 level for four degrees of freedom.

Despite their failure to refer to politics when asked why they had seen a party broadcast, it transpired that the unselective viewers differed significantly from the indifferent non-viewers.[16] They were both more knowledgeable and more interested in the

---

[15] It was permissible to combine these two groups into a single one for the purpose of these analyses, for it was found that they resembled each other very closely. For example, 50 per cent of the politically concerned viewers identified three party policies or more correctly, compared with 49 per cent of the non-viewers who regretted having missed the September party broadcast. And 44 per cent of the former group were rated 'very strong' in motivation for following the forthcoming election campaign, compared with 45 per cent of the latter.

[16] Unless otherwise stated, the chi-square test was used in this and all subsequent tests of significance mentioned in this book.

imminent election than the latter. Figure 4.1 shows how each of the groups in the analysis fared when asked to say which political party had proposed each of six policy measures. It can be seen that a half of the politically interested group identified three or more party policies correctly, compared with three-eighths of the unselective viewers, and three-tenths of the in-different non-viewers. Only seven per cent of the unselective viewers were unable to answer any of the information questions correctly, compared with 21 per cent of the indifferent non-viewers.

The differentiation was even more noticeable when interest in the forthcoming election campaign was considered – as in Figure 4.2.[17] This shows that 44 per cent of the politically interested group were rated 'very strong' in their motivation to follow the 1964 campaign, compared with 30 per cent of the unselective viewers, and only 15 per cent of the indifferent non-viewers.

Figure 4.2. REACTIONS TO THE LABOUR BROADCAST OF SEPTEMBER 11, 1964, BY STRENGTH OF MOTIVATION FOR FOLLOWING THE FORTHCOMING ELECTION CAMPAIGN

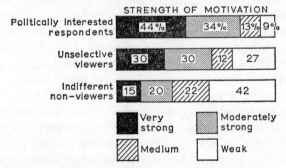

Significant at P = ·001 level for six degrees of freedom.

Two conclusions may be drawn from these findings. First, they suggest that the television audience which politicians address, though heterogeneous, and ranging, as Lord Windlesham has said, 'from the politically well informed and interested

[17] The nature of the measure used here is explained in some detail in Chapter 7.

to the completely uninformed and uninterested',[18] is somewhat above the general average in political knowledgeability and interest. For example, all those who saw the Labour broadcast of September 11, 1964, identified 2·3 party policies correctly on the average, compared with only 1·8 among those who had failed to see it; and 36 per cent of these viewers were rated 'very strong' in motivation for following the forthcoming election, compared with only 22 per cent of the rest of the sample.

Second, even though, in conditions of choice, many of the unselective viewers would have probably watched some other programme, their willingness to leave a party broadcast on under the present system seems to stand for something more than a rather uncritical reliance on their sets. This extra factor can probably be interpreted most suitably as a *toleration* of the presentation of politics on television.

Reasons for watching party broadcasts

These findings also underline the appropriateness of considering the particular gratifications which people may hope to satisfy by watching a party broadcast. Up to a half of the viewers refer spontaneously to the political content of such a programme, when asked why they watched it, and even the willingness of the rest of the audience to stay tuned in is politically significant in at least a minimal sense. It is relevant, therefore, to ask: Once they have left (or switched) it on, what do the viewers hope to get out of a party broadcast?

Two bodies of information have helped us to answer this question. One consists of open-ended material which was supplied by the participants in our first exploratory survey in February 1964. Sixty-nine of the 79 respondents said that they definitely would, or that they might, watch some party broadcasts during the official election campaign due to be held sometime in that year. When asked to give their 'main reasons for doing so', 16 individuals provided no clear answer and Table 4.4 shows how the replies of the others were classified.

Although the range of gratifications listed in Table 4.4 is wide, the most frequently mentioned reasons for watching party

[18] Lord Windlesham, *Communication and Political Power*, Jonathan Cape, London, 1966, p. 215.

Table 4.4. REASONS FOR WATCHING PARTY BROADCASTS
IN THE FORTHCOMING CAMPAIGN—AS STATED BY
53 RESPONDENTS, FEBRUARY 1964*

	No. of respondents
For general surveillance of politics (To keep up with, learn, see what is going on—in the country, at the election, in politics, in the world)	15
To see what some party would do should it win the election	14
To compare some party's election promises with its performance after the election	9
To enjoy the excitement of the election race	9
To judge what political leaders are like	7
To help make up my mind how to vote	5
To judge which party is likely to win the election	5
To use in discussion of the election with other people	5
To enjoy a feeling of superiority over politicians (to see how silly they are, pick holes in their arguments)	3
To remind me of my party's strong points	2
For intellectual satisfactions (to follow the arguments)	2

* Respondents could state more than one reason.

broadcasts reflected the interest of our respondents in what might be called *surveillance of the political environment*. Each of the first three rows in the table suggests that political broadcasts are regarded largely as a source of information about political affairs, and this appears to have both a general and a more specific meaning. In the more general sense, watching political television is most analogous to tuning in to the news. It is the sort of thing that a citizen does simply to keep in touch with events and trends in the wider world around him. But, more specifically, it is also a way of finding out what might be in store for him, his family, or some group he identifies with, should one or another party win an election and obtain power. It is evident from this material (see in particular the third row of the table), as well as from other data that we collected, that this specific element was often connected with sensitivity to the promises and pledges which electioneering politicians make when campaigning on behalf of their parties.[19]

The second body of evidence was collected in September 1964 from the members of our main sample, who were questioned about the gratifications they sought when watching party broadcasts. Using a more structured item on this occasion, those individuals who told the interviewer that they would, or might, watch some party broadcasts during the forthcoming campaign were presented with a card containing eight reasons for doing so and were asked to indicate any that applied to them. This list was drafted with the intention of covering economically most of the important motives that the open-ended questioning had disclosed in February.

Of the 677 television owners in the sample, 119, or 18 per cent, asserted that they would not watch any election broadcasts. Table 4.5 shows how each of the individual reasons on the card appealed to the would-be viewers among our respondents. (The percentages are based, however, on all the television owners and not merely those who expected to see some party broadcasts.)

Table 4.5. REASONS FOR WATCHING PARTY BROADCASTS IN THE FORTHCOMING CAMPAIGN—AS ENDORSED BY TV OWNERS, SEPTEMBER 1964*

	%
To see what some party will do if it gets into power	55
To keep up with the main issues of the day	52
To judge what political leaders are like	51
To remind me of my party's strong points	36
To judge who is likely to win the election	31
To help make up my mind how to vote	26
To enjoy the excitement of the election race	24
To use as ammunition in arguments with others	10
N =	677

* Respondents could endorse more than one reason.

The results reaffirm the importance of surveillance of the political environment as a paramount reason for following party broadcasts. The first two items on the list, which undoubtedly

[19] The significance of this interest in election promises is discussed more fully in Chapter 6.

66

belong to this category, were both endorsed by just over a half of all the set owners—a much higher proportion than any other item elicited except 'to judge what political leaders are like'. The impression is conveyed again that many voters use party election broadcasts, specifically, in order to find out what lies in store for them, should either the Labour or Conservative Parties win power, and, more generally, as a way of keeping up with current affairs. The fact that a 'leader-judging' item was almost as popular as the first two may reflect the public's appreciation of the unique opportunity which television affords of seeing political personalities in action, but there is evidence to suggest that this gratification is also connected with an interest in surveillance—as if the qualities of leading politicians form a part of that environment about which many citizens wished to be informed.[20]

Table 4.5 shows that several other interests may influence election broadcast viewing as well. Of the items on the card, only the activist's wish to obtain ammunition for use in political arguments was endorsed by quite a small minority. The excitement engendered by the conflicts and uncertainties of electioneering appealed, apparently, to between a fourth (item 7) and three-tenths (item 5) of the owners of television sets. Perhaps in viewing a party election broadcast they tended to find something analogous to a spectator's enjoyment of a competitive sport. It is of particular interest that fairly large numbers claimed to be prompted by more narrowly political reasons for seeing party broadcasts—that is, by motives which related their expected viewing to considerations of party allegiance and choice. A third of the set owners professed to seek a reinforcement of their existing political outlook; in fact the phrase which expressed this motive ('to remind me of my party's strong points') was endorsed more heavily than any other item on the card, except those which stood for surveillance. In addition, a quarter of the viewers hoped that seeing election broadcasts would help them to make up their minds how to vote.

Table 4.5 provides an approximate guide, then, to the relative importance of the various gratifications that are associated with party broadcast viewing, but can any additional meaning be extracted from these endorsements? In further analyses we

[20] See the analysis of inter-correlations of item endorsements on pp. 75–77.

explored three additional questions. First, we asked whether there was a significant *pattern* in the motives that people acknowledged as helping to explain their political viewing. How, if at all, is an acceptance of one item on our list related to an acceptance or rejection of the others? Second, we enquired whether viewers differed–according to groupings of age, sex, and class–in the gratifications which appealed to them. Are some groups of electors moved by interests in political television to which other groups are substantially indifferent? Finally, we considered the significance of the discovery that an interest in political surveillance is the predominant positive motive behind the viewing of party broadcasts. How can this be explained, and can it be reconciled with what we know already about the political behaviour of the average citizen? We begin, however, by reporting what we have learned about the relationship between the two most directly political motives for viewing party broadcasts: a desire for reinforcement and a need for help in deciding how to vote.

Political motives for receiving broadcast propaganda

It is important to grasp the nature of this relationship in order to clear up some confusions about the political meaning of exposure to party propaganda in an election campaign. After noting the stability of most voting intentions throughout a campaign, American students of voting behaviour have tended to assume that the typical elector seeks mainly a reinforcement of his existing loyalties from political communications. But Trenaman and McQuail concluded from their study of the British General Election of 1959 that the 'ordinary voter' in this country was 'more sceptical and also more tolerant than the somewhat bigoted person described' in various American surveys.[21] And, as we have noted already, Anthony Downs has argued that the party-committed voter could readily dispense with political propaganda altogether.

According to our evidence, however, there is no such thing as a 'typical voter' in these matters, and it is a mistake to look for one. It would be more accurate to visualize electors as if they were distributed along a dimension stretching between two

[21] Trenaman, J. and McQuail, Denis, op. cit., p. 150.

opposed poles. At one end we would find a number of staunch reinforcement seekers and at the other end a somewhat smaller number of vote-guidance seekers. And although the remaining citizens probably lean one way or the other, they are really much less moved by either of these reasons for receiving political materials than are the individuals at the poles. In estimating how many electors want reinforcement, and how many seek help in deciding how to vote, however, our original figures, as presented in Table 4.5, should be lowered. The need for this adjustment can be considered in conjunction with Table 4.6.[22] This shows that, although most of those who endorsed one of the political items on our checklist rejected the other,[23] some individuals claimed that both items applied to them. Further analyses indicated, moreover, that the members of this group with mixed political motives were very similar in many other ways to those individuals who had endorsed *neither* item.[24] If, for this reason, the mixed group is eliminated from our calculations, the proportion of genuine vote-guidance seekers is closer to 15 per cent than a quarter of the electorate, and

Table 4.6. DISTRIBUTION OF ENDORSEMENTS OF POLITICAL MOTIVES FOR FOLLOWING BROADCAST PROPAGANDA

		%
1. Sought guidance for voting, but not reinforcement	Vote-guidance seekers	15
2. Sought both vote-guidance and reinforcement	Mixed political motives	11
3. Sought reinforcement but not vote-guidance	Reinforcement seekers	23
4. Sought neither vote-guidance nor reinforcement	No political motives	51
		100
N =		748

[22] This table (and all the other tables in this section) refers to the whole sample of eligible electors and not just the television owners. Respondents without television were asked about their reasons for listening to party broadcasts on the radio.

[23] Such a pattern of dissociation is also confirmed by the analysis of inter-relationships between item endorsements on pp. 75–77 below.

[24] See Figures 4.3 and 4.4 and Tables 4.7 and 4.8 below.

the proportion of reinforcement seekers is more like a quarter than a third.

The picture of pure reinforcement seekers and pure vote-guidance seekers as standing at opposite ends of a continuum from each other was built up from several findings which revealed marked differences between these groups. Figure 4.3 shows, for example, that, when the 1964 campaign opened, the reinforcement seekers were far more certain about how they would eventually vote than were the vote-guidance seekers. Only eight per cent of the former admitted to any degree of uncertainty about the ultimate destination of their vote, compared with 42 per cent of the latter.

Figure 4.3. THE RELATIONSHIP BETWEEN STRENGTH OF PRE-CAMPAIGN VOTE INTENTION AND POLITICAL MOTIVES FOR FOLLOWING BROADCAST PROPAGANDA

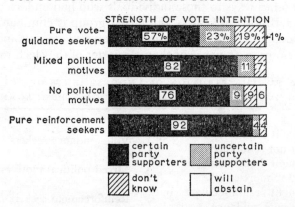

The vote-guidance seekers were also politically more volatile than the reinforcement seekers throughout the campaign as a whole. When, for example, we looked only at those individuals who had supported a party in September (ignoring the 'don't knows' and the 'won't votes'), we found that 19 per cent of the pure vote-guidance seekers had voted on Polling Day for a different party from the one they had favoured at the start of the campaign (15 out of 81), compared with only eight per cent of the pure reinforcement seekers (14 out of 155). This difference was statistically significant at the five per cent level. And when the 'don't knows' were included in the analysis, it transpired that a third of the vote-guidance seekers had decided how to vote during the campaign (33 out of 99), compared with less than an eighth of the reinforcement seekers (19 out of 161).

Yet another guide to the differences between these groups was provided by a finer measure of intensity of party support. This was the 'partisanship score', which measures the degree to which an elector prefers one of the major political parties over the other, and which can range between + 9 (indicating maximum support for the Conservative Party) and — 9 (maximum support for the Labour Party).[25] In preparing Table 4.7, the respondents who identified themselves as Labour or Conservative supporters at the outset of the 1964 campaign were distinguished according to their endorsements of the political motives for following party broadcasts, and then an average partisanship score was calculated for each sub-group. It can be seen that, for both groups of party supporters, the pure reinforcement seekers were strongest and the vote-guidance seekers were weakest in partisanship.

Table 4.7. THE RELATIONSHIP BETWEEN PRE-CAMPAIGN
PARTISANSHIP LEVELS (BY PARTY) AND POLITICAL
MOTIVES FOR FOLLOWING BROADCAST PROPAGANDA

| | Average partisanship scores | |
	Labour supporters	Conservative supporters
Pure vote-guidance seekers	− 3·13 (52 cases)	+ 3·69 (26 cases)
Mixed political motives	− 3·89 (53 cases)	+ 4·42 (26 cases)
No political motives	− 4·13 (149 cases)	+ 4·23 (124 cases)
Pure reinforcement seekers	− 4·36 (84 cases)	+ 4·85 (75 cases)

At first sight this finding might appear to specify the political characteristics of the reinforcement seekers in an unexpected way. 'Reinforcement' seems to stand for the idea that a group of doubters wish to be reassured about the merits of a party which they have traditionally supported. Yet our evidence shows that the typical reinforcement seeker is already convinced of his party's superiority. Why, then, does he wish to be

[25] The partisanship score is explained more fully on pp 21–24 and p. 192.

reminded of its 'strong points'? Why does he not conform to Downs' model and ignore political propaganda altogether?

The evidence which is presented in Figure 4.4 suggests that the answer lies in the salience of party allegiance to him. Three-fourths of the pure reinforcement seekers claimed to care 'a great deal' who won the 1964 election, compared with less than a half of the pure vote-guidance seekers. Since being a Conservative or a Labour supporter is exceptionally important to him, the reinforcement seeker is keenly aware of the imminence of the forthcoming campaign and anxious for his party to do well in it. To assess its progress, however, he must familiarize himself with at least some of the claims and arguments advanced by the opposition, and, in order to maintain his faith in his party's superiority, he wishes, through party broadcasts, to be reminded of its strong points.[26] As a staunch Labour supporter put it to one of our interviewers in February 1964:

> I know our theme, but I like to see our own star men on television. Are they going to make an impact on the average person? I want them to win–and if they put a dud on, I'm sorry. I like to watch our own party to see what kind of an image they are presenting.

This finding highlights the weakness of any attempt, like that of Downs, to explain exposure to political information in a competitive democracy solely with the aid of an economic model. The deficiency of such a model is that it cannot take account of the role of party *loyalty* as distinct from party *choice*. A strong preference for a political party is not just a matter of knowing with a high degree of certainty how one intends to vote. It is also a source of concern that one's own party should

[26] This interpretation is consistent with evidence that has been collected in other countries about the relationship between strength of party identification and the political knowledge and communications behaviour of electors. It was found, for example, in a recent Norwegian study that those voters who identified most strongly with their own political party were also exceptionally knowledgeable about the policy proposals of the *rival* parties. This might help to account for the reported tendency of the strong identifiers to read their party's newspapers and to attend its election meetings to a high degree. (See Valen, Henry, and Katz, Daniel, *Political Parties in Norway*, Tavistock Publications, London, 1964.) It seems that highly partisan voters are keen, through exposure to political communications, to reinforce a position which they feel strongly about in the face of the challenge of opposing policy stands with which they are familiar.

be victorious at the election–not merely as a means to consumer satisfaction but as an end in itself.

Figure 4.4. THOSE SEEKING REINFORCEMENT FROM PARTY BROADCASTS TENDED TO CARE MORE THAN OTHER ELECTORS DID ABOUT THE OUTCOME OF THE 1964 ELECTION

Q: Do you care who wins the election a great deal, somewhat, or not very much?

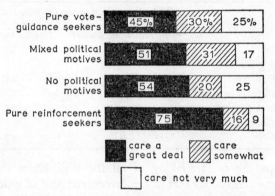

There were several other differences between those who sought reinforcement from party broadcasts and those who wanted help in deciding how to vote. The former tended to be older than the latter, and, if they supported the Labour Party, they worked in less skilled occupations.[27] In addition, there were significantly more political opinion leaders among the reinforcement seekers (36 per cent) than in the rest of the sample (25 per cent).[28] Some reinforcement seekers may rely

[27] See pp. 77–80 below.

[28] This was significant at P = ·01 level for one degree of freedom. The criterion of opinion leadership used in our survey was adapted from the work of other investigators, notably Milne, R. S. and Mackenzie, H. C. (*Straight Fight*, Hansard Society, London, 1954), and Katz, Elihu and Lazarsfeld, Paul F. (*Personal Influence: The Part Played by People in the Flow of Mass Communications*, The Free Press, Glencoe, Illinois, 1955). In calculating the figures given in the text, a respondent was treated as an opinion leader if he said he had discussed the election issues with other people during the campaign *and* thought of himself as more likely, or just as likely, as other people to be asked for his political views; or if he thought of himself as more likely to be asked for his views, although he did not discuss the election with anyone during the 1964 campaign.

on party broadcasts, then, not only because they wish to bolster their own high opinion of the party they support, but also as a source of material which they intend to relay to other people when trying to convince them of its merits.

Table 4.8. A MARKED TENDENCY FOR LABOUR RATHER THAN CONSERVATIVE SUPPORTERS TO WATCH THE LABOUR BROADCAST OF SEPTEMBER 11, 1964, WAS FOUND ONLY AMONG THE REINFORCEMENT SEEKERS

	Proportions viewing the broadcast among:	
	Conservative supporters	*Labour supporters*
	%	%
Pure vote-guidance seekers	35	44
Mixed political motives	24	29
No political motives	21	24
Pure reinforcement seekers	8	47

Perhaps the most striking of all the differences that were found between the seekers of reinforcement and of guidance in deciding how to vote concerned their actual usage of party broadcasts. This is illustrated by Table 4.8, which is based upon the pre-campaign supporters of the Conservative and Labour Parties, who are further sub-divided according to their endorsements of the political motives on our checklist for receiving broadcast propaganda. The percentages show what proportions of each of the sub-groups actually viewed the Labour broadcast of September 11, 1964. It can be seen that, for each motivational category, more Labour supporters than Conservatives watched that programme. It is also clear that the vote-guidance seekers, whatever their party affiliations, were strongly inclined to see it.[29] In the case of the reinforcement seekers, however, viewing of the broadcast was quite dramatically differentiated by party support. Forty-seven per cent of the Labour reinforcement seekers saw the programme, compared with only eight per cent of the Conservative reinforcement seekers. This tendency to differential exposure also

[29] The reliance of vote-guidance seekers on party broadcasts throughout the 1964 campaign as a whole is discused further in Chapter 8.

applied (though less markedly) to the viewing by reinforcement seekers of party election broadcasts throughout the entire campaign.[30]

Patterns of audience motivation

Do any other meaningful patterns lie behind the reasons for watching party broadcasts which the viewers accepted as applying to themselves? An instrument that helped us to answer this question was the phi coefficient, which is a statistical measure of the association between endorsements of pairs of items. This was calculated for the endorsements of each item with those of every other item on our checklist, and in the first instance all the phi coefficients of ·30 or higher (a level which is most unlikely to be reached by chance) were picked out. Figure 4.5

Figure 4.5. CLUSTERS OF ASSOCIATED REASONS FOR
WATCHING PARTY ELECTION BROADCASTS (PHI
COEFFICIENTS OF ·30 AND HIGHER)

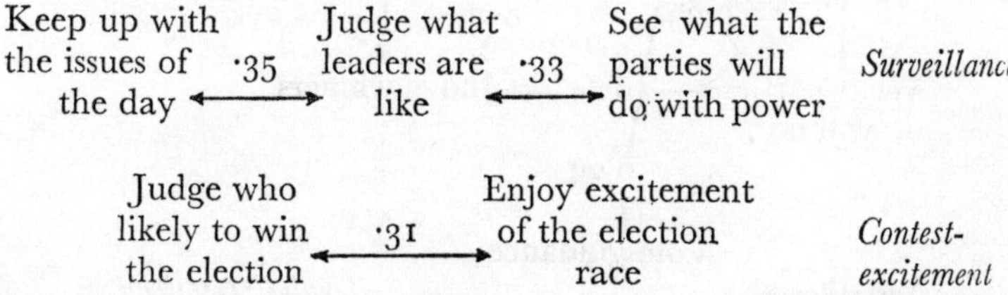

Keep up with the issues of the day	·35	Judge what leaders are like	·33	See what the parties will do with power	*Surveillance*

	Judge who likely to win the election	·31	Enjoy excitement of the election race	*Contest-excitement*

shows that this located two different clusters of associated reasons for watching party broadcasts, which seem to stand, respectively, for surveillance of the political environment, and for the excitement of a contest. The coefficients indicate that an endorsement of one of the surveillance items is not usually a random occurrence, since it often goes with acceptance of another item in this cluster. (The figure also confirms that a desire 'to judge what political leaders are like' belongs in the category of surveillance motives for following political television.) The same tendency

[30] Taking only those Conservative and Labour supporters who saw at least one election broadcast of any kind during the campaign, it was found that the mean excess in the number of broadcasts of their own party seen, over those of the major rival party seen, was 0·53 in the case of the pure vote-guidance seekers and 0·71 in the case of the pure reinforcement seekers. The behaviour of the rest of the sample tended to resemble that of the vote-guidance seekers (a mean excess of 0·59).

75

is found in the items which should tap the disposition of viewers to seek excitement when following a campaign. And at this level of the analysis these two clusters are distinct; they are not connected with each other.

When we took account next of the phi coefficients of ·20 and higher, a more complex web of interconnected motives for following party broadcasts emerged. Figure 4.6 portrays the resulting pattern.

Figure 4.6. CLUSTERS OF ASSOCIATED REASONS FOR WATCHING PARTY ELECTION BROADCASTS (PHI COEFFICIENTS OF ·20 AND HIGHER)

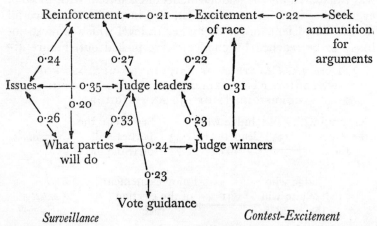

One feature of the figure is the isolated position of the vote-guidance seekers. Their motive for watching party broadcasts stands almost on its own and is not connected with any other item except an interest in judging what political leaders are like. In fact there were quite low inter-correlations between vote-guidance seeking and an interest in ammunition for use in arguments with others (·05) and a desire for reinforcement (·11).

Unlike vote-guidance seeking, a desire for political reinforcement is not an isolated motive for following party broadcasts. The figure shows that it is connected with both the excitement and the surveillance clusters. Perhaps surveillance helps the reinforcement seeker to judge how his party is likely to fare on Polling Day, anxiety about which generates in turn an extra measure of tension and excitement about the election.

At this level of the analysis some contact is also established between the gratifications of surveillance and excitement. From the pattern it appears that some electors find it exciting to compare the performances of the rival political leaders during the campaign, as well as the pledges and promises which their parties put forward.

Finally, an interest in judging political leaders appears to be a rather central motive for viewing party broadcasts. Perhaps because it is a distinctively televisual reason for following a campaign, it is associated with endorsements of six out of the seven other items on the checklist.

Other differences between viewers

Another approach to the study of motivational differences in the party broadcast audience followed lines of demographic demarcation. This aimed to find out whether the gratifications sought from political television depended upon the sex, age, educational background or occupation of the respondents. In general age and occupation proved more important than either sex or education in discriminating between the motives of party broadcast viewers.

The sexes differed little in their reasons for following political television. Although reinforcement seeking was slightly more common among men, and vote-guidance seeking was more prevalent among women, these differences were not statistically significant.[31] In fact the only statistically significant difference between the sexes arose from their interest in using television to judge the qualities of party leaders, and, perhaps surprisingly, it was found that men endorsed this reason for viewing political broadcasts more often than women.[32]

Educational background too was only moderately important. The main difference reflected a tendency for the better-educated respondents to endorse each of the surveillance items more

[31] Thirty-nine per cent of the men and 33 per cent of the women wanted reinforcement from party broadcasts; 24 per cent of the former and 28 per cent of the latter wanted help in deciding how to vote.

[32] Fifty-eight per cent of the men endorsed the 'leader-judging' item, compared with only 46 per cent of the women. This was significant at $P = \cdot 01$ level for one degree of freedom.

heavily than did those who had left school at 14. This proved statistically significant in the case of the item, 'to keep up with the issues of the day'.[33]

Table 4.9. REASONS FOR WATCHING PARTY ELECTION
BROADCASTS BY AGE

	Age groups			
	21–29 %	30–44 %	45–65 %	66 + %
*Political motives**				
Reinforcement	30	29	41	43
Vote-guidance	35	29	22	23
Surveillance				
Judging what leaders are like	35	56	51	58
Seeing what the parties will do	58	51	55	57
Keeping up with the issues	44	51	53	54
Excitement				
Seeing which party will win	24	27	34	38
Excitement of the race	18	27	24	23
N =	84	219	293	81

* The table does not refer to an interest in obtaining ammunition for use in arguments because that item was so little endorsed by the sample as a whole.

In each case, however, the analysis by age and by occupation picked out a group with a distinctive set of interests in political television. A reading of Table 4.9 will show that the youngest voters differed markedly from the rest of the electorate in their reasons for watching party broadcasts. In addition to feeling slightly less excited about the prospects of an election fight, the members of the 21–29-year-old age group were more interested in materials that might help them to decide how to vote[34] and

[33] Sixty-four per cent of those who stayed at school until they were 16 or older endorsed this item, compared with 50 per cent of those who had left school at 14. This difference was significant at $P = \cdot 05$ level for one degree of freedom.

[34] This is consistent with other survey evidence which indicates that young voters are less certain about their party preferences than are their elders. See Abrams, P. and Little, A., 'The Young Voter in British Politics', *British Journal of Sociology*, Vol. XVI, No. 2, pp. 95–109.

strikingly indifferent to the potential of television for use in judging political leaders. (Abrams and Little have also reported that, of various reasons which can be given for voting for a political party, young voters are least impressed with the criterion of having 'the best leader'.)[35] Reinforcement of their existing party preferences, on the other hand, was sought mainly by the middle-aged and elderly electors in our sample.[36]

The role of occupation in determining the gratifications sought from political television is illustrated by Table 4.10. Here the group with a distinctive set of interests was the body of non-skilled workers. Their anticipation of election excitement was well above the average, they expressed relatively little interest in using television to keep up with the issues of the day, and they were exceptionally concerned to be reminded of their party's strong points.[37] The incidence of some motives, however, was determined by the distinction between non-manual and manual workers (skilled and non-skilled alike). Guidance in deciding how to vote, for example, was more likely to be sought by the manually employed respondents than by the white-collar electors.[38] But the non-manual voters proved much keener

---

[35] Ibid.

[36] The difference between the 21–29 age group and the rest of the sample in endorsing the leader-judging reason for watching party broadcasts was statistically significant at P = ·001 level. The difference between the 20–44 and 45+ age groups in endorsing the reinforcement seeking item was significant at P = ·01 level. A control for education showed, however, that the above-average interest of the middle-aged and elderly electors in reinforcement was characteristic only of those who had left school at the age of 14.

[37] The following percentages of endorsement of the reinforcement item by different groups of non-skilled workers show that this was a phenomenon of (a) Labour support, and (b) high partisanship. (The latter was measured by the partisanship score, a description of which is provided in Chapter 11.)

	High partisans	Low partisans
Conservative supporters	38%	27%
Labour supporters	53%	41%

[38] Vote-guidance seeking was characteristic mainly of manual supporters of the *Labour* Party, as the following percentages show:

	Conservative	Labour
Non-manual	18%	16%
Manual	21%	32%

79

than the manual workers to judge what political leaders were like from their performances on television.[39]

Table 4.10. REASONS FOR WATCHING PARTY ELECTION BROADCASTS BY OCCUPATION

	Occupation Groups		
	Non-manual	Manual	
		Skilled	Semi- and unskilled
Political motives	%	%	%
Reinforcement	32	34	48
Vote-guidance	19	30	27
Surveillance			
Judging what leaders are like	61	47	47
Seeing what the parties will do	59	51	55
Keeping up with the issues	60	52	37
Excitement			
Seeing which party will win	28	31	39
Excitement of the race	23	22	35
N =	203	331	127

Surveillance of the political environment as the dominant motive for viewing party broadcasts

The participants in this survey have provided an unequivocal answer to Katz and Feldman's question about the meaning of

[39] See Chapter 6 for further confirmation of the finding that middle-class electors are more preoccupied with the role of personality in politics than are working-class voters. Of the differences set out in Table 4.10 in the text, the following proved statistically significant:
Reinforcement seeking—between the non-skilled group and the rest—at P = ·01 level.
Keeping up with the issues—between the non-skilled and the rest—at P = ·001 level.
Seeing which party will win—between the non-skilled and the rest—at P = ·05 level.
Excitement seeking—between the non-skilled and the rest—at P = ·01 level.
Vote-guidance seeking—between the manual and non-manual workers—at P = ·01 level.
Leader-judging—between the manual and non-manual workers—at P = ·001 level.

high exposure to election television.[40] Although diverse motives are typically involved, British viewers are more concerned to obtain information about their political environment from party broadcasts than to satisfy any other interest. The predominance of this motive may be unexpected, but, under closer examination, the finding appears both reasonable and consistent with a view of the average elector as only moderately involved in political affairs.

All the evidence suggests that no other gratification could account for high levels of political viewing. Only a minority seek help in deciding how to vote, for example, because most citizens have already made up their minds before campaigning starts, and they stick to their early decisions right up to Polling Day. At the other end of the political spectrum, only a minority of electors are sufficiently partisan to seek reinforcement from political communications. It is equally difficult to imagine how a television campaign, as it is usually waged in Britain, could arouse more intense hopes of excitement than were reflected in our findings. There were even signs that many electors make a distinction between following politics and following a sport. The excitement of a sport arises partly from elements of conflict and aggression. But many participants in our first exploratory survey objected spontaneously to the attacks of politicians upon each other as if they were pointless and interfered with their reception of the information they wanted.[41] The modest role of contest-excitement in the motivation of our sample is also consistent with Richard Rose's finding that, 'while four-fifths of electors regard voting as a duty, more

---

[40] See p. 55.

[41] Seventy-nine participants in that survey were asked whether there were any campaigning methods which they particularly disliked. Of 55 individuals who could think of an objectionable tactic of campaigning, 19 referred to the tendency of politicians to abuse their opponents. Only one other practice (unreliable promise-making) was mentioned more frequently (23 times). When, in addition, the members of our main sample were asked about this by means of a forced-choice question, 38 per cent said they 'usually' objected to the attacks made upon each other by politicians during an election campaign, 25 per cent said they 'occasionally' objected, and only 30 per cent 'rarely' objected (seven per cent did not know). It was also found that the information seekers in that sample were more likely to object to politicians' attacks on one another than were those who sought excitement from a campaign, as the figures at the foot of p. 82 show.

than half felt no emotional reaction – whether of enjoyment or annoyance – during an election campaign.'[42]

But why do voters seek information about their political environment when following an election campaign? Two explanations can be derived from much of the open-ended material that was spontaneously supplied by the participants in our exploratory survey of February 1964. One is that some individuals see this as a way of discharging their minimal obligations as citizens. It is not only voting, but also the attempt on their part to acquire information about some of the problems facing the country, that electors regard as a duty. Even if this sentiment tends to lie dormant between elections, an imminent campaign will draw the attention of voters to the roles they are supposed to fulfil as citizens and thus encourage a measure of 'obligatory' information seeking. Guilt about past neglect of this role may even facilitate such behaviour. This interpretation is supported by the remarks of those individuals who explained their intentions to view party broadcasts along the following lines:

I think that you should always listen to political programmes, especially during an election campaign when it will be up to you to decide who you want to govern the country.

I shall see a lot of them, though they won't alter my opinions. It's just to give you as broad a view as possible of the subjects they're dealing with. When all is said and done you want to know what the government is like and what it is going to do.

Because the whole future depends on it – at least the next few years.

Motives endorsed for watching party broadcasts	Proportions stating they 'usually' objected to politicians' attacks on each other
	%
To keep up with the main issues of the day	43
To judge what political leaders are like	42
To see what some party will do if it gets into power	39
To judge who is likely to win the election	39
To enjoy the excitement of the election race	28

[42] Rose, Richard, 'For the People, not by the People', *The Times*, April 18th, 1966.

And I'm interested to know who will get in. I don't want the country to go to rack and ruin.

The country is in the throes of a great danger. And I'm wondering which party will be able to cope with the changes we are up against. There's automation, changes in wages structure, and nationalization. I want to judge what party will get in and what it would do about these problems if it did.

When the campaign heats up, I will listen to them. To see what they have to say. Just so that I'll know what's going on–know something about it. It's like reading the paper–to see why Home is blowing his nut about the H-bomb. Then I can figure out what I think. It's all just for your own little idea.

An even larger number of respondents related their interest in political information to their own personal stake in the outcome of political processes:

Just to hear what they have to say for themselves. I'm interested only in things that affect me.

I'm interested in what affects me personally–the schools and my children and what they're going to do about it.

I want to know what they promise to do if they get into power.

I want to know what they will do about housing problems, schools, and education and the such like. Not that they ever keep their promises.

I want to hear what they'll do. I put it on to see what they promise. In my young days there weren't the same chances as today. I want to hear what they'll do for me. I haven't much and can't afford much, though I've tried to save a bit. So I want to know what they'll do for my pension.

To see how things are going on. To see if the old-age pensions are going to go up and the rents to be reduced.

It's interesting to see what the different parties say. I'm interested particularly to see what the Labour Party will do about nation-alization because, having had some money left to me, I'm personally interested–and it is invested in stocks and shares.

My husband is in the building trade, and I want to see what effect the proposals of the various parties might have on his work.

WHY DO PEOPLE WATCH

Despite its obvious lack of sophistication, there is a sense in which the approach of these voters to propaganda may be said to be guided by rationality. Apparently, many of them were interested less in judging the competence of the parties (although that was sometimes involved) than in forming some impression of how political developments might affect the tangible circumstances of their own lives in the near future. That is why there was so much concern to find out from political broadcasts what the parties proposed 'to do'–about rents, pensions, schools, mortgages, roads, etc. And if trying to plan one's life in the light of information about the various circumstances that can affect it–including those which result from the measures of government–is rational, then this should count as a rational basis for following political television.[43]

---

[43] Political theorists differ keenly over the realism of the expectation that the citizens of a democratic state should orient themselves rationally to political affairs. A resolution of this issue depends not only on the facts about electoral behaviour, but also on the particular criterion of rationality which is applied to those facts. The authors will attempt to indicate briefly here what model of rational political behaviour they consider is most suited to the investigation of these matters.

The utilitarian model of the rational citizen as an *efficient calculator*, which underlies the thought of Anthony Downs, is more rigorous, philosophically, than any other, but it is ill-adapted to the analysis of actual situations of political choice. As John Plamenatz pointed out some years ago ('Electoral Studies and Democratic Theory: A British View', *Political Studies*, Vol. VI, No. 1, 1957, pp. 1–9):

> If we met a man who claimed to take all the issues
> at an election seriously, and to place them in their
> order of importance, we should say to ourselves: If
> you were a candidate I should not vote for you.
> None but a fool knows all the answers or even many
> of them.

A different criterion of political rationality has been advanced more recently in a posthumous publication by V. O. Key, Jr. (*The Responsible Electorate*, Harvard University Press, Cambridge, Massachusetts, 1966). This defines the rational citizen as a *consistent voter*–as someone whose policy preferences are compatible with his voting intentions. Instances of such consistency could derive, however, not from deliberation and choice, but from the dissonance-reducing forces of party loyalty.

We believe that appropriate standards for evaluating the quality of democratic life, which are neither too demanding nor too indulgent, can be derived from what we would term a *debate model of political campaigning*. This portrays the rational citizen as someone who is prepared to follow

POLITICAL PROGRAMMES?

These findings do not conflict with other sources of evidence about the attitudes of the general public towards politics, although they illustrate the need to ensure that the depth and extent of political apathy is not exaggerated. It is one thing to insist that many people engage in their personal affairs to the exclusion of most forms of political activity and another to imply that they perceive little or no *connection* between the world of politics and their immediate concerns. According to our evidence, many citizens recognize that political developments impinge upon their personal circumstances, and they wish to acquire information that might help them to grasp how they are likely to be affected by that connection. After all, if most electors regarded politics as irrelevant to their material needs, it would be difficult to explain why voting behaviour is associated so powerfully with socio-economic status.

We do not claim that the drive of the average citizen to obtain politicial information is usually strong or intense. Many other pursuits are undoubtedly far more attractive and absorbing. Nevertheless, a moderate degree of interest in surveillance of the political environment does seem to lie behind much exposure to political broadcasting. This may help to explain why many voters actually acquire previously unfamiliar information about party policies through exposure to political television during an election campaign.[44]

political materials as if a debate were being conducted of which he was trying to make sense. The participants in such a debate would state their order of priorities and outline their proposals for dealing with outstanding political problems; seek to clarify the main differences between their policies and those of their opponents; and give reasons for preferring themselves to their rivals. An assessment of the rational potential in the audience of electors would turn, then, on whether they could respond appropriately to a campaign mounted in such a fashion—not necessarily by wearing their votes on their sleeves, but by trying to grasp what has been proposed and to sift some of the main arguments in the light of their own experiences and values. We do not claim that this is an accurate description of the actual conduct of democratic politics but that it provides the most relevant notion of rationality to apply when judging the performance of campaigners and the capacity of their audiences.

[44] See Ch. 9 below.

CHAPTER 5

WHAT KIND OF POLITICAL TELEVISION DO VIEWERS WANT?

The area of enquiry

Consideration of viewers' reasons for following politics on television leads logically to an area of controversy over the uses that are made of television by the broadcasting authorities and more particularly by the political parties (since control is ultimately in their hands). Whereas the foregoing chapter was devoted to the gratifications viewers seek from political broadcasting, this chapter presents their opinions about the alternative forms it can take. Much criticism of the role of political television was aired at both the 1964 and the 1966 elections, and the issues are still unsettled. As Martin Harrison pointed out after the earlier campaign, 'The rules of the political broadcasting game have never been so controversial.'[1] As much concern was expressed over the unexplored possibilities, and what was left undone, as over what was actually presented. Evidence collected during our survey has some bearing on a range of questions that can be asked about these matters.

How, for example, did the public respond to those innovations in election broadcasting which were pioneered during the 1964 campaign and repeated in 1966? They include the BBC's *Election Forum* (a series of three programmes in which each of the party leaders was asked questions sent in by viewers) and the decision to allow the national current affairs programmes to stay on the air and comment on the progress of the campaign.

What was the reaction of the electorate to the much-canvassed proposal to broadcast a party-leader debate on the

[1] Harrison, Martin, in Butler, D. E., and King, Anthony, op. cit., p. 156

Kennedy–Nixon model? The rejection of this idea was ascribed, according to public statements, largely to grounds of principle in 1964 and in 1966 to practical difficulties–although the politicians were undoubtedly swayed on both occasions by strategic considerations as well.[2] The preferences of voters would not seem to have entered into the discussion, and we have been particularly concerned to ascertain viewers' opinions about the relative merits of a debate format compared with other ways in which politicians might appear on television. More specifically, we have also asked whether they were keen to see the top leaders themselves debate the election issues on television.

How many viewers regard an election campaign as a tedious affair which tends to occupy too much air time on television? The Audience Research Department of the BBC noted in 1964 that opportunities for their respondents to complain spontaneously about the domination of television by the election had been used only rarely.[3] And Martin Harrison pointed out that audience levels for political programmes did not decline during

[2] After a meeting in February 1964 of representatives of the political parties and the broadcasting authorities, a statement was issued which mentioned the following objections to confrontations: that they were more suited to a presidential than a parliamentary system of government; that the Liberal leader would be difficult to fit in; and that viewers might become satiated with too many election programmes. Shortly before the 1964 campaign officially opened, the leader of the Labour Party challenged the Conservative Prime Minister to engage in a televised debate, but this was dismissed as a pre-election tactical manoeuvre. In 1966 no consideration was given, at any of the pre-campaign meetings between the broadcasters and the politicians, to the possibility of arranging party-leader debates. When questioned on February 28th on *Panorama* and *This Week*, however, each of the three leaders expressed willingness to participate in some form of confrontation. It soon transpired that Mr. Wilson would accept only a three-sided format, whereas Mr. Heath insisted on debating solely with Mr. Wilson (leaving out Mr. Grimond). At one stage Mr. Heath proposed a complex series of three two-sided debates (in which each leader, including Mr. Grimond, would take part twice). In the middle of the campaign a three-sided invitation was issued to all the leaders on behalf of the independent network, and the BBC put forward a compromise suggestion, whereby a single programme would incorporate both a two-sided and a three-sided format. The entire affair eventually petered out in an irritable exchange of correspondence and recriminations.

[3] 'The 1964 General Election', op. cit., p. 14.

the latter stages of either the 1964 or the 1966 campaign.[4]
Nevertheless, a widespread feeling developed in 1964 that
something had gone wrong with the television campaign as a
whole.[5] By 1966 even the Prime Minister found it expedient to
sympathize in his first election broadcast with those voters who
could not muster much enthusiasm for the impending skirmishes.
Although various causes unconnected with broadcasting were
cited for the suspected increase in boredom with election politics
—e.g. the apparent lack of any ideological distinction between
the major parties, and in 1966 the near certainty of the eventual
outcome plus the subdued campaign strategy adopted by
Labour—there was also a 'commonly held view that there is
. . . too much politics on your set at this time.'[6] Many of the
complaints were directed specifically at the party broadcasts,
which were criticized as either too numerous or for taking up
all available channels when transmitted.[7] But were viewers as
resentful of the role of these programmes as were their more
vocal critics?

Another set of questions concerns the possibility of televising
the proceedings of Parliament. How many viewers would welcome the opportunity to see how the House of Commons
conducts its business—and for what reasons? What is the extent
of public indifference to this proposal? Although this area of

[4] Harrison, Martin, in Bulter, D. E. and King, Anthony, op. cit., pp.
181–3; and Harrison, Martin, 'Television and Radio', Ch. VII in Butler,
D. E. and King, Anthony, *The British General Election of 1966*, Macmillan,
London, 1966, pp. 143–5.

[5] Blumler, Jay G., 'Campaign on Television', op. cit.

[6] This particular statement was made in *Television and the General Election*,
a Granada programme which was broadcast on March 22, 1966. The
Audience Research Department of the BBC reported that election broadcasts received consistently lower reaction indices from members of their
viewing panel in 1966 than from their counterparts in the 1964 campaign.
The Department suspected that this was due to 'a change in the attitude
of the audience rather than in the broadcasts themselves.' ('The 1966
General Election', Audience Research Department, British Broadcasting
Corporation, LR/66/498, p. 11.)

[7] See in particular Martin Harrison's portrayal of simultaneous transmission of party broadcasts as the last outpost of elite paternalism in
British broadcasting (*Sunday Times*, October 11, 1964) and Mary Crozier's
discussion of the anomalies that could arise if simultaneous transmission
was retained despite a long-term increase in the number of television
channels in use (*The Guardian*, May 14, 1964).

questioning had no direct bearing on the use of television at election time, by exploring it we hoped to gain some insight into the potential of a popular and trusted mass medium for involving the individual citizen in what may often seem to him to be rather remote processes of government.

Television and electioneering

Opinions about these matters cannot be considered in isolation. They need to be examined in the context of voters' perceptions of electioneering itself, as a process to which they are subjected, and of which they form certain impressions when following a campaign in the mass media. Some questions which can arise in this connection, and which receive more extensive treatment in Chapter 6 below, include: What do electors notice most about the activities of campaigning politicians? How do they feel about the bombardment of competitive party propaganda which an election unleashes? Do they find its barrage of conflicting claims and counter-claims confusing or clarifying? If the democratic persuasive process leaves many electors unsatisfied, can reform of the pattern of election television help to improve the situation?

Unlike a number of other queries that might be posed about electioneering, these questions are 'voter-oriented' and not 'party-oriented'. The subject of enquiry here is not whether the tactics of the political parties are effective in marshalling electoral support[8] but whether the organization and conduct of campaigning meets the felt needs of voters. At least two major American writings in the field of political science have adopted something like this perspective in analysing the electoral process. One is the previously mentioned work of Anthony Downs, *An Economic Theory of Democracy*, which develops the *logical implications* for parties and for voters of the assumption of rational political behaviour. Downs concludes that in a two-party system

[8] It has been maintained in two recently published books that British politicians do not in fact campaign so 'rationally' as they might—that is, in a manner which is deliberately calculated to maximize the securing of electors' votes. See Ch. III of Butler, D. E. and King, Anthony, *The British General Election of 1964*, op. cit., and Rose, Richard, *Influencing Voters*, op. cit.

the would-be rational voter will tend to be frustrated by the campaign strategies followed by the politicians. He maintains that democratic electioneering engenders a 'rationality crisis', a phrase which he uses to refer to the paradoxical fact that it is rational for politicians to foster irrational voting behaviour in the electorate at large. In competing for the support of the uncommitted moderate voter, for example, both major parties tend to promulgate vague and ambiguous platforms which converge near the centre of the political spectrum. The similarity of the resulting policies deprives the citizen of a rational basis for choice and encourages him to vote on relatively irrelevant grounds—such as the appeal of a candidate's personality. Downs was unhopeful about the prospect of overcoming this condition: the 'rationality crisis' was built into the situation and was unlikely ever to be resolved. [9]

In another substantial study of electioneering, Stanley Kelley, Jr. has considered the defects of campaigning from an *ethical* standpoint. His analysis consists, in part, of a sustained critique of the presidential contest in 1956 between General Eisenhower and Mr. Adlai Stevenson. Kelley complains that in that campaign, '. . . both candidates described their policy positions in terms so general that their statements lacked any clear relation to issues on which voters had to make decisions.' Too much attention was devoted to areas of agreement which were irrelevant to the voters' choice, and even when disagreements emerged, '. . . the candidates either failed to take account of important points made by their opponents or re-stated them in ways that made them more vulnerable to attack.' They '. . . tended to "talk past each other" almost as though they were participating in two different elections.' In addition, the candidates often proclaimed their support of various lofty goals

[9] Downs, Anthony, op. cit., Ch. 8. Downs considers and dismisses two possible methods of counteracting the shortcomings of democratic campaigning. He concludes that legal regulation would be unenforceable in this sphere. Somewhat more practicable would be the institution of a multi-party system, which would counteract the tendency in a two-party system for the struggle to concentrate on the uncommitted centre. Such an arrangement would lead to even greater difficulties for the rational voter, however (who could not predict the terms of the compromises on which the various parties might be prepared to agree to work together in a coalition government which would have to be formed after the election).

without indicating how exactly they proposed to advance them. A notorious example was the following Republican spot announcement on television:

> Voice: Mr. Eisenhower, what about the high cost of living?
> Eisenhower: My wife, Mamie, worries about the same thing. I tell her it's our job to change that on November 4th.[10]

Unlike Downs, however, Kelley was cautiously optimistic about the corrigibility of democratic electioneering. He ascribed low standards of campaign argument neither to weaknesses in the electorate nor to unchangeable imperatives of party strategy. According to Kelley the level of campaign discussion depends on the conditions under which it takes place; and it could be raised substantially if candidates would agree to meet each other more often in a debating situation. In a debate it is to a speaker's advantage to establish the distinctive merits of his own policy proposals, to meet any objections raised by his opponent, and to challenge his weaker positions in turn. A debate also '. . . sets up certain checks on the accuracy of the information that is brought to it', for 'It is not advisable for a debater to misquote his opponent or to give an obviously distorted version of what his opponent has said.' 'Raising the level of campaign discussion', Kelley concluded, 'is not an inherently unrealizable goal.'[11]

The relationship between campaigning and the needs of voters has been considered from both a *logical* and an *ethical* standpoint, but what, then, about an *empirical* approach to these matters? Do the electors themselves feel thwarted by the practices cited by Downs and Kelley? Their dissatisfaction cannot be taken for granted, for both the analyses outlined above derive from the contentious premise of rational voting behaviour—in the first case as the axiom of a logical model and in the second as a morally desirable condition.[12] Since most

[10] Kelley, Stanley, Jr., *Political Campaigning: Problems in Creating an Informed Electorate*, The Brookings Institution, Washington, D.C., 1960, Ch. IV.   [11] Ibid., Ch. II.

[12] Kelley states in Chapter I, for example, that:
> This study will attempt to show . . . that much . . . dissatisfaction with the character of our campaigns is eminently justified if one basic assumption is granted: that campaign discussion should help voters make rational voting decisions.

electors know well in advance of Polling Day how they are
going to vote, it can be argued that the alleged shortcomings of
electioneering should not trouble them unduly. But if–as we
have maintained in Chapter 4–many citizens are moved by
other, and equally serious, reasons for following a campaign,
they might well be sensitive to its more blatant defects. In that
event it would also be appropriate to try to find out whether
voters consider that there are ways in which political television,
suitably organized, could help them to make more sense of a
democratic campaign.

Is there too much politics on television?

In charting consumer reactions to political television and the
form it should take, we begin by considering the total amount
that is provided. David Riesman has alleged that there is a
general tendency for the mass media to '. . . pay more attention
to politics than their audience seems to demand', ascribing this
to a 'desire of those who work for [them] to do what is considered to be right by those to whom they look for leadership.'[13]
If so, British television might be thought to tax the tolerance of
its patrons particularly severely, for its news bulletins pay
proportionately more attention to domestic political affairs than
do many morning newspapers, and the two main channels
offer the viewer little choice in this respect (the quantity of
political material being almost identical on BBC and ITN).[14]
Riesman's implication that all media personnel are animated
by a common desire to provide a respectable political menu is
probably mistaken. Interviews with current affairs producers
working in British television suggest that the degree of their
concern depends in part on the particular roles they assume:
it is strongest among the specialist political reporters and interviewers. Nevertheless, it is true that at least some television

[13] Reisman, David, *The Lonely Crowd*, Yale University Press (paperbound
edition), New Haven and London, 1961, p. 197.
[14] These points have been documented by means of a content analysis of
television news bulletins, carried out by Malcolm Warner, then of the University of Essex, in July 1966. They appear in an unpublished duplicated
paper, 'The Political Element in Television News: A Preliminary Analysis
by Content of a Week's Output'.

journalists are keen to convey their own appreciation of political problems to viewers–an emphasis which could conceivably be noticed and resented by many in the audience.

In fact there was little evidence in our survey that viewers are dissatisfied with the amount of attention that is normally paid to politics on television in an *out-of-election* period. When asked in June 1964 whether they would 'like to see less, more, or about the same time given to politics on television as there is now', just over half the owners of TV sets in our sample (52 per cent) endorsed the existing level of provision. Thirteen per cent even expressed a wish for more political programmes, and those who actually wanted a reduction accounted for only 24 per cent of the viewers (11 per cent offered no opinion). It seems reasonable to interpret this overall pattern of response as reflecting a widespread acceptance of the *status quo* at that time.

Why are there so few complaints about the volume of political television? Perhaps the level which is actually reached does not really interfere with popular enjoyment of entertainment programmes and the desire of many viewers to use their sets for relaxation and diversion. There may even be a feeling that television *should* screen rather more political fare than the majority would normally choose to consume–thus exerting a legitimate pull against the viewer's indulgent inclination to see many light-weight programmes. So long as the provision of such a counter-balance is not taken to fanatical lengths, many citizens may see the point of having it.[15] But these findings may not apply to a campaign situation when many more political programmes are scheduled. What do viewers think about the amount of time that television tends to devote to an election? And how, specifically, do they feel about party broadcasts?

[15] The results of an American survey have suggested that although many viewers regard television predominantly as a source of entertainment, they may experience guilt feelings about their tendency to use it to excess for this purpose. This can give rise in turn to a demand for the provision of reality materials on the medium. See Steiner, Gary A., *The People Look at Television*, Alfred Knopf, New York, 1963.

Party broadcasts and the 1964 campaign on television

Party broadcasting in this country is completely sheltered from competition with any other kind of programme. It is clear from Table 5.1 that a majority of viewers dislike this system and would welcome the possibility of switching to an alternative. The size of the minority which claims to support the existing arrangement, however, is surprisingly large (nearly three-eighths of those with television) – especially since the question posed an issue of viewers' freedom.[16] Freedom of choice is undoubtedly more popular than paternalism, but the fact that this preference is not overwhelming hints again at the influence of a belief that politics is something which citizens should follow despite their own inclinations.[17]

Table 5.1. VIEWERS' OPINIONS ABOUT THE SIMULTANEOUS TRANSMISSION OF PARTY BROADCASTS ON ALL CHANNELS

Q: When party political broadcasts are televised, they go out on both BBC and ITV at the same time. Do you like or dislike that arrangement?

	%
Like	36
Dislike	47
Don't know	17
	100

N = 677 set owners

The signs of popular dissatisfaction with party broadcasting were more pronounced once the election campaign was over. We asked the sample after Polling Day to say, first of all,

[16] When questioned in late 1965 on behalf of the ITA, 36 per cent of the members of a national sample of viewers also endorsed the existing system.

[17] Such a belief is probably most common among the most politically interested electors. When the viewers in our sample were divided into four groups according to a measure of their strength of motivation for following the election campaign, it was found that a majority of those who were rated most keen actually professed to 'like' simultaneous transmission of party broadcasts. This contrasted with a proportion of only a sixth who endorsed the existing arrangements among the least enthusiastic viewers. One advantage of simultaneous transmission to the politically minded person should not be forgotten: it protects him from the clamour of less keen members of his household to switch over to some other programme.

whether they thought that 'the amount of time spent on politics during the campaign was about right? Or were there too few or too many political programmes?' Table 5.2 illustrates the majority's firm conviction that the broadcasting authorities had been too obsessed with the campaign. Such a finding does not contradict evidence from other sources of the sustained buoyancy of audience levels for political programmes as Polling Day approached. The climax of even an unsatisfactory campaign will generate an additional increment of interest and excitement –especially if, as in 1964, the outcome is uncertain. It is not that the viewers experienced a progressive and mounting sense of boredom and fatigue. They just considered that the campaign as a whole had been unsatisfactory and expressed that judgement by complaining about the transmission of too many political programmes.

Table 5.2. VIEWERS' REACTIONS TO THE NUMBER OF POLITICAL PROGRAMMES BROADCAST ON TELEVISION DURING THE 1964 CAMPAIGN

Had been:	%
Too many	55
About right	39
Too few	1
Don't know	4
	99

N = 672 respondents with access to TV during the campaign

But what exactly was at fault? How would our respondents have reduced the demands of the campaign? Most viewers welcomed the various innovations in political television of the 1964 campaign, even though the total amount of time devoted to the election was consequently increased. For example, nearly four-fifths of all those who claimed to have seen at least one *Election Forum* endorsed it as a 'good idea'. Fifty-five per cent of those with access to television thought that it had also been a 'good idea' to allow the regular current affairs programmes (*Gallery* and *This Week*) to stay on the air and comment on the issues of the election.[18]

[18] During a two-month period of the Belgian election campaign in 1965, ten programmes (*Face à l'Opinion*), which were similar in format to the

Satiation with the 1964 campaign was accounted for, then, almost exclusively by the party broadcasts. This was confirmed when we asked all the sample members, except those who said that 'too few' programmes had been transmitted, to indicate whether any of the following measures should have been adopted: have less campaign news in the TV news bulletins; cut down the number of party election broadcasts; transmit party broadcasts on one channel only; or keep special political programmes like *Gallery* and *This Week* off the air for the period of the campaign. Only those items on this list which referred to the party broadcasts were endorsed by large numbers of respondents. Whereas 13 per cent said that *Gallery* and *This Week* should have been suspended, and 22 per cent wanted fewer campaign items in the news bulletins, 37 per cent opted for the transmission of party broadcasts on one channel only, and 34 per cent recommended a reduction in the total number of party broadcasts.

The focusing of dissatisfaction on party broadcasts is further illustrated by Table 5.3, which presents the replies only of those viewers who complained of 'too many' political programmes. The data have been regrouped to show how many of these critics confined their attacks to the party broadcasts alone, how many endorsed cuts in the non-party programmes exclusively, and how many wanted reductions in both sides of the political output. According to the top row of the table a majority of this group would have taken action against the party broadcasts only. And when the figures of the first two rows are added together we find that some reduction in party broadcasting was desired by 83 per cent of the critics. This contrasts with a corresponding figure (obtained by adding the figures in the second and third rows together) of only 39 per cent who wanted any cut-back at all in the non-party political provision.

BBC's *Election Forum* (except that panels of party spokesmen appeared instead of the top leaders only), were transmitted to the French-speaking areas of the country. A team of investigators at the Free University of Brussels found that these programmes attracted higher audiences on the average than the conventional party broadcasts and that the proportion of viewers who felt dissatisfied with them never exceeded 20 per cent. (Cf. Clausse, Roger, 'Presse, Radio et Télévision Belges dans la Campagne Electorale de Mai 1965', *Res Publica*, Vol. VIII, No. 1, 1966, pp. 24–66.)

Table 5.3. CRITICS OF THE TV COVERAGE OF THE
CAMPAIGN MAINLY SINGLED OUT PARTY BROADCASTS
FOR COMPLAINT

	%
Would cut down on:	
Party broadcasts only	56
Party broadcasts and non-party political programmes	27
Non-party political programmes only	12
No specific measures endorsed	5
	100

N = 372 respondents with access to television who complained of 'too many' political programmes during the 1964 campaign

The proposal to televise parliamentary proceedings[19]

We have seen that several innovations in political television enjoyed broad support among viewers when actually tried out during the 1964 campaign. A number of other questions, which were put in the June 1964 round of interviewing, tested the warmth of their welcome for certain *proposed* innovations. One sought their reactions to the idea of televising the proceedings of Parliament. The response is shown by the figures set out in Table 5.4. They indicate the presence of a moderate degree of public interest in seeing how Parliament conducts its business on television. Although there is no overwhelming demand for the televising of Parliament, neither is interest in the proposal confined to a tiny minority. In fact the proportion of a third professing to like the idea 'very much' is a fairly impressive result.[20]

[19] Much of the material presented in this section first appeared as Appendix 22, 'Survey of Viewers' Reactions to the Proposal to Televise the Proceedings of Parliament', to the *First Report from the Select Committee on Broadcasting etc. of Proceedings in the House of Commons*, Her Majesty's Stationery Office, London, 1966, pp. 138–41.

[20] This pattern of response has since been confirmed in a national sample which was contacted by the National Opinion Poll in December 1966. Asked 'how interested' they would be 'supposing the debates in Parliament were televised' 31 per cent said 'very interested'. (The other replies were distributed as follows: 33 per cent 'quite interested', 19 per cent 'not very interested', and 17 per cent 'not at all interested'.)

Table 5.4. VIEWERS' REACTIONS TO THE IDEA OF
TELEVISING PARLIAMENT

Q: It has been suggested recently that the proceedings of Parliament
should be televised, although some people don't like the idea
very much. What do you think? Do you like this idea very
much, like it somewhat, or doesn't it matter to you one way or
the other?

	%
Like very much	33
Like somewhat	20
Indifferent	42
Don't know	5
	100

N = 677 TV set owners

The best predictor of respondents' replies was not a social
category (age, sex, class, etc.) but an index of general interest
in following political argument. Table 5.5 shows how indifference to seeing the deliberations of Parliament on television
mounted as the general level of viewers' respect for political
argument fell. This suggests that a special programme, containing an edited version of the day's debates, would cater
mainly for those individuals whose interest in politics is already
above the average, and that it would have little potential for
attracting or informing those citizens whose involvement in
politics is minimal. If, however, MPs were willing to allow
extracts from their proceedings to be transmitted in news
bulletins and weekly current affairs programmes, the proportion
of the population that would then become increasingly familiar
through television with the work of Parliament would be considerably enlarged.[21]

After the respondents had endorsed one of the three alternative
responses to the question about televising Parliament, they were
asked to explain their answers ('Why do you say that?'). It

[21] Fear of the consequences of giving television journalists unlimited
access to the tapes of the proceedings, which they could then edit as they
wished, was an important factor in the decision of the House of Commons
(November 24, 1966) to reject a proposal for an experimental closed-
circuit trial of parliamentary television. See Blumler, Jay, 'Parliament and
Political TV', *Encounter*, March 1967, pp. 52–6 and *Parliamentary Debates*
(*Hansard*), Vol. 736, No. 103, November 24, 1966, cols. 1606–1732.

TELEVISION DO VIEWERS WANT?

Table 5.5. At higher levels of interest in political argument there was a greater readiness to approve the idea of televising parliament

	Level of interest*		
	High	Moderate	Low
	%	%	%
Like very much	49	32	23
Like somewhat	18	22	21
Indifferent	32	44	50
Don't know	2	2	6
	101	100	100
N =	204	225	221

* This index was based on the amount of attention that the informants thought voters should normally pay to the arguments of campaigning politicians ('a lot', 'some', and 'a little' or 'none').

would be misleading to try to quantify the resulting material, but several interesting themes appeared in many replies—especially those of individuals who welcomed the idea. Some interviewees emphasized the revelatory character of television as a medium—as if admission of the cameras into the Houses of Parliament would help viewers to see what this part of the political system was *really* like.

> A very good idea. We can get an impression of the people who are running the country without having it second-hand. We can see it for ourselves and judge it for ourselves.

> I'd like to listen to the debates at first-hand. I'd like to form my own opinions about what is going on.

> I think it would be very interesting and educative; you would see what goes on behind the scenes.

> It would be very interesting to know what really happens inside instead of just hearing about it.

> It would be nice to see what is actually happening.

Other members of the sample expressed an interest in obtaining information about the organization and workings of Parliament. Although, some of them implied, the man in the street occasionally hears about parliamentary events from various sources, his knowledge is fragmentary and sketchy, and it does not add up to a meaningful picture. It was hoped that the introduction of television at Westminster would help to fill in some of these gaps. The following comments illustrate this expectation:

> It would help to give us a better understanding of it. Half of it is double dutch to me now.

> You never seem to have an idea of what is happening. The papers use such terms as party whips, etc., but people do not know what is meant by those terms or by the other terms used.

> Because you have to have a mind like a lawyer to read about Parliament, but if we saw it we would know more about it.

Some viewers thought that they might be able to form a better impression of what politicians themselves were really like:

> I think that watching it live would be very interesting. Well, to see people–politicians I mean – live gives one a better insight as to what politicians are like.

> It would be rather interesting. It would seem a more natural state of affairs than seeing politicians reading prepared statements.

The last comment hints at yet another theme. This was a feeling that electors must rely to a considerable extent at present on 'processed', and possibly biased, interpretations of political affairs, giving rise to some uncertainty about what to accept and believe. Some of the respondents whose remarks are cited below evidently felt that the televising of Parliament would reduce their dependence on such second-hand sources:

> So that everyone can see what is going on. It would be first-hand information, not what the papers would like to tell you.

> It would be a good idea. It would let you know what was going on in Parliament without the newspapers twisting it. And it would show who is who in Parliament.

> You would get it first-hand instead of just being reported. It's given to bias then and may not be impartial.

Debates between party leaders

Another proposed innovation evoked a response which suggests a similar degree of faith in the revelatory power of television. There was massive support in June 1964 for the staging of a confrontation on television between the leaders of the three main political parties. The exact wording of the question used, and the distribution of the replies among the viewers in our sample, are set out in Table 5.6. It can be seen that two-thirds of the set owners claimed that they would 'definitely watch' a televised debate between Sir Alec Douglas-Home, Harold Wilson, and Jo Grimond if one was arranged during the 1964 campaign. Only seven per cent were sure that they would not tune in to such an event.[22]

Table 5.6. Viewers' intentions to watch a televised party-leader debate

Q: Suppose that a TV debate was arranged between Sir Alec Douglas-Home, Harold Wilson, and Jo Grimond during the forthcoming campaign. Do you think that you would definitely watch, might watch, or would definitely *not* watch such a debate?

	%
Definitely would watch	68
Might watch	24
Definitely would not watch	7
Don't know	1
	100

N = 677 set owners

Such a high degree of public backing for party-leader debates accords with evidence collected during the presidential election of 1960 in the United States when John F. Kennedy and Richard Nixon met each other in a series of four confrontations. The Gallup Poll reported before their transmission that 55 per cent of the American electorate was looking forward to them with 'a lot' of interest. It was estimated subsequently that four-fifths of the adult population had seen at least one of the debates and that 55 per cent had viewed all four. The proportions of audience members who indicated their approval of this

[22] According to the Gallup Poll, 60 per cent of a national sample welcomed the idea of a TV meeting between Sir Alec Douglas-Home and Harold Wilson when asked in February 1964. In March 1966, 69 per cent of a sample contacted by the National Opinion Poll said they would like Harold Wilson and Edward Heath to face each other on television.

form of political television ranged between two-thirds and four-fifths (depending on the particular survey). It is not surprising, therefore, that the Kennedy–Nixon debates have been described as 'one of the great political assemblages of all time'.[23]

It is possible that many voters share the feeling of Stanley Kelley, Jr. that the distinctive elements of a party's policy and leadership are more likely to emerge clearly from a debating situation than from any other format in which politicians can appear. This is suggested by the figures given in Table 5.7, which indicate how the members of our sample replied when they were asked to say which of three kinds of political programme would be most likely to help them to weigh up the qualities of a political leader. Their response demonstrates an overwhelming preference among viewers for those forms of political television in which politicians do not have things all their own way but must respond to a challenge from some independent source. A half of the set owners believed that a debate with an opponent would provide the best basis for judging the true qualities of a politician, compared with two-fifths who preferred an interview with a reporter, and only a tenth who thought that a straight talk would be more revealing than either of the other alternatives.

Table 5.7. TYPES OF POLITICAL PROGRAMMES
PREFERRED BY VIEWERS

Q: If you wanted to weigh up the qualities of some political leader who was appearing on television, which of the following kinds of programme do you feel would help you most?

	%
A debate with an opponent	48
An interview with a TV reporter	39
A straight talk	10
Don't know	4
	101

N = 677 set owners

In fact the interest of our respondents in confrontations between the three party leaders survived the 1964 campaign more or less intact—despite other signs of their disenchantment

[23] Katz, Elihu and Feldman, Jacob J., in Kraus, Sidney, op. cit., p. 190.

after Polling Day with election politics on television. When asked in October 1964, 58 per cent of the set owners said they wished that some debates between leading political figures had been arranged during the campaign (compared with only 33 per cent who did not want them).[24]

[24] This result contrasts sharply with developments in American opinion at about the same time. Whereas 61 per cent of a national American sample welcomed the idea of a televised debate between Lyndon Johnson and Barry Goldwater when interviewed in June 1964, only 39 per cent said after Election Day in November that such a meeting would have helped them to form a better appreciation of the campaign issues and of the merits of the two candidates. (Cf. Elmo Roper and Associates, op. cit., p. 21.)

CHAPTER 6

TELEVISION AND THE CREDIBILITY OF CAMPAIGNING POLITICIANS

If the diverse findings of the previous chapter have a common theme, it is *the preference of electors for challenging forms of political television*. They are unenthusiastic about programmes which enable politicians to put their case in the best possible light without fear of any contradiction. They favour instead a type of presentation in which politicians can be observed reacting, in a freely developing situation, to a challenge that has been mounted from some genuinely independent source. Typical expressions of this sentiment include: nearly unanimous dismissal of the straight political talk as unrevealing; massive support for the idea of a top-level party-leader confrontation; strong approval of *Forum*-type programmes; and some of the reasons which viewers have given for welcoming the proposal to televise the proceedings of Parliament. But what accounts for this preference?

The excitement of a contest

Probably the appeal of challenging political television arises in part from the promise of a gladiatorial contest. An interview, for example, is similar in some respects to fencing. Can the reporter penetrate the politician's guard, or will his subject be able to parry even the most searching questions convincingly? A confrontation between political opponents combines several sources of excitement: anticipation of direct conflict; the unpredictability of the course which the argument is likely to follow; and uncertainty about who will emerge from the encounter as the victor. As one person explained, when he was asked why he preferred debates to straight political talks: 'It is more interesting when there is a bit of opposition. When you have opposition, you have a good fight'.[1]

But even if challenging programme forms are more entertaining than a conventional party speech, it does not follow that viewers enjoy displays of blatantly aggressive behaviour by politicians on television. Their disapproval of 'slanging' and 'mud-slinging' suggests that in fact they would prefer the participants in a confrontation to deal directly and constructively with the current issues and with each other's arguments. Although the criteria which viewers apply when evaluating a televised debate have never been investigated systematically, it is our impression that many would be disappointed if a confrontation amounted to little more than an exchange of mutual abuse without clarifying some of the problems under discussion. As another respondent pointed out, in explaining his preference for interviews:

> When interviewed by a reporter it shows a leader as he is. It shows his authenticity more than in a talk where he is able to evade issues. He's got to answer the questions put by a reporter.

And as three viewers replied, when they were asked why they wanted televised debates:

> It would be very good. Every time one politician said something, or made a promise, he'd have to prove it to the other.

> If they are put on the spot by each other, they can't have prepared answers.

> A debate would help us to find out who is 'bulling'.

[1] A hint of a connection between a desire for excitement and a liking for challenging programmes emerged when viewers' reasons for watching party broadcasts were sorted against their answers to the question which asked them to choose between a debate, an interview, and a straight political talk. Since 86 per cent of the entire sample opted for debates or interviews, there was very little scope for any significant difference to appear. But it is worth noting, at least, that 92 per cent of those who endorsed the item, 'to follow the excitement of the election race', as a reason for seeing a party broadcast, chose one of the more challenging formats. This proportion was exceeded in only one other group: 93 per cent of the vote-guidance seekers preferred interviews or debates.

TELEVISION AND THE CREDIBILITY

Fears about the persuasive process

These comments suggest that the thrill of a conflict is not the only factor in the popularity of challenging political television. This preference is also rooted, according to much of our evidence, in two sources of uncertainty about the persuasive process in politics. One is an awareness of the unreliability of the statements of party spokesmen, who are regarded as having an interest in painting as rosy an impression as they can of their own achievement and as black a picture as possible of the record of the opposition. The other is the elector's fear of his own gullibility when exposed to the wiles of the politicians—and particularly when those wiles are projected on the supposedly seductive medium of television. In the context of these anxieties two main functions are conferred on challenging political television: first to provide a searchlight, exposing what politicians wish to conceal; and second, to erect a shield, protecting viewers from their own susceptibility.

The unreliability of campaigning politicians

The first source of uncertainty reflects a mistrust of campaigning politicians which is as common as the preference for challenging programmes. Its full extent is shown by the answers our respondents gave when asked the following two questions:

1. During an election campaign, politicians often make pledges and promises. Do you ever feel that they cannot be relied on to be kept?
2. Politicians often quote various facts and figures during an election. Do you ever think that they might be misleading?

Anyone who replied affirmatively to either question was asked further whether he thought that the pledges of campaigners (or their statistical data) were 'usually', 'occasionally', or 'rarely' unreliable (or misleading). Table 6.1 shows how the answers to these questions were distributed. It can be seen that those who were prepared, on either count, implicitly to trust the statements of politicians amounted at the most to only 15 per cent of the respondents. Two-fifths of the sample found them 'usually' unreliable and misleading.[2]

Table 6.1. MANY ELECTORS MISTRUST THE STATEMENTS
OF CAMPAIGNING POLITICIANS

Campaign pledges and promises are:	%	The facts and figures cited in a campaign are:	%
Usually unreliable	39	Usually misleading	41
Occasionally unreliable	38	Occasionally misleading	32
Rarely unreliable	4	Rarely misleading	3
Never unreliable	10	Never misleading	12
Don't know	9	Don't know	11
	100		99

N = 748

Perceptions of campaigning as a promise-making activity

This sensitivity to the unreliability of political argument is connected with the way in which many voters perceive the

[2] The reactions of our respondents to these questions may be compared with those of a sample of 702 American electors to the statement that, 'The party leaders make no real effort to keep their promises once they get into office'. Only a third unreservedly disagreed with this statement, as the following figures show:

	%
Strongly agree	6
Agree	30
Disagree/Agree	28
Disagree	31
Strongly Disagree	2
Don't know	4
	101

See Dennis, Jack, 'Support for the Party System by the Mass Public', *American Political Science Review*, Vol. LX, No. 3, 1966, pp. 600–15. It seems that voters find party propaganda less credible than Anthony Downs expected they would. He argued that since the rational voter would value party reliability (defined as an ability to predict its future conduct from its past statements), competing parties would wish to establish a reputation for having this quality (Ch. 7, op. cit.). Electors' uncertainty about campaign promises may be greater than Downs anticipated because the ever-changing flux of complex political circumstances gives almost unlimited scope to governments to present plausible alibis for their failure to implement particular pledges.

nature of campaigning as an activity in itself. We have not studied their perceptions exhaustively, and much scope certainly remains for a more sustained investigation of them. But we were impressed, in our first attempt (in February 1964) to explore voters' notions of campaigning, by the frequency with which it was spontaneously described as *a promise-making activity*. This tendency emerged from the replies of the respondents to certain open-ended questions which approached these matters obliquely.

When, for example, we asked what methods of campaigning they disliked most, two tactics were mentioned far more frequently than any others. One, as we noted elsewhere,[3] was back-biting and the abusive attacks which party spokesmen direct at each other. But even more unpopular was the making of false, insincere or rash promises. One individual said that, 'I don't care much what they do. But about their promises, it wouldn't be so bad if they kept them, would it?'. Another referred to '. . . old-age pension promises. It is a gimmick. They offer it, and you pay for it. It draws votes, and then up goes the National Insurance stamp.' A third person spoke of '. . . the general trend of saying that the other party hasn't done this, hasn't kept their promises–but *they* are going to. The trouble is nobody knows if they win whether they really can keep their promises.' Altogether, 42 per cent of the individuals who could think of any objectionable methods of campaigning complained about unreliable election promises.[4]

Another line of questioning which elicited many spontaneous references to political promises concerned the reasons why viewers intended to watch party broadcasts. When asked about this, the third largest group in the exploratory sample put forward the extraordinarily elaborate idea of seeing what a party promised to do in order to be in a position to judge later whether it had kept its promises (supposing that it formed the government).[5] For example, one voter said that he wanted to 'get an idea of the promises of both parties to see if they are carried out later'. Another stated that, 'Most parties make promises, and I want to see which they make and which they keep.' And a third individual said, 'They've promised lots of things, and I want to see if they climb down on them.'

[3] See p. 81.   [4] See Note 39, Chapter 4.   [5] See Table 4.4, p. 65.

OF CAMPAIGNING POLITICIANS

We had hoped that interviews with the main sample would enable us to compare the prevalence of this perception of campaigning with any other notions that voters might have formed. Unfortunately, we could not afford to prolong the interview by adopting a probing line of open-ended questioning about these matters, and we had to rely in the end on a single forced-choice question. Four different ideas of the nature of electioneering were formulated, and the sample members were asked to pick out two (in order of importance) which they tended to 'notice most often about the politicians taking part in an election campaign'. The alternatives were worded as follows: the promises which politicians make; the personalities of politicians; the opinions which politicians express on current issues; and the principles which politicians say they stand for. Table 6.2 shows how the respondents' first endorsements of these features of a campaign were distributed.

Table 6.2. WHAT ELECTORS NOTICE ABOUT CAMPAIGNING POLITICIANS (FIRST CHOICE)

	Number of respondents	%
Their promises	241	32
Their principles	237	32
Their opinions on issues	116	16
Their personalities	113	15
Don't know	41	5
	748	100

It can be seen that the responses were scattered over all the available answers. Nevertheless, the sample members were somewhat more inclined to regard campaigning as a promise-making activity than as an occasion for the propagation of political principles, for the definition of party stands on particular issues, or for the projection of leaders' personalities. And when the second endorsements from the list were considered, it was found that 57 per cent of the respondents were aware of the promises of campaigning politicians.

It is difficult to deduce anything definitive from this evidence about the importance of other notions of electioneering; but there is no doubt that many voters regard campaigning as a process in which rival politicians engage in competitive promise making. Those who take this view perceive an election as a bidding situation in which the parties aim to attract additional support by the electoral appeal of their promises. This is 'market politics': just as commercial advertisers seek custom by promising to provide a brighter wash, so do campaigning politicians seek votes by promising to build more houses and to increase the old-age pension.[6] What is more, this way of interpreting a campaign often reflects the influence of one of two other elements in the political psychology of the elector.

Promises as a concrete aid to political understanding

A tendency to concentrate on party promises when following an election is a symptom, in many cases, of the voter's relative lack of political sophistication. It shows that, amidst all the conflicting arguments, analyses, and trends which a campaign brings to his attention, the promise-noticing elector is looking for something concrete which he can grasp firmly and understand clearly. Pledges and promises provides this type of voter with a comprehensible anchor of attention.

Two pieces of evidence point to this interpretation. One emerged when we sorted the various features of a campaign which the interviewees claimed to notice against their responses to a request to choose three qualities (out of a list of 12) which a politician should have if he was to help to run the country well. This analysis yielded only one statistically significant relationship. The 'promise-noticers' in the sample valued the quality of 'straightforwardness' in politicians much more highly than all the other respondents did.[7] Those who focus on party promises, then, are impatient with complexities and are particularly anxious that political leaders should express themselves simply and directly and without equivocation.

Another sign of their lack of sophistication appears in Table

[6] The expression 'market politics' was first coined in order to describe this feature of electioneering by Dr. Mark Abrams, the Chairman of Research Services, Ltd.

[7] Of 241 promise-noticers, 114, or 47 per cent, preferred political leaders to be straightforward, compared with only 39 per cent of the rest of the sample. This was significant at $P = \cdot05$ level.

6.3, which provides particulars of their educational and occupational backgrounds. Only 13 per cent of those who had left school at the age of 16 or later were initially inclined to notice the promises of campaigning politicians–compared with 36 per cent of those who had left school at 14 or earlier. In the former group promises were noticed less often than each of the other itemized features of campaigning; in the latter group they topped the list. The table also shows that there is an inverse relationship between promise-noticing and occupational status.[8]

[8] The authors of *The American Voter* have also commented on the propensity of the unsophisticated voter to perceive campaigning as a promise-making activity, a tendency which first emerged in their surveys, as in ours, in responses to open-ended questioning about other matters. National samples were asked during the 1952 and 1956 presidential elections to evaluate the good and bad points of the Democratic and Republican Parties and their candidates. The investigators then ranked the replies according to the levels of conceptualization which they seemed to reflect– whether the respondents preferred a party or its candidate for ideological reasons, for expected group benefits, or just out of some simple readiness to equate a party with the goodness or badness of the times. In discussing the remarks of those respondents, whom they classified in the category of 'group benefits', the authors drew attention to a theme deserving of 'special comments', notably a tendency to refer to specific party promises. This passage then follows:

> In the upper ranges, particularly among the full ideologues, references to promises made or broken are almost non-existent. But as we depart from the upper level, references of this sort increase in frequency to the point at which they become almost the centre of any attention paid to content with policy implication. The political 'promise' in the form retained by the respondent, has characteristics that contrast sharply with the sorts of concerns associated with ideology. . . . Promises arise *de novo* with each campaign; they have minimal roots in either a party tradition or a long-range program. The time perspective they imply is foreshortened in the future as well as the past, because they create expectations of immediate results. . . . The tendency to focus upon these pledges as the issue core of politics seems to token narrow time perspectives, concrete modes of thought, and a tremendously oversimplified view of causality in social, economic, and political process.

See Campbell, Angus, Converse, Philip E., Miller, Warren E., and Stokes, Donald E., *The American Voter*, John Wiley and Sons, Inc., 1964, p. 237.

Table 6.3. THE HIGHLY EDUCATED AND THE NON-MANUAL
ELECTORS WERE LEAST INCLINED TO NOTICE THE PROMISES
OF CAMPAIGNING POLITICIANS AND MOST INCLINED TO
NOTICE THEIR PERSONALITIES

What was noticed first about campaigning politicians:	School-leaving age			Occupation		
	14 and under	15	16 and older	Non-manual	Skilled manual	Semi- and unskilled
	%	%	%	%	%	%
Their promises	36	34	13	26	35	36
Their personalities	13	16	26	20	15	7
Their principles	31	29	37	32	30	34
Their opinions on issues	15	14	19	18	15	15
Don't know	5	8	5	3	6	7
	100	101	100	99	101	99
N =	522	118	108	217	364	149

Class and an interest in political personalities

It is convenient to draw attention here to another striking
feature of Table 6.3. This is the influence of educational and
occupational background on the tendency of voters to notice
the *personalities* of campaigning politicians. In contrast to what
we expected, high-status electors are much more aware of the
personalities of politicians than are manual workers and voters
who left school at the age of 14. Twenty per cent of the white-
collar respondents admitted that they noticed politicians' personalities most often when following a campaign, compared
with only seven per cent of the non-skilled workers in the
sample. This is consistent with a finding, presented in Chapter
4, which showed that the middle-class viewer was more likely
than his working-class counterpart to watch party broadcasts
in order 'to judge what political leaders are like'.[9]

How can the emergence of this pattern be explained? It may
be significant that the least privileged elements in the community
are most indifferent to the play of personality in politics. Perhaps non-skilled workers think of themselves *as* low-status
citizens who, because they are highly dependent on tangible

[9] See pp. 79–80.

help from governments to improve their material circumstances, wish politicians to specify clearly the exact benefits they would provide if elected to power. According to this interpretation, it is mainly the better-off voter who can afford the luxury of regarding electioneering as an arena in which the leading politicians vie with each other to make their mark on events and to show the stuff of which they are made.

Promises and political scepticism

The tendency to regard an election campaign as consisting mainly of a competitive exchange of promises is not solely to be accounted for by the concern of the less sophisticated voter to learn in fairly simple terms what the parties propose to do if elected and how their proposals could affect the material circumstances of his life. It is closely involved also with a sceptical reaction to the reliability of politicians' statements. That is, election promises not only provide tangible clues to the policy intentions of the parties; they are also a source of uncertainty, for they can be broken, ignored, overridden and reinterpreted as easily as they were made.

Table 6.4. SCEPTICAL ELECTORS TENDED TO REGARD
CAMPAIGNING AS A PROMISE-MAKING ACTIVITY

	Amount of attention deserved by politicians' arguments			
	A lot	Some	A little	None
Percentage who noticed campaign promises most often	27%	36%	32%	52%**
N† =	227	238	149	69

† Includes all those who noticed some feature of campaigning but leaves out the 'don't knows'.

** Significant at P = ·01 level for three degrees of freedom.

The empirical relationship between distrust of politicians' arguments and sensitivity to their campaign promises is illustrated by Table 6.4. This distinguishes the members of our sample according to the amount of attention which they thought that politicians' arguments usually deserved, and, reading from left to right, it shows what proportion of each of the four increasingly sceptical groups was also inclined to notice promises. It can be seen that only a quarter of the least sceptical electors (those who would pay a 'lot' of attention to politicians) noticed promises more often than any other feature of a campaign, compared with over a half of the most sceptical respondents (those who said that politicians' arguments deserved no attention).

The view of campaigning as a promise-making activity which emerges from this analysis is quite a complex perception. For a campaign promise is regarded both as a moral commitment, which should be kept, and as a manipulative weapon in the persuasive armoury of politicians, which should be distrusted. Those who most need the specific policy statement as an anchor to their understanding are also most wary of its use in the hands of politicians.

Some tension is inherent in this situation, and part of the appeal of challenging political television may derive from its ability to relieve the strain. We have seen that the least sophist-icated electors (those who depend most on television for their access to current affairs) find it easier to follow party promises than the other elements introduced by politicians into a campaign. We have seen that those promises may have a material bearing on their future life-chances. We have also seen that party promises tend to be regarded as intrinsically unreliable. Challenging political television, then, may seem to offer a means of distinguishing between those promises which it would be reasonable to count on and those which are most extravagant and untrustworthy.

Television and the fear of being duped

The desire to be helped in this way may be strengthened by an elector's fear of his own gullibility and of being duped by politicians who are accustomed to presenting themselves plausibly on television. Such a fear is unlikely to be acknowledged openly. One hint of its existence emerged, however, from a piece of research which was recently commissioned by the Independent Television Authority. This showed that, whereas only 15 per cent of the members of a national sample who had ever seen a party broadcast thought that their *own* views had been affected, 51 per cent surmised that party broadcasts could influence the opinions of *other* viewers.[10] It is as if these respondents regarded party broadcasts as clever exercises in persuasion which could deceive a viewer unless he deliberately built up some defences against them (which most claimed, of course, to have done already).

In our sample the characteristic reaction to the deceptive potential of political television was one of ambivalence. Viewers' attitudes were a mixture of *confidence* in their ability to judge what politicians were really like from their TV appearances and of *wariness* about the dangers of being taken in by a spurious image. The note of confidence was firmly sounded when they were asked to choose, from a list of 12 qualities, three characteristics that it was most desirable for politicians to have if they were to run the country well, and three that television was most able to reveal. Table 6.5 shows how each quality was ranked by the holders of television sets in both respects.

Table 6.5. COMPARISON OF VIEWERS' OPINIONS ABOUT LEADERSHIP QUALITIES IMPORTANT TO GOOD GOVERNMENT WITH THOSE TELEVISION CAN SHOW

Most important for running the country well		*Qualities in politicians*	*Most likely to be revealed by TV*	
No. of mentions	*Order of mention*		*Order of mention*	*No. of mentions*
285	1	Straightforward	3	301
269	2	Hardworking	9	101
261	3 (tied)	Sincere	2	313
261	3 (tied)	Strong	7	125
238	5	Confident	1	318
219	6	Fairminded	4 (tied)	198
148	7	Inspiring	8	114
110	8	Able	10	50
78	9	Persuasive	4 (tied)	198
75	10	Likeable	6	163
24	11	Kindly	12	37
13	12	Unassuming	11	47

The results facilitate a number of intriguing comparisons—

[10] 'Report on a Survey of Attitudes towards News, Current Affairs and Documentary Programmes on Television', op. cit., p. 26.

depending on how the qualities themselves are grouped.[11] The viewers apparently perceived likeability, kindliness, and lack of conceit (which appear in the bottom three rows of the table) as rather personal traits that were unimportant in a political leader but more likely to be revealed in television performances. This contrast was reversed by the respondents' reactions to the strong and hard-working characteristics of a politician – which, though highly relevant to good government, were much less likely to be disclosed on television. (Together with ability, these qualities received half as many endorsements for revelation by TV as for their importance in running the country well.) It is also tempting to ascribe the relatively low standing on both lists of being 'inspiring' to the rather humdrum style of political leadership that has prevailed in Britain throughout the 1960s!

Despite these differences, however, several important qualities occupied similar positions in both lists. This suggests that the average elector feels some confidence in his own ability to make a true estimate of those leaders who appeal for his vote by observing their behaviour on the television screen. It is noticeable that this conviction was focused upon the qualities of straightforwardness, sincerity, and self-confidence – which were regarded both as very important in a political leader and as readily detectable from the appearances of politicians on television.

Two implications of this emphasis deserve further consideration. First, it is striking that the importance to statesmanship of these qualities should have been stressed at the expense of other presumably more relevant traits – such as ability, which the sample ranked only eighth when the needs of good government were considered. The tendency to prize straightforwardness even above ability is partly a function of educational background. Table 6.6 shows that it is mainly the minimally educated voter who lacks confidence in his capacity to follow and grasp what politicians say and who appreciates straightforwardness in his leaders, therefore, and relies on TV to disclose its presence.

[11] The authors are indebted to Professor Paul F. Lazarsfeld for drawing their attention to the implications of the comparisons which are discussed here and in the following three paragraphs.

Table 6.6. THE ELECTORS WITH LEAST EDUCATION
VALUE STRAIGHTFORWARDNESS IN POLITICIANS, AND THEY
BELIEVE IT IS REVEALED ON TELEVISION, IN CONTRAST TO
THE HIGHLY EDUCATED WHO TEND TO VALUE ABILITY†

	School-leaving age	
	14 or 15	*16 or older*
	%	%
Value straightforwardness in leaders	44	33*
Find that TV shows straightforwardness	47	28***
Value ability in leaders	14	29***
Find that TV shows ability	7	9
N =	580	97

† In the analysis of endorsements by educational background significant differences were found only for these qualities.
** Significant at P = ·05 level for one degree of freedom.
* Significant at P .05 level for one degree of freedom.

Second, it may be feared that the average viewer's preoccupation with straightforwardness, sincerity, and self-confidence creates an opportunity to deceive him by appearances. We have no direct evidence that voters have actually been influenced by the efforts of individual politicians to cultivate a reputation for such supposedly perceptible traits.[12] Nevertheless, confidence, directness and sincerity are probably the qualities that a self-conscious image-maker is most likely to try to project on television. The high regard of electors for these same qualities,

[12] Our own sample's impressions of the party leaders who fought the 1964 campaign were modified most substantially on those scales that stood for strength, self-confidence, persuasiveness, and being inspiring (see Chapter 12 below). Although David Butler considers that television usually shows those who appear on it 'in a fairly true light', he has also described Harold Wilson (before the devaluation crisis) as:

> . . . probably the ablest exploiter of television the country has yet produced. He can speak straight to camera with unmatched force and clarity conveying statesmanship and sincerity . . . But the qualities of ingenuity and cunning which so impress those who deal closely with him, friend and foe alike, are totally absent from his television *persona*.

Cf. Butler, D. E., 'Political Television', Seventh Annual Lecture, Research Students' Association, The Australian National University, Canberra, 1967, p. 5.

then, could favour a manipulative style of campaigning, and perhaps it illustrates the vulnerable position of the public in the television age.

But it would be a mistake to suppose that most voters are blithely unaware of these dangers. The very data that we have been considering reflect the presence of certain undercurrents of uneasiness about televised persuasion. For example, the public's concern to be led by rulers who are straightforward and sincere is itself probably a symptom of electoral anxiety. Riesman noted some years ago that: 'Forced to choose between skill and sincerity, many in the audience prefer the latter. They are tolerant of bumbles and obvious ineptness if the leader tries hard.'[13] He pointed out further that such a stress on the importance of sincerity often arises when people have some reason to suspect that they are targets of persuasion which have been mounted to advance not their own interests but those of the persuaders. A classic instance of this phenomenon is described in Robert Merton's study of the attempt of Kate Smith, an American radio entertainer, to sell a large number of war bonds in the course of a 24-hour marathon programme during the Second World War. He found that those individuals who had responded favourably to her appeal often contrasted:

> . . . her integrity with the pretences, deceptions and dissembling which they observe in daily experience. On every side they feel themselves the object of manipulation. They see themselves as the target of ingenious methods of control through advertising which cajoles, promises, terrorizes; through propaganda that . . . guides the unwitting audience into opinions which may or may not coincide with the best interests of themselves or their affiliates; through cumulatively subtle methods of salesmanship which may simulate values common to both salesmen and client for private and self-interested motives. So our informants live in a climate of reciprocal distrust which, to say the least, is not conducive to stable human relationships.[14]

Yet another sign of an awareness on the part of our respondents of the misleading potential of television was provided by their views about persuasiveness as a political quality. Although it

[13] Riesman, D., op. cit., p. 195.
[14] Merton, Robert K., *Mass Persuasion*, Harpers, New York, 1946, pp. 142–3.

was rated only ninth when the demands of good government were considered, persuasiveness was placed fourth in the list of qualities that television was supposed to project. It is seen, therefore, as something of an extraneous factor which television specifically brings into the campaigning situation, and one which is regarded rather ambivalently. We found, for instance, that when they were asked directly to estimate how easy it was 'to get a true picture of what a politician is like from his appearances on television', more viewers maintained that it was 'usually difficult' (42 per cent) than thought it was 'usually easy' (32 per cent).[15] When, further, we compared these two groups in terms of their opinions about the qualities which television can reveal, two interesting differences emerged. Table 6.7 shows that those who were most conscious of the difficulties of judging leaders from their television appearances were particularly sceptical about its ability to convey the prized trait of straightforwardness. They were also more likely to see television as projecting the persuasive qualities of politicians. This implies that persuasiveness carries a pejorative connotation, and that many viewers find it difficult to penetrate the televisual plausibility of politicians when judging their worth.

This complex of reservations is empirically connected with the desire of voters to be served by more challenging political programmes. A preference for interviews and debates is clearly associated with opinions about the difficulty of judging politicians on television. For example, only 28 per cent of those viewers who preferred politicians to give straight talks admitted that it was 'usually difficult' to judge what leaders were like from their appearances on television. But of those preferring an interview with a reporter, 39 per cent found leader-judging difficult, and of those wanting debates between political opponents, the corresponding figure was 46 per cent. We may infer that lack of

---

[15] The full breakdown of the response to this question was as follows:

	%
Usually difficult	42
It depends	22
Usually easy	32
Don't know	4
	100
N =	677 TV owners

Table 6.7. THOSE WHO FIND IT EASY TO JUDGE POLITICIANS
ON TV THINK THAT TV REVEALS THE QUALITY OF
STRAIGHTFORWARDNESS, WHILE THOSE WHO FIND IT
DIFFICULT BELIEVE THAT TV SHOWS PERSUASIVENESS†

	Judging politicians on TV is:	
	Usually easy	Usually difficult
	%	%
Find that TV shows straight-forwardness	54	41**
Find that TV shows persuasive-ness	20	35***
N =	220	281

† In the analysis of endorsements by estimated difficulty of judging
politicians on television, significant differences were found only for these
qualities.
** Significant at P = ·01 level for one degree of freedom.
*** Significant at P = ·001 level for one degree of freedom.

confidence in their ability to assess political qualities accurately
led many of our respondents to look for help to those types of
programme in which an independent challenge is posed to the
politicians concerned.[16]

A substitute for 'the challenge of events'

In concluding this analysis it is appropriate to make one final
interpretive point. This arises from the conviction of some
voters that anyone wishing to assess the calibre of a political
leader or his party would do better to examine their record of
past deeds than to heed their fair words. Such sentiments were
voiced by a number of participants in our first exploratory

[16] Opinions about many of these matters were associated strongly with
age. Younger voters were far more suspicious of the misleading potential
of television and more enthusiastic about challenging political programmes
than their elders. This relationship is shown by the following figures:

	Age			
	21–29	30–44	45–65	66 +
	%	%	%	%
Believe that it is 'usually easy' to judge politicians on TV	20	29	38	36
Find that TV shows persuasiveness	40	33	27	16
Prefer challenging political television (interviews or debates)	92	91	84	74
N =	84	219	293	81

survey when they were asked about the point of attending to politicians' arguments. The following remarks illustrate their outlook quite well:

> You should just judge by what you've seen, not by what they say. By what's gone on in the past years and that. For example, Labour got the country into a mess, and it was up to the Conservatives to get the country out.

> I think you should go by what a party has done when it was in power previously. I don't think that you can judge by what they promise. What has been done is the important thing.

> I think you should pay more attention to their record than their arguments. Arguments needn't be true. It's what they've done that counts. If you look back in the past, you'll see they promise all sorts of things, but they don't always do what they say.

These electors seem to be implying that the best way to judge a party or a politician is to see how they have measured up to what might be called 'the challenge of events'. Unfortunately this advice is not easy to follow during an election campaign, which is concerned as much with the future as with the past. Precisely when the onset of a campaign heightens the average citizen's receptivity to politics, the supply of relevant 'challenges of events' tends to dry up. Foreign crises are often obligingly postponed, and typically Budget Day is a long way off. Then in fact there are only the notoriously unreliable words of the politicians to go by. Seen in this perspective, the preference for interviews and debates as a form of political broadcasting during an election can reasonably be interpreted as a search for a television substitute for 'the challenge of events' to the authenticity of campaign claims.

CHAPTER 7

THE MEASUREMENT OF DISPOSITION TO FOLLOW A TELEVISION CAMPAIGN

Our interest in public attitudes towards election television was not restricted to an exploration of their *distribution* in a sample. In addition, we aimed to examine their *role* in facilitating or impeding the persuasive force of propaganda. This required the preparation of special instruments for dividing our respondents into attitudinally homogeneous groups, within each of which the association between opinion change and campaign exposure could be examined separately. This chapter outlines our approach to this task and some of the measures that were considered for this purpose. The most important instrument to emerge from our research was an index of the strength of a viewer's motivation for following an election campaign on television. In the pages that follow we describe the construction of this measure; present the results of some tests of its validation; and show how it was distributed in our sample. But first let us consider exactly why this line of enquiry was pursued.

The lessons of communications research

The need for such a refinement in studying the impact of a campaign derives ultimately from a major conclusion of much previous research in the field of mass communications. This refers to the importance in the communications process of the *initial predispositions* of members of an audience towards the materials they are about to receive. Such predispositions are regarded as mediating factors which filter the reception of a message and help to shape whatever impact it has. As a recent summary of the literature has pointed out, 'People respond to persuasive communications in line with their predispositions, and they change or resist change accordingly.'[1] So far as politics specifically are concerned, presumably differential reactions to party propaganda can normally be expected. If all voters happened to share identical feelings about political materials, their initial dispositions would not matter (they would be held constant). But since, as William A. Glaser has pointed out, '... users approach the media with a variety of needs and predispositions', then 'any precise identification of the effects of television watching on voting must identify the uses sought and made of television by the various types of viewer'.[2]

It is easier to frame such a recommendation, however, than to carry it out. In fact studies of political communications have typically been designed mainly to take account of the influence of certain demographic particulars (such as age, sex, occupation etc.) and of party support. The Audience Research Department of the BBC has shown, for example, that party preference consistently influences the reaction indices (measures of audience satisfaction with transmitted programmes) for party broadcasts.[3] But what has not yet been examined in any study of changing political attitudes is the part played by the type and degree of an individual's *interest in receiving political communications*. Our own object, then, was to give a central place in the study of political persuasion to an exploration of the role of variations in motivation for following an election campaign.

[1] Berelson, Bernard, and Steiner, Gary, *Human Behaviour: an Inventory of Scientific Findings*, Harcourt, Brace and World, Inc., New York, 1964, p. 540.

[2] Glaser, William, 'Television and Voting Turnout', *Public Opinion Quarterly*, Vol. XXIX, No. 1, 1965, pp. 71–86.

[3] The following table of mean reaction indices for party election broadcasts televised in the 1964 campaign is set out on p. 11 of 'The 1964 General Election', op. cit.:

	Pro	Anti	Uncommitted
Labour broadcasts	72	42	57
Conservative broadcasts	66	38	53
Liberal broadcasts	71	53	58

Political motives for receiving broadcast propaganda: reinforcement and vote-guidance seeking

On the face of it one division in our sample was directly suited to this purpose. It had been established that some electors look to the mass media for guidance when deciding how to vote, while others seek a reinforcement of their existing political opinions and allegiances. Several other differences also clustered around this distinction. The reinforcement seekers were more partisan, older and employed in less skilled jobs, tended to act more often as 'opinion leaders', and were politically less volatile than the vote-guidance seekers. In addition, selective exposure played a greater part in their reception of political broadcasts (they saw relatively more programmes produced by their own party).[4] It seemed appropriate, therefore, to see whether these groups also differed in the responses of their political attitudes to propaganda. But although such an investigation was undertaken, more use was made in the end of yet another motivational variable.

Strength of motivation for following election television

This other variable stood for differences between viewers in the *strength* (not the type) of their disposition to follow an election on television. Such differences seemed especially relevant to the situation in Britain. Communications research has shown that the two most important determinants of exposure to a message are (*a*) an interest in its content and (*b*) accessibility to it.[5] In an election, specifically, big doses of exposure to party materials are usually due to a keen political interest on the part of the voter. But in Britain the simultaneous transmission of party broadcasts on all available channels maximizes the accessibility of propaganda—with the result that heavy exposure to political television may be attributable *either* to strong interest *or* to habitually frequent usage of the TV set. This is to say that the highly exposed group of electors may include, on the one hand, many keen followers of *politics* and, on the other hand, many inveterate *television* addicts. Such a lack of homogeneity would

[4] See Chapter 4.
[5] Berelson, Bernard, and Steiner, Gary, op. cit., p. 531.

not matter in a study of the impact of a campaign if strength of motivation itself has no bearing on the persuasibility of voters. But if this variable affects susceptibility to influence, then differences in it among those who have followed an election extensively–unless allowed for in the research design–might obscure and even obliterate any connection between attitude change and campaign exposure.

In the early stages of this study two simple and opposed hypotheses about the role of motivation were formulated. The first expected to find a direct connection between disposition and influence: those who, though exposed to party broadcasts, were uninterested in them, would pay too little attention to be affected by them. The second postulated a direct connection between motivation and strong attitude defences: those who were least receptive to political communications would be more open to influence because they would bring a less definite set of pre-formed political opinions to the viewing experience.

In order to test these expectations, we sought to devise a measure of differences between viewers in the degree of their willingness to receive broadcast propaganda. Some further characteristics of the required instrument can be specified here. It should be related to, but not identical with, an index of general interest in politics (some politically minded electors might not be keen to follow a campaign specifically on television). It would not measure merely the degree to which viewers like or dislike political television, since a disposition to follow a campaign may arise from a sense of duty as well as expected enjoyment. And since we were interested in the interaction between this disposition and the impact of deliberate persuasive efforts, the measure should refer to a vehicle of party propaganda–that is, to party election broadcasts.

Reactions to a particular party broadcast

One device which might have met these requirements was the categorization of respondents in terms of their reactions to a particular party broadcast that had actually been transmitted. As was shown in Chapter 4, it was possible, by detailed questioning shortly after the appearance of a single party broadcast, to classify electors according to whether they had given political reasons for watching it, had watched it without mentioning any such political reasons, had expressed regret at missing the programme, or had missed it without regret.[6] Several advantages attracted us to this procedure at first. Realistic responses might be encouraged by using an actual instance of viewing behaviour as a basis for assessing the degree of motivation. In addition, we had evidence that the main sample's reactions to a pre-campaign Labour broadcast had successfully predicted exposure to the subsequent campaign. Of those who were classified as having political reasons for seeing that programme (or as having regretted missing it), 41 per cent had later viewed eight or more of the 13 party election broadcasts—in comparison with proportions of 24 per cent among the unselective viewers and 17 per cent among the indifferent non-viewers, respectively.

Nevertheless, certain drawbacks were eventually responsible for an abandonment of this approach to our problem. One was its inability to discriminate sensitively between the numerous individuals who happened not to have seen the particular party broadcast to which the measure was anchored. Each time the test was applied more than half of the body of television owners fell into a single category—that of indifferent non-viewers—although important gradations of interest presumably existed within this large group. In addition, the party of origin distorted the results. When a Labour broadcast was shown the politically motivated group of viewers consisted disproportionately of Labour supporters (and contrariwise when a Conservative broadcast was used). Finally, an empirical reason for discarding this instrument emerged from the fact that an alternative index of strength of motivation was associated more closely with the key variables it should reflect. How was this other measure derived?

The chosen measure: ratio scores

We have stressed several times that public feeling towards party broadcasts is ambivalent: the various gratifications that electors derive from following politicians on television are counteracted by reservations about the staleness and unreliability of party propaganda. This mixture eventually provided

[6] See pp. 57–64.

the key to the methodological problem posed in this chapter, for it transpired that the strength of an individual's disposition to receive political communications on television could be conceived as the outcome of a set of pulls and pushes. If he had many reasons for wanting to watch party broadcasts and none for disliking them, he would tend to be strongly motivated to follow them; and, if the position was reversed, he would be strongly disposed to avoid them. Our measure of strength of motivation for following election television was derived, then, from the *ratio* of the number of reasons for *watching* election broadcasts that viewers endorsed (out of eight on a checklist) to the number of reasons for *avoiding* party broadcasts (out of nine) which they accepted as applying to them.

The utility of this device was discovered at first by accident. When analysing the data collected in the exploratory survey of February 1964, it was found that if the respondents were ranked in descending order according to their ratio scores, a crucial cutting point appeared less than a third of the way down the list: most of the respondents above it (with such high scores as 3:0, 4:0, 4:1, 5:1, etc.) had either given political reasons for watching the party broadcast to which that survey was 'tied', or had regretted missing it; and many below the cutting point were either unselective viewers of the broadcast or had not minded missing it. Altogether, the classification in terms of the ratio score accorded with the previous classification of sample members (as interested or uninterested viewers and interested or un-interested non-viewers of a particular party broadcast) in 85 per cent of the cases. The ratio score, then, was a very good predictor of the freely-given replies to the open-ended question that had been the basis of our first measure of motivation. But the ratio score had the additional advantage of providing comparable information about all our participants.

When this measure was calculated for members of the main sample, about 50 different ratio scores were obtained, and, to facilitate analysis, it was necessary to group the respondents in a small set of categories. Various arrangements were tried, and in the end the system of classification set out in Table 7.1 was adopted. This divides the sample, according to their ratio scores of June 1964, into five main strength-of-motivation groups (descending from the strongest to the weakest) and one very

Table 7.1. How the ratio scores were distributed
in june 1964 among the tv owners in the main sample*

Classification of motivation	Ratio scores	N	%
1. Very strong	At least three reasons for watching, and up to one for avoiding party broadcasts endorsed: 3:0, 3:1, 4:0, 4:1, up to 8:0, 8:1	118	17
2. Moderately strong	All other respondents with more reasons for watching than for avoiding party broadcasts, up to a maximum of two of the latter: 1:0, 2:0, 2:1, 3:2, 4:2, up to 8:2	162	24
3. Medium	All even ratio scores: 0:0, 1:1, 2:2, up to 8:8	181	27
4. Moderately weak	One less reason for watching than for avoiding party broadcasts: 0:1, 1:2, 2:3, up to 8:9	98	14
5. Very weak	All other respondents with more reasons for avoiding than for watching party broadcasts: 0:2 up to 0:9, 1:3, up to 1:9, 2:4 up to 2:9, etc.	98	14
6. Ambiguous	More reasons for watching than for avoiding party broadcasts, but at least three of the latter endorsed: 4:3, 5:3, up to 8:3, 5:4 up to 8:4, etc.	20	3
		677	99

* If non-owners had a radio set they were given the items on the checklist with a slightly revised wording. The percentage distribution of ratio scores over the whole sample of 748 electors was as follows:

	%
1.	17
2.	24
3.	26
4.	16
5.	14
6.	3
	100

small residual ambiguous category. For some purposes the sample can be divided three ways, with a strong motivation group consisting of most of the individuals who endorsed more reasons for watching party broadcasts than for avoiding them; a medium group containing all the 'even' ratio scores; and a weak motivation group including all the viewers who endorsed more reasons for avoiding than for watching party broadcasts. And when the relationship between attitude change and campaign exposure was examined, it proved sufficient to dichotomize the sample into two large groups, the medium category joining the respondents rated weak in motivation for this particular purpose.[7]

The checklists of items from which the ratio scores were derived were administered to the members of the main sample on two occasions. During the first round of interviewing, in June 1964, they were asked to pick out those items which had ever applied to their viewing or avoidance of party broadcasts in the *past*; and in the second round in September they were asked to specify the reasons that might affect their viewing and avoidance of election broadcasts during the *forthcoming* campaign. In most subsequent analyses, however, the June ratio scores were used to measure viewers' strength of motivation. Three considerations governed this choice. First, it seemed likely that an individual's explanation of his past behaviour in an actually experienced situation would provide a more accurate indication of his attitudes than a speculative attempt to estimate how he would feel in a hypothetical state of affairs

[7] Although the 20 viewers in the residual group endorsed more reasons for watching party broadcasts than for avoiding them, they stated that at least three of the latter applied to them. This response was treated as ambiguous, for the distribution of their answers to other questions indicative of political interest could not be ranked consistently in relation to the replies of members of the other groups. For example, a large proportion of the ambiguous respondents (85 per cent) cared who won the election 'very much', only a moderate number (40 per cent) said they liked the idea of televising Parliament 'very much', and very few (10 per cent) wanted more political programmes than were generally available on television. In response to exposure to election communications, however, there were signs that the political attitudes of the ambiguous viewers had developed along lines characteristic of the voters who were rated weak in motivation. But because of their ambiguous situation, they were excluded from all rigorous analyses of the relationship between opinion change and exposure.

THE MEASUREMENT OF DISPOSITION

in the future. Second, the ambiguous category had more than
tripled from June to September (containing 73 cases at the
latter interview, compared with only 20 in the earlier one),
and we were reluctant to exclude as many as 11 per cent of the
viewers in our sample from the additional analyses that we

Table 7.2. Answers to a direct question about interest
in the campaign were associated more closely with
June ratio scores than with two other measures
of motivation*

Degree of interest in following the forthcoming campaign	June ratio scores			September ratio scores			Reactions to Sept. broadcast		
	Strong	Medium	Weak	Strong	Medium	Weak	Strong	Medium	Weak
	%	%	%	%	%	%	%	%	%
1. Very	61	45	23	57	35	30	61	56	38
2. Somewhat	30	33	30	29	41	29	26	37	33
3. Not much	9	21	45	13	22	41	13	7	28
4. Don't know	—	1	2	—	2	—	—	—	1
	100	100	100	99	100	100	100	100	100
N =	280	181	196	309	110	185	145	71	421

* In preparing this table a three-fold division of the ratio scores was used,
bringing together groups 1 and 2 (the very and moderately strong); 3
(medium); and 4 and 5 (the very and moderately weak). For reactions to
the Labour Party broadcast of September 11th, the strongly motivated
group consisted of the politically interested viewers and the individuals who
minded missing it, and the weak category included unselective viewers and
the individuals who did not regret missing it. A 'medium' category was
fabricated out of the replies of some of the individuals who had been difficult
to place in the fourfold classification usually applied to this material. The
figures suggest, however, that this attempt was unsuccessful, for the 'medium'
group did not really fall halfway between the others.

planned. Finally, the June ratio scores seemed to be associated
somewhat more closely than their September equivalents with
several other indicators of interest in television politics.

One example of its superiority in this respect is provided by

Table 7.2. This shows how the answers of our respondents to a direct question about their interest in following the forthcoming campaign were distributed by each of the three possible measures of strength of motivation at our disposal: the June ratio scores; the September ratio scores; and the open-ended reactions to viewing (and not viewing) the Labour party political broadcast of September 11, 1964. By reading along row 3 of the table it can be seen that both sets of ratio scores were more effective than the particular broadcast reactions in picking out the most apolitical viewers. And a comparison of the June and September ratio scores shows that the discriminatory power of the former was marginally superior to the latter. A more comprehensive set of tabular comparisons between these three possible measures of strength of motivation for following election television is provided in Appendix D.

The activation of motivation by the approaching campaign

The differences between the June and September ratio scores may have arisen from different methods of administering the checklist, but there were signs that they also reflected the impact on the sample of the approach of the coming campaign. This strengthened our confidence in the measure. Table 7.3 shows how the ratio scores were distributed across the various motivational categories in June and September, respectively. It can be seen that attitudes towards campaign television had tended to polarize between the two interviews (the 'very strong' and 'very weak' groups were both slightly larger in September than in June). And by the later date there was a quickening of public interest in television politics (45 per cent of the viewers were rated strong in motivation in September, compared with 41 per cent in June).

The imminence of the campaign had apparently awakened the interest of two distinct groups in the electorate. One consisted of elderly people past the age of retirement. Table 7.4 records a big increase between June and September in the proportion of electors aged 66 and over who were rated strong in motivation. It appears that between elections the elderly tend to feel indifferent about and cut off from civic affairs – but that the approach of a campaign helps to revive their previous

Table 7.3. HOW THE DISTRIBUTION OF RATIO SCORES
CHANGED BETWEEN JUNE AND SEPTEMBER, 1964

Classification of motivation	June %	September %
Very strong	17	23
Moderately strong	24	22
Medium	27	16
Moderately weak	14	9
Very weak	14	18
Ambiguous	3	11
	99	99

N = 677

interest in politics.[8] In contrast to this development, it is noticeable that the youngest members of the sample, whose average level of motivation also seemed rather low in June, were not similarly activated by the campaign.

Table 7.4. THE OLDEST ELECTORS WERE MOST LIKELY
TO HAVE THEIR INTEREST AROUSED BY THE APPROACH
OF THE CAMPAIGN

Proportions rated strong in motivation in:	Age groups			
	21–29	30–44	45–65	66 +
June	34%	42%	45%	36%
September	37%	48%	46%	50%
N =	84	219	293	81

Second, there was an interesting relationship between developments in voting intentions and arousal of interest in the forthcoming campaign. This is illustrated by Table 7.5. The individuals who eventually voted for a different party from the one they had supported in September (the so-called inter-party changers) were far more interested in the campaign immediately before it opened than they had been 2½ months earlier. It was apparently not indecision as such that prompted this activation (for the second column in the table shows that the September 'don't knows' were unmoved by the approach of

[8] This was but one of several signs in our evidence of a resumption of contact by the elderly with national politics through the impact of an election. See pp. 194–5.

the campaign), but the entertaining of doubts about the merits of a party which the voter had previously supported. Perhaps this kind of elector hopes that the campaign will help to resolve some of his more painful conflicts of loyalty.

Table 7.5. INTEREST IN THE APPROACHING CAMPAIGN WAS AROUSED MOST NOTICEABLY AMONG THOSE WHO EVENTUALLY SWITCHED FROM SUPPORT OF ONE PARTY TO ANOTHER

Proportions rated strong in motivation in:	Developments between September vote intention and October vote			
	Consistent party supporters	Late deciders	Inter-party changers	Non-voters
June	46%	45%	23%	21%
September	47%	40%	53%	28%
N =	525	60	64	78

Validation of the June ratio scores

When tapping a previously unexplored attitude, it is important to validate the instrument intended to measure it. This can be attempted in two main ways: (*a*) by examining evidence of the kind of behaviour in which the attitude should be expressed; and (*b*) by testing it against other opinions to which the attitude should be related. The former called for a scrutiny of the actual exposure patterns of the differently motivated viewers to the various scources of the 1964 campaign. However, the results of this acid test of validation appear in the following chapter, which is devoted to a full discussion of the influence on viewing behaviour of a wide range of audience dispositions and opinions.

Meanwhile, we can consider here how the June ratio scores were associated with the answers our respondents gave to certain questions in three other areas of relevant opinion. First, we had asked a direct question about their intentions to view party broadcasts during the campaign. Figure 7.1 shows how the answers were distributed among each of the motivation groups in the sample (except the residual category). By portraying the results for all five ratio score categories, the figure reveals the fine gradations of response which this instrument can sometimes

THE MEASUREMENT OF DISPOSITION

record. For example, the proportion stating that they would 'definitely' view a party broadcast during the campaign increased progressively from 15 per cent of the 'very weak' respondents to 86 per cent of the 'very strong' viewers.

Second, we had tapped various expressions of electoral feeling about the activities of campaigning politicians and especially about the credibility of political argument. Table 7.6 reveals the strong associations which emerged when the ratio scores were plotted against the responses to two of these items. It can be seen that only 13 per cent of the very strongly motivated

Figure 7.1. LEVEL OF MEASURED MOTIVATION WAS CLOSELY ASSOCIATED WITH ANSWERS TO A DIRECT QUESTION ABOUT VIEWERS' INTENTIONS TO WATCH PARTY ELECTION BROADCASTS

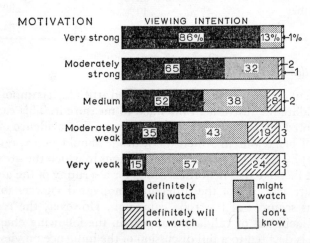

viewers believed that campaign arguments deserved merely a little or no attention. This contrasts with a figure of 50 per cent among those who were rated 'very weak' in motivation. Similarly, the proportions who thought that campaign promises were 'usually' unreliable ranged from 28 per cent in the 'very strong' motivation group to 54 per cent of those in the 'very weak' group.

Third, we had data about viewers' reactions to the election campaign on television after its completion. Table 7.7 shows that even when a question was asked about this at the final

Table 7.6 As LEVEL OF MEASURED MOTIVATION DECLINED, SCEPTICISM ABOUT CAMPAIGNING INCREASED

Attention deserved by campaign arguments	Motivation				
	Very strong	Moderately strong	Medium	Moderately weak	Very weak
	%	%	%	%	%
A lot	47	35	27	21	13
Some	41	39	30	32	26
A little/none	13	25	38	42	50
Don't know	—	1	5	5	11
	101	100	100	100	100
Find campaign promises 'usually unreliable'	28%	33%	38%	48%	54%
N =	118	162	181	98	98

Table 7.7. STRONGLY MOTIVATED VIEWERS WERE MORE SATISFIED WITH THE TV COVERAGE OF THE CAMPAIGN THAN WERE THOSE WHOSE MOTIVATION WAS WEAK

	Motivation		
	Strong (very or moderately)*	Medium	Weak (very or moderately)*
	%	%	%
Campaign about right (or too few programmes provided)	51	37	26
Too many programmes	44	55	66
Don't know	6	8	8
	101	100	100
N =	280	181	196

* The fivefold distinction in this case introduced no more variation in the response.

stage of the panel survey, almost four months after the motivational classification had been made, there was a clear relationship between viewer disposition and an overall judgement about the coverage provided on TV. A majority of the strongly motivated viewers felt that the amount of time given to the campaign had been about right–compared with only three-eighths of the intermediate group and a quarter of those rated weak in motivation.

The distribution of interest in election television

How is keenness to follow a campaign on television distributed throughout the electorate? Figure 7.2 shows the proportions of strongly motivated viewers that were detected by the June ratio scores in each of several demographic groups in our sample. It

Figure 7.2. PROPORTIONS OF VIEWERS IN VARIOUS
SUB-GROUPS RATED STRONG ('VERY' OR 'MODERATELY') IN
MOTIVATION TO FOLLOW ELECTION TELEVISION

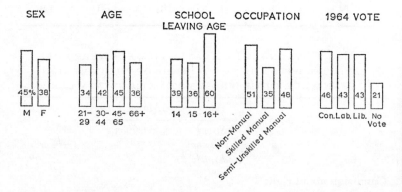

can be seen that educational background affected this disposition more powerfully than did any other variable. Three-fifths of those who left school at the age of 16 or later were strongly disposed to watch election broadcasts, compared with only about two-fifths of the minimally educated. Sex and age made little difference to the distribution of the ratio scores, although there was a tendency for women, young voters, and the elderly to be below-average in motivation.[9] Non-manual

[9] In fact age affected only those sample members who had received a minimal education. The respondents who had attended school until at least the age of 16 were uniformly strong in motivation regardless of their ages at the time of the interview.

workers recorded higher ratio scores than the manually employed, but when differences in skill among the latter were
taken into account, a curvilinear relationship emerged, and the
less skilled workers proved nearly as interested in television
politics as the white-collar workers were.[10]

The right-hand bars of the figure illustrate the relationship
between 1964 vote and the distribution of the ratio scores.
Only a very small proportion of those who abstained on Polling
Day were classified as strong in motivation for following the
campaign on television. But among the voters, party support
was unrelated to strength of motivation. Our results confirm a
finding, taken from a sample in Newcastle under Lyme, that,
'Political interest appears spread fairly evenly among supporters
of both political parties. Labour has a slight disadvantage,
but . . . the discrepancy between the two parties is not very
large.'[11] Of course it was vital in a study of this kind that a
measure which was intended to be used as an intervening
variable in investigating the process of political attitude change
should prove to be independent of party support.

[10] It is difficult to determine whether this is a distinctive feature of our
local sample. Some investigators who have related political interest to
occupation have examined only the gross differences between non-manual
and manual workers, although others have shown that the least skilled
elements are lowest in political interest. But it may be pointed out that
we also administered the items from which the ratio scores were calculated
to members of the Viewing Panel recruited by the Audience Research
Department of the BBC. Again the results (which apply to September 1964)
yielded a curvilinear relationship by occupation, as the following percentages show:

Rated strong in motivation
%

Non-manual	51
Skilled manual	42
Semi- and unskilled	48

[11] Bealey, Frank, Blondel, J., and McCann, W. P., *Constituency Politics:
A Study of Newcastle under Lyme*, Faber and Faber, London, 1965, p. 193.

CHAPTER 8

THE AUDIENCE FOR ELECTION
TELEVISION

We have examined electors' opinions about political broad-casting from a number of perspectives so far. We have considered the strength of their disposition to follow election television; the particular motivations which underlie viewing; preferences about the form which political television should take; and the uses which viewers wish to make of it, given the widespread feelings of mistrust that surround political propaganda. Now we turn to the connection between voters' views about these matters and the uses they *actually* make of the various political materials that are available during a General Election. We want to find out whether differences in what is sought from a campaign—and about the value of following it—are reflected in differential patterns of exposure to it.

Despite their seemingly direct relevance, it cannot be taken for granted that the opinions we have tapped will condition the public's reception (and rejection) of campaign communications. Caution about the predictive power of our measures of attitude is called for on at least two grounds. First, as the authors of a recently published textbook on the psychology of attitudes have pointed out, 'It is dangerous to assume that a knowledge of attitudes is in itself predictive of behavioural consequences in specific situations.'[1] Discrepancies between expressed attitudes and the type of behaviour which is expected to flow from them have often emerged from investigations

[1] Jahoda, M., and Warren, Neil (eds.), *Attitudes*, Penguin Modern Psychology Readings, Penguin Books, Ltd., Harmondsworth, Middlesex, 1966, p. 211.

designed especially to study this relationship.[2] In addition to this general source of doubt, however, there is a second and more specific reason in this case for expecting attitudinal distinctions to be blurred when exposure to the main channels of election communication is charted. The organization of political broadcasting, and the general habits of set use which prevail among viewers, ensure that every television owner has an easy access to political programmes. We might even expect to find, as a result, a total absence of association between intentions and interests on the one side and exposure to political broadcasts on the other.[3] In that event, the audience for political television might seem like a rather featureless and undifferentiated mass—an anonymous aggregate of viewers whose behaviour reflects but slightly those numerous differences of interest in following politics through the mass media which are professed verbally.

To explore the effect of audience predisposition on the volume and type of electoral exposure to campaign materials, the following five characteristics of our respondents were intensively studied:

1. Strength of motivation for following the election on television (as measured by the June ratio scores);

2. Customary habits of television set usage;

3. Acknowledgement of a direct political motive for receiving broadcast propaganda—e.g. a need for reinforcement and a desire for guidance in deciding how to vote;

4. Scepticism about the credibility of campaign arguments;

[2] Cf. De Fleur, Melvin L., and Westie, Frank R., 'Verbal Attitudes and Overt Acts: An Experiment on the Salience of Attitudes', *American Sociological Review*, Vol. XXIII, No. 6, 1958, pp. 667–73; and Rokeach, Milton, 'Attitude Change and Behavioral Change', *Public Opinion Quarterly*, Vol. XXX, No. 4, 1966–7, pp. 529–50.

[3] In any case, as an American authority has pointed out, discrepancies between measures of interest in certain programmes and actual viewing behaviour are quite common outside the political field: 'While opinion surveys . . . show considerable differences in the preferences of various population groups, actual audience measurements indicate fewer differences than might be expected in the extent to which various segments of the audience actually view programmes of different types.' Cf. Bogart, Leo, *The Age of Television*, Crosby, Lockwood and Son, Ltd., London, 1958, p. 91.

5. A readiness to designate themselves as opinion leaders–
that is, as individuals whose political views are sought
by other people in the circles in which they happen
to move.

The interaction of strength of motivation and habitual set usage

At the outset of this enquiry we postulated that exposure to a
television campaign would be determined by the independent
operation of two different factors: the strength of a viewer's
attachment to television itself; and the degree of his interest in
politics. The evidence presented in this section shows how far
these expectations were confirmed. It also provides the results
of a behavioural test of the validity of our measure of strength
of motivation for following an election on television.

Table 8.1. USUAL VIEWING HABITS AFFECTED EXPOSURE
TO THE TELEVISION CAMPAIGN

	Heavy viewers	Medium viewers	Light viewers
	%	%	%
Saw four or more party election broadcasts	68	60	47
Saw the main news at least three times per week	69	67	54
Saw late election news bulletins at least three times per week	29	24	16
Scored three or more for viewing non-party political programmes*	49	48	32
N =	257	266	152

* This takes account of exposure to *This Week, Election Gallery, Question
Time, Marathon* and *Look North*. The range of possible scores was 0–14, and
the method of scoring is explained in Appendix C.

According to the figures presented in Table 8.1, an individual's consumption of political television certainly depends,
in the first place, on his more general viewing habits and his
overall reliance on TV. The set owners in our sample were
divided into 'heavy', 'medium' and 'light' viewers of television,
respectively, according to their answers to two questions which
had been asked in June 1964–about the number of evenings
in a typical week when they usually engaged in some viewing,

and about the number of hours in an average evening which were devoted to viewing. The table shows that on each of four different measures of actual exposure to election television, the heavy viewers saw more of the 1964 campaign than did the medium viewers, while the medium viewers in turn saw more political programmes than did the light viewers. The relationship is undoubtedly progressive in the case of party election broadcasts—for the heavy viewers saw 5·6 of these programmes on the average, compared with 4·9 by the medium viewers and 3·5 by the light viewers.

Figure 8.1. FEWER HEAVY USERS OF TV WERE FOUND AMONG THE STRONGLY MOTIVATED VIEWERS THAN AMONG THOSE WHOSE MOTIVATION WAS WEAK

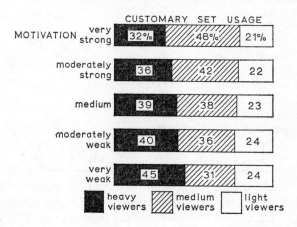

But is the volume of political viewing also affected by a motivational factor? Before presenting the evidence on this point, it is important to understand how our measures of strength of disposition to follow election television, and of customary viewing habits, were related to each other. Figure 8.1 shows that the association between these two variables is *inverse*. That is, at each step down the strength-of-motivation scale, an increasingly large proportion of heavy viewers is found. Thus, among the respondents who were rated 'very strong' in their motivation for following election television, only 32 per cent were normally heavy viewers—compared with 45 per cent in the group rated 'very weak' in motivation. This means that if our strength-of-motivation variable is to show a positive association with political viewing, it must first overcome the 'dragging' effect of its inverse relationship to customary set usage.

Table 8.2. STRENGTH OF MOTIVATION FOR FOLLOWING ELECTION TELEVISION AFFECTED EXPOSURE TO THE TELEVISION CAMPAIGN

	Motivation				
	Very strong	Moderately strong	Medium	Moderately weak	Very weak
	%	%	%	%	%
Saw four or more party election broadcasts	68	68	63	54	35
Saw the main news at least three times per week	75	69	65	62	55
Saw late election news bulletins three times weekly	30	29	24	18	13
Scored three or more for viewing non-party political programmes	56	44	45	40	24
N =	118	162	181	98 ·	98

Nevertheless, it transpired that degree of exposure to the television campaign of 1964 varied directly according to the strength of a viewer's motivation for following it. The trends which affected our four indices of political viewing are set out in Table 8.2. The top row of the table shows that the strongly motivated viewers saw many more party election broadcasts than did those individuals whose prior interest in the election was only slight. Expressed in terms of average figures, those who were rated strong in motivation saw about 5½ party broadcasts during the campaign, compared with only three among those whose motivation was 'very weak'.[4] The figures for the

[4] The average number of party election broadcasts seen by the respondents in each of the motivation groups was as follows:

Very strong	Moderately strong	Medium	Moderately weak	Very weak
5·4	5·6	4·8	4·5	3·0

latter group even seem to reflect a positive *avoidance* of propaganda, since 35 per cent of its members saw no party broadcasts at all (compared with only 14 per cent of the very strongly motivated viewers). Judged by their ability to predict viewer acceptance of campaign programmes, then, the June ratio scores clearly passed the acid test of validity with flying colours.

The other rows of the table show how the various motivation groups responded to the programmes put out by the television authorities themselves (as opposed to the parties' own broadcasts). It seems that predisposition is least likely to affect exposure to ordinary television news, for there is a fairly substantial amount of claimed viewing at each motivational level. The use of late election news, however, is quite strongly influenced by motivation, a result which is presumably attributable both to its exclusively political content (as compared with the main news) and to the greater degree of deliberate effort involved in seeing it. In addition, the viewing of such discussion programmes as *This Week* and *Election Gallery* was directly proportional to degree of measured motivation. Perhaps there is most scope for motivation to affect exposure in the case of those programmes which are exclusively political and which do not monopolize all available channels.

Having found that participation in the television campaign was influenced both by general viewing habits and by specific political inclinations—factors which even seemed to be pulling against each other—we decided to examine their interaction more closely. The results appear in Table 8.3, which holds set usage constant, and which shows the effect of motivation at each level of habitual weight of viewing by recording the average number of party election broadcasts that were watched during the campaign. It can be seen, first, that when reliance on television generally is heavy, motivation is virtually impotent to influence exposure to political programmes. The top row of the table shows that, among the normally heavy viewers, only those who were rated 'very weak' in motivation had seen a small number of party broadcasts. There were no consistent differences in the number of political programmes seen by all the rest of the heavy TV users—from those rated 'very strong' to those deemed 'moderately weak' in motivation. But second, where, as in the second and third rows of the table, television

AUDIENCE FOR ELECTION TELEVISION

is typically used only moderately or infrequently, motivational level becomes a powerful determinant of the volume of political viewing.

Table 8.3. AVERAGE NUMBER OF PARTY ELECTION BROADCASTS SEEN: BY CUSTOMARY WEIGHT OF VIEWING AND BY STRENGTH OF MOTIVATION FOR FOLLOWING ELECTION TELEVISION

Customary weight of viewing	Motivation				
	Very strong	Moderately strong	Medium	Moderately weak	Very weak
Heavy viewers	5·6	6·6	5·3	6·2	3·6
Medium viewers	6·0	5·4	4·8	4·0	2·9
Light viewers	4·0	4·3	3·9	2·6	1·9

This analysis underlines the need for information about both customary set usage and motivation before a confident interpretation of the forces responsible for a given pattern of viewing figures can be provided. Otherwise one cannot be sure whether a high level of exposure to a certain class of programme is due to habit or to keenness—two characteristics which, in the political field at least, are in a sense opposites.

Political motives for receiving broadcast propaganda as they affect exposure

Among the various motives for attending to party broadcasts discussed in Chapter 4, two distinctively political ones were located: a concern for the reinforcement of existing loyalties and a wish for guidance in coming to a voting decision. The so-called reinforcement seekers and vote-guidance seekers were seen, respectively, to have a high and a low degree of party commitment. It was also noted that the vote-guidance seekers, in so far as they had declared a provisional party preference, were more inclined to view broadcasts put out by the opposing side, whereas the reinforcement seekers received proportionately more material from their own party.

But how did these groups compare with each other in their overall use of the various channels of campaign communication during the 1964 election? It might be expected, *a priori*, that

144

the vote-guidance seekers should avoid the party broadcasts and rely especially on less partisan and biased sources – notably the news broadcasts and the discussion programmes which are independently provided by the television authorities. Surprisingly, this expectation is not confirmed by the findings presented in Table 8.4. The figures in the top row show that the vote-guidance seekers relied on party election broadcasts more extensively during the 1964 campaign than did any other group in our sample – including even the reinforcement seekers. Although the difference between the vote-guidance and reinforcement seekers is not substantial,[5] its full significance emerges when the other kinds of exposure are also considered. For each of the other television exposure variables, as well as for following politics in the press, the reinforcement seekers obtained higher scores than did the vote-guidance seekers. In comparison with the other groups represented in the table, then, the vote-guidance seekers were not only high consumers of party broadcasts; they also *depended* on them in contrast to their usage of the *other* main sources of campaign materials. The reinforcement seekers, on the other hand, were avid followers of political speeches in the press. It may be that they tend to subscribe to newspapers with editorial leanings that correspond to their own party preferences (but this could not be verified by the data at our disposal).

The evidence of Table 8.4 suggests that it would be a mistake to dismiss party broadcasts out of hand as vehicles for reaching the less committed electors. The so-called vote-guidance seekers

[5] The differences between these groups in exposure to party broadcasts proved rather more complex. Vote-guidance seekers were particularly likely to have seen four or more party election broadcasts, as Table 8.4 in the text shows, but many reinforcement seekers were found at exceptionally high levels of exposure – as the following detailed figures indicate:

No. of party election broadcasts seen

	0	1	2	3	4	5	6	7	8	9	10	11	12	13
Vote-guidance seekers	27	3	5	3	5	14	11	14	10	8	6	1	1	1
Reinforcement seekers	31	12	14	11	11	18	13	13	15	12	5	5	6	8

This shows that relatively few vote-guidance seekers saw a small number of party broadcasts, while a blanket absorption of all available propaganda materials on television was more likely to characterize certain reinforcement seekers.

Table 8.4. POLITICAL MOTIVES FOR RECEIVING BROADCAST
PROPAGANDA AND EXPOSURE TO THE CAMPAIGN[6]

	Vote-guidance seekers	Rein-forcement seekers	Mixed motives	No political motives
	%	%	%	%
Saw four or more party election broadcasts	65	61	60	49
Saw the main news at least three times per week	59	65	65	56
Saw late election news bulletins at least three times per week	18	25	28	20
Scored three or more for viewing non-party political programmes	48	52	38	33
Scored two or more for exposure to politics in the press*	49	60	64	43
N =	109	174	85	380

* The range of possible scores was 0–5.

constitute an important target for political campaigners and
could provide up to a fifth of the audience for any single party
broadcast. It is not quite clear why these individuals should
turn so often to party broadcasts for the information they
want, but it may be that they welcome the first-hand contact
with party spokesmen and their claims which these programmes
provide. Although they are often no more than exercises in
public relations, they do at least give the viewer some opportunity to see and hear a politician choosing his own words and
mounting his own arguments.[7] In considering these matters,
however, it should be appreciated that the vote-guidance

[6] In this table, and those which follow in this chapter, only variables of
press and television exposure are included. Partly this is in order to simplify
presentation, but it is also because little of interest emerged from the
relations between our various measures of audience disposition and exposure
to radio programmes and involvement in the local campaign.

[7] This explanation would be consistent with evidence showing an above-
average involvement in the local campaign by the vote-guidance seekers.
Seventy-four per cent of the members of this group achieved a score of
two or more (out of a maximum possible score of five) for attending to the
local campaign, compared with 69 per cent of the reinforcement seekers.
The comparable figures for those endorsing both and neither items were
69 per cent and 63 per cent, respectively.

AUDIENCE FOR ELECTION TELEVISION

seekers were also very inclined, when asked to state their preferences for different forms of political television, to favour the more challenging varieties. This suggests that they might derive at least as much benefit from a debate format as they apparently did from following the conventional party broadcasts.

Political scepticism and exposure to the campaign

Although political campaigning naturally provokes much suspicion and distrust, there is a particular group of electors whose scepticism about the credibility of party argument is intense and deep-seated. Participation in the 1964 campaign, however, was related less closely to our measures of this outlook than it had been to the other variables considered in this chapter. In order to examine the influence of political scepticism on the communications behaviour of our respondents, we divided them according to their replies to a question (asked in June 1964) about the amount of attention which the arguments of campaigning politicians usually deserved. Differences in those replies certainly tended to reflect other attitudinal differences in our sample. For example, of those who maintained that 'little' or 'no' attention should be paid to political argument, only 34 per cent stated a definite intention to watch any party election broadcasts during the campaign, compared with a figure of 67 per cent for those who thought that 'a lot' or 'some' attention should be given. But Table 8.5 shows that the gap between the same groups, in their exposure to the main channels of election communication, was much narrower than these figures about pre-campaign intentions had led us to expect.

Some relationship of the expected kind between scepticism and actual exposure is discernible in the figures in the table, but the similarity between the groups is almost more noticeable than their differences. Although, for example, those with a positive attitude to political argument saw 4·8 party election broadcasts on the average, their more sceptical counterparts managed to view 4·2. In fact the gap between the groups almost closed in respect of exposure to political materials in the press, and it completely disappeared for use of the late election news on TV.

147

Table 8.5. POLITICAL SCEPTICISM AND EXPOSURE TO THE
CAMPAIGN

	Attention deserved by campaign arguments	
	A lot/some %	A little/none %
Saw four or more party election broadcasts	60	50
Saw the main news at least three times per week	63	53
Saw late election news bulletins at least three times per week	23	23
Scored three or more for viewing non-party political programmes	46	33
Scored two or more for exposure to politics in the press	54	48
N =	473	239

It is difficult to understand why political scepticism virtually failed to block the transmission of election materials from the parties to the public. The imperfections of our measure of this attitude may be responsible for this result, but its close association with other indicators of attitudes to campaigning tends to undermine the plausibility of this explanation. We surmised that the behaviour of the sceptics might have been affected by their normal habits of TV usage, but we found, on pursuing this possibility, that there were actually more light viewers, proportionately, in the sceptical group than in the rest of the sample.[8] Alternatively, scepticism may not present so formidable a barrier to the reception of political communications as we had initially supposed it to do. Perhaps some sceptical viewers derive a wry satisfaction from seeing political performers confirm, through their television appearances, the already low opinions which they had previously formed of them. Whatever the explanation, it would seem, on the basis of the evidence, easy to exaggerate the problem of contacting those who express anti-political views. When the time comes they behave very

[8] Twenty per cent of those who believed that 'a lot' or 'some' attention should be paid to campaign arguments were classified as 'light' viewers, according to their normal habits of television usage—compared with a figure of 28 per cent among those who thought that political claims deserved 'little' or 'no' attention.

much as others do, and they certainly do not seem to screen themselves very effectively from political communications.

The reliance of opinion leaders on different sources of the campaign

Previous research on the audience for mass communications suggests that an important distinction can be drawn between a group of individuals who serve as opinion leaders in a defined sphere of public attitudes and other individuals who are inclined to turn to them for comment and advice within that field.[9] Special investigations have even been designed to trace the passage of communications from a mass medium to opinion leaders to opinion followers (based on the assumption that the transmission of messages proceeds according to a 'two-step flow').[10] Such a study, however, which requires a peculiarly composed sample, could not have been superimposed on the design of our own survey. We cannot shed any light, therefore, on the processes of interaction between political opinion leaders and their 'clients' during the 1964 election, nor can we state whether opinion leaders tend to filter the influence of media materials by interpreting them for other voters, or whether (as has been argued recently) television has by-passed the two-step flow of political communications and established a more direct line of access to large numbers of otherwise uninvolved citizens.[11] It was possible, however, by means of criteria developed in previous studies, to pick out certain members of our sample as opinion leaders, and to examine the sources of information they used when following the 1964 campaign. Although we

[9] Cf. Katz, Elihu and Lazarsfeld, Paul F., op. cit.

[10] Ibid and Katz, Elihu, 'The Two-Step Flow of Communication: An Up-to-date Report on an Hypothesis', *Public Opinion Quarterly*, Vol. XXI, No. 1, 1957, pp. 61–78, as well as Troldahl, Verling C., 'A Field Test of a Modified "Two-Step Flow of Communication" Model', *Public Opinion Quarterly*, Vol. XXX, No. 4, 1966–7, pp. 609–23.

[11] Stein Rokkan has raised this question without having been able to settle it decisively. He notes the 'distinct increase in the exposure of the population to national politics with the spread of the new medium' and comments: 'I shall be asked: has not television broken down these barriers in the system of social interaction and made the parties much less dependent on any such infrastructure of organized networks?'. Cf. Rokkan, S., *Readers, Viewers, Voters*, Guildhall Lectures, Granada TV Network, Manchester, 1964, pp. 30–1.

do not know how much of what they received was passed on to others, we can say that *if* there are political opinion leaders, *then* certain channels of communication are strategically significant because of the dependence on them of the members of this key group.

As in many other studies, the opinion leaders in our sample were self-designated. To locate them, two questions were asked in the final round of the survey, as follows: 'Did you discuss the issues of this election with anyone other than a canvasser during the campaign?'; and 'Compared with most people you know, are you more likely or less likely to be asked your views about politics?'. The sample was then divided, on the basis of the replies to these questions, into the following three groups: (*1*) opinion leaders by the most stringent definition, consisting of 79 individuals who had discussed the election with others and who thought they were more likely than most of their acquaintances to be asked for their political views; (*2*) opinion leaders by a more loose definition, consisting of 129 individuals who either were as likely as other people to be asked for their views and who had engaged in election discussions, or who were more likely to be asked for their opinions, although they had not discussed the 1964 election with anyone else; and (*3*) the rest of the sample, totalling 540 informants.

The opinion leaders who were designated by these criteria (especially those in the stringently defined group) had some distinctive characteristics in addition to their proclaimed political role. Many of them, for example, were men (75 per cent of the stringently defined group, compared with only 40 per cent in the non-opinion-leading majority). The opinion leaders were also better educated than the rest of the sample and more likely to be employed in white-collar jobs.[12] They did not lean significantly towards any single political party, but their measured motivation for following the election on television was high.[13] An examination of their particular reasons for

[12] Twenty-four per cent of the stringently defined opinion leaders had been at school at least until the age of 16, and 39 per cent were in non-manual occupations, compared with figures of 13 per cent and 27 per cent, respectively, for the non-opinion leading majority.

[13] Forty-seven per cent of the stringently defined opinion leaders were rated 'strong' in motivation for following the campaign on television compared with 37 per cent of the non-opinion leaders.

watching party broadcasts also disclosed a tendency for the opinion leaders to endorse reinforcement seeking and 'ammunition seeking' ('to use as ammunition in arguments with others') motives for receiving broadcast propaganda more often than did the majority of the respondents.[14]

The communications behaviour of the opinion leaders during the 1964 campaign is illustrated by the figures presented in Table 8.6. Two features characterize their exposure patterns. First, the opinion leaders were relatively high consumers of all forms of election materials. Their concern to keep in touch with

Table 8.6. OPINION LEADERSHIP AND EXPOSURE TO THE CAMPAIGN

	Opinion leaders (stringent definition)	Opinion leaders (loose definition)	Others
	%	%	%
Saw four or more party election broadcasts	62	67	52
Saw the main news at least three times per week	67	67	57
Saw late election news bulletins at least three times per week	29	28	19
Scored three or more for viewing non-party political programmes	54	46	37
Scored two or more for exposure to politics in the press	83	67	42
N =	79	129	540

political developments was evidently responsible for an above-average involvement in campaign communications of all kinds. But second, there were definite signs that the opinion leaders relied exceptionally heavily on certain political channels rather than others.

In fact the table seems to draw a firm line between less specialized and more specialized sources of information. The former category includes the party broadcasts and the main news, exposure to which was influenced only slightly by the

[14] Thirty per cent of the stringently defined opinion leaders wanted to be reminded of their party's strong points, and 22 per cent sought ammunition for use in arguments, compared with figures of 21 per cent and eight per cent, among the non-opinion leading majority.

role of opinion leadership. Into the latter category we would place the late election news, non-party political television programmes, and the press, since each of these sources was used quite extensively by the sample's opinion leaders. Their reliance on these more specialized channels was most pronounced in the case of the press. Nearly a half of the 79 fully fledged opinion leaders achieved a maximum possible score for following newspaper reports of the election, compared with only 15 per cent in the non-opinion-leading group. This may be related to the characteristic which the sample generally assigned to the press as giving much greater coverage in depth to political issues than does television.[15] But the opinion leaders were also keen to follow the non-party political programmes like *This Week* and *Election Gallery*—in contrast to their relative neglect by the rest of the sample.

Two points about the social and political role of the regular current affairs programmes on television are suggested by this last finding. First, if opinion leaders do watch these programmes frequently, politicians cannot afford to be indifferent to the impression they create when they appear in them. Second, in out-of-election periods those regular current affairs programmes which deal with controversial issues may be able to exert an influence exceeding that which would be expected from their audience sizes alone.

Is the viewing public a mass audience?

In the opening paragraphs of this chapter we raised a general issue about the nature of the audience for political television. This may be approached by considering how its heterogeneous composition poses a problem of communication for the politician who plans to use the medium. Rokkan has pointed to some of the difficulties facing campaign managers in a modern political system:

> Differentiated appeals require differentiated channels: the mass media address themselves indiscriminately to a generalized public and the only safe channels for pinpointing electoral appeals are the organizational and the personal.[16]

¹⁵ See p. 43.   ¹⁶ Rokkan, S., op. cit., p. 15.

AUDIENCE FOR ELECTION TELEVISION

In the case of television, specifically, there is seemingly no way of singling out target groups for special attention, no way of engineering the appeal to the public so that the emphasis may be altered to suit the audience – to take account of different shades or different degrees of support. Awareness of this situation sometimes fosters a conception of the viewing public as a huge mass audience, to which only generalized appeals, ignoring individual differences, are addressed, and which tends to respond with like uniformity.

Some of the findings presented in this chapter suggest that this view should be modified. It is true that, so long as present policies of control continue, the composition of audiences for political programmes on television is likely to remain much more representative of the electorate than, say, the readership groups of different newspapers (the major alternative means of communicating political information and comment). Nevertheless, we have found, by focusing on attitudinal parameters, that the television audience does tend to be structured somewhat more than is often supposed – particularly when different kinds of programmes are taken into account. We have seen, for example, that one element in the party broadcast audience is a highly motivated stream of viewers. We have seen that the vote-guidance seekers are differentially dependent on party broadcasts, while the opinion leaders turn more often to the programmes which are originated by the broadcasting authorities themselves. All in all, it appears that the audience for political television, though large and heterogeneous, can be divided in significant ways, the important distinctions relating to interests and motives which have not been given sufficient weight in the past. A fuller appreciation of the degree to which members of the viewing public do have positive expectations, needs, likes and dislikes, which can and do affect their behaviour, must modify any conception of the television audience as simply an undifferentiated mass.

PART III

THE IMPACT OF THE 1964 CAMPAIGN

CHAPTER 9

THE COMMUNICATION
OF PARTY POLICIES

Having considered how electors regard the activities of campaigning politicians, and the uses they wish to make of television when following an election, we turn now to the impact of the 1964 campaign itself on their political outlook. The General Election of 1964 marked a watershed in the recent political history of this country. Labour was elected to office for the first time in nearly 15 years. The major parties referred more frankly and forcibly than at any previous election to Britain's persistent domestic failure to attain economic viability and to the ambiguities of her international role. In addition, both the Conservative and Labour Parties set aside some of their traditional ideological preoccupations and adopted a more pragmatic approach to the prevailing issues. This is the broader context which lends some significance to a study of the development of public opinion during the General Election of 1964 and of the part played by the mass media in shaping it.

Specifically, we examined the effects of the 1964 campaign on the public's stock of *information* about party policies; on perceptions of the key *issues* facing the country; and on attitudes towards the three main *parties* and their *leaders*. In each case we raised and tried to answer three kinds of questions. First, how did public opinion evolve during the campaign? Second, how did television and the other mass media contribute to any changes that occurred? Third, how did the motivation of electors to follow the election affect their susceptibility to persuasion? In answering the first two questions comparisons have occasionally been drawn between our findings and those which emerged from the survey of 1959. The role of motivation in opinion change constitutes a new avenue of exploration, however, and what we have to say about this cannot be compared with the results of any previous study.

According to *Television and the Political Image*, the impact of the 1959 campaign was quite modest. Developments in issue salience were unremarkable, and most of the changes in political attitude that occurred were unrelated to any form of exposure to propaganda in the mass media. Only the public's understanding of party policies had apparently been affected. As Trenaman and McQuail put it, the main result of the 1959 campaign 'was merely that the electorate came to know more of the proposals of the politicians' (a consequence which they attributed largely to the influence of television).[1] In contrast to that outcome, the effects of the 1964 campaign proved less restricted–including, yet ranging beyond, changes in levels of political information. This chapter discusses the factors associated with a growth in the electorate's understanding of party policies, and the following chapter is devoted to the issues of the 1964 election. The last two chapters in this Part deal, respectively, with developments in public attitudes towards the political parties and their leaders.

How electoral understanding of party policies developed

The effect of the campaign on political knowledge was measured by a list of six policies, and electors were asked in both the pre-campaign and post-election interviewing rounds to identify the party that had put forward each one. This followed the procedure adopted in 1959, except that we attempted to incorporate a more specific set of policy proposals in our scale than had been used in the previous study.[2] It should

[1] Trenaman, J. and McQuail, Denis, op. cit., p. 165.

[2] Trenaman and McQuail described their test as 'less a measure of knowledge of specific policies than a general index of awareness of what the parties stand for'. For example, an item of Conservative policy was worded as follows: 'Give more freedom to individual enterprise in business.' Our aim in 1964 was to prepare a list of nine policies, each of which could unequivocally be identified with only a single party. Of the full list used in the pre-campaign questionnaire, however, only six items eventually tallied with the actual course of campaign argument. One source of difficulty

be stressed that any such measure of political information can only provide an approximate index of campaign change–and certainly not a complete picture of what happened. The proposals that were actually used are listed in Table 9.1, which also shows the percentages of respondents correctly identifying each policy before and after the campaign.

Table 9.1. THERE WAS A DEFINITE, THOUGH UNEVEN, INCREASE IN KNOWLEDGE OF PARTY POLICIES OVER THE PERIOD OF THE CAMPAIGN

Policy	Party of origin	Correct Identifications Pre-campaign %	Post-campaign %
1. Keep Britain's independent nuclear deterrent	Conservative	54	77
2. Public ownership of most building land	Labour	66	71
3. Stress variety in secondary education and not insist on abolition of the 11-plus examination	Conservative	35	34
4. Set up elected regional councils with powers to plan and spend for local needs	Liberal	7	15
5. Set up new government ministries of economic affairs and overseas development	Labour	31	40
6. Fix rates according to the value of sites	Liberal	4	9

The comparison between the percentage figures reveals an increase in correct attribution of policies to parties over the course of the campaign on all items except one. The increase is uneven, however, and two points about developments on particular items are noteworthy. One is that the Conservative campaign on behalf of Britain's independent nuclear deterrent

was a tendency for the policy stands of two or more parties to overlap. Another was the need to choose particular measures for our pre-campaign test before the parties' election strategies had been fully revealed. Nevertheless, consultation of party documents proved useful, and advice in sifting prospective items was obtained from the publicity officers of all three parties.

undoubtedly succeeded if judged as an exercise in the transmission of a party policy to the electorate.[3] It does not follow necessarily that this strategy was wise, or that voters' attitudes towards the Conservative Party became more favourable as a result. Exactly how those attitudes may have been affected by the Conservative stand on the nuclear deterrent is considered below,[4] but it is at least clear that the Conservatives generated a broad public understanding of their policy on this matter. Three-fourths of the sample identified this Conservative position correctly after Polling Day, compared with only a half just before the campaign began. This is a much greater proportionate gain than the largest change recorded for a policy item in the comparable test of 1959.[5]

A second feature of the table is its revelation of the extent of public ignorance about Liberal policy. At both interviews remarkably few respondents identified the two Liberal proposals on the list correctly (although the number of accurate attributions had approximately doubled by the end of the campaign). It seems clear that the electorate does not ascribe a distinctive set of policies to the Liberal Party. When interviewed after Polling Day, however, Liberal *voters* were better informed than any other group in the sample about the proposals of their party (identifying 0·5 correctly, on the average, compared with 0·3 by Conservative voters, 0·2 by Labour voters, and 0·1 by those who had abstained). Their superior grasp of Liberal policy was entirely a product of the campaign, for no differences by party support were detected as a result of the September interviews.

An analysis of performance on the test as a whole showed that the sample correctly recognized 1·97 of the six policy items on the average when interviewed before the campaign opened and 2·47 after Polling Day—an increase of 25·4 per cent. This level of achievement falls below that of the 1959 sample, whose members correctly identified an average of 4·06 items out of eight policies in the pre-campaign interview and

[3] See Appendix E for the results of a content analysis of party broadcast scripts. This shows that Conservative propagandists devoted considerable attention to the deterrent.

[4] See. pp. 172–4 and pp. 210–15.

[5] From 42 per cent to 60 per cent knowing that Labour would abolish the 11-plus examination.

4·66 after Polling Day. The difference between the two findings probably reflects the increased difficulty that our interviewees faced in responding to a test which aimed to refer only to specific policies and to avoid more general descriptions of party characteristics.

The impact of the campaign

The part played by the election campaign in communicating party policies to the public is illustrated by the figures presented in Table 9.2. If we treat the number of party election broadcasts which electors viewed as an index of their exposure to the campaign, there is a clear tendency for low levels of exposure

Table 9.2. HIGH LEVELS OF EXPOSURE TO PARTY BROADCASTS WENT WITH HIGH INITIAL INFORMATION LEVELS AND WITH SUBSTANTIAL GAINS IN KNOWLEDGE DURING THE CAMPAIGN

Number of party election broadcasts seen	Average no. of policies identified correctly pre-campaign	Average campaign gain	No. of respondents
0	1·61	+ 0·28	191
1–3	1·79	+ 0·37	142
4–6	2·15	+ 0·71	192
7–9	2·32	+ 0·66	136
10 +	2·16	+ 0·49	87

to be associated with limited knowledge gain and for high levels to go with greater gain. The table also shows that the minimally exposed were already rather ill-informed at the start of the campaign. It can be said, then, that they failed to take advantage of the greater scope they had for improving their political knowledge scores. This replicates a finding of the 1959 survey and emphasizes once again both the dependence of the general public on the mass media for political information and the isolation from civic affairs of that minority who are not open to influence via public means of communication.[6]

If the figures in the table are inspected in detail, however, it can be seen that the connection between information gain and the number of party broadcasts viewed is not sustained at the

[6] Trenaman, J., and McQuail, Denis, op. cit., pp. 169–70.

highest levels of exposure. Although the association of exposure with gain is progressive up to the viewing of six party broadcasts, it falls off thereafter—especially in that minority who claimed to have seen as many as ten or more of the 13 programmes that were transmitted. No such 'kick-back' was noticed in 1959, and an attempt to explain it—which draws both upon strength of motivation for following an election and upon customary habits of television usage—is presented below.

From which communication channels did electors acquire information about party policies during the 1964 campaign? Trenaman and McQuail reported after the 1959 election that only television had enlarged the political knowledge of voters. Their conclusion was based upon a significant correlation of 0·11 between information gain in the sample as a whole and an index of exposure to all forms of political broadcasting on television (including news bulletins and other miscellaneous programmes as well as party broadcasts). (Correlation co-efficients range from $+1$ to -1, a plus sign standing for a positive association between two variables, and a minus sign for a negative association.) When they separately examined the individual components of their exposure index Trenaman and McQuail also found that information gain was associated slightly more strongly with party broadcast viewing than with any other part of the TV output.[7] In analysing the comparable data collected in 1964, we calculated correlations between information gain and six sources of the campaign: three different television components (party broadcasts, news bulletins and all other political programmes) plus political materials in the press and on the radio and participation in the local campaign. The figures appear in Table 9.3.

These results confirm the previous designation of election television as the major source of the public's information about party politics. They indicate too that in 1964 party broadcasts were a more important factor in information gain than any other channel of political communication. The low correlations for exposure to political materials in the press and on the radio are almost identical with those that were obtained in 1959. (In the earlier study the correlation of information gain with press exposure in the whole sample was ·04, compared with ·03 in

[7] Ibid, pp. 187–9.

1964, and with radio exposure it was – ·06, compared with – ·04, in 1964.) The one noticeable departure from the 1959 pattern is the significant correlation of ·09 for the association between information gain and participation in the local campaign (in 1959 the corresponding figure was only ·03).

This suggestion that in 1964 some party policies may have been communicated to the electorate by means of the local campaign was somewhat unexpected. Of the several activities incorporated into our index of exposure to the local campaign, reading an election address and recalling the visit of a canvasser were probably the most important, and it may be that a certain amount of political information was conveyed successfully by these parochial but personal methods. It is also possible, how-

Table 9.3. CORRELATION COEFFICIENTS BETWEEN VARIABLES OF EXPOSURE TO THE 1964 CAMPAIGN AND CAMPAIGN GAINS IN POLITICAL INFORMATION

Total number of party broadcasts viewed	·10**
Television news	·06
Other non-party political television	·07*
Local campaign	·09*
Press	·03
Radio	— ·04

* Significant at P = ·05 level.
** Significant at P = ·01 level.

ever, that our measure of local involvement is reflecting the influence of some other concealed variable. Without support from another survey, it would probably be rash to regard the local campaign as an important channel of political communication. But the finding provides a salutary warning that it might be premature, despite the ubiquity of the modern mass media, to dismiss the impact of constituency activities altogether.

The role of motivation

Does the motivation of electors for following a campaign have any effect upon their absorption of political information?

At first glance our evidence seemed to suggest that in the acquisition of political information only exposure level mattered and motivation could be discounted. It was true that the minority of strongly motivated electors knew more about party policies when the campaign started than did the less keen electors – and that they even learned marginally more as a result of the campaign.[8] But this was ultimately traceable to an exposure difference: keen voters had learned more than apathetic ones because they had received more political communications. In one test of this interpretation we divided the sample between the respondents who were rated strong and weak in motivation, respectively, and separately examined the relationship between information gain and exposure in each group. This showed that exposure was just as powerful in its association with information gain among the individuals who were relatively indifferent to the election as among those who were more interested in it.

Nevertheless, at certain key points motivation can affect the process whereby political information is disseminated to the electorate. Two instances of this appeared in our data when particular sub-groups in the sample were examined separately. In one case we divided the respondents according to the extent of their exposure to election television, looking then at the relationship between information gain and strength of motivation at different exposure levels. The results are presented in Table 9.4.

The relationships illustrated by the table are certainly imperfect, but the figures for average information gain along the bottom row re-emphasize the fact that with a low level of exposure there is little likelihood that a citizen will add substantially to what he knows about party policies during an election campaign – regardless of the strength of his motivation. The effect of proceeding to a medium level of exposure is to increase information gain at almost every point, but degree of

---

[8] The figures were as follows:

	Motivation Groups		
	Strong	Medium	Weak
Average no. of policies identified correctly, pre-campaign	2·32	1·84	1·66
Average campaign gain	+ 0·54	+ 0·50	+ 0·40

COMMUNICATION OF PARTY POLICIES

motivation for following the campaign still has no effect. When
we reach the highest level of exposure, however, we see that
average information gain has ceased to rise, and that strength
of motivation influences the results for the first time. In other
words, the table suggests that as exposure increases, a point can
be reached where the amount of information likely to be
acquired depends on the viewer's strength of motivation for
following the election. It is as if strength of motivation 'takes
over' where amount of exposure 'leaves off'–in this case where
seven or more party election broadcasts had been seen. The calculation of a correlation coefficient between degree of motivation
and amount of information gain at each of the three levels of

Table 9.4. STRENGTH OF MOTIVATION FOR FOLLOWING
ELECTION TELEVISION WENT WITH INFORMATION GAIN ONLY
AT THE HIGHEST LEVEL OF EXPOSURE TO THE CAMPAIGN

Exposure to party broadcasts	Motivation to follow the campaign					Correlation coefficient of increasing gain with increasing motivation*
	Very strong	Moderately strong	Medium	Moderately weak	Very weak	
High (7+)	+0·73	+0·43	+0·65	+0·57	+0·29	0·41
Medium (4−6)	+0·82	+0·38	+0·61	+0·88	+1·33	−0·10
Low (0−3)	−0·07	+0·79	+0·31	+0·10	+0·19	0·06

* To calculate these correlation coefficients numerical weights were
attached to the index of strength of motivation (1 for 'very weak' to 5 for
'very strong').

exposure confirms that motivation is uniquely effective among
the highly exposed.

This may help to explain the previously mentioned 'kick-
back': the tendency for degree of information gain to fall off
at the highest levels of exposure. Much of such exposure may be
due more to habit and chance than a deliberate intention to
view, and if strength of motivation distinctively affects the
learning of the most highly exposed individuals, their overall
gain could be pulled back. This explanation is reinforced by
the fact that a marked increase in the proportion of habitually
heavy television users was found at precisely that point where
the 'kickback' in information gain began (between those who

viewed 4–6 election broadcasts and those who saw seven or more).[9]

The second sign that exposure does not always provide a sufficient explanation of information gain emerged when the sample was examined in terms of the respondents' particular reasons for watching party broadcasts. It transpired that the

Table 9.5. CAMPAIGN INFORMATION GAINS AMONG THE VOTE-GUIDANCE SEEKERS DID NOT DEPEND ON THE NUMBER OF PARTY BROADCASTS THEY SAW

No. of election broadcasts seen	Average information gain	No. of vote-guidance seekers
0	+ 0·59	27
1–3	+ 1·00	11
4–6	+ 0·73	30
7–9	+ 0·41	32
10 +	+ 0·11	9

109 vote-guidance seekers had responded distinctively to the campaign. They were initially highly knowledgeable, and they had acquired much further information about party policies between the two interviewing rounds.[10] Nevertheless, political information gain in their case was not progressively related to the extent of their exposure to the campaign. The absence of any such association is illustrated by Table 9.5.

[9] The distribution of customary viewing patterns among the various exposure groups in the sample was as follows:

Customary set usage	No. of party election broadcasts seen			
	0	1–3	4–6	7 +
	%	%	%	%
Heavy	29	32	38	47
Medium	35	44	40	39
Light	36	24	22	14
	100	100	100	100

[10] The figures were as follows:

	Vote-guidance seekers	Reinforcement seekers	Rest of the sample
Average no. of policies identified correctly, pre-campaign	2·21	2·20	1·84
Average campaign gain	+ 0·58	+ 0·51	+ 0·49

COMMUNICATION OF PARTY POLICIES

The detailed figures show that those vote-guidance seekers who saw relatively few party broadcasts actually learned more about party policies than did some of their more highly exposed counterparts. In this case it seems that those voters for whom information was relevant to a *choice* they had to make managed to obtain it even if their opportunities to do so were limited.

CHAPTER 10

THE ISSUES OF A DYNAMIC
CAMPAIGN

In the past students of British elections have invariably reported that all was quiet on the issues front. Any campaign changes in the issues that concerned voters most have typically proved slight in extent and uninteresting in direction. When, for example, in 1951 a sample of Bristol electors was given a list of eight issues (and asked to designate the three most important), the first four were ranked in the same order both before and after the election.[1] After another sample in the same city was invited in 1955 to choose three issues from a list of six, the investigators observed that, 'When opinions on the most important issues *after* the election are compared with those on the most important issues at the start of the campaign, little change is apparent.'[2] In 1959 Trenaman and McQuail offered the electors of Pudsey and West Leeds a longer list, containing 15 issues, out of which four were to be selected. Once again (they noted), 'The remarkable thing [was] the stability of opinion on these issues, and the lack of any widespread reaction in the population as a whole to the mass of relevant material to which they were exposed during the election campaign.'[3] A statistically significant increase in percentage endorsements was registered on only one item—an issue that had already proved most popular in the pre-campaign round of interviewing ('keep the cost of living down').

There is something puzzling about these findings, for, of all

---

[1] Milne, R. S. and Mackenzie, H. C., *Straight Fight*, op. cit., p. 103.

[2] Milne, R. S. and Mackenzie, H. C., *Marginal Seat, 1955*, The Hansard Society, London, 1958, p. 111.

[3] Trenaman, J. and McQuail, Denis, op. cit., p. 173.

the ingredients that make up an election campaign, issues seem potentially to provide the most dynamic element.[4] Traditional party loyalties and social position are far and away the most important determinants of the vote, of course, but a political party can do little to affect them. Even a leader's personality cannot really be tailored to fit the supposed requirements of the popular image of an ideal politician. But a political party has some freedom of manoeuvre to choose the issue ground on which it will fight. It may seem surprising, therefore, that British psephologists have detected so few traces of the endeavours of the parties in the results of their election surveys.

Trenaman and McQuail explained these findings in terms of the continuity of public opinion between the period which precedes a campaign and that of the campaign itself. Even before a campaign opens, they argued, 'The majority of the electorate . . . has a fairly soundly based and well-informed view of what at any particular moment are the main problems facing society.' 'During an election', therefore, 'little of the argument and counter-argument can be novel.'[5] This analysis is particularly likely to be valid in a period of relative stability, when the main political currents are running smoothly and lacking in complexity. At a time of greater change and uncertainty, however, some citizens might become aware of new problems and needs only through that acceleration of political communications which accompanies an election campaign. An examination of developments in the salience of issues to the electorate during the 1964 campaign may shed some light on this possibility.

The issues of the 1964 election

The public's appreciation of political issues was affected more profoundly by the General Election of 1964 than by any other campaign that has been studied systematically in this country. In plotting these developments, previously tried procedures were followed. A list of 16 issues, which one or more of the

[4] See Pool, Ithiel de Sola, Abelson, Robert P. and Popkin, Samuel, *Candidates, Issues and Strategies*, The MIT Press, Cambridge, Massachusetts, 1964, pp. 8–9.
[5] Trenaman J. and McQuail, Denis, op. cit., p. 176.

parties were expected to emphasize in the campaign, was prepared and administered to the sample before the campaign and after Polling Day. They were described as 'questions that matter to everybody', and the respondents were asked to choose the five they considered 'most important for the next government [or the new government] to tackle'.[6] Table 10.1 shows how the members of the sample ranked each issue before and after the campaign and what the significant changes in issue salience between the two interviews were.[7]

It can be seen that the position of many issues was little disturbed by the campaign. Three social welfare items–pensions, housing and full employment–topped the list after both interviews. It is also noticeable that those items which were intended to measure the sample's recognition of the need for radical changes in industrial organization (modernization, automation and incomes policy) never exerted more than an esoteric appeal at either stage of the campaign. And although the Conservatives devoted much of their TV propaganda to the superiority of private enterprise over public ownership, the issue of nationalization was as dead after Polling Day as it had been when the pre-campaign interviews were held.

Nevertheless, there were significant changes in the percentage endorsements of five items on the list. The most spectacular reflected the rise to prominence of the issue of economic growth ('get fast and steady growth of the economy'). Endorsed by a third of the sample in October, compared with only a fifth in September,[8] this issue moved up from eleventh to sixth place in the rank order. On the basis of this evidence it is no exaggeration to assert that economic growth was virtually what

[6] In order to prepare the issues lists the speeches and statements of party headquarters and spokesmen were followed closely for a period of about eight months before the campaign began. Although it was anticipated that certain issues would be stressed by one party more than another, care was taken in the wording of each item to ensure that a supporter of any party could endorse it if he felt so inclined.

[7] These were established by use of the McNemar test for the significance of changes. This test was invariably applied whenever differences in issue endorsements between the pre-campaign and post-election interviews were examined.

[8] Altogether one-fifth of the sample acknowledged the importance of economic growth in October without having endorsed it in September.

Table 10.1. Issue salience before and after the
1964 election

Order of endorsement		Issues	Percentage of endorsements	
Pre-campaign	Post-campaign		Pre-campaign %	Post-campaign %
1	1	Give old people better pensions	70	63**
2	3	Provide more houses at reasonable prices and fair rents	49	45
3	2	See there is no return of unemployment	47	49
4	8	Deal with road and traffic problems	40	28***
5	4	Raise Britain's standing in the world	36	39
6	7	Improve the health and hospital services	35	32
7	5	Maintain and raise the general standard of living	35	38
8	9	Provide a better education for all children	27	27
9	11	Make a new approach to unemployment and sickness benefits	26	21*
10	10	Settle the future of Britain's nuclear deterrent	22	27*
11	6	Get fast and steady growth of the economy	21	33***
12	12 (tied)	Work out an incomes policy with the unions and employers	20	21
13	12 (tied)	Meet the challenge of auto-mation and the scientific age	20	21
14	14	Modernize British industry	16	19
15	16	Avoid unnecessary govern-ment restrictions	15	14
16	15	Decide the future of nationalization	13	14

*   Significant at P = ·05 level.
** Significant at P = ·01 level.
*** Significant at P = ·001 level.

the 1964 campaign had been about. In addition, there was a significant increase in the salience of the nuclear deterrent issue. The table suggests that these gains were won partly at the expense of welfare questions (notably pensions and social insurance) and of road and traffic conditions (a remarkably popular item before the campaign opened). The decline of the latter after the election confirms a tendency noted in 1959 for issues ignored by the parties during a campaign to be displaced by others.

These changes seemed in turn to reflect certain issue strategies which both the major parties followed at the 1964 election. This parallel was confirmed by the results of a content analysis of the themes that were developed in party election broadcasts on television during the 1964 campaign.[9] In contrast to the 1959 campaign, when the Conservative and Labour Parties addressed much of their propaganda to questions already prominent in electors' minds,[10] they tried in 1964 to generate an appreciation of a few issues that lacked any immediate bread-and-butter appeal. Labour, for example, stressed the need for economic growth in its party broadcasts more often than any other single issue.[11] The Conservatives paid most attention to the desirability of maintaining a high standard of living,[12] but they devoted nearly as much television time to the nuclear deterrent as well.

The issues front of the 1964 campaign was buffeted, then, by conflicting cross-currents. The Conservatives treated the deterrent as a 'position issue', which distinguished the substance of their defence policy from that of Labour, and they succeeded in increasing electoral awareness of it. The argument over economic affairs was dominated instead by what has been called a 'valence issue' (one on which the competing parties

[9] See Appendix E.

[10] Trenaman, J. and McQuail, Denis, op. cit., pp. 173–5.

[11] According to Butler, D. E. and King, Anthony, economic growth and planning had already become 'the dominant theme' in Labour propaganda about a year or so before the 1964 election (*The British General Election of 1964*, op. cit., p. 62).

[12] The reversion of Conservative propagandists in the spring of 1964 to the 'standard of living' theme which had been projected with conspicuous success in 1959 is described in Butler and King, ibid, p. 93; Lord Windlesham, op. cit., Ch. 3; and Rose, Richard, *Influencing Voters*, op. cit., Ch. 2.

do not mark out opposed policy positions but try to persuade voters of their superior competence to realize a widely shared goal).[13] This struggle turned interestingly on how the issue itself should be defined, the Conservatives presenting it as one of sustaining a steady increase in an already high standard of living, and Labour proclaiming the need to achieve economic growth without recurring crises. According to opinion trends in our sample, the Labour Party won this battle to define the central economic question facing the government in 1964.

It still remains to be seen whether such issue gains can be translated into more direct political rewards. We pursued this question by examining changes in issue salience among those of our respondents who had decided how to vote during the campaign (those who were undecided when the campaign began and those who switched from one party to another during it). We found that the members of this group did not endorse the deterrent issue significantly more often after Polling Day than they had when interviewed in September. And although there was a significant increase in their endorsement of the economic growth item, it was no greater than the corresponding development among the undeviating party supporters. Neither major party profited at the ballot box, then, from the changes in issue salience which occurred in 1964. The only hint that an altered awareness of issues had affected voting emerged from a tendency for those individuals who decided to vote Liberal during the campaign to be attracted disproportionately to items about industrial modernization and scientific advance. The significance of this tendency is considered more fully in Chapter 13.[14]

Despite their seeming failure to capture any votes through the issues around which they built their campaigns, the efforts of the major parties were not entirely vain. An economic growth item on our party attitude scale ('would get the economy moving') was regarded as true of the Labour Party by significantly more electors in October than in September (and as true of the

[13] A detailed discussion of the distinction between a 'position issue' and a 'valence issue' appears in Stokes, Donald E., 'Spatial Models of Party Competition', *American Political Science Review*, Vol. LVII, No. 2, 1963, pp. 268–77.
[14] See p. 267.

Conservative Party by a significantly smaller proportion of the sample). On a foreign affairs item ('would weaken Britain's voice in world affairs') there were contrary, though less pronounced, shifts which benefited the Conservative Party and harmed Labour.[15] The same cross-currents that had influenced our respondents' opinions about the issues of the election had apparently affected their attitudes to the major parties as well. Even if no vote gains were harvested immediately, it looked as if the issue strategies which were applied in the 1964 campaign had begun to reshape the criteria by which the public assessed the parties and to alter the content of party images.

Who responded to the issues of the 1964 campaign?

Whenever electors are questioned about political issues, they respond partly according to their party and demographic group affiliations, and our respondents conformed to this pattern. When interviewed before the campaign, for example, the manual workers endorsed social welfare items more frequently than did the non-manual workers–who tended in turn to be more sensitive to issues of foreign policy and economic management. Similarly, whereas the elderly voters worried exceptionally about pensions, young people tended to emphasize education; and women were more interested than men in housing but less conscious of certain industrial questions (like modernization and incomes policy).

According to Trenaman and McQuail, one function of an election campaign is to narrow these gaps between groups in their appreciations of political issues. They maintained that election communications help to extend 'an individual's view

[15] The whole sample applied these items to the major parties as follows:

	True of Conservative Party		True of Labour Party	
	Pre-campaign	Post-campaign	Pre-campaign	Post-campaign
Would get the economy moving	47%	37%***	47%	55%***
Would weaken Britain's voice in world affairs	18%	17%[NS]	29%	31%[NS]

*** = Significant at P = ·001 level
[NS] = Not significant

of the world', so that he adopts an order of priorities which accords not only with his group interests but also with wider community needs as voiced in campaign materials.[16] But such a process of mutual accommodation was less evident in the data that were collected in 1964.[17] Most of the campaign changes in issue salience either affected all groups in the sample more or less equally or were concentrated to an exceptional extent in certain groups only. Perhaps Trenaman and McQuail's finding does not apply to an election at which the overall position in relation to issues is relatively fluid.

Occupation undoubtedly stood out as the most important demographic particular which mediated developments in issue salience in 1964. There were, for example, five statistically significant changes in the endorsement of issues by non-manual workers, and only one by the semi-skilled and unskilled. Four of the five changes in the non-manual group affected issues on which whole sample change had also been statistically significant: economic growth, the deterrent, pensions and road and traffic conditions.[18] It seems that the most sophisticated part of the electorate is reached first when new issues are injected into a dynamic campaign.

In view of the importance of economic growth as a political issue—both during the election we studied and afterwards—it is of interest to see how the various sections of the public represented in our sample responded to it in 1964. Although, according to the figures given in Table 10.2, endorsement of this issue increased significantly in almost every major group

[16] Trenaman, J. and McQuail, Denis, op. cit., pp. 179–81.

[17] In 1959, for example, endorsements of the pensions issue increased in the 21–44 age group from 42 per cent to 51 per cent, while they fell in the 45 + age group from 63 per cent to 57 per cent. In 1964, however, endorsements of the identical issue declined in both groups, and the fall was greater in the younger half of the sample, as the following figures show:

Endorsement of pensions issue	Age	
	21–44	45 +
Pre-campaign	65%	73%
Post-campaign	56%	69%

[18] The only difference between non-manual change and whole sample change arises from the fact that the former included a significant decrease in endorsement of health and hospitals as an issue instead of unemployment and sickness benefits.

THE ISSUES OF A DYNAMIC CAMPAIGN

in the population, the role of occupation was outstandingly influential. Even at the beginning of the campaign occupation discriminated responses to the issue of economic growth more powerfully than did any other demographic variable. Nevertheless, the gap between the various occupational groups had widened still further by Polling Day–especially if one compares the non-manual workers with the semi- and unskilled respondents. Forty-seven per cent of the former group endorsed this item after the election. In fact by Polling Day non-manual

Table 10.2. THE SALIENCE OF ECONOMIC GROWTH INCREASED DURING THE CAMPAIGN IN ALMOST ALL MAJOR DEMOGRAPHIC GROUPS, WITH THE EXCEPTION OF THE NON-SKILLED WORKERS

	Endorsements of the economic growth issue		No. of respondents
	Pre-campaign	Post-campaign	
By occupation	%	%	
Non-manual workers	37	47*	217
Skilled manual workers	14	29***	364
Semi- and unskilled workers	15	19	149
By sex			
Male	27	37**	349
Female	15	29***	399
By age			
21–44	26	36**	321
45 and over	17	30***	427

* Significant at P = ·05 level.   ** Significant at P = ·01 level.
*** Significant at P = ·001 level.

workers regarded economic growth as a more urgent question for the government to face than any other issue on the list. In contrast to the very high order of priority, the semi- and unskilled workers rated it merely twelfth in importance. The keynote of Labour's 1964 campaign was particularly congenial, then, to an occupational group that had traditionally resisted its appeal. Perhaps this helps to explain why Labour drew a somewhat higher proportion of its support in the country at large from the middle class in 1964 than it had in 1959.[19]

[19] Cf. Butler, D. E. and King, Anthony, *The British General Election of 1964*, op. cit., p. 297.

THE ISSUES OF A DYNAMIC CAMPAIGN

A still more precise specification of the electors who were reached by the dynamic issues of the 1964 campaign is provided in Table 10.3. If we divide up the sample, first according to major party vote, and then according to occupation, we find an interesting tendency, affecting both groups of party supporters, for the supposedly more sophisticated electors (the professional and white-collar workers) to be more inclined to adopt the issue emphasized by their own party. It is true that there were general upward movements in almost all groups on both issues –

Table 10.3. CAMPAIGN CHANGES IN THE SALIENCE OF THE ECONOMIC GROWTH AND NUCLEAR DETERRENT ISSUES BY VOTE AND OCCUPATION

	Endorsements of the economic growth issue by:			
	Conservative voters		Labour voters	
	Non-manual %	Manual %	Non-manual %	Manual %
Pre-campaign	45	14	29	17
Post-campaign	51	25*	47	27**
	Endorsements of the deterrent issue:			
Pre-campaign	25	27	31	20
Post-campaign	42**	32	29	25
N =	119	117	51	267

* Difference between pre-campaign and post-campaign endorsements significant at P = ·05 level.

** Difference between pre-campaign and post-campaign endorsements significant at P = ·01 level.

and especially that of economic growth. But the substantial move to adopt the economic growth issue shown by the middle-class electors turns out to be distinctively a shift among the non-manual Labour voters. This phenomenon is paralleled in the Conservative camp by a tendency for increased endorsements of the nuclear deterrent issue to be confined virtually to the non-manual supporters of that party. This suggests that the major parties were most successful in communicating their new issue emphases to the middle-class elements among their own supporters.

THE ISSUES OF A DYNAMIC CAMPAIGN

Issues, exposure to the campaign and motivation for following it

How were the new issues of the 1964 election communicated to the public? Did they impress mainly those electors who had followed the campaign extensively? What was the role of motivation for receiving campaign materials? We have already noted a close correspondence between the dominant propaganda themes of the major parties' election broadcasts and the issues that voters became more conscious of during the campaign, but it does not follow that our respondents had been influenced directly by those programmes. The importance of economic growth, for example, could have been underlined for many people simply by the announcement on September 30th (two weeks before Polling Day) of a large increase in the balance-of-payments deficit.

Table 10.4. IN THE SAMPLE AS A WHOLE, EXPOSURE TO PARTY BROADCASTS DID NOT SIGNIFICANTLY AFFECT THE SALIENCE OF THREE IMPORTANT ISSUES

| | Endorsements of the issues of: | | | | | |
| | Economic growth | | Deterrent | | Standard of living | |
	High	Low	by Exposure: High	Low	High	Low
	%	%	%	%	%	%
Pre-campaign	25	16	23	20	35	34
Post-campaign	37***	27***	28	26	41	35
N =	415	333				

*** Difference between pre-campaign and post-campaign endorsements significant at P = ·001 level.

To test whether party broadcast viewing had been associated with developments in issue salience, the sample was divided into two groups: those who had seen relatively few election broadcasts (three or less) and those who had seen a large number (four or more). We then examined issue endorsements separately in each group to see whether a significant increase in

178

THE ISSUES OF A DYNAMIC CAMPAIGN

any item had occurred distinctively among the highly exposed viewers. No differences emerged from this comparison. Any statistically significant change which appeared in the high-exposure group was present as well among those who had seen relatively little of the campaign. This outcome is illustrated by Table 10.4, which presents the figures for three of the issues to which the major parties devoted much of their TV time—economic growth, the nuclear deterrent, and the standard of living. It can be seen that on each of the issues—and especially economic growth—there was a higher level of *pre-campaign* endorsement among those who subsequently were heavily exposed to the campaign. But *campaign change* on each of these items was equally substantial in both groups.

Table 10.5. AMONG THE STRONGLY MOTIVATED
RESPONDENTS, EXPOSURE TO PARTY BROADCASTS ONLY
AFFECTED THE SALIENCE OF ONE ISSUE SLIGHTLY

	Endorsements of the issues of:					
	Economic growth		Deterrent		Standard of living	
			by Exposure:			
	High	Low	High	Low	High	Low
	%	%	%	%	%	%
Pre-campaign	30	23	22	22	30	36
Post-campaign	38[NS]	30[NS]	27[NS]	32[NS]	42*	38[NS]
N =	193	113				

* Difference between pre-campaign and post-campaign endorsements significant at P = ·05 level.
[NS] Difference between pre-campaign and post-campaign endorsements not significant.

The picture changed only slightly when we took account of strength of motivation for following the campaign. In this analysis, before testing for the effects of campaign exposure, the sample was divided between those who were rated strong in motivation and those who were regarded as medium or weak in motivation. When this was done, no exposure effects were detected in the less keen part of the sample and only one

179

in the more politically interested group. Table 10.5 provides details about the relationship, among the strongly motivated respondents, between exposure to the campaign and changes in the salience of the three issues that the parties stressed. It can be seen that the degree of change recorded by those who had been highly exposed to the campaign was statistically significant only on the standard-of-living issue.

Despite these largely negative results, it transpired that one motivational factor had substantially affected respondents' reactions to the election issues. It was not their general *strength* of motivation which mattered, however, so much as the particular *type* of political motive that had encouraged them to follow the campaign. The vote-guidance seekers were virtually impervious to the issues emphasized by the major parties, and in general they did not adopt any item on the entire list to a significantly greater extent after Polling Day than they had at the pre-campaign interview. The reinforcement seekers, however, shifted significantly in favour of three issues—and precisely towards those that have all along been central in this analysis (economic growth, the standard of living, and the nuclear deterrent). The importance of a desire for reinforcement was most noticeable in connection with the nuclear deterrent issue. Although the individuals who wished to be reminded of their own parties' strong points comprised only 23 per cent of the sample, they accounted for as many as 74 per cent of the increased endorsements of the nuclear deterrent item that the campaign stimulated.[20]

Although much of this increased endorsement of the nuclear deterrent item was supplied by highly partisan *Conservative* supporters, the reinforcement seekers did not discriminate otherwise between the issues of the 1964 election campaign according to their own party affiliations. That is, the Labour

[20] The differences between the reinforcement seekers' endorsements of the three issues in the pre-campaign and post-campaign interviews were statistically significant as follows:

Nuclear deterrent	—	at P = ·001 level
Economic growth	—	at P = ·05 level
Standard of living	—	at P = ·05 level

There was only one statistically significant increase in the issue endorsements of those who acknowledged no directly political motive for following the campaign—on economic growth (significant at P = ·01 level).

reinforcement seekers responded no less positively to the standard-of-living issue than did their Conservative counterparts, and the latter equalled the former in their mounting concern for economic growth. A desire for reinforcement, then, was allied to a high degree of sensitivity to the key issues at stake in the 1964 election – regardless of the party that had projected them into the limelight.

An interpretation of developments in issue salience

The foregoing evidence suggests that, in contrast to earlier elections, the 1964 campaign was remarkable for having directed the attention of many voters to certain issues which had not previously seemed important to them – notably that of economic growth but to a lesser extent that of the nuclear deterrent as well. Although these developments reflected the major parties' propaganda strategies, there was little sign that amount of exposure to the campaign itself had been a major factor in determining whether a voter would become more appreciative of these issues. More important than the extent of an electors' exposure to the campaign was the type of person he was.[21]

There were several signs of this, all pointing to the conclusion that those who respond to the new issues of a dynamic campaign consist largely, though not entirely, of sophisticated voters who are seeking a reinforcement of their previously established political loyalties. Middle-class electors in general were reached most readily by the issues of the 1964 campaign, and there was a tendency for non-manual Labour supporters to become more interested in economic growth, while non-manual Conservatives increasingly adopted the deterrent issue. In addition, there were strong movements among those individuals whom we had already classified as reinforcement seekers towards the key issues of the 1964 campaign. As noted above, the sensitivity of this group was not selective in any party sense.

[21] Amount of exposure to the 1964 campaign was not divorced entirely from changes in issue salience. But its role, as it was finally tracked down, proved complex and was inextricably bound up with changing attitudes towards the political parties – to which the next chapter is devoted. A more exact statement of the part played by campaign exposure in fostering changes in issue salience in conjunction with changing opinions about the parties may be consulted there.

THE ISSUES OF A DYNAMIC CAMPAIGN

Reinforcement seekers seem to be attuned to those issues that have been injected into the political struggle regardless of their party of origin. Perhaps their need for reinforcement is logically connected in part with their awareness of such issues. They wish to be reminded of the strong points of their own party when faced with the issue challenges posed by the propaganda of their rivals.

The role of reinforcement explains another feature of our evidence: the failure of the major parties to exploit their issue gains at the ballot box. In a sense their persuasive efforts proved most effective with those who were already converted. Perhaps those who were looking for guidance in deciding how to vote felt relatively indifferent towards themes that derived from such staunchly partisan sources. But even if few votes were influenced by the new issues of the 1964 campaign, it does not follow that they remained electorally insignificant thereafter. We have seen that some reinforcement seekers aim to act as opinion leaders, and it may be that their perspectives on the problems that matter to the country's welfare were disseminated in the longer run to a wider circle of electors. In the years that followed the General Election of 1964, economic growth in particular may have provided a criterion by which a growing number of voters were prepared to judge the merits of the rival parties.

CHAPTER 11

THE FORTUNES OF THE POLITICAL PARTIES

Although an election campaign may convey information to the electorate about party programmes, and focus its attention on particular issues, the crucial question is how far it can swing opinion in favour of one side or another. So far as *votes* are concerned, it has seemed that elections were won or lost well before the official campaign opened. And although a considerable amount of change was detected in the single study which examined the development of *attitudes* during the period of an election, no connection with exposure to propaganda and comment in the mass media was established. The material presented below shows, however, that these conclusions do not apply with the same force when some other lines of enquiry are pursued. The most important new departures include (*1*) an investigation of attitudes towards the Liberal Party and (*2*) a study of the role in persuasion of the disposition of voters to follow an election. In fact, by taking account of electoral motivation, it was even possible to locate some campaign effects on the public images of the major parties.

Changes of allegiance during the 1964 campaign

Exactly how large were the adjustments that occurred in party allegiance during the 1964 campaign? Table 11.1 provides a detailed comparison of the voting intentions that were declared before the campaign, with the actual votes reported after Polling Day, by the 725 individuals who were willing to answer our questions about these matters.[1]

Table 11.1. RESOLUTION OF VOTING INTENTIONS DURING THE 1964 CAMPAIGN

		1964 Vote				
		Conservative	Labour	Liberal	None	Total
	Conservative	210	8	15	14	247
	Labour	9	277	19	31	336
Pre-	Liberal	7	3	38	3	51
campaign	Other	—	3	—	1	4
intention	Don't know	15	25	13	12	65
	None	3	3	1	15	22
	Total	244	319	86	76	725

It can be seen that only a minority (but a fairly substantial one) participated in some form of campaign change as measured by developments in their voting intentions. The 64 switchers from one party to another amounted to nine per cent of the respondents. The 60 late deciders (individuals who eventually voted, although they could not support a party in the pre-campaign interview) added another eight per cent. The 76 abstainers (only 15 of whom had expected not to vote in September) accounted for yet another ten per cent. All those electors who fell outside the ranks of the undeviating party loyalists, then, totalled 27 per cent–a proportion which was almost identical, both in size and in composition, with the pattern that was found in a sample drawn from the same constituencies in 1959.[2]

[1] Seventeen individuals refused to declare a vote intention when interviewed in September 1964 and six others refused to state how they had actually voted. All these have been excluded from the discussion of campaign vote change. But a few respondents who indicated how they had voted in October, after having declined to state a vote intention in September, are included in those analyses below to which only the reported vote is relevant.

[2] The following proportions of different types of electors, who were not consistent party supporters, were found in the 1959 and 1964 samples, respectively:

	1959 %	1964 %
Inter-party changers	7·9	8·6
Late deciders	9·8	8·0
Abstainers	10·7	10·4

FORTUNES OF THE POLITICAL PARTIES

Did any single party profit from the net changes that occurred? Neither *major party* managed to advance during the 1964 campaign, for both received slightly fewer votes than they had been 'promised' in the pre-campaign interviews. The fall in Labour support somewhat exceeded the Conservative loss mainly because of a differential wastage through absentions – to which, traditionally, it has always been more vulnerable. In general the inter-election period of 1959–64 appears to have been more important than the 1964 campaign itself in deciding the fate of the major parties, since Labour enjoyed a substantial lead over the Conservatives in our sample at the beginning of the campaign – and had not relinquished it by Polling Day.

There is little point in preparing a more detailed comparison of the inter-campaign and intra-campaign vote swings that occurred in our sample. We asked our respondents how they had balloted in 1959, but it is known that the replies of floating voters in particular to questions about their voting behaviour at a previous election are highly unreliable. This was demonstrated, when, after Polling Day in 1964, we asked the surviving members of Trenaman and McQuail's 1959 sample (whose 1959 vote was already known) to indicate how they had voted in 1964 and also to recall their 1959 vote. Ninety-three per cent of those who did not change between the two elections remembered their 1959 vote correctly, compared with only 50 per cent of those whose voting position in 1964 differed from that of 1959. In most cases the effect of the error was to render the 1959 vote consistent with that which had been cast in 1964.[3] For what it is worth, however, it can be mentioned that the inter-campaign swing in our freshly drawn sample reflected

[3] This finding confirms a theoretical expectation of Philip E. Converse (Cf. 'Information Flow and the Stability of Partisan Attitudes', Ch. 8 of Campbell, Angus, Converse, Philip E., Miller, Warren E., and Stokes, Donald E., *Elections and the Political Order*, John Wiley and Sons, Inc., New York, 1966, p. 138), which was formulated as follows:

> The . . . theory which predicts that the less involved are more susceptible to party change suggests that the less involved will also give less accurate accounts of past political behavior. For simple psychological reasons, we would expect them to distort past behavior in the direction of current preference. Such distortions build in a false impression of stability . . .

the anti-Conservative trend of the period between 1959 and 1964–from 43 per cent support for the Conservatives among those who voted in 1959 to 40 per cent of the pre-campaign intentions of those who expected to vote in 1964.[4]

The evidence suggests that first-time voters gravitated to Labour in 1964. Of the 50 individuals in our sample who were ineligible to vote in 1959, 21 voted for the Labour Party in 1964, and only 13 supported the Conservatives. This result is compared in Table 11.2 with the equivalent finding in 1959– when those who had come on to the electoral register since 1955 favoured the Conservatives. It may be that new electors have no consistent preference for a particular party, but tend to respond to the political currents prevalent when they cast their first vote.

Table 11.2. VOTES OF FIRST VOTERS,
1959 AND 1964 COMPARED

	1959 %	1964 %
Conservative	44	26
Labour	35	42
Liberal	6	10
No vote	15	22
	100	100
N =	48	50

The fortunes of the *Liberal Party*–in marked contrast to those of its larger rivals–were virtually transformed by the 1964 campaign. Whereas the third party was named before the campaign opened by only eight per cent of those who intended to vote for some party (51 of 638), it actually received 13 per cent of the ballots of those who reported a vote (86 of 649).

[4] The table below refers only to those individuals who were eligible to vote in 1959 and excludes abstainers and 'don't knows' at each stage:

	Reported 1959 vote %	Intention Sept. 1964 %	1964 vote %
Conservative	43	40	38
Labour	51	52	49
Liberal	6	8	13
	100	100	100

FORTUNES OF THE POLITICAL PARTIES

The bulk of this Liberal gain derived from inter-party switching. Of the 64 individuals who transferred their allegiance from one party to another during the campaign, just over a half (34) were converted to Liberal support.[5] In addition, the Liberal Party received somewhat more than its fair share of the votes of the late deciders (14 of 60, or 23 per cent). It can be concluded from this that the party which stood no chance of winning the 1964 *election* had won the preceding *campaign*.[6]

Less than a half of the Liberal vote in our sample was delivered, then, by people who had expected to vote Liberal before the campaign began (38 of 86). We cannot generalize firmly from these Yorkshire results to the pattern of national support for the Liberal Party (which may vary according to differences in the regional character, social composition, and political traditions of the constituencies where Liberal candidates stand).[7] If, however, the trends in our sample were

[5] These derived more or less equally from pre-campaign supporters of the Labour (19) and Conservative (15) Parties.

[6] The pattern of an upward trend in Liberal support during the 1964 campaign, accompanied by a slight decline in major party support, was confirmed by the findings of four of the five main opinion polls in operation at the time: Gallup quota, Gallup random, *Daily Express*, and Research Services. (See Butler, David E. and King, Anthony, *The British General Election of 1964*, op. cit., p. 208.) In addition, the National Opinion Poll conducted some interviews with identical respondents at various stages of the campaign (amounting to approximately 1,000 electors, sampled on a national basis). NOP has showed us a turnover table in which the various inter-party movements that occurred between the earlier and later interviews are summarized. This discloses only a very slight pro-Liberal shift (a movement from nine per cent to ten per cent support for the third party in the whole sample). The discrepancy between that result and our own can almost certainly be explained by technical factors, of which the most important involves the timing of the interviews. The final NOP interviews were held four or five days *before* Polling Day (October 15th), whereas ours all took place after that date. And in general the period between interviews was much shorter in the NOP study than in our survey—as the following comparisons show:

	NOP	LEEDS
'Pre' interviews	Three surveys combined: September 17th–20th September 24th–27th October 1st–4th	September 12th–20th
'Post' interviews	October 10th–11th	October 16th–25th

[7] Three excellent analyses of variations in the Liberal gain between 1959

187

typical of electoral behaviour in many other areas, it would
follow that a considerable part of the Liberal revival of 1959–64,
in which the third party's share of the national poll advanced
from 5·9 per cent to 11·2 per cent, was not an inter-campaign
development but an outcome of the 1964 campaign itself. This
impression of the importance of the campaign was not dispelled
when we looked separately at trends among our respondents
from Pudsey (where a Liberal had stood in 1959) and from
West Leeds (where there had been no Liberal candidate at the
previous election). In both cases a majority of the new Liberal
votes that were won since 1959 were apparently products of
the 1964 campaign.[8]

Public attitudes towards the parties in 1964

Developments in voting intentions may provide an incomplete
picture of the effects of an election campaign. Those who make
up their minds (or change them) during the three weeks before
Polling Day, are an untypical minority, and trends of opinion
that may have affected the rest of the electorate also deserve
some attention. That is why we devised measures of the attitudes
of all our respondents towards the Conservative, Labour, and
Liberal Parties. The resulting scales consisted of nine statements
–five favourable and four critical–which seemed germane to
the concerns that were uppermost in electors' minds in 1964.[9]
The respondents were asked to go through the full list of items
three different times–stating which were true and which untrue

and 1964 have been published. They include Steed, Michael, 'An Analysis of
the Results,' Appendix II to Butler, D. E. and King, Anthony, *The British
General Election of 1964*, op. cit.; Berrington, H. B., 'The General Election
of 1964', *Journal of the Royal Statistical Society*, Series A (General), Vol. 128,
Part I, 1965, pp. 17–66; and Lees, J. D., op. cit.

[8] The table below illustrates the point. Inevitably, the first line depends
on the imperfect memories of electors.

	Number of Liberal supporters in:	
	West Leeds	Pudsey
Recalled 1959 vote	13	24
September 1964 intention	19	30
1964 vote	39	47

[9] See Appendix B for an account of the procedures by which the nine
items were chosen.

of each of the political parties in turn. Table 11.3 shows how the whole sample applied the individual items of the scale to the various parties at the pre-campaign interview and again after the election.

Table 11.3. STATEMENTS APPLIED TO THE LABOUR, CONSERVATIVE, AND LIBERAL PARTIES BEFORE AND AFTER THE CAMPAIGN BY ALL ELECTORS

	True of:					
	Labour Party		Conservative Party		Liberal Party	
	Before %	After %	Before %	After %	Before %	After %
1. Out for the nation as a whole	58	67***	51	51	45	51**
2. Out to raise the standard of living for the ordinary man in the street	76	76	45	42	47	49
3. Disunited and badly organized	28	17***	23	29*	32	20***
4. Would weaken Britain's voice in world affairs	29	31	18	17	30	29
5. Would get the economy moving	47	55***	47	37***	23	28***
6. Has a good team of leaders	51	56***	50	42***	21	28***
7. Has no clear policy	22	14***	24	28	38	33*
8. Would know how to run the country well	45	50*	52	47**	21	27**
9. Don't keep to their promises	38	34	49	49	20	19

*   P = significant at ·05 level
** P = significant at ·01 level
*** P = significant at ·001 level

It can be seen that Labour improved its overall position during the campaign, while impressions of the Conservative Party became less favourable. The gap between the major parties widened most noticeably on two items. It was increasingly felt that Labour 'would get the economy moving', and that the Conservatives could not achieve this objective. Labour was also accorded significantly more credit after the campaign for having 'a good team of leaders'—a quality which was ascribed to the Conservatives less often after Polling Day. Another area of substantial Labour gain—though not of corresponding Conservative weakness—was located by the phrase, 'out for the nation as a whole'. In percentage terms the Labour Party was regarded most favourably at both interviews for being 'out to raise the standard of living for the ordinary man in the street', but it made no further headway on this item during the campaign itself. There was a general tendency for critically worded items to be applied less frequently to the Labour Party, and more often to the Conservatives, at the post-election interview, but, against the run of most of these assessments, the campaign increased doubts about Labour's ability to represent Britain abroad ('would weaken Britain's voice in world affairs'), while improving the Conservatives' standing on this point. This is an instance in the party ratings of those cross-currents of opinion which were shown in the previous chapter to have affected the endorsements of issue items.

Table 11.4. HOW THE STANDING OF THE CONSERVATIVE PARTY AS 'OUT FOR THE NATION AS A WHOLE' DECLINED, AND THAT OF LABOUR IMPROVED, BETWEEN 1959 AND 1964

	'Out for the Nation as a whole'			
	Deemed true by Conservative voters of the:		Deemed true by Labour voters of the:	
	Conservative Party %	Labour Party %	Conservative Party %	Labour Party %
October 1959	91	28	53	79
September 1964	85	33	29	80
October 1964	88	41	26	91

This material suggests that electors' perceptions of the major parties had changed in at least one important respect between 1959 and 1964. This development can be traced by showing how the 1959 and 1964 samples, respectively, rated the Conservative and Labour Parties on one item that was common to the party attitude scales on both occasions: 'Out for the nation as a whole'. In providing this information, Table 11.4 holds party support constant by distinguishing between the responses of the Conservative and Labour voters in both samples.

Trenaman and McQuail reported that in 1959 the Conservative Party was seen largely as a national party, whereas Labour was regarded alternately as a party of the common people (by its own supporters) or as *not* a party of the nation (by its opponents).[10] The results of two other surveys which were conducted in late 1959 confirmed the influence of this distinction.[11] Table 11.4 suggests, however, that in the ensuing five years there was a considerable decline in the public's awareness of this contrast. Two different trends are evident. In the period *between* the campaigns, the Conservatives lost much of the respect which they had formerly enjoyed among their opponents as a national party (the proportion of Labour supporters who thought the Conservatives were 'out for the nation as a whole' having fallen from 53 per cent to 29 per cent). There was very little inter-campaign change in Labour's standing on this item; but *during* the 1964 campaign, opponents and supporters alike were increasingly inclined to regard Labour as a party of the whole nation. In the post-election interviews of 1964, then, 91 per cent of the Labour voters claimed that their party was 'out for the nation as a whole' (compared with 79 per cent five years earlier); and 41 per cent of the Conservative voters acknowledged Labour's national representativeness (compared with only 28 per cent in 1959).[12]

---

[10] Trenaman, J. and McQuail, Denis, op. cit., Chapter III.

[11] See Abrams, Mark, Rose, Richard and Hinden, Rita, *Must Labour Lose?*, Penguin Books, Ltd., 1960, Part I, Ch. 1; and Bealey, Frank, Blondel, J. and McCann, W. P., op. cit., Chapter 10.

[12] There were also signs that the 'traditional-versus-radical axis', along which many of the differences in party ratings by members of Trenaman and McQuail's sample had fallen, had become less important to the electorate in 1964 than in 1959. A component analysis of endorsements of party attitude items by one of our preliminary samples suggested that instead of applying this traditional/radical distinction, voters were rating the parties more pragmatically according to their general ability to govern well – and especially to manage economic affairs competently. See Appendix B.

FORTUNES OF THE POLITICAL PARTIES

Some correlates of attitude change during the 1964 campaign

The extent and direction of attitude change during the 1964 campaign may be summarized conveniently by deriving two composite scores from the endorsements of the individual items on the party attitude scale. One (it will be recalled from a previous explanation)[13] is a party attitude score, which ranges from $+ 5$ to $- 4$, and which can be calculated for any party by subtracting the total number of critical items which an individual regarded as true of it from the total number of favourable items that he applied to it. Such a score has been used, for example, to express the attitudes of our respondents at both stages of the campaign to the Liberal Party. In studying attitudes to the major parties, however, we have usually relied upon a so-called partisanship score, which stands for the difference between an individual's opinion of the Conservative Party and his views about Labour. This ranges from $+ 9$ to $- 9$ and is computed by subtracting the Labour Party attitude score from the Conservative Party attitude score (a positive result signifying a Conservative leaning and a negative quantity a pro-Labour opinion). These general measures are indispensable for any analysis of the relationship between attitude change and other variables– for example, party identification, demographic particulars, and exposure to various channels of election communication.

Our composite scores confirm that two main waves of attitude change were generated by the election campaign of 1964. One was a movement in favour of the Labour Party, which is reflected in the fact that in the sample as a whole the average partisanship score was $- 0.30$ as a result of the pre-campaign interview and $- 1.16$ after Polling Day. This shift of something approaching a whole point is similar in magnitude to the pro-Conservative swing which (according to Trenaman and McQuail) the 1959 campaign produced.[14] Second, there was a strong groundswell in favour of the Liberal Party. The Liberal Party attitude score (the range of which is half as extensive as that of the partisanship score) went up from an

---

[13] See pp. 21–4.
[14] Trenaman, J. and McQuail, Denis, op. cit., p. 151.

FORTUNES OF THE POLITICAL PARTIES

average of + 0·33 in September 1964 to + 0·81 in October–or
approximately half a point.

Were all groups in the sample affected more or less equally
by these changes of outlook, or did some participate in them
more wholeheartedly than others? One influence on attitude
change was the *party identification* of the voter. This was in
marked contrast to the position in 1959, when Trenaman and
McQuail found that their entire sample had shifted in favour
of the Conservative Party–Labour supporters by half a point,
on the average, and Conservatives by a whole point.[15] But in
1964 the Conservative voters staunchly resisted that pro-Labour
swing by which all the other voting groups in the sample had
been moved–as the left-hand column of figures in Table 11.5
shows.

Table 11.5. AVERAGE PARTISANSHIP AND LIBERAL PARTY
ATTITUDE SHIFTS BY 1964 VOTE

1964 Vote	*Mean partisanship shift*	*Mean Liberal shift*	*No. of respondents*
Conservative	− 0·12	− 0·11	246
Labour	− 1·44	+ 0·48	321
Liberal	− 0·64	+ 1·47	86
Abstained	− 0·83	+ 1·00	78

Another feature of attitude change in the 1964 election was a
tacit Lib–Lab alliance. It can be seen from the table that many
Labour voters became more appreciative of the Liberal Party
as a result of the campaign, but that the Conservatives stood
out against the general trend again and actually became
slightly more hostile to the Liberals. The Liberal voters recipro-
cated the favourable opinions of the Labour supporters. At
the beginning of the campaign they were exactly neutral between the parties (average partisanship score: 0·00), but after
Polling Day they stood firmly on Labour's side of the divide
(average partisanship score: − 0·64). In the inter-election
period of 1964-66 some observers commented on a tendency
for Labour and Liberal voters to support that party at by-
elections which had the best chance of defeating the Conservative
candidate. If any such alliance was operating at the polls at

[15] Ibid.

193

that time, it was apparently an outgrowth of the 1964 campaign itself.

How can we explain the immunity of the Conservative voters to those waves of opinion change which swept through the rest of the electorate during the 1964 campaign? They may have closed their ranks in solidarity against what they perceived to be a concerted attack on their party from both Labour and Liberal quarters. But it is also possible that the very factors which accounted for sagging Labour morale in 1959 helped to sustain the spirits of the Conservatives in 1964. In *Television and the Political Image*, Trenaman and McQuail portrayed the typical Labour supporter as cross-pressured between his party identification and his affinity to 'the prestige values of the whole social structure . . . and to . . . the whole cultural life of the community'– which Conservatism seemed to represent.[16] If, as a consequence, Labour voters were vulnerable to Conservative propaganda at a time when the Conservatives were on top, the same forces may have helped the Conservative voters, when the tables were turned, to withstand appeals to which most of their compatriots were responding. If Labour voters are cross-pressured, Conservatives are probably twice armed: by their ordinary party loyalties and by an extra element of confidence in their party's embodiment of the enduring values of British society and culture.[17]

Table 11.6. PARTISANSHIP SCORES BY AGE BEFORE AND
AFTER THE 1964 CAMPAIGN

Age group	Average pre-campaign partisanship score	Average campaign shift in partisanship score	Average post-campaign partisanship score	Number of respondents
21–29	− 1·59	− 0·21	− 1·80	94
30–44	− 0·38	− 0·89	− 1·27	227
45–65	− 0·17	− 0·90	− 1·07	318
66 +	+ 0·58	− 1·12	− 0·54	109

[16] Ibid, p. 158.

[17] If, however, the distinction between the Conservatives as a national party and Labour as a class party is becoming less clear in electors' minds, Conservative supporters may draw less strength from it in the future than they have done in the past.

Changes in attitudes towards the major parties also depended on *age* and *occupation*. The influence of the former is shown by Table 11.6, which relates the ages of our sample members to their partisanship scores.

Before the campaign pro-Conservative views were most common among the oldest electors. This was consistent with an NOP pre-election finding (based on 12,000 interviews) that 'the over-65s were the only age group with a decided preference for the Conservatives'.[18] During the campaign, however, the pro-Labour swing in our sample became increasingly pronounced with advancing age.[19] Perhaps Labour's election programme, with its promise of higher pensions, appealed distinctively to the elder part of the electorate, although we cannot demonstrate that this was the case.[20] It is worth noting in this connection that, according to NOP, the swing to Labour between the two elections of the mid-1960s was greater among the over-65s than in any other age group.[21] An alternative possibility, however, is that a mass campaign promotes a consensus in the political outlook of the various age groups in the population. This would be consistent with a view of elder citizens as normally rather isolated from current trends–but brought back into touch with the climate of opinion by the stimulus of an election.

To appreciate the relationship between occupation and

[18] The citation is taken from Butler, D. E. and King, Anthony, *The British General Election of 1964*, op. cit., pp. 296–7.

[19] It was interesting to find that these trends were equally evident even when the data by age were separately examined in the different voting groups of the sample.

[20] With only one exception (electors aged 21–29 in the pre-campaign interview), all the age groups in our sample accorded a higher priority to pensions than to any other issue at both stages of the campaign. Nevertheless, the over-65s were exceptionally concerned with this issue, 80 per cent having endorsed it before the campaign and 77 per cent after Polling Day (compared with about 60 per cent of the youngest electors). On other issues the patterns of campaign change among the elderly resembled those found in the rest of the sample–but at a lower level of endorsement overall. For example, endorsements of the economic growth issue by the over-65s shot up during the campaign from 11 per cent to 22 per cent, but the latter figure was still well below that of 34 per cent for all other respondents.

[21] Cf. Butler, D. E. and King, Anthony, *The British General Election of 1966*, op. cit., p. 264.

partisanship shift, it is necessary to hold the vote constant. When they examined the role of occupation in 1959, Trenaman and McQuail reported that the *less* skilled Conservatives in their sample had been pulled towards Labour, while the *more* skilled Labour supporters had been pulled towards the Conservatives. These counter-movements seemed to reflect the activation by the campaign of social pressures on the most affected groups.[22] In 1964, however, this phenomenon did not recur—as Table 11.7 shows.

Table 11.7. PARTISANSHIP SCORES BY OCCUPATION OF LABOUR AND CONSERVATIVE VOTERS BEFORE AND AFTER THE CAMPAIGN

	Average pre-campaign score	Average campaign shift	Average post-campaign score	Number of respondents
Labour voters:				
Non-manual workers	− 2·37	− 1·92	− 4·29	51
Skilled manual	− 3·62	− 1·41	− 5·03	179
Semi/unskilled manual	− 4·25	− 1·06	− 5·31	88
Conservative voters:				
Non-manual	+ 3·99	− 0·12	+ 3·87	119
Skilled manual	+ 3·73	+ 0·08	+ 3.81	90
Semi/unskilled manual	+ 4·44	− 0·44	+ 4·00	27

Instead the role of occupation in attitude change was virtually the same in both major party voting groups. The figures suggest that the campaign had helped to strengthen the party allegiances of the *higher-status supporters* of both the Labour and Conservative Parties. This tendency was most noticeable in the Labour camp, where, of the three occupational groups, it was the non-manual category which swung most sharply in favour of its own party. On the Conservative side, both the non-manual and skilled manual supporters held steadfastly to their previous attitude positions in the face of the general anti-Conservative swing of the time—to which, however, the non-skilled workers succumbed. These developments mirrored the changes which occurred in the same groups in their appreciations of the key

[22] Trenaman, J. and McQuail, Denis, op. cit., pp. 152–5.

issues of economic growth and the nuclear deterrent.[23] All this
lends further support to the hypothesis, which was advanced
in the previous chapter, that relatively sophisticated voters are
more likely to absorb appeals mounted by their own parties and
to be reinforced in their political outlook as a result.

Age and occupation did not influence the changing pattern
of attitudes towards the Liberal Party, however–all demographic groups in the sample having been affected to a similar
extent by the pro-Liberal swing. That shift in favour of the
Liberals, it should be pointed out, was at least as substantial
as the changes in our respondents' attitudes towards the major
parties. The average movement in the whole sample's Liberal
Party attitude score was + 0·49, compared with + 0·44 for
the Labour Party attitude score, and — 0·22 for the Conservative Party attitude score. In fact nearly a half of the
participants in our survey were more favourably disposed to
the Liberals at the end of the campaign than they had been at
the outset.[24] How did exposure to the various sources of the 1964
campaign affect this trend? We may now consider the role of
television and the other mass media–first, in facilitating the
Liberal vote gains of 1964, and second, in promoting pro-
Liberal attitudes.

Election communications and the new Liberal vote

The upsurge of Liberal support at the polls in 1964 was
powerfully assisted by exposure to the preceding campaign.

[23] The following figures show that degree of change in the salience of
these two issues was inversely related to occupational status when vote was
held constant:

	Non-manual	Skilled manual	Semi/unskilled manual
Endorsements by Labour voters of economic growth issue	%	%	%
Pre-campaign	29	17	16
Post-campaign	47	29	23
Endorsements by Conservative voters of nuclear deterrent issue			
Pre-campaign	25	27	30
Post-campaign	42	37	18

[24] Forty-six per cent of the whole sample inclined more favourably to the
Liberal Party after Polling Day than they had in September 1964. Twenty-
one per cent did not change, and 32 per cent became more critical.

FORTUNES OF THE POLITICAL PARTIES

Election television was centrally involved in this development, and the greatest contribution was apparently made by the party election broadcasts–especially those which the Liberal Party originated. These conclusions emerged from a detailed inspection of the exposure patterns to the main campaign sources of the various stable and vote-changing electors in our sample. The role of party broadcasts is illustrated by the figures presented in Table 11.8.

Table 11.8. RESOLUTION OF THE VOTE AND EXPOSURE TO
PARTY ELECTION BROADCASTS

	Average number of Liberal broadcasts seen	Average number of election broadcasts seen (all parties)	Number of respondents
Inter-party changers			
To Liberal	1·4	5·4	34
To Conservative and			
Labour	0·9	4·3	30
Late deciders			
To Liberal	0·9	3·4	14
To Conservative and			
Labour	1·1	5·3	46
Consistent party supporters			
Liberal	1·0	4·4	38
Conservative and Labour	1·0	4·6	487
Non-voters	0·6	3·3	76

It can be seen that the changers from the other parties to a Liberal vote (from which, it will be recalled, the bulk of the Liberal gain derived) absorbed more party broadcasts as a whole, and more Liberal broadcasts, than did any other group in the sample–and substantially more, for example, than did the consistent supporters of the Conservative and Labour Parties. In the case of Liberal broadcasts the mean excess represents about 40 per cent more exposure on the average. It is true that the members of this key group also followed the campaign to a high degree through most of the other available communications channels–for example, the late election news bulletins on television, the other non-party political TV programmes, and the press. But their differential reliance on these sources was not nearly so pronounced as in the case of party broadcast viewing.[25]

A limitation of this analysis arises from its dependence on data supplied by only a tiny proportion of the electorate (amounting, in the case of the inter-party changers to Liberal support, to five per cent of the sample). To arrive at a more comprehensive picture of the influence of election communications on Liberal fortunes in 1964, it is necessary to examine the association in the whole sample between changing attitudes to the Liberal Party and indices of exposure to the main sources of the campaign. Our interest in this broader analysis centred on two areas of enquiry. First, was there an association in the sample at large between television viewing and pro-Liberal swing, and if so, how far was it independent of other factors? Second, how far were distinctions of motive for following the election relevant to the process of persuasion?[26]

Pro-Liberal attitudes, exposure to the campaign, and strength of motivation for following it

When political viewing scores were plotted against changing attitudes towards the Liberal Party in our sample, the resulting findings upheld the central conclusion of the previous section. Television had apparently promoted pro-Liberal attitudes in

[25] The exposure patterns of the various voting groups to these other campaign influences were as follows:

	Average exposure scores		
	Late election news (TV)	Other non-party political TV	Press
Inter-party changers to Liberal	1·9	2·9	2·5
Inter-party changers to major party	1·5	1·9	1·7
Late deciders to Liberal	1·3	3·8	2·4
Late deciders to major party	1·1	2·7	2·2
Consistent Liberal supporters	1·3	2·7	2·5
Consistent major party supporters	1·6	2·5	2·3
Non-voters	1·2	1·6	1·3

[26] Before leaving the area of Liberal *vote* gain, it should be pointed out that we have not considered the possible influence of any non-exposure variables in this section. It is more convenient to consider their role, in conjunction with the impact of television, in one of the concluding chapters (see Chapter 13 below).

the electorate during the 1964 campaign. When the role of television was examined in the *whole sample*, however–disregarding differences of motive–its impact seemed rather modest. This point is illustrated by Figure 11.1, which shows the mean shifts in the Liberal Party attitude scores that were registered by those individuals who saw 0, 1, 2, and 3 Liberal party election broadcasts, respectively.

Figure 11.1. IN THE SAMPLE AS A WHOLE, HIGH EXPOSURE TO LIBERAL ELECTION BROADCASTS WENT WITH ATTITUDE CHANGE IN FAVOUR OF THE LIBERAL PARTY

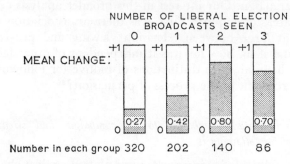

Except for a slackening off at the highest level of exposure, there is a clear differentiation between the viewing groups and a progressive relationship between the number of broadcasts seen and change in favour of the Liberal Party. The more election programmes an individual watched, the more likely he was to experience a high degree of pro-Liberal change in attitude. A chi-square test showed that this association was just statistically significant (it could have arisen by chance on only five occasions out of 100).[27]

[27] $\chi^2 = 7 \cdot 90$ when applied to the following distribution:

	Number of Liberal broadcasts seen		
	0	1	2 or 3
	%	%	%
Shifted in favour of the Liberal Party	41	47	53
No change or shifted against the Liberal Party	59	53	47
	100	100	100
N =	320	202	226

P = significant at ·05 level for two degrees of freedom.

Now let us see what happens when disposition to follow the election on television is injected into the analysis. Its effect is depicted in Figure 11.2, which deals separately with those respondents who were rated strong in motivation for following the campaign, and those whose motivation was deemed medium or weak. The figure shows that the introduction of a motivational variable has transformed what was a modest dependence of pro-Liberal shift on campaign exposure into a powerful association–and one that is concentrated entirely among *the less interested electors*. The zig-zag pattern on the left-hand side of the figure indicates that, among the more keen voters, there was no consistent relationship between the development of pro-Liberal views and the number of Liberal programmes that had been seen. But among those whose concern to follow the election via broadcasting was only lukewarm (see the right-hand side of the figure), there was a strong and progressive relationship between pro-Liberal change and party broadcast exposure which would have arisen by chance only once in a hundred times.[28] This suggests that the qualitative dimension of the viewing experience is highly relevant to what is gained from it and that the interaction between political communication and attitude change can be understood properly only if the disposition of the individual to receive propaganda is taken into account.[29]

[28] $\chi^2 = 12.75$ when applied to the following distribution:

	Number of Liberal broadcasts seen		
	0	1	2 or 3
	%	%	%
Shifted in favour of the Liberal Party	38	52	57
No change or shifted against the Liberal Party	62	48	43
	100	100	100
N =	200	113	107

P = significant at ·01 level for two degrees of freedom.

[29] It should be pointed out that the result is not improved if the respondents are subdivided further according to the strength of motivation variable. That is, the association between Liberal shift and exposure is not greater among those who were deemed 'very weak' in motivation for following the campaign than among those whose motivation was classified as 'moderately weak' or 'medium'. The most powerful effect emerges from dichotomizing the sample, as in Figure 11.2.

Figure 11.2. THE ASSOCIATION BETWEEN PRO-LIBERAL
SHIFT AND EXPOSURE TO LIBERAL BROADCASTS WAS
CONFINED TO THOSE RESPONDENTS WHOSE MOTIVATION
FOR FOLLOWING THE CAMPAIGN WAS MEDIUM OR WEAK

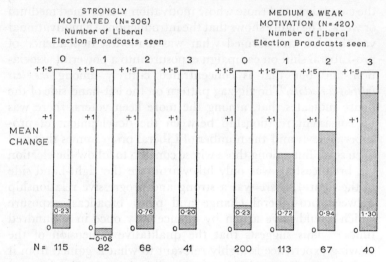

STRONGLY MOTIVATED (N=306)
Number of Liberal Election Broadcasts seen

MEDIUM & WEAK MOTIVATION (N=420)
Number of Liberal Election Broadcasts seen

It cannot be concluded from this analysis that Liberal broadcasts proved uniquely effective in fostering pro-Liberal attitudes.
A number of other exposure variables were also related positively
to the development of those attitudes – and in each case the
association between exposure and change was confined to that
60 per cent of the sample whose interest in the campaign was
only moderate or weak.[30] Why a motivational distinction
should mark off the persuasible from the unsusceptible voters
so firmly calls for interpretive comment which is provided in
the concluding section of this chapter. The immediate practical
implication of the results presented here was that we could

[30] For example, when Liberal attitude change is related to the viewing of
late election news on television, we find that amongst the strongly motivated
group, 41 per cent of those with a high level of exposure (having watched it
at least three times a week) moved favourably to the Liberal Party, compared with 46 per cent of those who saw relatively few late election news
bulletins. In this case there is even a negative relationship between the two
variables. Amongst the less keenly motivated respondents, however, a
strong relationship appears, since 59 per cent of the highly exposed individuals show a pro-Liberal movement, compared with only 44 per cent
of those with a low level of exposure.

FORTUNES OF THE POLITICAL PARTIES

concentrate further investigation exclusively on the vulnerable group of electors when trying to disentangle the influence of television from any other factors that could have created favourable impressions of the Liberal Party.

Which were the most influential campaign sources?

Separate analyses of the role of each individual exposure variable cannot clarify their relative importance in disseminating a favourable image of the Liberal Party in 1964. In the weakly motivated group more than one measure of exposure was positively related to pro-Liberal attitude change, and on the face of it the strength of the association did not differ greatly from one variable to another. The root cause of this difficulty is the high degree of inter-correlation between the exposure variables themselves, which is illustrated by the correlation coefficients presented in Table 11.9. They reflect the fact that an individual who followed the campaign extensively in one communication channel probably received much election material from several other sources as well. Nevertheless, a close reading of the table discloses the presence of some differential exposure patterns. For example, all the television variables in the table are highly inter-correlated, while the measurements of exposure to the press and the local campaign are related more closely to each other than either is to any form of TV exposure. All the correlations of radio usage with the other exposure variables are quite low. These patterns suggest that the people who rely on radio for political information nowadays are cut off from most of the other sources of election communications. The remainder are divided between those who depend largely on television for keeping up with politics and those who turn more often to the press and the local campaign.

The task which remained was one of disentangling the independent contributions to an effect (e.g. the development of pro-Liberal views among the politically indifferent electors) of a number of interacting variables (e.g. exposure to the different sources of the campaign). A statistical technique which can help an investigator to unravel the influences at work in such a situation is known as regression analysis. So-called simple linear regressions can chart the individual associations

203

between an effect and each of the explanatory influences separately, thus suggesting which of the latter had been most powerful. And by means of a multiple regression it is possible to measure the extent of the independent contribution of some variable when allowance has been made for the effects of one or more of the other variables.

Table 11.9. CORRELATION COEFFICIENTS FOR INTER-
RELATIONSHIPS AMONG EXPOSURE VARIABLES
(RESPONDENTS RATED MEDIUM AND WEAK IN MOTIVATION)

	Liberal broad- casts	Major party broad- casts	TV News	Other non-party political television	Radio	Press
Liberal broadcasts						
Major party broadcasts	·67					
TV news (main and late news combined)	·42	·53				
Other non-party political television	·37	·45	·42			
Radio	− ·04	·02	− ·04	·05		
Press	·22	·21	·18	·23	·08	
Local campaign	·18	·20	·16	·23	·16	·33

Before a series of such regression analyses could be undertaken, however, it was necessary to decide which variables deserved to be included in the calculations. In the event, all the exposure variables listed in Table 11.9 were incorporated into the simple regression stage of the analysis—together with a measure of changing attitudes towards the major parties: the difference between the pre-campaign and post-campaign partisanship scores.[31] We included none of the standard demographic particulars (age, sex, education, and occupation), because we

[31] This was chosen to stand for the connection between major party allegiance and Liberal shift (whereby Labour voters had become more favourable to the Liberal Party while Conservatives had become more critical). It was superior to 1964 vote for inclusion in a regression analysis, which requires the use of continuous variables (ones that mount progressively by increments on a single dimension, as the partisanship score does, and as differences in party vote do not).

had no evidence that they were associated with changing attitudes towards the Liberal Party.[32]

In preparing the simple linear regressions, the degree of change in the Liberal Party attitude score for each respondent was matched up against the degree of his exposure to each campaign source in turn. (A similar operation related the degree of shift in Liberal Party attitude to the degree of change in each individual's partisanship score.) The resulting correlations, which appear in Table 11.10, measure the association between Liberal Party attitude shift and each of the other variables, when they are considered one at a time. The F-ratio values in the table estimate the *genuineness* of each correlation – i.e. the probability that an association was real and so differed from a situation where the variables concerned were unconnected with (statistically independent of) each other. The results of this part of the analysis show, then, that although five sources of exposure were significantly associated with pro-Liberal attitude change, the most important single influence on the development of pro-Liberal views was exposure to television news.

Table 11.10. RESULTS OF SIMPLE REGRESSIONS OF
EXPLANATORY VARIABLES ON LIBERAL PARTY
ATTITUDE SHIFT

	Correlation coefficients	F-ratio values
Television news	·17	12·29***
Liberal broadcasts	·15	8·99**
Major party broadcasts	·13	7·14**
Local campaign	·10	4·52*
Press	·10	4·14*
Non-party political television	·08	2·65
Radio	·02	0·17
Partisanship shift	− ·06	1·74

* Significant at P = ·05 level.
** Significant at P = ·01 level.
*** Significant at P = ·001 level.

[32] The strongest association was with occupation. Fifty-three per cent of the non-skilled workers shifted in a pro-Liberal direction, compared with 45 per cent of the skilled manual workers and 43 per cent of the non-manual workers. But when tested by chi-square, this trend was not statistically significant, and to a considerable extent it reflected the influence of a political variable – of which account was already being taken by inclusion in the analysis of the measure of partisanship shift.

In using multiple regression to examine these influences further, we aimed mainly to see whether any campaign source, taken singly or in combination, had independently supplemented the effect of television news on pro-Liberal attitude change. We found that the largest extra contribution to that of television news was made by the viewing of Liberal broadcasts, but even that increment was not statistically significant at the five per cent level. And only television news contributed significantly to the other variables and combinations. Three general conclusions may be drawn from these results. First, in promoting favourable impressions of the Liberal Party, television was a more important medium than, say, the press or the local campaign. Second, in facilitating this shift of opinion, the two most powerful television variables–the news bulletins and the Liberal broadcasts–worked to a considerable extent in harness, each doing more or less the same job as the other. Third, when the extra contribution of each variable, beyond the area of its overlap with the others, was assessed, only television news proved distinctively effective.

There seems to be no doubt that the appearance of Liberal spokesmen, and the presentation of the Liberal case on television, were more advantageous to the Liberal Party than any other means of political communication in 1964. It is true that the actual amount of change in Liberal Party attitude scores which our exposure variables explain is somewhat limited.[33] Extra-communications factors must have helped to stimulate that movement of opinion from which the Liberals benefited so strikingly at the polls in 1964. Nevertheless, these findings point to some conditions of success for a third party in the British political situation–first, the availability of a large group in the electorate who are prepared to tolerate political messages without being keen to receive them, and second, access to a channel of communication through which this group can be reached. Television is the medium that met the latter criterion in 1964. It satisfied this requirement, partly because of its high popularity and the heavy use made of it by the more vulnerable viewers, partly because the Liberals received a

[33] The F-ratio value for the multiple regression equation of all eight explanatory variables was 2·24–which was statistically significant at the 5 per cent level.

relatively generous share of TV time, and partly because of the sheltered status that politics enjoys in the programme schedules of British broadcasting. It is noteworthy in this connection that the difference between the influential TV variables and the single uninfluential one (non-party political programmes) is that habitual exposure accounts for a great deal of exposure to the former, whereas watching the latter is more likely to derive from a definite choice. This is consistent with the assumption that high political viewing among lukewarm electors must also be due largely to the force of habit.

But before offering a full explanation of the susceptibility of the politically indifferent viewers to Liberal propaganda on television, it is instructive to look at the part played by strength of motivation in mediating the effects of the campaign on attitudes to the Labour and Conservative Parties. Its role in partisanship shift proved different from, but not inconsistent with, its significance for Liberal shift. The evidence presented below strengthens the impression that motivation is of more than casual importance in the process of political persuasion.

Attitudes towards the Conservative and Labour Parties: exposure to the campaign and strength of motivation for following it

Although there was little net change in the number of electors who intended to vote for either major party, attitudes shifted during the 1964 election away from the Conservatives and in favour of Labour. The average change in partisanship score of -0.86 was sufficiently large to suggest that a genuine movement of opinion had occurred during the period of the campaign. Was this development connected with exposure to television or to any other vehicle of political communication? Or was there—as Trenaman and McQuail found in 1959—a veritable barrier shielding attitudes towards the major parties from the main sources of the campaign?[34]

When the entire 1964 sample was taken as the unit of analysis, and campaign shifts in partisanship scores were plotted against indices of media usage, the findings of 1959 were replicated. There was no indication that responsibility for the increasingly pro-Labour mood of our respondents could be traced to any

[34] Trenaman, J. and McQuail, Denis, op. cit., pp. 190–3.

single source of political comment or propaganda. Table 11.11
presents a typical pattern of findings.

Table 11.11. IN THE SAMPLE AS A WHOLE, PRO-LABOUR
ATTITUDE CHANGE WAS NOT RELATED TO THE VIEWING
OF PARTY BROADCASTS

Number of party election broadcasts seen	Shifted in favour of the Labour Party %	Number of respondents
0	55	191
1–3	54	142
4–6	52	192
7–9	48	136
10 +	49	87

It can be seen that higher exposure (which is measured in
this case by the total number of party election broadcasts
viewed) was not attended by an increasing shift in favour of
the Labour Party. On the contrary, there was a slight tendency
for exposure to be related *inversely* to pro-Labour shift. When
probed further, this was explained by the fact that more of the
highly exposed voters had shifted in favour of the Conservative
Party than did those who had seen only a few election broadcasts. When, for example, the sample was divided between
those who had seen four or more party election broadcasts, and
those who had watched three or less, it was found that 36 per
cent of the former had become more pro-Conservative in outlook after the campaign than they had been before it opened—
compared with 28 per cent of the latter. When tested by
chi-square, however, this difference was not statistically
significant.[35]

[35] $\chi^2 = 5.44$—not significant at two degrees of freedom—for the following
distribution:

	Low exposure (Viewed 0–3 party broadcasts) %	High exposure (Viewed 4+ party broadcasts) %
Pro-Conservative shift	28	36
No change	17	14
Pro-Labour shift	55	50
	100	100
N =	333	415

FORTUNES OF THE POLITICAL PARTIES

Was this negative result sustained when our strength-of-motivation variable was introduced into the analysis? Its impact is illustrated graphically by Figure 11.3.

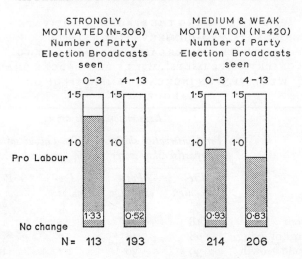

Figure 11.3. AMONG THE STRONGLY MOTIVATED RESPONDENTS, HIGH EXPOSURE TO PARTY BROADCASTS APPEARED TO CHECK THE SWING TO LABOUR

It can be seen that the division of the sample into its strongly motivated and relatively indifferent members has picked out a group of electors whose attitudes have responded to exposure. In contrast to the outcome of the parallel analysis of Liberal attitudes, however, it is *the more interested voters* who proved susceptible to influence in this case. It is not that campaign exposure helped to produce favourable attitudes to the Labour Party in either group. Instead, the effect of high campaign exposure can be visualized as a braking action on the attitudes of the strongly motivated voters—checking the extent of their pro-Labour swing. Thus 37 per cent of those individuals in this group who had watched four or more party election broadcasts had shifted in favour of the Conservative Party after the campaign, compared with only 24 per cent of those who had viewed three such programmes or less. This relationship is statistically significant, according to the chi-square test, and would have occurred by chance on only five out of 100 occasions.[36]

The sources of attitude change in the politically interested electorate

Our investigation of the sources of this association followed a different track from the one that was pursued in the case of

Table 11.12. AMONG THE STRONGLY MOTIVATED
RESPONDENTS, PRO-CONSERVATIVE ATTITUDE CHANGE
WENT WITH AN INCREASED EMPHASIS ON TWO
'CONSERVATIVE ISSUES', WHILE PRO-LABOUR CHANGE
WENT WITH AN INCREASED EMPHASIS ON ONE
'LABOUR ISSUE'

| | *Issue endorsements among:* | | | |
| | *Pro-Conservative shifters in partisanship scores* | | *Pro-Labour shifters in partisanship scores* | |
	Pre-campaign %	*Post-campaign* %	*Pre-campaign* %	*Post-campaign* %
Deterrent	18	31*	24	27
Standard of living	28	48**	37	35
Economic growth	30	30	27	39**
N =	99		163	

* Difference between pre-campaign and post-campaign endorsements significant at P = ·05 level.

** Difference between pre-campaign and post-campaign endorsements significant at P = ·01 level.

[36] $\chi^2 = 6·06$–significant at P = ·05 level for two degrees of freedom—when applied to the following distribution among the strongly motivated respondents:

	Low exposure (*Viewed 0–3 party broadcasts*) %	*High exposure* (*Viewed 4+ party broadcasts*) %
Pro-Conservative shift	24	37
No change	15	14
Pro-Labour shift	61	49
	100	100
N =	113	193

pro-Liberal attitude change. A regression analysis was unnecessary, since, of our various measures of exposure, only party broadcast viewing was associated at a statistically significant level with shifts in partisanship scores. It transpired, however, that this connection was a product in part of two other tendencies – neither of which had affected the less politically minded members of the sample.

First, certain changes in *issue salience* were allied meaningfully to shifts in partisanship attitudes among the highly motivated electors. The signs of this link are presented in Table 11.12, which distinguishes between two groups of respondents: those whose partisanship scores had developed in favour of the Conservative Party during the campaign; and those who had veered towards Labour.

It can be seen that the right-shifting respondents became significantly more sensitive to the standard-of-living and deterrent issues, but that their views about economic growth did not change at all. Among the left-shifters this pattern was exactly reversed. They became much more aware of the need for economic growth but remained unmoved by the standard-of-living and deterrent issues. Since this pattern was found only among the politically interested voters,[37] it follows that the

---

[37] The figures below apply to those individuals who were less keen to follow the campaign. They show no significant increases in the salience of the deterrent and standard-of-living issues among either the right- or left-shifters, although both groups became significantly more appreciative of the importance of economic growth.

Issue endorsements among:

	Pro-Conservative shifters in partisanship scores		Pro-Labour shifters in partisanship scores	
	Pre-campaign %	Post-campaign %	Pre-campaign %	Post-campaign %
Deterrent	21	24	22	28
Standard of living	43	42	32	34
Economic growth	19	31*	14	30***
N =	138		218	

* Difference between pre-campaign and post-campaign endorsements significant at $P = \cdot 05$ level.

*** Difference between pre-campaign and post-campaign endorsements significant at $P = \cdot 001$ level.

FORTUNES OF THE POLITICAL PARTIES

strength of motivation distinction has located a section of the electorate whose opinions about the issues of a campaign really do march hand in hand with their attitudes towards the major parties.

Second, these changes in issue salience depended in turn upon the actual *party direction* of the election broadcasts that the highly motivated viewers had seen. We know that Labour emphasized the need for economic growth in its TV broadcasts and that the Conservatives devoted considerable attention to the standard-of-living and deterrent issues. The evidence presented in Table 11.13 suggests that these emphases were communicated effectively to those viewers who were keen to follow the election.

Table 11.13. AMONG THE STRONGLY MOTIVATED RESPONDENTS, AN INCREASED AWARENESS OF THE STANDARD-OF-LIVING ISSUE WENT WITH THE VIEWING OF CONSERVATIVE BROADCASTS, WHILE AN INCREASED AWARENESS OF THE ECONOMIC GROWTH ISSUE WENT WITH THE VIEWING OF LABOUR BROADCASTS

	Issue endorsements among those whose exposure to:†							
	Conservative broadcasts was:				Labour broadcasts was:			
	High		Low		High		Low	
	Pre-campaign	Post-campaign	Pre-campaign	Post-campaign	Pre-campaign	Post-campaign	Pre-campaign	Post-campaign
	%	%	%	%	%	%	%	%
Standard of living	31	44*	33	38	32	34	33	44*
Economic growth	29	34	25	35*	25	39*	28	33
Deterrent	22	32	22	27	22	28	22	29
N =	117		189		110		196	

† High exposure: 3–5 broadcasts seen.
  Low exposure: 0–2 broadcasts seen.
  * Difference between pre-campaign and post-campaign endorsements significant at P = ·05 level.

The respondents are divided in two ways in the table: first, according to whether they saw a large number of Conservative broadcasts (three or more) or only a few (two or less); and second, according to the number of Labour programmes they watched. Nothing that emerges from the figures has a bearing on the salience of the deterrent issue. Those viewers, however, who saw a large number of Conservative broadcasts became significantly more aware of the standard-of-living issue–but not of the need for economic growth. Those who were highly exposed to Labour propaganda on television reacted in just the opposite way: they endorsed economic growth as an important issue significantly more often after the campaign than they did in mid-September–but not the standard-of-living item. And when the role of party vote was examined in an even more detailed analysis, it was found that much of this difference derived from selective viewing by certain major party supporters (from their tendency, that is, to see many of their own side's broadcasts while ignoring most of those put out by their opponents).[38] Again no equivalent pattern emerged

[38] The table below records the changes in the salience of the key issues of the campaign that occurred among four different groups of Conservative and Labour voters, who are each distinguished according to their patterns of exposure to Conservative and Labour broadcasts. It can be seen that the greatest shift on the economic growth item occurred among those Labour voters who saw many Labour broadcasts but few Conservative ones. Contrariwise, the greatest move towards adoption of the standard-of-living and deterrent issues occurred among those Conservatives who were high in exposure to Conservative broadcasts but low in exposure to Labour ones.

Endorsements of key issues by:	Economic growth		Standard of living		Nuclear deterrent		N
	Sept.	Oct.	Sept.	Oct.	Sept.	Oct.	
	%	%	%	%	%	%	
Conservative voters							
High Con/Low Lab	50	55	30	50	20	50	20
High Con/High Lab	29	38	54	46	33	46	24
High Lab/Low Con			LOW N				4
Low Lab /Low Con	36	41	38	39	25	36	64
Labour voters							
High Con/Low Lab			LOW N				8
High Con/High Lab	29	33	19	29	17	31	42
High Lab/Low Con	23	46	26	31	27	15	26
Low Lab/Low Con	15	18	34	36	20	28	61

High exposure: 3–5 party election broadcasts seen.
Low exposure: 0–2 party election broadcasts seen.

when the same kind of analysis was undertaken among the politically less keen viewers.

These additional pieces of evidence do not explain the whole of the link between political viewing and the changing attitudes of the interested voters towards the major parties during the 1964 campaign.[39] They illustrate, nevertheless, the operation of two important forces within this group. One is a move towards consonance in political outlook which arises from its members' sensitivity to the issue content of a campaign. Unlike the less politically minded part of the electorate, highly motivated voters are capable of grasping the issues projected by the contending parties at election time and of adjusting their political attitudes accordingly.

The other factor at work in this group is a process whereby existing political attitudes are reinforced as a result of the campaign. It is as if some of the voters who were relatively keen to follow the election had bolstered their opinions of the worth of the parties they initially supported by aligning their views about the issues that mattered with the themes that their own parties were projecting on television. It was shown in the

[39] For example, the tendency of keen Labour supporters to become more tolerant of the Conservative Party after the campaign did not depend on the party direction of the broadcasts they had viewed. This particular shift was most noticeable, however, among those Labour voters who had initially recorded very high pro-Labour partisanship scores at the pre-campaign interview. It may be accounted for in part, therefore, by the fact that the design of our attitude scale made it easier for them to show a pro-Conservative shift than a pro-Labour change. It is curious, nevertheless, that this particular effect should have occurred in this strongly partisan group *only* among those who had been highly exposed to the campaign. The relevant details apply to the highly motivated Labour voters.

	Exposure *			
	High		Low	
	Pro-Con shift	No pro-Con shift	Pro-Con shift	No pro-Con shift
Strongly pro-Labour in September (−4 to −9)	30	22	5	18
Not so strongly pro-Labour (−3 to +9)	5	36	1	20

* High exposure: 4–13 party election broadcasts seen.
  Low exposure: 0–3 party election broadcasts seen.

previous chapter that the reinforcement seekers of both major parties were exceptionally responsive to the key issues of the 1964 campaign. In addition, it may be pointed out here that high and differential exposure to broadcasts transmitted by their own party characterized the television usage of the reinforcement seekers (especially the Conservatives among them) in the strongly motivated group.[40] It seems from all this that reinforcement in the political field is neither a comprehensive nor a near-universal consequence of exposure to mass communication. It occurs selectively among those who look for it or whose prior attitudes towards the content of a communication encourage a reinforcing result.

The responses to the campaign of the vote-guidance seekers

Of course a political party cannot hope to win many votes through such reinforcement effects, because they occur mainly among those electors whose party identifications are already rather firm. What about the so-called vote-guidance seekers – where the scope for attracting support is obviously greater? We have previously seen that they were little impressed by the issues which the major parties emphasized in 1964.[41] But how did their party attitudes respond to the election campaign of that year? There was no sign that this more open-minded body of electors had swung decisively towards either major party. The

[40] The distinctive exposure patterns of the highly motivated reinforcement seekers can be seen from the following figures:

		Reinforcement seekers intending to vote Conservative	Other Conservative supporters	Reinforcement seekers intending to vote Labour	Other Labour supporters
		%	%	%	%
Exposure to	High (3–5)	51	31	43	29
Conservative	Low (0–2)	49	69	57	71
broadcasts		—	—	—	—
		100	100	100	100
Exposure to	High (3–5)	24	24	57	41
Labour	Low (0–2)	76	76	43	59
broadcasts		—	—	—	—
		100	100	100	100
	N =	49	66	56	80

[41] See p. 180.

most characteristic feature of their political opinions was relative volatility. This is illustrated by the figures presented in Table 11.14, which compares the vote-guidance seekers with three other groups in the sample. The percentages refer to the individuals in each group whose party attitude scores (towards the Liberal, Conservative, and Labour Parties) did *not* change between the pre-campaign and post-campaign interviews. In each case the attitudes of the vote-guidance seekers proved substantially less stable than those of all the other electors.

Table 11.14. THE POLITICAL ATTITUDES OF THE
VOTE-GUIDANCE SEEKERS WERE LESS STABLE THAN
THOSE OF OTHER GROUPS

	Proportions whose party attitude scores did not change during the 1964 campaign among:			
	Vote-guidance seekers %	*Reinforcement seekers* %	*Mixed political motives* %	*Neither political motive* %
Liberal Party attitudes	12	22	16	24
Conservative Party attitudes	17	31	27	24
Labour Party attitudes	23	28	33	27
N =	109	174	85	380

Despite such volatility, however, attitude change in this group was unrelated to degree of campaign exposure. For example, of those vote-guidance seekers who had seen no Liberal broadcast, 55 per cent shifted after the campaign in a pro-Liberal direction, compared with the following percentages among those who had viewed one, two, and three Liberal programmes, respectively: 48 per cent, 67 per cent, 42 per cent.[42] Even though vote-guidance seekers are disposed to change their political opinions, then, and although they are also prepared to watch a large number of party broadcasts, they

[42] Similarly an analysis of partisanship shift showed that 34 per cent of those who saw relatively few party broadcasts (three or less) shifted in a pro-Conservative direction, compared with 32 per cent of the highly exposed (having viewed four or more party broadcasts).

appear to be resistant to deliberate persuasive efforts. They may be willing to reconsider their political positions, but they like to make up their minds for themselves.

Strength of motivation as a condition of communication effects

A prominent feature of the evidence presented in this chapter is the differential role of motivational level in mediating the impact of political communications upon party attitudes. Whereas opinions of the strongly motivated voters were influenced by major party propaganda, the politically less keen electors responded favourably to presentation of the Liberal case. Furthermore, these findings seemed genuinely to reflect the influence of motivation and not some other factor with which it was associated.[43] Clearly, strength of motivation is not related straightforwardly to persuasibility. Why, then, did motivational level act differently in the cases of Liberal shift and partisanship shift?

[43] In the case of Liberal shift, this was put to the test by seeing whether strength of motivation continued to function as a condition of communication effect when 1964 vote was held constant. (The expectation that this outcome might disappear arose from the association of Liberal shift with party allegiance.) By reading along the top row of the following table it can be seen that in each voting group exposure to Liberal broadcasts is clearly associated with a greater degree of pro-Liberal movement among those rated weak or medium in motivation. In contrast with this, the figures for the strongly motivated group show a reverse tendency in three of the four cases.

Proportions shifting in favour of the Liberal Party among:

	Labour voters		Conservative voters		Liberal voters		Abstainers	
	Ex-posed	Not Ex-posed	Ex-posed	Not Ex-posed	Ex-posed	Not Ex-posed	Ex-posed	Not Ex-posed*
	%	%	%	%	%	%	%	%
Medium and weak in motivation	59	33	39	30	79	57	55	48
Strongly motivated	45	41	39	42	50	67	38	75

* 'Exposed' refers to anyone who saw at least one Liberal broadcast; 'Not Exposed' to all those who saw none.

A similar reaffirmation of the independent action of motivation emerged when the association of occupation with partisanship shift was tested in the same way. It can be seen from the following table that exposure is more

FORTUNES OF THE POLITICAL PARTIES

The discovery that the most powerful television effects were experienced by the politically more indifferent electors was consistent with one of the hypotheses that influenced the design of this study. In a situation where much television viewing arises from habit, and where the political content of the medium is suddenly enlarged by the launching of an election campaign, the group most likely to undergo a substantial increase in exposure to political communications will consist of those individuals who would not normally seek out political programmes but who are unwilling to give up viewing television during an election. If our measure of motivation is accurate, almost the whole of this group should be found within the weakly motivated portion of the sample. It could be deduced, moreover, from our major quantitative hypothesis – that a greater degree of exposure will be reflected in a greater degree of attitude change – that the most substantial shifts overall should occur among those for whom the election campaign provides relatively the biggest increase in exposure above the level of political communication previously received. This captive, mildly tolerant, but rather passive audience relies differentially on television for its political impressions, since the positive effort required to seek out campaign materials from the press or elsewhere would be out of character in the case of individuals who have no burning desire for political enlightenment. Consequently, it was mainly television, and only marginally the press and the local campaign, which precipitated the major attitude change that affected the less motivated respondents.

It is not only their distinctive communications habits that explain the responses of the less keen electors to the 1964 campaign. Their prior orientation to politics may have played

influential with the strongly motivated respondents in both the non-manual and manual categories.

	Non-manual workers Exposure		Manual workers Exposure*	
	High	Low	High	Low
Medium and weak in motivation	35%	33%	35%	29%
Strongly motivated	35%	18%	39%	26%

* Viewing four party broadcasts or more counted as high exposure; three or less as low exposure.

a part as well. As a consequence of political indifference, they may have been less well-prepared to meet broadcast propaganda with counter-arguments of their own. This source of vulnerability could have been reinforced by the unpurposive political viewing in which they are probably inclined to indulge. As Bernard Berelson has pointed out, when exposure to a communication is accidental rather than deliberate, '. . . defenses against new ideas are presumably weaker because preconceptions are not so pervasively present.'[44] Recent research in the United States has underlined this interpretation by indicating that distracted exposure to a communication can enhance its persuasive force by stifling the *sub voce* framing of counter-arguments against its message.[45] Ironically, the successful penetration of our less interested respondents by televised propaganda may have been due in part to the relatively casual attention they paid when their sets were tuned in to party election broadcasts.

But why was the Liberal Party the sole beneficiary of these effects? It may have gained from its central position in what is essentially a two-party system. If major political loyalties are bi-polar, it is easier for adherents to the two foci of identification, in so far as their political outlook changes at all, to shift in favour of the middle and neutrally conceived party, than to look more favourably upon their traditional rivals. Social elements in the viewing situation could work in the same direction. A viewer in a Labour household who expressed appreciation of a Conservative broadcast might provoke ridicule that would be withheld if he voiced a similar degree of approval for a Liberal broadcast.

In addition, lukewarm feelings about the major parties among the politically indifferent electors may have facilitated their pro-Liberal responses. In other words, their receptivity to Liberal propaganda may have arisen from mistrust of the dominant forces in British politics, which they found embodied

[44] Berelson, Bernard, 'Communication and Public Opinion', in Schramm, Wilbur (Ed.), *The Process and Effects of Mass Communication*, University of Illinois Press, Urbana, Illinois, 1955, p. 352.

[45] Festinger, Leon, and Maccoby, Nathan, 'On resistance to persuasive communication', *Journal of Abnormal and Social Psychology*, Vol. LX, No. 4, 1964, pp. 359–66.

in the Conservative and Labour Parties. Some support for this interpretation is provided in Table 11.15. When pre-campaign vote intention is held constant, and the Labour and Conservative Party attitude scores of the less motivated respondents are compared with those of the strongly motivated electors, we find that in every case except one (Conservative supporters rating the Labour Party) the former are lower on the average than the latter.

Table 11.15. AT THE START OF THE CAMPAIGN THERE WAS A TENDENCY, WHICH WAS INDEPENDENT OF VOTE INTENTION, FOR THE STRONGLY MOTIVATED ELECTORS TO RATE BOTH MAJOR PARTIES MORE FAVOURABLY THAN DID THOSE WHOSE MOTIVATION WAS WEAKER

	Vote intention			
	Labour	Conservative	Liberal	All other
Mean Labour Party attitude scores of those rated:				
Strong in motivation	+ 3·76	− 0·77	+ 1·10	+ 1·94
Medium and weak in motivation	+ 3·56	− 0·74	− 0·21	+ 0·95
Mean Conservative Party attitude scores of those rated:				
Strong in motivation	− 0·18	+ 3·88	+ 1·95	+ 1·77
Medium and weak in motivation	− 0·52	+ 3·50	+ 0·83	+ 0·66

It may also be important that between election campaigns the Liberal Party receives less coverage in the mass media (including television) than it does at election time. It follows that in the inter-election period the average citizen, who is not actively seeking political information but taking it as it comes, will find the Liberal Party getting more remote from his thoughts. He will become less aware of its political stance, and his attitudes towards it will become more fluid and in a sense more out of touch. If so, it is understandable that such an elector should be strongly affected when he receives a con- siderably stepped-up dosage of exposure to the ideas and

FORTUNES OF THE POLITICAL PARTIES

leaders of the Liberal Party. This happens particularly on television, which, unlike the press, is obliged to devote a definite proportion of its attention to the Liberals during an election campaign.

Some factual evidence in support of this interpretation can be introduced by the figures presented in Table 11.16. At the pre-election stage, those who were measured as weak or moderate in motivation had lower Liberal Party attitudes scores, on the average, than did those who were rated strong in motivation. The table shows that the difference was largely independent of party identification. The attitudes of Conservative supporters to the Liberal Party did not vary according to motivation, but otherwise the difference was consistent, and overall there was a gap of a quarter of a point, on the average, between the two motivation groups. This pattern closely parallels the previously shown motivational difference in voters' ratings of the major parties.

Table 11.16. AT THE START OF THE CAMPAIGN THERE WAS A TENDENCY, WHICH WAS INDEPENDENT OF VOTE INTENTION, FOR THE STRONGLY MOTIVATED ELECTORS TO RATE THE LIBERAL PARTY MORE FAVOURABLY THAN DID THOSE WHOSE MOTIVATION WAS WEAKER

	Vote intention				
	Labour	Conservative	Liberal	all other	All groups
Mean Liberal Party attitude scores of those rated:					
Strong in motivation	+ 0·24	+ 0·30	+ 2·95	+ 0·91	+ 0·52
Medium and weak in motivation	+ 0·03	+ 0·29	+ 2·28	− 0·07	+ 0·25

During the campaign, however, the gap in ratings of the Liberal Party closed. The average Liberal Party attitude score of the strongly motivated group as a whole moved up by 0·27 of a point to 0·79, while that of the less motivated group moved up by 0·56 to 0·81. The effect of the campaign in this case was to bring the less strongly motivated electors into line with the rest of the sample. It should be noted that no such movement affected attitudes towards the major parties.[46] It seems that the campaign–partly because the Liberals were thrust suddenly into the limelight, and partly because the group we are considering found itself watching them on television whether it wanted to or not–gave these viewers a chance to assess the third party afresh and to bring their attitudes up to date.

No part of this structure of interpretation is undermined by the discovery of a connection between exposure to the campaign and partisanship shift in the strongly motivated group of electors. That link was forged with the help of elements which are likely to prove influential only among politically keen voters. It involved an adjustment of party attitudes to the issue content of the 1964 campaign–which presupposes a capacity to grasp and to respond to arguments mounted in such terms. In addition, some of the developments in this group may be interpreted most suitably as reinforcement effects, which tend again to be sought and experienced mainly by those individuals whose political opinions are already rather firm and definite. Change in response to exposure was less pronounced in this group than among the more indifferent electors, because their own political views could be brought into play more readily whenever campaign materials were being received. And perhaps they were impressed less by Liberal propaganda than by the efforts of the Conservative and Labour Parties, because they tend to perceive campaigning itself as an activity

[46] The average Conservative and Labour Party attitude scores recorded at both stages of the campaign by the strongly motivated respondents and those rated weak and medium in motivation are given below:

	Strongly motivated	Medium and weak in motivation
Mean Conservative Party attitude score		
Pre-campaign	+ 1·38	+ 1·01
Post-campaign	+ 1·40	+ 0·61
Mean Labour Party attitude score		
Pre-campaign	+ 1·68	+ 1·53
Post-campaign	+ 2·15	+ 2·01

FORTUNES OF THE POLITICAL PARTIES

in which the major parties expose their differences in terms
of defined issues.[47]

[47] It may be asked whether any of the currents of opinion reported in this
chapter could have been influenced by the fact that our post-campaign
measures of political attitudes were drawn from interviews conducted after
Polling Day. There are two main types of 'halo effect' which could have
arisen from the informants' awareness of the election result itself. One is that
a marginal group of waverers had claimed falsely to vote for the winning
party. The plausibility of this thesis is considerably diminished, however,
by the finding that in our sample the Liberal Party, not Labour, was the
net beneficiary of campaign vote change. The other possibility is that the
winning of an election enhances the prestige of the victorious party, helping
thereby to improve public attitudes towards it. Although such a factor
cannot be entirely ruled out as an explanation of the overall pro-Labour
movement of attitudes in the sample, its plausibility is reduced by the
unevenness of the shift and in particular by the virtually complete failure
of the Conservative members of the sample to share in it.

In any case it would be difficult to ascribe the two main communications
effects discussed in this chapter to the influence of a 'halo'. There is no
logical connection between the election result and the responsiveness of the
less politically minded members of our sample to Liberal propaganda on
TV. And, in the more strongly motivated group, attitudes towards the
major parties appear to have developed, not in response to the election
result, but to issue themes which had been projected by the Labour and
Conservative Parties *during* the campaign.

CHAPTER 12

THE IMAGES OF THE PARTY
LEADERS

The disputed sources of leader images[1]

Political television itself has an image. It is frequently said that its major function is to project to the electorate some impression (either genuine or fabricated) of those qualities which well-known politicians apply to their tasks of government, party management, and the leadership of public opinion. What this common belief ignores is the role of party allegiance in shaping voters' views about political leaders. Such assessments

[1] Although much confusion surrounds the use in politics of the term 'image', we have found it convenient to refer in this chapter to 'leader images' when presenting evidence about the qualities electors ascribe to outstanding politicians. Much of the current popularity of the term derives from its use in advertising and market research, and John Downing has recently noted that the expression 'brand image' is falsely associated for many people with certain manipulative advertising techniques. (Cf. Downing, John, 'What is a Brand Image?', *The Advertising Quarterly*, No. 2, Winter 1964–5, pp. 13–19.) Downing supplies a definition of the brand image, however, which, with an appropriate substitution of terms, could represent the concept as we have tried to use it here: 'a constellation of feelings, ideas and beliefs associated with a brand by its users and non-users mainly as a result of experience of its advertising and performance.' Despite possible misinterpretations, the term serves a useful purpose by drawing attention to the facts (*a*) that political attitudes are structured and inter-related, and (*b*) that they derive from diverse sources, both near-to-hand and more remote, of information, discussion, and propaganda. No other expression refers so succinctly to these features of political attitudes. There is no necessary connection with manipulative techniques of persuasion, and we would stress that a leader's image has no independent existence of its own. Its empirical basis lies entirely in the recorded expressions of attitude and opinion of electors.

do not float so freely on the shifting seas of public opinion that they can be altered dramatically by a single impressive or disastrous appearance on television. Popular attitudes towards political personalities are anchored with at least some degree of firmness in prior party loyalities.

Nevertheless, many features of this relationship are still imperfectly understood. How deeply rooted in political partisanship are the sources of leader images? Can such perceptions ever be prised loose from the bonds of party affiliation? Are all judgements of leaders' traits—whatever the quality in question—affected equally by party support, or do partisan leanings determine some rather than others? Turning to an election situation, in which efforts are made to *change* voters' attitudes, can the performance of a politician during a campaign substantially improve (or undermine) his own reputation? If so, which dimensions of judgement about him tend to change most readily? Do most of the resulting changes merely reflect altered opinions about the suitability of his party? Or can exposure to material about a politician in the mass media affect his public image independently of attitudes to the party he represents? In that case how powerful is the influence of television?

These questions are connected in turn with certain fundamental and unresolved issues of political psychology. There are two main schools of thought about the sources of popular impressions of political leaders. In gist, one opinion maintains that leader images are 'perceiver determined', while another insists that they are 'stimulus determined'. The first of these positions arises from an assumption that the attitudes of most people are affected by a 'strain to consistency'. Many social psychologists consider that individuals experience a need to keep the various beliefs which matter to them in a state of consistent balance with each other.[2] If one such belief seems to

[2] The literature of this theory is extensive, but the leading writings in which it has been developed are as follows:

Heider, Fritz, 'Attitudes and Cognitive Organization', *The Journal of Psychology*, Vol. XXI, First Half, 1946, pp. 107–12.

Newcomb, Theodore M., 'An Approach to the Study of Communicative Acts', *Psychological Review*, Vol. LX, No. 6, 1953, pp. 393–404.

Osgood, Charles E., and Tannenbaum, Percy H., 'The Principle of

conflict with another, discomfort will ensue, which the affected individual will feel impelled to resolve. When applied to political opinions, this doctrine implies that the function of perception is to avoid stress. Consequently, the supporters of one party will tend to rate its leader well above that of the rival party. They 'will see in a preferred candidate what they wish to see–even if it is unrelated to objective reality.'[3] Their impressions of politicians will be perceiver-determined.

A rival point of view has been called the image thesis. This states that voters' impressions of a leader depend not so much on their other political preferences as on his speeches, actions, coverage in the mass media, etc. These convey an image to the electorate of what the leader is like, which will be subscribed to until other similarly derived impressions override or alter it. That image is stimulus-determined.

So far neither theory has received overwhelming support from the available survey evidence. For example, during the American presidential election of 1960, Joseph and Marion McGrath asked 80 Young Democrats and 39 Young Republicans to rate John Kennedy and Richard Nixon along 50 pairs of attributes (dynamic/relaxed, light/heavy, intellectual/practical, etc.). They found that on 29 of these combinations the two party groups agreed in assigning Kennedy towards one and Nixon towards the other end of the opposed pairs. They concluded from this that 'perceptions of political figures are stimulus-determined rather than perceiver-determined for a large number of attributes.'[4] This interpretation was sub-

Congruity in the Prediction of Attitude Change', *Psychological Review*, Vol. LXII, No. 6, 1955, pp. 42–55.

Festinger, L., *A Theory of Cognitive Dissonance*, Row, Peterson, Evanston, Illinois, 1957.

Zajonc, Robert B., 'Balance, Congruity, and Dissonance', *Public Opinion Quarterly*, Vol. XXIV, No. 2, 1960, pp. 280–96.

A cogent critique of the theory may be found in Chapanis, Natalia P., and Chapanis, Alphonse, 'Cognitive Dissonance: Five Years Later', *Psychological Bulletin*, Vol. LXI, No. 1, 1964, pp. 1–22.

[3] Sigel, Roberta S., 'Effect of Partisanship on the Perception of Political Candidates', *Public Opinion Quarterly*, Vol. XXVIII, No. 3, 1964, pp. 488–96.

[4] McGrath, Joseph E. and McGrath, Marion F., 'Effects of Partisanship on Perceptions of Political Figures', *Public Opinion Quarterly*, Vol. XXVI, No. 2, 1962, pp. 236–48.

sequently challenged by Roberta S. Sigel, who argued that the attributes studied 'were not likely to produce stress, which would be produced only in politically relevant areas'. It was not difficult for a Republican to agree with a Democrat that Kennedy, say, was 'light' and that Nixon was 'heavy'. She then presented evidence (collected during the same campaign from 1,350 Detroit voters) which showed that Democrats were more likely than Republicans to assign traits to Kennedy which corresponded to their own image of an ideal President–and *vice-versa* in rating Nixon. She concluded that '. . . perception is stimulus-determined when perceivers look at a candidate's personality, appearance, objectively verifiable circumstances, etc., but it is perceiver-determined when respondents view the candidate's political traits.'[5] In other words, Miss Sigel distinguished between the political and personal components of a leader's reputation, and she maintained that while the former was determined largely by party feeling, the latter was open to influences from the mass media and elsewhere.

However, neither of these studies had a dynamic element which comes from interviewing the members of a panel on two or more occasions over a period of time. In a strict sense, therefore, they failed to investigate the actual responses of leader images to a definite *stimulus*–such as an election campaign undoubtedly provides.[6] Our own study of the British General Election of 1964 does not suffer from this limitation, but before considering the light it can shed on the stimulus thesis, a variant of the approaches outlined above should be noted. After examining the results of many studies of the Kennedy–Nixon debates of 1960, Elihu Katz and Jacob Feldman recommended

[5] Sigel, Roberta S., op. cit.

[6] A more recent Australian enquiry used such a panel design, but its findings proved rather inconclusive. An audience of approximately 250 electors was invited to watch a televised address by Sir Robert Menzies (then Prime Minister and Leader of the Liberal Party), which was delivered in the early stages of the 1963 Federal election campaign. In the short run opinion change seemed to be perceiver-determined, for, immediately after the screening of his speech, ratings of Mr. Menzies tended to develop favourably among Liberal supporters and unfavourably among Labour voters. Over the longer period of the campaign as a whole, however, there was little net attitude change in either party group. Cf. Hughes, Colin A. and Western, John S., *The Prime Minister's Policy Speech: A Case Study in Televised Politics*, Australian National University Press, Canberra, 1966.

THE IMAGES OF THE PARTY LEADERS

that future political research should consider 'in general whether images can change independently of voting intentions'. If they can, they went on to ask, 'How do people isolate one from the other . . .?' This introduced, they said, 'the whole area of cognitive balance, which is so much in the forefront of current socio-psychological research.' If a Nixon supporter considers that Kennedy has some of the qualities of an ideal President, how does he cope with such a contradiction?[7] The framing of these questions suggests that Katz and Feldman were unwilling to treat the theories of perceiver- and stimulus-determination as mutually exclusive alternatives. Although their preoccupations arose from the doctrine of perceptual balance, they seemed to recognize at the same time that leader images at odds with party loyalties could emanate from stimulus sources. At that point, they implied, certain (unspecified) mechanisms might help the voter under stress to achieve a balanced political outlook without jeopardizing his party loyalties.

Bearing these issues in mind, let us now consider how the electors of West Leeds and Pudsey regarded the leaders of the Conservative, Labour, and Liberal Parties before and after the General Election of 1964, and whether their impressions were influenced in any way by exposure to the campaign in the mass media.

Campaign developments in leader images

At both the pre-campaign and the post-election interviews the members of our sample were asked to rate Sir Alec Douglas-Home, Harold Wilson and Jo Grimond for their possession of 12 different qualities. These impressions were elicited by means of the so-called semantic differential—an instrument for measuring attitudes which was developed in the United States by Osgood, Suci, and Tannenbaum.[8] This device converted each of the dozen qualities into a pair of opposed adjectives (strong/weak, sincere/insincere, etc.), between which seven spaces,

[7] Katz, Elihu, and Feldman, Jacob, Ch. 11 of Kraus, Sidney, op. cit., pp. 214–15.

[8] Osgood, Charles E., Suci, George J., and Tannenbaum, Percy H., *The Measurement of Meaning*, University of Illinois Press, Urbana, Illinois, 1957.

228

standing for different shades of judgement, were placed. An impression of the layout of the scales can be formed from the figure below. If an informant thought that Mr. Wilson, say, was 'very strong', he was instructed to tick the space nearest the word 'strong', and if 'very weak', the space at the opposite end of the scale. Other gradations allowed for included 'fairly strong' (or weak), 'slightly strong' (or weak) and neither strong nor weak. In the analysis itself scores were then allotted to these ratings—ranging from + 3 for the most favourable to − 3 for the most critical judgements.

Figure 12.1. SPECIMEN OF A SEMANTIC DIFFERENTIAL
LEADER-RATING SCALE
HAROLD WILSON

Weak — — — — — — —	Strong
Likeable — — — — — — —	Disagreeable
Inspiring leader — — — — — — —	Uninspiring leader

The semantic differential has many advantages: ease of administration; proven reliability; sensitivity to relatively slight shifts of opinion; and confirmation of its utility in several American election surveys.[9] The convenience of the semantic differential is not an unmixed blessing, however, for a respondent may be tempted to rate something about which he really has no opinion at all. But many of the participants in our survey were apparently willing to reveal their unfamiliarity with a leader by consistently ticking the centre (neutral) space for all 12 qualities. In September 1964, for example, a quarter of the sample members signified their complete ignorance of Jo Grimond's personality in this way.[10]

How did the party leaders stand with the voters of West Leeds and Pudsey a month before Polling Day in 1964, and how were they affected by the subsequent campaign? The evidence for the sample as a whole (disregarding differences of

[9] Ibid., Ch. 3, and Kraus, Sidney, op. cit., Chs. 15 and 16.
[10] One hundred and eighty three of the 748 participants in our survey applied such a ticking pattern to the page of the questionnaire on which they were asked to rate the Liberal leader. In contrast, only five per cent of the sample responded similarly to the Labour and Conservative leaders (40 informants having no definite opinions about Harold Wilson and 38 about Sir Alec Douglas-Home).

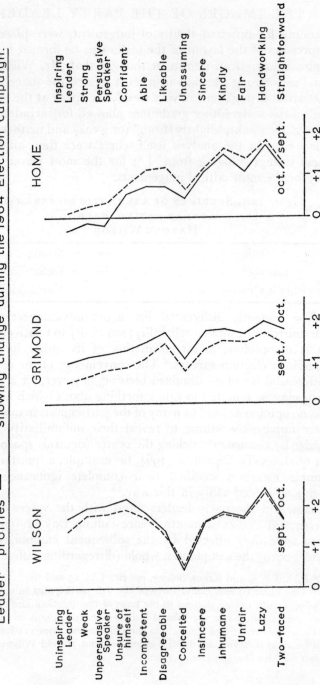

Figure 12.2

Leader profiles — showing change during the 1964 Election campaign.

party allegiance) is summarized here in two different forms—
in Figure 12.2 and Table 12.1, respectively. The figure presents
the pre-campaign and post-election ratings of Sir Alec, Mr.
Wilson and Mr. Grimond as leader-profiles across each of the
12 attributes for which they were judged. The table provides
a numerical expression of campaign change—using averages to
represent the degree of shift in public attitudes which affected
the ratings of each leader on each quality.

Table 12.1. MEAN SHIFTS IN RATINGS OF THE PARTY LEADERS
DURING THE 1964 CAMPAIGN (BASED ON SCORING RANGE OF
+ 3 TO − 3)

Qualities*	Sir Alec Douglas-Home	Harold Wilson	Jo Grimond
Inspiring	− ·47	+ ·36	+ ·44
Strong	− ·36	+ ·21	+ ·44
Persuasive	− ·55	+ ·20	+ ·37
Confident	− ·21	+ ·24	+ ·41
Able	− ·40	+ ·10	+ ·34
Likeable	− ·45	+ ·09	+ ·25
Unassuming	− ·21	− ·10	+ ·31
Sincere	− ·14	·00	+ ·39
Kindly	− ·15	+ ·04	+ ·27
Fair	− ·26	+ ·03	+ ·18
Hardworking	− ·12	+ ·08	+ ·24
Straightforward	− ·09	·00	+ ·30

* In this and all subsequent tables only the positive meaning of the qualities for which the leaders were rated is given.

Diverse findings can be extracted from this material. It
reveals a tendency for the electorate to treat party leaders as if
they shared certain occupational characteristics, *qua* politicians,
in common. It points to some distinctive features of public
feeling about the leader of the third party. It shows that there
was a substantial gulf in a particular area of judgement between the charted images of the two major party leaders. And
it locates a cluster of scales on which a considerable part of
campaign-induced change was concentrated.

There are two signs in the leader profiles that voters may
regard top politicians as members of a single occupational
species. One is the fact that Sir Alec, Mr. Wilson, and Mr.

Grimond were uniformly rated as highly industrious. Each was judged more favourably at both interviews for being 'hard-working' than for any other quality on the list.[11] Another less marked indication of a consensus was the sample's tendency *not* to expect a successful politician to be modest in the proclamation of his own virtues! Mr. Wilson's average score for being 'unassuming' was much lower than for any other trait, and both Sir Alec and Mr. Grimond received their fourth lowest ratings on this scale.[12] It seemed, nevertheless, to locate a particular weakness in the Labour leader's otherwise quite impressive public image. Of the 12 qualities on the list, Mr. Wilson's overall standing declined after the campaign only on the unassuming/conceited scale. Even Labour voters acknowledged his weakness in this respect. Whereas at both interviews the consistent Labour supporters accorded their leader very high average scores for every other attribute on the list (between + 2 and the maximum of + 3), they bumped him sharply down for conceit to an average of + 1·45 in September and + 1·58 in October.[13]

The profiles also enable us to compare the popularity of the three leaders at both stages of the campaign. It can be seen that in September Mr. Wilson was already a clear favourite with the voters of West Leeds and Pudsey, and that Mr. Grimond came second.[14] After the campaign Jo Grimond sub-

[11] Such a consensus should not be dismissed as insignificant, since industriousness was chosen more often than any other trait on the list, except straightforwardness, when the respondents were asked to rank the same qualities for their importance if a politician was to help to run the country well.

[12] A similar tendency affected ratings of Sir Robert Menzies in the 1963 Australian study. Sir Robert was credited less often as being 'modest' than for having any of nine other favourable qualities for which he was rated. And he was regarded more often as 'arrogant' and 'pompous' than for having any of eight other unfavourable characteristics. Cf. Hughes, Colin A., and Western, John S., op. cit., p. 25.

[13] This was probably the least damaging weakness of which Mr. Wilson could be accused, however, for the sample regarded modesty as less important for running the country well than any other quality on the list.

[14] The pre-campaign superiority of Harold Wilson over Sir Alec was not due merely to the preponderance of Labour voters in the sample. It also arose from the extra measure of confidence which Labour supporters had in certain qualities of their leader—in contrast to the Conservatives' somewhat weaker feelings for Sir Alec. Undecided voters were also tending to lean towards Mr. Wilson at that time.

stantially improved his standing with the whole sample, making gains on all the qualities for which he was rated. Sir Alec, on the other hand, lost ground on all the scales. And, despite his relatively favourable image at the pre-campaign stage, Harold Wilson had managed by the end of the campaign to improve his public reputation yet further.

Certain features of Mr. Grimond's image should be noted. At the outset of the campaign he stood between the Labour and Conservative leaders on all the scales—except those which represented modesty and likeability, where his reputation was marginally superior to that of both his rivals. After the campaign, however, Mr. Grimond not only widened the gap between himself and the other leaders on the likeable/disagreeable scale; he also shot ahead of them when rated for sincerity and straightforwardness. This result is open to two interpretations. It could represent a tribute to the directness and frankness of Mr. Grimond's handling of the issues of the 1964 election. But it might also reflect the voters' sensitivity in an electioneering situation to the manipulative intentions of major party propaganda, and an associated feeling that, by comparison, the contributions to the campaign of the third party and its leader were more disinterested.

In terms of leader attitudes, perhaps the most important outcome of the 1964 campaign emerges when we consider where the greatest amount of net change occurred. Sir Alec lost the most ground (in order of magnitude) on the following scales: persuasive speaker/unpersuasive speaker, inspiring leader/uninspiring leader, likeable/disagreeable, able/incompetent, and strong/weak. Mr. Wilson's image improved most for the attributes of inspiration, confidence, strength and persuasiveness. Mr. Grimond's greatest gains were achieved on the scales which stood for strength, being inspiring, and for confidence, sincerity and persuasiveness. Persuasiveness, strength, and inspiration appear on all three lists and confidence on two. Although some substantial shifts of opinion took place outside this area, a very large part of the net change in the images of the party leaders during the General Election of 1964 arose from reassessments of their firmness, strength, and external effectiveness.

According to our evidence, this development had deep roots which extended into the very structure of public attitudes towards political leaders. It certainly reflected the electorate's awareness of a marked difference between the personalities of Sir Alec and Mr. Wilson even before the 1964 campaign was launched. This is illustrated by Table 12.2, which shows in the sample as a whole how far the ratings of Mr. Wilson were superior to those of Sir Alec on each quality, and how these differences were affected by the campaign. In September our respondents gave the Labour leader a decisive edge over Sir Alec only when considering the traits of strength, persuasiveness, inspiration, and confidence. And although after Polling Day the gap between the two contenders widened on all the scales to some extent, it yawned most visibly for ratings of persuasiveness and inspiring leadership.

Table 12.2. MEAN DIFFERENCES BETWEEN THE RATINGS OF
HAROLD WILSON AND SIR ALEC DOUGLAS-HOME BEFORE
AND AFTER THE 1964 CAMPAIGN

	Superiority of Wilson's rating over Home		
	Before the campaign	In campaign shift	After the campaign
Inspiring	1·2	·8	2·0
Strong	1·5	·6	2·1
Persuasive	1·4	·8	2·2
Confident	1·1	·5	1·6
Able	·6	·5	1·1
Likeable	·1	·5	·6
Unassuming	−·1	·1	·0
Sincere	·3	·2	·5
Kind	·1	·2	·3
Fair	·3	·2	·5
Hardworking	·4	·2	·6
Straightforward	·4	·1	·5

On the face of it each of the key scales where the greatest amount of campaign change occurred stood for some facet of a politician's forcefulness. But we have not yet demonstrated that the respondents themselves interpreted these qualities in this light. In order to pursue this question the structure of popular attitudes towards the party leaders was examined empirically by means of a component analysis. The results of such an analysis help to disclose the patterns by which judgements of one kind accompany judgements of another kind. Table 12.3 presents a list of factor loadings for the first three components that emerged from an analysis of the whole sample's ratings of each leader at the pre-campaign stage.

Factor loadings may range between $+1$ and -1, and it can be seen that those which are set out under the first component are uniformly high, with some reaching levels above ·80 and none falling below ·50. This means that the electors' ratings of each leader were based, first of all, on a tendency for a favourable judgement on one scale to go with positive opinions on most of the other scales (and *vice-versa* for unfavourable judgements). This suggests that the respondents reacted initially to a party leader as if they were simply 'for' him or 'against' him, and that, if they were 'for' him, they tended to rate him highly on all the scales they were asked to use. About a half of the variability in their assessments of the leaders could be accounted for by this general evaluative factor, and the qualities which seemed most representative of it were straightforwardness and fairness.[15]

The second component in the table locates a pattern of judgement which is next in importance when the differences due to the first factor are set aside. It can be seen that the cluster of scales which had attracted the greatest amount of campaign change also figured prominently in this component. Its loadings tend to contrast high negative values for persuasiveness, strength, confidence, and inspiration with high positive values for such qualities as kindliness, straightforwardness, and fairness. By and large, an identical pattern shaped each leader's second component (except that in the case of Mr. Wilson industriousness was substituted for inspiration). This hints at the presence of a way of perceiving politics itself—as a world in which those leaders who are strong are usually not very amiable, and those

---

[15] This initial lack of discrimination between scales was not just a reflection of party allegiance. We excluded the possible influence of party preference by carrying out separate component analyses on the ratings of Harold Wilson that were made by those who intended to vote for the Labour, Conservative, and Liberal Parties respectively, and by those who supported no party. The same pattern of uniformly high loadings on the first factor persisted in each case (although a few scattered loadings fell to between ·39 and ·50).

Table 12.3. FACTOR LOADINGS OF PRE-CAMPAIGN PARTY LEADER RATINGS

	I General evaluative factor			II Strength, or malevolent dynamism, factor			III Activity factor		
	Home	Wilson	Grimond	Home	Wilson	Grimond	Home	Wilson	Grimond
Inspiring	+·73	+·76	+·60	-·36	+·03	-·60	+·21	-·20	-·02
Strong	+·73	+·70	+·65	-·48	-·49	-·55	+·11	-·19	+·11
Persuasive	+·70	+·69	+·66	-·41	-·27	-·52	+·23	-·16	+·03
Confident	+·61	+·58	+·61	-·39	-·53	-·38	+·22	-·16	+·08
Able	+·78	+·79	+·78	-·09	-·12	-·13	+·12	-·05	-·13
Likeable	+·79	+·77	+·81	+·08	+·31	+·18	+·01	-·10	-·06
Unassuming	+·61	+·57	+·50	+·19	+·49	+·32	+·56	-·33	+·77
Sincere	+·73	+·80	+·70	+·14	+·07	+·12	+·35	-·11	+·11
Kindly	+·70	+·73	+·77	+·47	+·25	+·42	+·18	+·36	-·08
Fair	+·79	+·81	+·82	+·29	+·16	+·28	-·01	+·13	-·11
Hardworking	+·70	+·64	+·78	+·32	+·31	+·31	-·32	+·58	+·29
Straightforward	+·82	+·78	+·81	+·19	+·27	+·25	-·05	+·17	-·07

236

who try to be nice tend to be weak. It is as if the electors are implying that in politics being dynamic and being decent are mutually exclusive.[16] This contrast is reminiscent of a finding from an American study of the presidential election of 1952, in which it was reported that the members of a sample had rated a number of politicians along a dimension of 'malevolent dynamism . . . vs. benevolent insipidness'.[17] The emergence of this component in our results also confirms that the group of strength scales, which Table 12.2 showed to have sharply discriminated electoral reactions to Sir Alec from reactions to Mr. Wilson, and which tapped the biggest campaign swings, did indeed represent different facets of the same core of meaning to our respondents.

(The pattern of loadings under the third component is more difficult to interpret, but it seems to include a consistent tendency for high loadings of one sign on the unassuming/conceited scale to be opposed to high loadings of the reverse sign on the hardworking/lazy scale. This factor may stand for ratings of politicians for their activity. If so, such an outcome would be consistent with the results of many other uses of the semantic differential scale.)[18]

[16] When separate component analyses were carried out on the ratings of Wilson made by the supporters of different parties, this strength factor seemed to emerge slightly more prominently in the results for the would-be Conservative and Liberal voters than it had for the whole sample. This is shown by the following list of loadings on the most important scales in the Labour Leader's second component:

Second factor loadings of pre-campaign ratings of Wilson (whole sample and by party)

	Whole sample	Conservative supporters	Liberal supporters	Labour supporters
Strong	− ·49	− ·64	− ·55	− ·36
Persuasive	− ·27	− ·40	− ·38	− ·32
Confident	− ·53	− ·52	− ·50	− ·39
Hardworking	− ·31	− ·31	− ·27	− ·10
Likeable	+ ·31	+ ·30	+ ·39	+ ·30
Unassuming	+ ·49	+ ·47	+ ·61	+ ·58
Kindly	+ ·25	+ ·33	+ ·17	+ ·39
Fair	+ ·16	+ ·18	+ ·38	+ ·15
Straightforward	+ ·27	+ ·35	+ ·45	+ ·22

[17] Osgood, Charles E., Suci, George J., and Tannenbaum, Percy H., op. cit., pp. 121–22.

[18] Typically, the factor structure of judgements made by diverse samples of a wide range of concepts has consisted of Evaluation, Potency (or

THE IMAGES OF THE PARTY LEADERS

Many of these findings point, then, to one conclusion: the election campaign of 1964 provoked reassessments of the *strength* of the rival party leaders. Although some previous election studies have hinted at the influence of such a tendency,[19] this is possibly the first occasion on which it has virtually dominated the results of a large-scale survey of public attitudes towards party leaders. There is, however, one attempt in the relevant literature to interpret its emergence. This can be found in an account by Richard F. Carter of the responses of a small panel (60 Democrats and 60 Republicans) to the televised appearances of Messrs. Kennedy and Nixon in their famous debates of 1960. Carter noted that, out of eight qualities:

> The only major changes were on characteristics of *industrious* and *experienced* (Kennedy) and *tough* (both candidates). The debates are not found to have produced substantial changes on such characteristics as *hardworking, honest, sincere, intelligent,* and *imaginative*. It seems almost as if the audience searched for characteristics of strong leadership in the candidates, or perhaps, the candidates may have emphasized these characteristics as they sought to build acceptable images.[20]

Yet another, and in our view a more likely, explanation is that voters tend to perceive a campaign as presenting a challenge

Strength), and Activity components. See Osgood, Charles E., Suci, George J., and Tannenbaum, Percy H., op. cit., and Osgood, Charles E., 'An Exploration into Semantic Space', Ch. 2 in Schramm, Wilbur (Ed.), *The Science of Human Communication*, Basic Books, New York, 1963. The persistence of the factor structure of our sample's leader ratings through time was tested by carrying out a component analysis of shift scores based on differences in the whole sample's ratings of the three leaders between September and October. It was found that changing attitudes towards the party leaders reflected the same patterns that had already been implicit in the pre-campaign assessments.

[19] Cf. McGrath, Joseph E. and McGrath, Marion, op. cit., who stated, when describing what they regarded as the stimulus-determined characteristics of the Presidential candidates of 1960, that:

> Kennedy is seen by members of both parties as more ambitious, aggressive, striving, active, dynamic, rebellious, etc. Nixon, in contrast, is seen by members of both parties as less ambitious, more easygoing, contented, passive, relaxed, conforming, etc.

[20] Carter, Richard F., 'Some Effects of the Debates'. Ch. 14 in Kraus, Sidney, op. cit., p. 258.

to a leader to show his mettle. If he is believed to be performing well, he will be upgraded for qualities of strength, confidence, and persuasiveness. If he is considered to be responding inadequately, his standing on those traits will suffer accordingly. Since a typical campaign rarely poses any *moral* tests of a leader's worth, ratings of politicians for such qualities as fairness and straightforwardness are less likely to be affected. Jo Grimond's profile improved 'all across the board' in 1964, partly because some voters first made up their minds about him at that time, and partly in response to the pro-Liberal swing of opinion which swept the sample during the campaign. But otherwise the net effect of the 1964 election was to depress Sir Alec's – and to enhance Mr. Wilson's – public reputation for strength.

Leaders and parties

What happens when party differences are deployed in the analysis? Do they affect these trends in any way? We were able to examine this question from two main angles. First, we studied the *interaction* of campaign developments in leader images and party attitudes – seeing, for example, how far an altered view of Sir Alec Douglas-Home tended to accompany a revised opinion of the Conservative Party. Second, we considered whether shifts in leader ratings depended at all on electors' *party allegiances*.

The first line of enquiry showed that altered impressions of a political leader usually marched in close conjunction with changed attitudes towards the suitability of his party. It was impossible to sort out relations of cause and effect in this association. Nevertheless, we found variations in the strength of the tie between party attitude shift and leader attitude shift when different pairs of rated objects were considered (Wilson/ Labour Party, Home/Conservative Party, and Grimond/Liberal Party). This suggested that there might be an area of some leeway in which leader images could change independently of party attitudes. Consequently, it was an object of a further investigation to establish whether (within that area where party attitudes were inoperative) our respondents' impressions of the three leaders had been influenced by their exposure to the mass media during the campaign.

THE IMAGES OF THE PARTY LEADERS

A statistical interpretation of the association between changing attitudes towards each leader and evaluations of his party is provided in Table 12.4. It lists the F-ratio values that were obtained when the correlations between leader attitude shifts and corresponding party attitude shifts (which were derived from simple regression analyses) were tested for their significance.

Table 12.4. F-RATIO VALUES FOR SIMPLE REGRESSIONS OF PARTY ATTITUDE SHIFTS ON LEADER ATTITUDE SHIFTS

	Attitudes towards:		
Respondents rated:	The Labour Party and Wilson	The Conservative Party and Home	The Liberal Party and Grimond
Strong in motivation to follow the campaign			
Strength	27·86***	5·55*	5·90*
Ability	13·42***	7·39**	10·51**
Likeability	18·31***	15·70***	7·30**
Fairness	5·32*	5·08*	0·11^{NS}
Medium and weak in motivation			
Strength	23·35***	13·13***	26·82***
Ability	22·89***	2·12^{NS}	14·22***
Likeability	16·23***	3·96*	3·58^{NS}
Fairness	17·70***	4·31*	6·82**

*   P = significant at ·05 level.   ** P = significant at ·01 level.
*** P = significant at ·001 level.   NS = not significant.

The form of the table is governed by the fact that the calculations were carried out by the Leeds University computer, to which the data were submitted separately for the two main strength-of-motivation groups into which the sample had been divided for other purposes. Economy required a reduction in the number of semantic differential scales to be used in the analysis. The results of our component analysis had shown that four scales shared a common meaning: persuasive speaker/unpersuasive speaker, inspiring leader/uninspiring leader, strong/weak, and confident/unsure of himself. This justified a decision to combine movement on these scales into one average score, which stood for changes in electors' perceptions of a leader's strength. In addition, shift scores for altered ratings of

THE IMAGES OF THE PARTY LEADERS

the ability, likeability, and fairness of the leaders were incorporated into the analysis.

It can be seen that of the 24 tested associations between party attitude shift and leader attitude shift, only three were not statistically significant, six were significant at the five per cent level, four at the one per cent level, and as many as 11 at the ·1 per cent level. The table also suggests that judgements about a leader's party were linked more closely to impressions of his strength than to any other facet of his image. In four out of the six sets of figures, the F-ratio value was higher for the relationship between party attitude shift and shift in a leader's rating for strength than for any other tested leader scale—and this was the only association that invariably proved significant. In addition, the table shows that the complex of shifting sentiments towards a party and its leader differed according to the politician concerned. Of the three individuals who fought the 1964 campaign, popular attitudes towards Mr. Wilson developed in most intimate association with feelings about his party. All the tested relationships for the Wilson/Labour pair were statistically significant. In fact seven of the eight F-ratio values reached a ·1 per cent level of significance—compared with only two in the cases of Sir Alec and Mr. Grimond.

Yet another difference is illustrated by Table 12.5 below. It divides the respondents, first of all, according to their changed party attitudes. Then it shows, at each of several levels of party attitude shift, how ratings of that party's leader for strength had developed during the campaign. The first column of figures indicates that Mr. Grimond's reputation for strength improved throughout virtually the entire sample—and even with some of the electors who had shifted *against* his party. Only the most extreme anti-Liberal shifters (with scores for campaign change of − 5 to − 9) also regarded Mr. Grimond as a weaker leader after the election than they had perceived him at the pre-campaign interview. For Sir Alec Douglas-Home this pattern was virtually reversed: his strength rating declined even among many of those sample members whose party attitudes had become more pro-Conservative. Mr. Wilson fell somewhere between the other two leaders—his pattern having resembled that of Mr. Grimond somewhat more than that of Sir Alec. In other words, appreciations of Jo Grimond seemed to run in advance

241

THE IMAGES OF THE PARTY LEADERS

of changing opinions about the Liberal Party during the 1964 campaign, while Sir Alec's image fell behind that of his party, and Mr. Wilson's standing developed more or less in harness with the evolution of public sentiments towards Labour.

Table 12.5. CAMPAIGN SHIFTS IN THE LEADERS' STRENGTH RATINGS SHOWED GRIMOND RUNNING AHEAD, WILSON STAYING LEVEL, AND HOME FOLLOWING BEHIND CHANGES IN ATTITUDES TOWARDS THEIR RESPECTIVE PARTIES

Levels of party attitude shift*	Average campaign shift in strength†		
	Grimond	Home	Wilson
+ 5 to + 9	+ 0·96	0·00	+ 1·19
+ 3 and + 4	+ 0·76	+ 0·41	+ 0·31
+ 1 and + 2	+ 0·52	− 0·32	+ 0·40
0	+ 0·34	− 0·28	+ 0·26
− 1 and − 2	+ 0·22	− 0·60	+ 0·02
− 3 and − 4	+ 0·14	− 0·63	− 0·07
− 5 to − 9	− 0·92	− 0·87	− 1·06

* In dividing the groups Labour Party attitude shift scores have been used for Mr. Wilson, Conservative Party attitude shift scores for Sir Alec, and Liberal Party attitude shift scores for Mr. Grimond.
† Four strength scales combined.

But what about the role of party allegiance itself? In examining its influence on developing leader images, the floating voters in the sample should be distinguished from the more consistent party supporters. The floaters break down in turn into a number of small sub-groups, in many of which there was an expected tendency for leader attitude change to follow vote change.[21]

[21] The following table sets out the average leader shift scores (across all 12 scales combined) that were registered between the pre-campaign and post-campaign interviews by each of the different groups of floating voters in the sample:

	Average leader shift			Number of
	Wilson	Home	Grimond	respondents
Inter-party changers				
To Liberal	− 0·42	− 0·05	+ 0·51	34
To Labour	− 0·07	− 0·59	− 0·02	14
To Conservative	− 0·33	− 0·05	− 0·21	16
Late Deciders				
To Liberal	+ 0·27	− 0·40	+ 0·57	14
To Labour	+ 0·49	− 0·07	+ 0·54	28
To Conservative	− 0·17	+ 0·05	− 0·19	18

However, the inter-party changers to Conservative and Labour support constituted an exception to this rule—having rated all three leaders *less* favourably after Polling Day than at the start of the campaign. Otherwise, it was evident that the Conservatives' vote gains owed little to developments in Sir Alec Douglas-Home's own image. And it was found that the crucial body of inter-party changers to Liberal support showed an unusual tendency—at a time when Mr. Wilson's credit with the sample at large was very high— to rate him far more critically at the post-election interview than they had in September, while substantially boosting Mr. Grimond's overall rating. It may be that for some electors in this category the choice was between a party led by Mr. Grimond and one led by Mr. Wilson.[22]

More clarification of the issues raised at the outset of this chapter is likely to be gleaned from the leader ratings of the consistent party supporters, for their responses will not have been 'contaminated' by a major change in party allegiance. For each of the three bodies of stable voters in our sample, Table 12.6 presents an average score of campaign change in attitudes towards each of the leaders (across all 12 scales combined). In addition, it shows how attitudes towards the parties themselves changed in the same electoral groups.

It seems that the consistent Liberal and Labour supporters behaved somewhat differently from the Conservative voters. In both the non-Conservative groups leader attitude shifts were broadly consistent with party attitude changes. In accordance with their Lib-Lab alliance, these individuals concurred in upgrading Jo Grimond and Harold Wilson and in downgrading Sir Alec (just as they had become mutually more appreciative of each other's party and more hostile towards the Conservative Party after Polling Day).

Among the Conservatives, however, net shifts in leader

[22] A detailed inspection of the Wilson profile of the inter-party changers to Liberal support suggests that this group was particularly inclined after the election to view Labour's leader through a perspective of 'malevolent dynamism'. Wilson's standing with this group declined most for being unassuming (average shift of − 0·81), likeable (− 0·78), sincere (− 0·69), and fair (− 0·66). His rating declined least for the strength cluster of qualities: (confident − 0·25, strong − 0·12, inspiring − 0·12 and persuasive + 0·09).

attitudes were not entirely consistent with movements in their party attitudes. They boosted Mr. Grimond's standing but not that of his party, and they failed to respond to Mr. Wilson although their impressions of the Labour Party became more favourable. Even more noteworthy was the absence of any party difference in ratings of Sir Alec Douglas-Home. The Conservative voters felt obliged to agree with the rest of the sample in finding their own leader less satisfactory after the campaign than he had seemed before–even though their attitudes towards the Conservative Party were improving at the same time. This suggests that impressions of party leaders are not always perceiver-determined.

Table 12.6. AVERAGE CAMPAIGN SHIFTS IN THE LEADER
AND PARTY ATTITUDES OF THE STABLE VOTERS

	Average scores of shift towards:						
	Labour Wilson	Party	Conservative Home	Party	Liberal Grimond	Party	Number of respondents
Stable supporters of							
Liberal	+0·25	+0·22	− 0·24	− 0·55	+0·20	+0·79	38
Labour	+0·19	+0·50	− 0·36	− 0·57	+0·37	+0·48	277
Conservative	+0·03	+0·36	− 0·24	+0·11	+0·31	0·00	210

But why are some assessments of a political leader apparently governed by party preferences while others are not? An interesting clue to the answer emerged from a scale-by-scale comparison of shifting attitudes towards the major party leaders by the consistent Conservative and Labour voters, respectively. In rating Mr. Wilson it was found that both these groups perceived him as a stronger personality after the campaign than he had seemed in September, but that the Conservatives placed more exclusive emphasis on this area of gain. Among the Conservatives, Mr. Wilson's image improved most on the four scales which individually represented different aspects of a leader's strength. In the case of the Labour supporters, only inspiration and confidence appeared among the first four scales on which the greatest amount of pro-Wilson shift occurred (the

THE IMAGES OF THE PARTY LEADERS

others were likeability and ability). Particularly impressive was the fact that the scale of persuasiveness occupied the third place in the batting order of pro-Wilson shift among the Conservatives and only eleventh place among the Labour voters. In effect the former were attributing much more of Mr. Wilson's success in 1964 to his plausibility than were the latter.

So far as Sir Alec was concerned, both party groups downgraded the Conservative leader for all 12 attributes as a result of the campaign. Nevertheless, the Conservatives were more sensitive than the Labour supporters to his lack of strength. Anti-Home shift among the Conservatives was greatest for persuasiveness, inspiration, and strength – qualities that appeared second, fourth, and sixth, respectively, in the equivalent batting order for the Labour voters. Again, the Conservatives seemed much more inclined to feel that their leader had not found a suitable way to put their party's case to the public.

A summary of these tendencies is provided in Table 12.7. This presents, for the consistent Conservative and Labour voters, two scores for mean shift in leader ratings: (a) on the four strength scales combined; and (b) on all the eight other scales combined.

Table 12.7. PARTY SUPPORT HAD LITTLE EFFECT ON CAMPAIGN CHANGE IN THE RATINGS OF WILSON AND HOME FOR STRENGTH, THOUGH IT DID AFFECT THE CHANGE IN THEIR STANDING ON OTHER SCALES

| | Shifts in ratings of: | | | | |
| | Wilson | | Home | | |
Stable supporters of:	For four strength scales	For eight other scales	For four strength scales	For eight other scales	No. of respondents
Labour	+ 0·24	+ 0·17	– 0·38	– 0·34	277
Conservative	+ 0·24	– 0·08	– 0·40	– 0·16	210

The table highlights an intriguing pattern of party differences and similarities. A horizontal reading of the figures shows that Mr. Wilson's image improved comprehensively among Labour supporters, while the Conservatives regarded him as a more powerful but a less worthy leader after the election than they

245

had supposed him to be before the campaign. Similarly, whereas Sir Alec's image deteriorated comprehensively among Labour supporters, the Conservatives distinguished between his attributes of strength (in which they expressed considerable disappointment after the campaign) and his other qualities (where any decline was less pronounced). The Conservatives in our sample differed from the Labour supporters, then, in the *selectivity* of their responses to the strength qualities of the party leaders. They upgraded Mr. Wilson and downgraded Sir Alec selectively for strength. But embedded in this pattern is an important similarity between the two voting groups—as a vertical reading of the same figures will show. The average amount of change recorded on the strength scales was virtually identical for both leaders among both the consistent Labour and Conservative supporters. In other words, party support determined attitude change when the more moral characteristics of the leaders were considered—but *not* when their strength qualities were under review.

The implications of this evidence can be summarized in three points. First, despite a general tendency for development in leader ratings to go with party attitude change, the stimulus thesis has received impressive support. On an important cluster of scales (those connoting strength) different groups of party supporters revised their opinions of leading politicians in the same way and to the same extent.

Second, this area of stimulus-determined change is not politically insignificant. Roberta Sigel's opinion that the stimulus thesis applies only to the personal image of a leader cannot be sustained.[23] Strength is undoubtedly one of the essential qualities

[23] Hughes and Western also disagreed with Miss Sigel's conclusion. They reported that among the Labour and Liberal supporters in their Australian sample '. . . there is agreement on the political image, but disagreement about the personal image' of Sir Robert Menzies (op. cit., p. 30). An inspection of their leader rating scales shows, however, that they classified the following items as 'political'—vigorous, brilliant, eloquent, able, weak, uninspiring, and practical—and the following as 'personal'—unreliable, hypocritical, honest, frank, good-natured, and tolerant. In our opinion the former list of qualities is highly suggestive of strength, while the latter is best interpreted as standing for an evaluative cluster of attributes. If accepted, this would yield a conclusion very similar to our own, which stresses party agreement over the strength image of leaders but disagreement about their more moral qualities.

which many voters expect to find in an effective politician. (Our own respondents, for example, ranked strength as third in importance when asked to rate a dozen qualities for their value in helping a politician to run the country well.)[24]

Third, a question reminiscent of that posed by Katz and Feldman can be asked in connection with the findings reported here. How did the Conservatives in our sample reconcile their continuing high regard for the Conservative Party with a waning respect for its leader? One answer could be that they experienced little pressure to harmonize these conflicting perceptions. If a party as such is a more salient focus of political allegiance than its leader, then it might not be too painful for a body of supporters to acknowledge the more obvious limitations of their standard-bearer.[25] Nevertheless, some support for the assumption of a 'strain to consistency' might be derived from the Conservatives' tendency to downgrade Sir Alec selectively on the scales which connoted strength. This could mean that his lack of vigour had served as a scapegoat to explain the failure of the Conservative Party to impress the electorate in 1964. Perhaps cognitive balance was sustained by the view that the party itself had been in good order and that it might have fared better had it not been (a) for the Machiavellian persuasiveness of the leader of the Labour Party and (b) for the weakness of the Conservative leadership.

---

[24] It is true that, in June 1964, only 33 per cent of the consistent Conservatives in our sample endorsed strength as an important quality in statesmen, compared with 42 per cent of the consistent Labour voters. This was the only substantial difference over the qualities needed for running the country well that divided supporters of the major parties, and it was statistically significant at the five per cent level. Perhaps this reflected an awareness among Conservative electors, even at that early stage, of their own leader's relative deficiency in strength.

[25] A detailed discussion of the implications of treating party identification as more salient to voters than certain other objects of political evaluation—including attitudes to a party's candidate—can be found in Sullivan, Denis G., 'Psychological Balance and Reactions to the Presidential Nominations in 1960', Ch. 11 of Jennings, M. Kent and Zeigler, L. Harmon (Eds.) *The Electoral Process*, Prentice-Hall, Inc., Englewood Cliffs, N.J., 1966.

THE IMAGES OF THE PARTY LEADERS

The role of sex and occupation

Before examining how exposure to the campaign affected leader images, two demographic influences deserve consideration. They are sex and occupation, each of which appeared to influence ratings of the leaders distinctively (and not judgements about the parties themselves)–and in particular those key qualities which stand for strength.[26]

The role of sex was expressed in the fact that our female respondents were much less critical of the weaknesses of Sir Alec Douglas-Home's campaign performance than were the males. Table 12.8 compares the ratings of the Conservative leader by men and by women on the four measures of attitude shift that were used in the computer analysis. There is a general tendency for anti-Home shift to be less pronounced among women than men, but this sex difference was twice as large when Sir Alec's strength was rated as it was for any other quality. Although on most other attributes, then, the sexes agreed in their post-election estimates of the Conservative leader, for strength the men accorded him a much lower rating than did the women.[27]

In considering the role of occupation, it should be recalled that one feature of the analysis of partisanship shift was the loyal reaction of the higher-status workers: the Conservatives

[26] There was one demographic influence (not described in the text above) which affected partisanship shift and leader attitude shift in like fashion. When the role of age was examined, it was found that the most elderly electors (aged 66 and over) were least aware of Mr. Wilson's strength and most impressed with that of Sir Alec's at the start of the campaign. After Polling Day, however, they shifted exceptionally favourably when rating the Labour Leader's strength. The similar pattern which was found when partisanship attitudes towards the major parties were examined was ascribed in Chapter 11 to the impact on a relatively isolated group of a restored exposure to current political materials (see p. 195).

[27] Sex did not affect assessments of Harold Wilson at any stage. In rating Jo Grimond, however, the women appeared to swing more substantially in his favour on all qualities after the campaign than the men did. This probably reflected the greater prevalence of ignorance of Mr. Grimond before the campaign among women. Since a definite rating of a leader on the semantic differential scale is a positive one more often than not, a shift from ignorance to familiarity with a leader tends to show up as a strong favourable swing.

Table 12.8. RATINGS OF SIR ALEC DOUGLAS-HOME BEFORE
AND AFTER THE CAMPAIGN BY SEX

	Average scores					
	Pre-campaign ratings		Campaign shift		Post-campaign ratings	
	Men	Women	Men	Women	Men	Women
Home's rating for:						
Strength*	0·37	0·42	−0·58	−0·23	−0·21	0·19
Ability	1·11	1·23	−0·40	−0·40	0·70	0·83
Likeability	1·29	1·17	−0·53	−0·37	0·76	0·80
Fairness	1·50	1·39	−0·32	−0·17	1·18	1·21

* Four combined scales.

among them had been most inclined to stand fast on behalf of their party; and the non-manual Labour supporters had shifted most noticeably in a pro-Labour direction.[28] Leader ratings, however, were not affected by such a tendency, and instead two other associations with occupation were detected. First, it was found that the least skilled workers—in all party groups—shifted more heavily against Sir Alec Douglas-Home, when assessing his strength qualities, than did the members of any other occupational category. This effect is illustrated by Table 12.9—the second column of which shows that the greatest amount of anti-Home shift occurred among the semi- and unskilled manual workers in each of three voting groups. Since this particular reaction was directed exclusively against Sir Alec, no comparable pattern having affected the ratings of Harold Wilson, it appears that the 1964 campaign helped to generate some class-based resentment of the rather patrician leader of the Conservative Party.

Second, it was noticeable that the non-manual Conservatives responded less favourably to Sir Alec Douglas-Home than to his party. In addition, they distinguished more sharply between a politician's moral and strength qualities when judging both the major party leaders than did the manual supporters of the Conservative Party. This difference is illustrated by Table 12.10 in connection with the ratings of Sir Alec and Mr. Wilson for strength and for fairness, respectively.

[28] See p. 196.

THE IMAGES OF THE PARTY LEADERS

Table 12.9. RATINGS OF THE STRENGTH OF SIR ALEC DOUGLAS-HOME BEFORE AND AFTER THE CAMPAIGN BY OCCUPATION AND VOTE

	Average scores (four combined strength scales)		
	Pre-campaign ratings	Campaign shift	Post-campaign ratings
Conservative voters			
Non-manual	1·45	− 0·43	1·02
Skilled manual	1·44	− 0·29	1·15
Semi- and unskilled	1·85	− 0·51	1·34
Labour voters			
Non-manual	− 0·37	− 0·29	− 0·66
Skilled manual	− 0·36	− 0·40	− 0·76
Semi- and unskilled	− 0·37	− 0·61	− 0·98
Other			
Non-manual	0·18	− 0·30	− 0·12
Skilled manual	0·01	− 0·20	− 0·19
Semi- and unskilled	0·56	− 0.52	0·04

Table 12.10. UNLIKE MANUAL CONSERVATIVE ELECTORS, NON-MANUAL CONSERVATIVES DISTINGUISHED BETWEEN THE QUALITIES OF STRENGTH AND FAIRNESS WHEN REASSESSING HOME AND WILSON AS A RESULT OF THE CAMPAIGN

	Average shift for strength (four combined scales)	Average shift for fairness	Difference in shift for strength and fairness
Ratings of Home			
Non-manual Conservative voters	− 0·43	+ 0·05	0·48
Manual Conservative voters	− 0·34	− 0·25	0·09
Ratings of Wilson			
Non-manual Conservative voters	+ 0·30	− 0·16	0·46
Manual Conservative voters	+ 0·07	− 0·17	0·24

THE IMAGES OF THE PARTY LEADERS

It can be seen that reappraisals of Sir Alec and his rival among the white-collar Conservatives were determined by a distinction between their strength and fairness which their blue-collar counterparts hardly applied at all. In other words, it was the non-manual Conservative voters in whom the campaign tended to implant an image of Sir Alec as a benevolently insipid, and of Mr. Wilson as a malevolently dynamic, political leader. This pattern of response may be connected with other signs of the exceptional sensitivity of the non-manual Conservatives to the 1964 campaign—from at least a part of which they had derived some reinforcement of their pre-election outlook. It will be recalled that they had tended to espouse the issues stressed in their party's propaganda, and that their pro-Conservative attitudes of partisanship had stood firm.[29] Having followed the campaign so closely, however, they presumably could not conceal from themselves the evidence it conveyed of the Conservative leader's weaknesses.

The impact of exposure to the campaign

It was more difficult to trace the influence of election communications on leader images than to study any other effect of the 1964 campaign. There were signs that exposure had helped to change some popular judgements of the party leaders. And, in line with our findings in the sphere of party attitudes, distinctions in terms of strength of motivation for receiving campaign materials pinpointed the most vulnerable electors. The main vehicle of influence seemed to be television—but the evidence of its impact was not strong enough to support the more vivid myths about its image-building power.

Precision in analysis was hampered mainly by a technical obstacle: that of devising accurate measures of the sample's exposure to relevant materials about the leaders as such. Two examples of such a difficulty may be given. When studying the influence of party broadcasts, a simple count of the total number a respondent viewed would not have sufficed, since Sir Alec had appeared in only two of the five Conservative programmes, Harold Wilson in the same number of Labour broadcasts, and Jo Grimond in but one of the three Liberal productions. We

[29] See p. 177 and p. 196.

decided, therefore, to take account of the individual broadcasts that had been seen–but of course there was no guarantee that attention had been paid specifically to the leaders' presence in them. Even more frustrating were the uncertainties which surrounded the sample's exposure to the most relevant programme of all–the BBC's *Election Forum*. This series of three broadcasts, which 'starred' each of the leaders in turn, was transmitted without advance notice in the week before the official campaign–in the middle, that is, of our own interviewing schedule. Consequently, some individuals had seen one or more *Forums* before they were contacted in the pre-campaign round, while others had watched them afterwards. We tried to exclude all instances of viewing before the interview by consulting the actual dates when the respondents were contacted, but the outcome was bound to be untidy. In addition, we were convinced that the members of our sample had grossly overestimated their own viewing of this series–having experienced some difficulty, perhaps, in distinguishing it from other vehicles of leader appearances on television.[30] We included a measure of *Forum* viewing in the analysis, nevertheless, partly because we suspected that it might at least stand for the degree to which our respondents had been exposed to leader materials on television generally; but the results certainly cannot provide an accurate measure of the impact of any particular programme.[31]

It is convenient to examine the evidence in stages: to provide a more general indication, first, of how exposure to the 1964 campaign affected the images of the party leaders; and then to look more closely at some further implications of the findings. The general picture may be built up from the information presented in Table 12.11. This summarizes the results of a computer analysis, in which simple regressions of each of our exposure variables were carried out on four measures of attitude change for each leader (an average score for shift on all four strength scales, plus scores for changing views about their

[30] Although the BBC estimated that only 12·1 per cent, 18·5 per cent, and 17·4 per cent of the adult population watched the *Forums* of Grimond, Wilson, and Home, respectively, the corresponding figures of claimed viewing in our sample were 32·8 per cent, 40·0 per cent, and 35·8 per cent.

[31] See Appendix C for details of the methods of scoring exposure to leader materials that were adopted.

THE IMAGES OF THE PARTY LEADERS

Table 12.11. SIGNIFICANT CORRELATIONS OF EXPOSURE
VARIABLES WITH MEASURES OF CAMPAIGN LEADER
ATTITUDE SHIFT BY DISPOSITION TO FOLLOW THE CAMPAIGN
(TESTED BY SIMPLE REGRESSIONS)

Strongly motivated respondents		Respondents rated medium or weak in motivation	

SIR ALEC DOUGLAS-HOME†

TV news	Strength*	TV news	Ability*
No. of party broadcasts viewed	Strength*	Press	Likeability*
Other non-party political TV ..	Strength*		
Election Forum }	Strength* Likeability*		

HAROLD WILSON†

		Other non-party political TV ..	Fairness*

JO GRIMOND

Press	Strength*	Viewing Grimond's party broadcast }	Likeability*** Strength** Ability** Fairness**
		TV news }	Likeability** Strength** Ability*
		Election Forums	Strength**
		Press	Strength**
		Local campaign }	Likeability** Strength* Ability* Fairness*

† The relationships for Sir Alec and Mr. Wilson among the respondents of medium and weak motivation were inverse: as exposure increased their images declined in favourability.

  *   Significant at P = ·05 level.

  **   Significant at P = ·01 level.

  *** Significant at P = ·001 level.

253

ability, likeability and fairness). The analysis was conducted separately within the two main strength-of-motivation groups in the sample, and the table lists all the relationships between some form of exposure and some dimension of attitude change for which the F-ratio values proved statistically significant.

Three main conclusions may be drawn from this material. They concern the fortunes of the leaders, the qualities on which they were judged, and the role of motivation. First, when the individual leaders are considered, we see that the public standing of Harold Wilson was not affected by the degree to which electors had been exposed to him, or to material about him, in any communication channel.[32] Instead the table is dominated by two major clusters of exposure effects—those relating to Sir Alec Douglas-Home and Jo Grimond.

Second, when the qualities involved in these effects are considered, the results underline the importance of the previously mentioned link between an election campaign and reappraisals of a politician's strength. Consistent evidence of the effect of exposure to political communications on Sir Alec's reputation is confined to the strength scales. And although the campaign apparently promoted a more widely based improvement in Mr. Grimond's image, only ratings of his strength were associated significantly with all the exposure variables in the table.

Third, the table shows that disposition to follow the election was as important in mediating campaign effects on leader attitudes as it had been on party attitudes. To all intents and purposes the exposure effects of the 1964 campaign on leader images were concentrated among the strongly motivated electors when Sir Alec was rated and among the less keen respondents when Mr. Grimond was judged.

It was also possible to explore the further implications of these findings in three directions. First, we wished to know whether they reflected a genuine response to campaign exposure of leader images as such—or whether they stemmed instead

[32] The isolated discovery of an association at the five per cent level between ratings of Mr. Wilson's fairness by the less keen electors and their exposure to other non-party political television does not provide an exception to this conclusion. Where so many relationships are being tested it is to be expected as a result of chance that at least one in twenty should prove statistically significant at this level. The same consideration applies to the other isolated associations which appear in the table.

THE IMAGES OF THE PARTY LEADERS

from a confounding of leader attitude shift with party attitude shift. Multiple regression analysis is suited to the investigation of such a problem, and analyses of all the variables that were significantly involved in altered ratings of the strength of Sir Alec and Mr. Grimond were carried out. In each case, the results showed that the impact of exposure remained significant even after the role of party attitude change was taken into account. Taking the Liberal leader, for example, when, to a group of influences that included Liberal Party attitude shift, the most powerful exposure variable was added, the F-ratio value for its extra contribution to Mr. Grimond's reputation for strength among the less politically minded respondents was 5·23—which was significant at the five per cent level. Similarly in the case of the Conservative leader, when, to a group of factors that included Conservative Party attitude shift, the most influential exposure variable was added, the F-ratio value for its extra contribution to ratings of Sir Alec's strength by the strongly motivated electors was 7·50—which was significant at the one per cent level.

Second, we wished to compare the relative effectiveness of the various media in projecting impressions to the electorate of the party leaders. Was television more important in this area than the other main sources of the campaign? So far as the imperfect evidence at our disposal permits a judgement, the answer is affirmative. In the case of the Liberal leader, for example, the regression analysis showed that all the campaign contributions to pro-Grimond shift could be encompassed within the influence of one television variable. Once its effect was taken into account, no other source of the campaign made a significant extra contribution. It so happens that this single variable was claimed viewing of *Election Forums*. Of course, this result cannot be accepted as a tribute to Mr. Grimond's response to the challenge of a new programme form, but it does lend some weight to our guess that the index of *Forum* viewing provided a more general measure of exposure to leader materials on television. The outcome of the comparable analysis of influences on Sir Alec's developing image was less ambiguous. A glance back at Table 12.11 will show that only TV variables were associated significantly with shifts in attitudes towards the Conservative leader. The multiple regression analysis indicated

255

THE IMAGES OF THE PARTY LEADERS

in turn that the whole of this influence could be expressed in
the impact of one such variable: exposure to the main and
late-night news bulletins on television.

Finally, we tried to explain one puzzling feature of the
connection in the highly motivated group between campaign
exposure and altered impressions of Sir Alec Douglas-Home.
Although in the main Sir Alec was regarded as a *weaker* leader
after Polling Day than he had seemed to be before the campaign
opened, the effect of exposure to election television was to
oppose this tend. That is, as viewers saw more of the television
campaign they became *less* critical of Sir Alec's lack of vigour.
This tendency is illustrated by the figures presented in Table
12.12. At each level of exposure to television news, the respondents regarded Sir Alec as a less forceful leader at the
post-election interview than they had perceived him to be a
month earlier. But the magnitude of this shift was greatest
among those who had seen little or nothing of the campaign
and relatively slight among the more highly exposed.

Table 12.12. AMONG THE STRONGLY MOTIVATED
RESPONDENTS, INCREASED EXPOSURE TO TELEVISION NEWS
CHECKED THE TENDENCY TO CRITICIZE HOME FOR LACK OF
STRENGTH

Score for exposure to TV news	Average shift for strength in rating Home
0	− 0·64
1 and 2	− 0·63
3	− 0·31
4 +	− 0·22

Why should the impact of television run counter to the net
effect of the campaign in changing the public's impression of
Sir Alec's strength qualities? Since the regression analysis had
taken account of the role of party attitude shift, some concealed
influence of a change in partisan feeling could be ruled out.[33]

[33] The probability that we were examining a distinctive contribution of
viewing to developments in Sir Alec's image alone was strengthened by
several other features of the evidence. First, there was no parallel link
between exposure and change in Harold Wilson's leader ratings among the
highly motivated respondents. Second, the effect of the campaign on ratings
of Sir Alec was not merely a reflection of the impact of exposure on partisanship attitudes in the same motivation group (reported in Chapter 11). A

THE IMAGES OF THE PARTY LEADERS

The relevant literature of political communications studies was culled for parallel instances, but only one remotely similar case was found. In an investigation of the American election of 1960, Tannenbaum, Greenberg, and Silverman divided 145 voters according to an index of their exposure to the Kennedy–Nixon debates and compared the resulting groups on ten different measures of change in their attitudes towards the presidential candidates. The authors reported '. . . a somewhat unexpected if not inconsistent finding across all 10 comparisons together, in that the least exposed of groups (little or no TV exposure) showed more (although not statistically significant) change' from the pre-campaign to the post-debates interviews. They dismissed this finding, however, stressing that '. . . any obtained differences may be as much a function of extraneous factors (e.g. party preference, degree of political interest, etc.) as of exposure to the debates proper.'[34]

detailed inspection of changes in attitudes towards the major parties separately showed that the net effect of exposure on partisanship shift was concentrated largely on opinions about *Labour* and not on judgements of the *Conservative Party*. This point is illustrated by the table below. Third, different exposure variables were involved in the campaign effects on partisanship shift and Sir Alec's leader rating shift. Whereas only exposure to party broadcasts mattered in the former case, several TV variables (most notably television news) played a part in the latter.

Exposure to party broadcasts and party attitude change
(strongly motivated respondents only)

	No. of party broadcasts seen	
	0–3	4–13
Conservative Party attitude change[NS]	%	%
Pro-Conservative	30	35
No change	26	23
Anti-Conservative	44	41
	100	99
*Labour Party attitude change**		
Pro-Labour	55	40
No change	19	33
Anti-Labour	26	27
	100	100
N =	113	193

* Differences between exposure groups significant at P = ·05 level.
[NS] = Differences between exposure groups not significant.
[34] Tannenbaum, Percy H., Greenberg, Bradley S., and Silverman, Fred R., 'Candidate Images', Ch. 15 in Kraus, Sidney, op. cit., p. 285.

THE IMAGES OF THE PARTY LEADERS

But neither of the grounds cited by Tannenbaum and his colleagues helped to explain our finding. Political interest had already been held constant by confining the analysis to the highly motivated respondents. And when party support was also held constant, the tendency for viewers to moderate the force of their criticism of Sir Alec, as they saw more election news on television, persisted to some extent in all groups. This is shown by the figures presented in Table 12.13.

Table 12.13. THE TENDENCY FOR EXPOSURE TO TV NEWS TO CHECK CRITICISMS OF HOME FOR LACK OF STRENGTH WAS INDEPENDENT OF PARTY SUPPORT

Score for exposure to TV news	Average shift for strength in rating Home by:		
	Conservative voters	Labour voters	All others
0	− 0·47	− 0·40	− 1·30
1 and 2	− 0·86	− 0·60	+ 0·05
3	− 0·43	− 0·14	− 0·17
4 +	− 0·15	− 0·24	− 0·44

We were obliged to conclude, then, that this particular effect of the campaign was genuine and that it had been projected uniquely through television. If this conclusion is accepted, a tentative interpretation of what happened might proceed along the following lines. The impression that Sir Alec had proved a weak leader of the Conservative Party was disseminated quite widely throughout the electorate and was accepted to some extent by the majority of voters. In fact this judgement was so common that measured degree of exposure to the campaign or any of its sources had no effect on the outcome. When viewing television, however, the more interested voters noticed the various difficulties which the Conservative leader had to face (such as the onslaughts of hecklers at meetings covered in the news, his initial unease before the cameras, etc.). Perhaps the more they watched him under these circumstances, the more they came to respect Sir Alec's mettle in at least trying to cope manfully with an admittedly difficult situation.

PART IV

CONCLUSIONS

CHAPTER 13

A LONG-TERM EFFECT OF
ELECTION TELEVISION

The concluding chapters of this study correspond to the two main research approaches that guided our investigation of the role of television in the General Election of 1964. The survey was designed both to examine the political impact of viewing and to explore the uses and gratifications associated with exposure to political programmes. The conclusions which can be drawn from its findings are similarly divisible. This chapter presents mainly an interpretation of what we have learned about the political effects of television. In Chapter 14 we consider, in the light of viewers' known preferences, the pattern of election television which the broadcasting authorities and political parties should aim to provide in the future.

There is a vast gulf between what we *know* about the political impact of television and what television is often *supposed* to have done to Britain's political life. The propositions which can be placed in the former class are undoubtedly much less numerous and dramatic than those which belong in the latter category. There are several reasons for this gap. First, television itself is such a dramatic medium that many observers have been tempted to exaggerate its effects and to discount the staunch firmness of popular resistance to persuasive campaigns. Second, the methodology of the social sciences is not yet so advanced that we can apply it successfully to all the questions we wish to ask about the political functions of the mass media. Finally, there is a legitimate area of speculation about the indirect impact of television–about, that is, those effects which stem not from its influence on political attitudes but from the subsidiary consequences for certain political processes of increasing public reliance on television.[1]

For example, television is often depicted as a personalizing medium in politics. Yet we have found that a desire to see what his leaders are like is only one among a number of concerns that may lie behind a voter's viewing behaviour. It is also clear that the measurable contribution of television to the shaping of leader images falls far short of popular expectation. Impressions of politicians are no more susceptible to media influence than are attitudes towards the parties. Nevertheless, the *reputation* of television as a medium which is suited to the projection of personality may influence the stress which is put in a party's publicity on the appeal of its leader. Also a leader's relative power, *vis-à-vis* any would-be rivals in his own party, may depend in part now on his reputation for using the medium effectively and confidently or ineffectually and uneasily.

A similar bevy of qualifications and reservations will surround any other proposition that might be advanced about the political significance of television. Does this medium draw the attention of voters to national issues and personalities at the expense of local ones? Despite a provision by both services of a number of regional news and current affairs programmes, television may on balance strengthen the centripetal forces in British politics, although its contribution in this respect may not be so influential as that of the morning papers with their nation-wide circulations. Does television help to moderate the tone of political argument by delivering a heterogeneous audience to the producers of party broadcasts? Even if a weakening of partisanship in public debate is partly attributable to the influence of television, it probably stems from more profound roots as well: the achievement of a more affluent society; the growth of a conviction that many modern problems call for practical, not ideological, solutions; and the shaping of party strategies by an awareness that the undecided voter is least likely to be swayed by fiercely partisan arguments. Can television help to stimulate electoral turnout at the polls? A careful

[1] The authors have been privileged to consult a perceptive account of some of these consequences in Becker, Samuel L., 'Broadcasting and Politics in Great Britain', 1966 (duplicated paper).

analysis of the use of televised reminders to vote in American elections gives little support to such an expectation.[2]

In fact until 1964 only one affirmative proposition could be placed firmly in the category of research-supported generalizations about the political impact of British television. Television had helped to increase the store of political information available to voters at the General Election of 1959–a phenomenon which was confirmed by the results of the 1964 survey. In a sense the later enquiry doubled our stock of tenable propositions, for it showed that television had also helped to boost the popularity of the Liberal Party at the General Election of 1964. Public attitudes towards the Liberal Party and its leader became more favourable during the campaign, and in the greater part of the sample this movement of opinion was associated progressively with exposure to election television. Furthermore, the wave of pro-Liberal sentiment washed many previous major party supporters into the Liberal camp on Polling Day, and in the generation of those ballot box gains television was also involved.

These findings pose an intriguing interpretive problem. Should we assume that a Liberal advance with the aid of television was uniquely a feature of the 1964 campaign? Or is there some reason to believe that similar developments occurred, without detection, at each election that has been held during the television age? Although it is not possible to offer a definitive answer to these questions (since the relationship between popular feeling about the Liberals and exposure to the mass media was never examined at any campaign other than that of 1964), we have been able to marshal a certain amount of evidence which bears indirectly on the generalizability of our findings. This problem deserves a sustained treatment if only because of its links to several deeper issues: the function of a third party in the British political system; the contribution of the rules which govern political broadcasting to that party's fortunes; and the place of the election of 1964 itself in the political history of this country. We shall argue in the rest of this chapter that our findings represent both a special case and an instance of a more general phenomenon. That is, we suspect that the Liberals have benefited to some degree from their share of broadcasting time ever since 1955, but that the political

[2] Glaser, William A., op. cit.

circumstances which prevailed in 1964 enabled them to exploit their opportunities to an exceptional extent.

Before considering why we have accepted this interpretation, the basic facts about post-war trends in the Liberal vote should be recalled. The increase in the national Liberal poll between 1959 and 1964, from approximately $1\frac{1}{2}$ to 3 million votes, was apparently part of a Liberal revival that had been gathering momentum at each successive election since 1951. (In that year the Liberal Party won only 2·5 per cent of the votes cast nationally, compared with 11·2 per cent in 1964.) In fact A. J. Allen maintained in late 1964 that, 'The most outstanding feature of British politics . . . in the past ten years or more has been the growth of the third-party vote.'[3] Yet his upward projection of this trend—based on the assumption that, as the Liberal vote increased, more and more electors would regard the third party as a serious contender for power—was confounded in 1966 when the Liberal share of the national vote fell to 8·5 per cent. Any interpretation of the contribution of television to the electoral standing of the Liberal Party must be consistent with these facts.

One explanation of the Liberal revival which was mooted after 1964 can, according to our evidence, almost certainly be dismissed. This related the growth in Liberal support to the gradual decline in electoral turnout from the peak figures that had been attained in 1950 and 1951. (Whereas 82·5 per cent of the electorate voted at the General Election of 1951, only 77·1 per cent went to the polls in 1964.) It was suggested that a vote for the third party might be equivalent to, and a substitute for, abstention. According to Hugh Berrington, for example, '. . . the view that non-voting and voting Liberal are part of the same phenomenon' deserved 'some support' because at the 1964 election 'turnout . . . fell less where Liberal candidates were standing'.[4] And Michael Steed also considered that, '. . . in 1964 . . . many people voting Liberal would otherwise probably have abstained.'[5]

---

[3] Contribution to a discussion at the Royal Statistical Society of a paper by Berrington, H. B., presented as 'The General Election of 1964', and published in the *Journal of the Royal Statistical Society*, op. cit.   [4] Ibid.

[5] Steed, Michael, 'An Analysis of the Results', Appendix II to Butler, D. E. and King, Anthony, *The General Election of 1964*, op. cit., p. 338.

Such an explanation is hardly consistent with our discovery that the Liberal voters of 1964 had been highly exposed to election television during the campaign. Many surveys attest to the fact that most individuals who fail to turn out on Polling Day virtually ignore the preceding campaign as well. But we were also in a position to examine the relationship between abstention and third-party voting more directly in two bodies of data. First, we analysed the pre-campaign intentions of the 86 Liberal voters in our 1964 sample and found that only one had expected to abstain. Two-thirds of the intending abstainers (15 of 22) actually failed to vote. In that sample at least the distinction between abstention and third-party voting was firmly maintained.

But perhaps many of the new recruits to the Liberal camp in 1964 had abstained *in 1959*. This possibility was explored through data supplied by our inter-election panel. Twenty-eight individuals in Trenaman and McQuail's sample who had abstained in 1959 were re-interviewed, of whom 13 abstained again in 1964, eight voted Conservative, three voted Labour, and only four voted Liberal. At 27 per cent, the Liberal share of the ballots of those former abstainers who went to the polls in 1964 was slightly higher than might have been expected, but its contribution to the full Liberal vote was infinitesimal. In 1964 the re-interviewed panel contained 70 Liberals, 50 of whom had not supported the Liberal Party in 1959. The four previous non-voters, then, amounted to only eight per cent of these 'new Liberals', 92 per cent of whom had voted for either the Conservative or Labour Parties in 1959. It seems fair to conclude that voting Liberal and abstaining are quite distinct phenomena.[6]

This brings us back to the main stream of the analysis. We know that many of the new Liberal voters of 1964 were weaned from the ranks of former supporters of the major parties and that television facilitated the severing of their old ties. Did this happen only during the 1964 campaign? Three features of our

[6] It should be pointed out that the situation in one of the two constituencies should have favoured conversion from abstention to Liberal support. Although a Liberal stood in Pudsey in both years, in West Leeds there was a straight fight between the major parties in 1959 and a three-cornered contest in 1964.

evidence encouraged us at first to regard the General Election of 1964 as an exceptional one.

First, the issue content of the 1964 campaign – and its impact on the electorate – seemed quite different from the corresponding features of 1959, when the Labour and Conservative Parties had devoted much of their propaganda to issues that were already prominent in the voters' minds. Consequently, no noteworthy developments in issue salience emerged from Trenaman and McQuail's survey of the 1959 election. In 1964, however, the major parties attempted to highlight issues which mattered relatively little to the electorate when the campaign opened. This not only produced impressive trends in our respondents' awareness of certain issues. It also helped to create a campaign atmosphere that appeared to be buffeted by conflicting cross-currents. Although Labour succeeded in awakening a sense of the urgency of improving Britain's record of economic growth, the Conservatives managed to communicate their emphasis on the standard of living and nuclear deterrent issues to many voters. These conflicts were reflected in the sample's ratings of the parties, whereby Labour, for example, was credited after the campaign with a greater ability to revive the economy but a diminished capacity to cope with foreign affairs.[7]

It seems possible that confusion about the strong and weak points of the major parties favoured the prospects of the Liberals among the undecided voters. In the main those electors who made up their minds to vote Liberal during the 1964 campaign tended in their ratings of the major parties to reflect the ambivalent pattern described above. Of course this might be expected as a natural product of the central position they had come to occupy by deciding to support the third party. There was, however, one hint of a distinctive development in issue salience among the 34 inter-party changers who voted

[7] Another difference between the Leeds surveys of 1959 and 1964 may be noted. In the earlier election the standing of the Conservatives improved consistently on all five favourable items in the party attitude scale that Trenaman and McQuail used, and that of Labour declined on all four critical items. In 1964 the Labour Party failed to make progress on one out of the five favourable items on the equivalent scale and the Conservative Party actually bettered its position on one of the four critical items that it contained.

OF ELECTION TELEVISION

Liberal in 1964. This group differed noticeably from the rest of the sample in its endorsement of two contemporary issues: 'meet the challenge of automation and the scientific age' and 'modernize British industry'.[8] The figures appear in Table 13.1, and they show that although the bulk of the sample was unmoved by these issues as a result of the campaign, large increases in their endorsement occurred among the 'new Liberals'. In fact after Polling Day the level of endorsement among the latter was twice the average for the rest of the sample. These results suggest that this strategic body of voters included many potential supporters of the Labour Party who were still unconvinced by the end of the campaign that Labour could provide a genuine modernizing impetus.

Table 13.1. THE LIBERAL VOTERS WHO HAD SUPPORTED A DIFFERENT PARTY AT THE START OF THE CAMPAIGN TENDED TO BECOME MORE AWARE OF CERTAIN 'MODERNIZATION ISSUES' DURING IT

	Endorsements of issues worded:				
	'Meet the challenge of the scientific age'		'Modernize British industry'		
	Pre-campaign	Post-campaign	Pre-campaign	Post-campaign	No. of respondents
	%	%	%	%	
Inter-party changers to Liberal	26	41	24	38	34
All other respondents	20	20	16	18	714

The General Election of 1964 definitely seemed distinctive, then, for the issues on which it had been fought: for their relatively deep-seated character; for the changes that had been precipitated in public opinion; for the failure of either major party to win an outright victory on this front; and for the

[8] The proportion of inter-party changers to Liberal support regarding economic growth as an important issue in October 1964, however, at 37 per cent, was not appreciably greater than the comparable figure for the rest of the sample (32 per cent).

267

opportunity this created for a Liberal advance. In contrast to the implications of this evidence, the other two indications that the 1964 campaign might have been exceptional did not stand up so well to sustained analysis. In fact they drew our attention eventually to certain persistent and enduring characteristics of electoral politics in Britain.

One feature of the 1964 election which impressed us from the very beginning was the magnitude of the campaign gains made by the Liberals and especially their feat in capturing more than half of all the inter-party switches in our sample. The outcome of the General Election of 1966 seemed only to strengthen this impression that 1964 had been an outstanding year for the Liberal Party. In the absence of a before-and-after campaign survey no firm evidence is available on this point.[9] But the campaign shift in favour of the Liberal Party which the opinion polls recorded in 1966 was much reduced in comparison with 1964.[10] Unfortunately, the opinion polls are not always able to measure the degree of third-party support in the electorate accurately. Michael Steed offers another clue by examining the returns in three constituencies where by-elections were held shortly before the General Election of 1966 (between early November 1965 and late January 1966). He points out that the votes for the Liberal candidates in these constituencies at the General Election in March 'recovered, compared to the by-elections, on average by 2·0 per cent.' This showed, he concludes, that '. . . the Liberal Party was able to improve in general election conditions on the immediately preceding by-elections.'[11] But even if the Liberals benefited slightly from the 1966 campaign, the scale of its gain was seemingly much less substantial than the Liberal advance in our sample had been

[9] Detailed results from panel interviews conducted by NOP during the 1966 campaign are presented on p. 176 of Butler, D. E. and King, Anthony, *The British General Election of 1966*, op. cit. These show little sign of a Liberal gain in vote intentions, but, as in the comparable survey of 1964, the gap between 'pre' and 'post' interviews did not span the entire duration of the campaign.

[10] Compare the figures given on p. 174 of *The British General Election of 1966* with those set out on p. 208 of *The British General Eection of 1964*.

[11] Steed, Michael, 'An Analysis of the Results', Appendix to Butler, D. E. and King, Anthony, *The British General Election of 1966*, op. cit., p. 290.

in 1964-from 8·0 per cent of the declared vote intentions to 13·3 per cent of the recalled vote.

What about the Liberal position in elections held before 1964? To answer this question, we re-examined evidence which had been collected by various academic investigators from constituency samples in surveys that had been mounted before and after each of the four General Elections of the 1950s. Against our expectations, our attention was drawn to a strong element of continuity between our findings of 1964 and those which applied to the earlier campaigns. We knew that Trenaman and McQuail had not reported the emergence of a pro-Liberal trend in 1959, but its presence could have been masked by the fact that the Liberals had fought only one of their two constituencies. And we found, when consulting their figures for Pudsey alone (the seat with a three-sided fight), that the extent of the Liberal campaign gain virtually matched the third party's achievement in the same constituency in 1964. The full details appear in Table 13.2, which also presents evidence culled from the Bristol studies of Milne and Mackenzie during the General Elections of 1955 and 1951 and from the Greenwich enquiry of Benney, Gray and Pear at the General Election of 1950.[12]

The table shows that it has been typical rather than unusual for the Liberal Party to benefit from election campaigns and to capture approximately a half of all the inter-party switches generated by them. It can be seen that since 1955 the Liberal Party has been the net victor of each campaign that has been studied in detail and that the scale of the reported gain increased steadily until the peak of 1964. It is noticeable too that the start of the Liberal revival coincided with the use of television in electioneering; that its acceleration paralleled the increasing domination of campaigns by television; and that in 1950, when the national Liberal poll was nearly as high as in 1964, but when television was unavailable, the Liberal campaign advance that was achieved was far less extensive than at any subsequent election.

---

[12] Benney, M., Gray, A. P., and Pear, R. H., *How People Vote*, Routledge and Kegan Paul, London, 1956; Milne, R. S. and Mackenzie, H. C., *Straight Fight*, op. cit.; Milne, R. S. and Mackenzie, H. C., *Marginal Seat, 1955*, op. cit.; Trenaman, J. and McQuail, Denis, op. cit.

Table 13.2. THE LIBERAL VOTE IN CONSTITUENCY ELECTION
STUDIES, 1950–64

	Sample Vote Intention	Vote	Liberal campaign gain	Liberal share of interparty switches†	Liberal share of national vote	Sample members viewing one TV election broadcast
	Dec. 1949 %	Feb. 1950* %	%		%	%
Green-Con.	36·8	33·8				
wich Lab.	59·3	61·8		35 %	9·1	—
1950 Lib.	3·9	5·4	1·5%	(22 of 62)		
	100·0	100·0				
Bristol North east 1951	No Liberal candidate				2·5	—
	Early May %	Late May %				
Bristol Con.	49·1	47·9				
North Lab.	45·0	43·2		54%	2·7	38
east Lib.	5·9	8·9	3·0	(19 of 35)		
1955	100·0	100·0				
	Sept. %	Oct. %				
Pud- Con.	56·6	56·6				
sey Lab.	33·7	29·8		48%	5·9	57
1959 Lib.	9·7	13·6	3·9	(10 of 21)		
	100·0	100·0				
	Sept. %	Oct. %				
Pud- Con.	49·3	49·5				
sey Lab.	39·8	34·8		53%	11·2	74
1964 Lib.	10·9	15·7	4·8	(17 of 32)		
	100·0	100·0				
Pudsey and West Leeds combined 1964			5·2	53% (34 of 64)		

A LONG-TERM EFFECT OF ELECTION TV

This evidence should only be regarded as suggestive. Differences in the constituencies that were studied and in the survey methods that were adopted impair strict comparability. And a temporal association between the Liberal revival of the years covered by the table and the expansion of television in British households is not necessarily causal; it could be fortuitous. Although, for example, the same period witnessed a decline in electoral turnout, we have not argued that television helped to precipitate an increasing number of abstentions. But it is instructive to consider why the long-term relationship between the growth of television and the Liberal vote is emphasized here, while ignoring a similar temporal link with non-voting. The reason is that the former is additionally supported by survey evidence whereas the latter is not. In sample surveys high exposure to political television generally accompanies, not a tendency to abstain, but above-average involvement in other facets of a campaign, including a disposition to vote. It is just because high television exposure was associated strongly in our 1964 survey with the generation of favourable attitudes to the Liberal Party that we are also inclined to give some weight to evidence which connects the longer-term recovery in Liberal fortunes with the increasing domination of election campaigns by the medium of television.

The other prominent feature of the 1964 election, which seemed to us to set it apart on first inspection, concerned the high levels of campaign exposure, political interest, and political information which were recorded by the inter-party changers to Liberal support. Like many political scientists, we had tended to think of such electors as an amorphous body of

---

* The figures for the Greenwich survey are taken from Table 45, p. 168 of *How the People Vote*, where the total number of respondents, at 736, appears to be 45 fewer than the 781 sample members used in preparing other tables. But this is the only available source of data about inter-party switching in the panel. Had the larger group been used the overall Liberal campaign gain would have been 1·0 per cent instead of 1·5 per cent.

† The Liberal Party's share of 'late decisions' (of the votes of those who were 'don't knows' and 'no votes' at the start of a campaign) has always been much smaller than its gain from inter-party switches. In 1955 it won only seven per cent of such decisions (four of 54); in 1955, 25% (six of 24); in Pudsey 1959, 24% (nine of 37); in Pudsey 1964, 24% (six of 25); and in Pudsey/West Leeds 1964, 23% (14 of 60).

apathetic individuals, the ultimate destination of whose ballots turned on relatively trivial considerations. Professor Blondel has aptly put the view of their behaviour to which we subscribed in the following words:

> Floating voters may play a central part in the British system of government. But they do not seem to be aware of their responsibilities. They do not seem to be drawn from the most politically conscious section of the community. The reasons for their change of allegiance are often trivial. They seem to be less committed, not because of a genuine independence of mind, but more out of apathy. They resemble abstainers more than they resemble the image of the perfect voter.[13]

As Table 13.3 shows, however, the newly created Liberals of 1964 failed strikingly to conform to this image. If, in each of the columns of the table, the figures for the inter-party changers to Liberal support are compared with those that apply to the other voting groups in the sample, the following points stand out: very few members of this crucial group were rated weak in motivation for following an election campaign; they were well above the average in knowledgeability when the campaign opened; they nevertheless acquired more political information as a result of the campaign than did any other voting group in the sample; and they watched a remarkably large number of political broadcasts, including many transmitted by the Liberal Party. In fact the new Liberal of 1964 seemed to embody some of the classic virtues of the rational democratic voter. And we reasoned from the discovery of this pattern that a political climate which could breed such an unprecedentedly serious kind of floating voter might have proved exceptionally conducive to mass media influence as well.

But a consultation of the literature of previous election studies demonstrated again that these 'new Liberals' were not so new after all. In particular, Milne and Mackenzie had discovered them and noted some of their characteristics in two

---

[13] Blondel, J., *Voters, Parties and Leaders*, Penguin Books, Ltd., Harmondsworth, Middlesex, 1963, p. 72. See too the statement of Professor Moodie: 'It is also of importance that those who change sides at election time tend to be less rather than more interested or learned in political affairs.' (Moodie, Graeme C., *The Government of Great Britain*, Methuen University Paperbacks, London, 1964, p. 63.)

Table 13.3. RESOLUTION OF THE VOTE AND INTEREST AND PARTICIPATION IN THE 1964 CAMPAIGN

	Rated 'weak' in motivation for following an election campaign in June 1964 %	Knowledge of party policies, Sept. 1964— Average no., out of six, correctly identified	Average campaign gain in level of knowledge	Average no. of party election broadcasts seen	Average no. of Liberal election broadcasts seen	No. of respondents
Inter-party switchers						
to Liberal	12	2·3	+ 0·8	5·4	1·4	34
to major parties	43	1·8	+ 0·5	4·3	0·9	30
Late-deciders						
to Liberal	29	2·4	+ 0·2	3·4	0·9	14
to major parties	30	1·6	+ 0·6	5·3	1·1	46
Consistent Liberals	24	1·4	+ 1·0	4·4	1·0	38
Other consistent voters	27	2·1	+ 0·5	4·6	1·0	487
Non-voters	51	1·4	+ 0·2	3·1	0·6	76

passages of *Marginal Seat, 1955* (their Bristol study of the General Election of that year). In the first of these passages they commented on the 'curious feature' that few of the new Liberals of 1955 had been ex-Liberals of 1950 unable to vote for the third party in 1951 because no candidate was standing. Instead, they remarked, 'In many cases the Liberal vote seems to have been a product of disillusion with a major party [and] perception of the Liberals as "in between" the major parties'. They considered that these voters could be described most suitably as 'Protest Liberals', and they pointed out that: '. . . a change from one major party to another in this country constitutes a relatively large step. A change to the Liberals . . . is a less formidable undertaking for the prospective changer.'[14] In their concluding chapter Milne and Mackenzie referred again to the 'Protest Liberals' as a 'puzzling aspect of the sample', drawing attention this time to their participation in the campaign:

> One might have supposed that they would resemble other voluntary floaters. However, they were far superior to these in political knowledge and activity although their interest in the election was lower. Indeed, apart from interest, they compared favourably with the other Liberals who had voted Liberal previously; their exposure to propaganda was actually slightly *higher* and their attribution of propositions *more acute*.[15]

Evidently the 'Protest Liberals' of 1955 shared certain traits with their counterparts of 1964 – particularly above-average levels of knowledgeability and involvement in the campaign.

To the characteristics detected by Milne and Mackenzie we have been able to add a few more. Politically, the major party supporters who eventually voted Liberal were less committed to the Conservative and Labour Parties at the outset of the 1964 campaign than the consistent supporters of those parties had been. When asked in September, for example, how 'certain' they were to vote Labour or Conservative, three-eighths of those who switched later to the Liberal Party admitted to some uncertainty compared with only six per cent of the unwavering

[14] Milne, R. S. and Mackenzie, H. C., *Marginal Seat, 1955*, op. cit., pp. 47–49.
[15] Ibid, p. 198.

Conservative and Labour supporters.[16] At the same time their pre-campaign Liberal Party attitude scores were already substantially higher than those of the consistent major party voters.[17]

The attitudes of this group to the election campaign itself also fluctuated according to an interesting cycle. The pattern is reflected in the figures set out in Table 13.4. The first two rows present the proportions in each of several voting groups in the sample who were rated strong in motivation for following the campaign, first in June 1964, and then in September 1964. They show that there was a phenomenal increase in interest in the forthcoming campaign among those electors who were to change *later* from their support of a major party to a Liberal vote. The third row shows that, in addition, many in this group were 'vote-guidance seekers', a large number having endorsed the statement, 'to make up my mind how to vote', as a reason that would apply to their viewing of election television during the campaign. When, however, the same individuals were asked after the election whether there had been too many or too few political programmes on television during the campaign, or whether the amount had been about right, the 'new Liberals' swung violently again, many of them asserting emphatically that the coverage by television had been excessive.

These various pieces of evidence can be assembled into a tolerably coherent account of the constant and variable forces which are likely to affect the size of the new Liberal vote generated in the course of any particular election campaign. As an election approaches, it seems that some previously committed electors begin to question their earlier identification with one or the other of the major parties. That is the meaning of the admission by the new Liberals, when questioned before the

[16] Among the inter-party changers to Liberal support, 12 felt uncertain about their pre-campaign major party vote intention, 20 felt certain, and two failed to reply. The corresponding figures for the consistent major party supporters were 30 uncertain, 496 certain, and 11 'no answers'.

[17] There follows the average Liberal Party attitude scores in September 1964 of:

Switchers from a Conservative intention to a Liberal vote (15)	+ 1·20	Consistent Conservatives (210)	+ 0·33
Switchers from a Labour intention to a Liberal vote (19)	+ 0·63	Consistent Labour (277)	+ 0·10

campaign began, of some uncertainty about their intention, as stated at that time, to vote for Labour or for the Conservatives.

Table 13.4. RESOLUTION OF THE VOTE AND ATTITUDES TO THE CAMPAIGN

	Inter-party changers to:		Late Deciders to:		Consistent voters		Non-voters
	Lib	Lab & Con	Lib	Lab & Con	Lib	Lab & Con	
	%	%	%	%	%	%	%
Rated 'strong' in motivation for following the campaign — June	29	17	64	39	47	46	21
Rated 'strong' in motivation for following the campaign — Sept	68	37	42	39	31	49	28
Would follow campaign on TV: 'To make up my mind how to vote'	50	27	71	28	18	25	18
Objected to 'too many' political programmes on TV during campaign	62	57	43	41	66	47	53
N =	34	30	14	46	38	487	78

It is also clear that these wavering electors are not, in the main, ill-informed or apathetic, as many abstainers and 'don't knows' are. It seems fair to assume, therefore, that they are aware of current social and political problems and that the strain on their old allegiances arises partly from doubts about the ability of the major parties to respond appropriately to modern needs and trends. The *size* of this vulnerable group, then, may depend very much on the political climate of the period in which an election falls. Those cross-currents, which influenced the endorsements of issue and party attitude items by the members of our sample, suggest that in 1964 the group of wavering major party supporters was probably larger than usual. In fact the empirical evidence points to something like the suggestion, advanced hypothetically by Butler and King, that in 1964:

> . . . many voters were torn between their desire, on the one hand, to bring to an end a period of Conservative government which had brought with it economic recession, scandal, and a decline in Britain's standing in the world, and, on the other hand, their doubts about the Labour Party's past disunity, its financial competence, and its administrative capacity.[18]

But why do so many of these susceptible electors wind up eventually in the *Liberal* camp? Two factors could be responsible for such an outcome. One, as Milne and Mackenzie noted a decade ago, is that the midway position of the Liberals favours a switch to them as an easier step than a move all the way to the other major party. The other factor involves the impact of television. We have already seen that the vulnerable voters fluctuate in their keenness to follow the campaign. Several months before it is due to begin, their interest in the campaign tends to be bunched at a middle level.[19] But as the campaign approaches, their uncertain loyalties, which were reflected in a prior disposition to regard the third party in the field with some favour, also give rise to a pronounced intensification of

[18] Butler, D. E. and King, Anthony, *The British General Election of 1964*, op. cit., p. 300.

[19] In June 1964 the interest of these individuals in following a campaign on television was rated as follows:

	%
Very strong	12
Moderately strong	18
Medium	56
Moderately weak	9
Very weak	3
Ambiguous	3
	100
N =	34

political interest. They hope that the forthcoming campaign will help them to decide how to vote. This helps to account for their very high degree of exposure to election materials. And such a high degree of general exposure entails in turn the receipt–via television particularly–of much Liberal propaganda, which strengthens their initial leanings to the Liberal Party. But since they have also seen many Conservative and Labour broadcasts, without being satisfied by either major party that it is fit to govern, they are inclined to feel at the end of it all that too many election programmes had been transmitted.[20]

The further implications of this analysis can be considered, first from the standpoint of the Liberal Party, and second, from that of the recent electoral history of this country. Despite its successes in the 1950s and 1960s, this analysis tends to show how little room for manoeuvre and the deployment of any independent initiative the Liberal Party has within the British political system. Its fortunes at each election are likely to depend on opportunities for advance that arise from the organization of campaigning, in particular the rules governing election television, and on opportunities for advance that arise from the political climate of the period. The former, however, are more or less fixed now, and the latter are largely out of the Liberals' control. Although the Liberals stand to gain both from their

[20] Except for its occupational characteristics the body of inter-party changers to Liberal support tended to resemble the rest of the population demographically (that is, in age, sex, and educational background). Occupationally, there was a tendency for the members of this group to derive disproportionately from the lower middle class side of the boundary between the working- and middle-class groups in the population as the following figures show:

	Inter-party changers to Liberal vote %	Rest of sample %
Higher non-manual	9	12
Lower non-manual (clerks, minor supervisory etc.)	26	17
Skilled manual	41	49
Semi- and unskilled manual	15	20
Unclassified	9	2
	100	100
N =	34	714

central position in the party spectrum and from the broadcasting facilities they enjoy, the use which they can make of these advantages is circumscribed by a wider set of constraints, which confine the Liberal Party mainly to the limited function, as Robert Alford has put it, of 'relieving temporary strains and tensions between [the other] parties and their supporters.'[21]

It is too soon to try to define the exact place of the General Election of 1964 in Britain's political history, especially since several violent fluctuations in party fortunes have intervened between that event and the present time of writing. It is interesting, however, to note a parallel between some of the evidence that has been presented here and an analysis which has recently been applied to the historical study of American presidential elections. That interpretation was first outlined in the late 1950s in two articles by V. O. Key, Jr.,[22] and it was further developed by Charles Sellers in an article which appeared in 1965.[23] Key concluded, after studying changes in the degree of party support given by various demographic groups to the Democratic and Republican Parties in the periods before and after the presidential elections of 1896 and 1928, that there is a category of widely spaced and so-called 'critical elections', which initiate a realignment of party allegiances in the population that eventually proves both sharp and durable. Sellers refers to the same events as 'realigning elections' and proffers three criteria for their recognition. It is intriguing to find that each of his criteria could have been applied to the British election of 1964.

First, Sellers says, a realigning election occurs in a period marked by 'events with widespread and powerful impact or issues touching deep emotions'.[24] It is conceivable that recognition of the persistence and gravity of Britain's economic crisis provided a stimulus for some voters to reconsider their

[21] Alford, Robert L., *Party and Society*, Rand, McNally, Chicago, 1963, p. 151.

[22] Key, Jr., V. O., 'A Theory of Critical Elections', *Journal of Politics*, Vol. XVII, 1955, No. 1, pp. 3–18, and Key, Jr., V. O., 'Secular Realignment and the Party System', *Journal of Politics*, Vol. XXI, 1959, pp. 198–210.

[23] Sellers, Charles, 'The Equilibrium Cycle in Two-Party Politics', *Public Opinion Quarterly*, Vol. XXIX, No. 1, 1965, pp. 16–38.

[24] Sellers takes over the wording of this criterion from Key's writings.

traditional party allegiances in the mid-1960s. Before the 1964 election most voters seemed to be concerned less about the underlying economic situation than about a number of other more immediate problems. As we have seen, however, the 1964 campaign itself provoked a dramatic and unprecedented upsurge of public concern about the need for fast but steady growth of the economy. And, in the period which followed that election, many voters undoubtedly continued to expect the government to give a high priority to the implementation of measures intended to overcome the chronic weaknesses of the economy.[25]

Second, Sellers notes that each realigning phase of American politics has been accompanied by a temporary increase in third-party voting, which provides a half-way house for established voters who cannot move all the way at once into a party against which their social groups have always previously identified. According to our evidence, a certain amount of load-shedding from major-party support to third-party voting has characterized a number of recent British elections. But these movements seemed to reach a post-war peak at the General Election of 1964, after which they apparently receded in 1966.

Finally, Sellers states that the electors who first become eligible to vote at a realigning election tend to support, not a third party, but the advantaged major party, because, as he puts it, the:

> ... 'events with widespread and powerful impact or issues touching deep emotions' are commanding enough to cause new voters, in the process of forming party identifications, to take their cues from the political environment rather than simply from the identifications of their parents.

Again evidence can be produced to show that at the General Election of 1964 the first-time voters were rather more pro-

[25] Because of differences in composition and wording, opinion poll measures of issue salience are difficult to compare with each other and with our results for the 1964 campaign. But when NOP asked a national sample just after the 1966 election which of three problems (out of a list of eight) they thought the new Government should tackle most urgently, the heaviest endorsement (62 per cent) was given to an item worded, 'deal with the balance of payment crisis'. See 'NOP Bulletin, April 1966', National Opinion Polls, Ltd., London, p. 8.

Labour than their predecessors of 1959 had been, and that the Liberal Party, which had improved its position in most other age groups, appealed only faintly to the youngest electors.[26]

According to these criteria, then, 1964 could be said to have witnessed a 'critical election',[27] marking the origins of a pro-Labour trend that gathered yet further momentum at the General Election of 1966. More recently, however, this development has apparently been drastically reversed, largely because of the persistence without relief of those fundamental economic problems that Labour had promised to resolve.

[26] See Table 11.2 p. 186. It can also be pointed out that, according to an NOP profile which was based on five pre-election polls taken in 1964, Labour support in the 21–24 age group was higher than in any other part of the electorate. Among the same group of young voters Liberal support was weaker than in any other age group except the over 65s. See Butler, D. E. and King, Anthony, *The British General Election of 1964*, op. cit., p. 296.

[27] Joseph Klapper points out in *The Effects of Mass Communication* (op. cit., p. 255) that:

> The elections on which the classic voting studies focus are not 'critical' by these criteria, but are rather occasions on which previously manifested alignments held more or less stable. What role mass communication may play in determining voters' decisions before a 'critical' election is not yet known.

If the British General Election of 1964 may be regarded as 'critical', the findings of this survey could help to fill the gap to which Klapper refers, although it would be rash to generalize firmly from the results of only one enquiry of this kind. Our impression is that, even in a critical election, the mass media would be impotent to effect major changes in voters' attitudes towards the leading parties and personalities. In our sample, for example, opinions about the Labour and Conservative Parties were not appreciably affected by exposure to propaganda. And we do not know whether the two main attitude changes reported in this study (the development of pro-Liberal opinions, and a reinforcement of the partisan feelings of the keenest Labour and Conservative supporters) occurred at some previous election, for no previous investigator was in a position to look for them. Perhaps the essential role of mass communication in a critical election is suggested by our findings in the area of issue salience. It may be hypothesized that in a critical election the mass media will help to shape electoral awareness of the most important issues that a government should tackle. If so, these changes may be registered initially in the thinking of the most partisan voters, but as they are disseminated more widely, corresponding changes in the public standing of the rival parties, themselves, may ensue.

CHAPTER 14

THE FUTURE PATTERN OF
ELECTION TELEVISION

It is difficult to believe that the existing arrangements for political broadcasting can survive, intact and substantially unmodified, to govern the flow of political communications in yet another British election. What, then, are the guiding lines that should shape any new pattern of provision? It is not easy to recommend an acceptable approach, partly because three conflicting but legitimate interests (the parties, broadcasters, and voters) have to be reconciled, but also because the *status quo* itself presents a complex mixture of weaknesses and areas of strength. The appropriate task of reform, therefore, is to put right what needs to be changed without sacrificing what deserves to be preserved.

Some virtues of the British system of election television

Some of the values upheld by the British system of political broadcasting stand out prominently when it is compared with the arrangements that prevail in other countries. It is at least a negative virtue, for example, that in Britain the provision of air time does not depend on the ability of a political party to pay for it. According to an authoritative estimate, the full cost to the American political parties of purchasing broadcasting time has escalated from a sum of approximately $10,000,000 in the presidential campaign of 1956 to nearly $25,000,000 in the contest of 1964.[1] Party spokesmen have reckoned recently that a single hour of network TV costs between $120,000 and

[1] Federal Communications Commission, *Survey of Political Broadcasting*, Government Printing Office, Washington, D.C., 1965, Tables 1 and 2.

$250,000, exclusive of production expenses.[2] The two main
dangers of this situation—which are largely avoided in this
country—are first, that minority parties may be priced out of
the market, and second, that those wealthy individuals who are
prepared to give donations and to stand as candidates can exert
a disproportionate influence in the counsels of even the majority
parties. It is not surprising, therefore, that one American
commentator has concluded that, 'Some method must be
found to regulate campaign expenditure so that one candidate
cannot virtually monopolize the electronic media during a
political contest.'[3]

Another abuse of electronic electioneering, which is not
perpetrated in this country, is the spot commercial. This is a
short political advertisement, lasting between 20 seconds and
five minutes, in which only one theme is projected—sometimes
with great dramatic force. A notorious example was a one-
minute spot which the Democratic Party prepared for use in
the 1964 campaign against Senator Barry Goldwater. This
opened with film of a small girl picking petals from a daisy and
counting them, as a male voice in the background counted
down from ten to zero. The production built up to a scene of
an atomic explosion, which was followed by a voice that urged
that, 'The stakes are too high for you to stay at home' on
Election Day. A disturbing feature of this use of television is its
whole-hearted and unrestrained attempt to exploit the presumed
irrationality of the voters. Whatever their other faults may be,
British party broadcasts have not yet abandoned all pretence of
appealing to the reason of viewers. On the contrary, as Martin
Harrison has pointed out, the trend during the 1964 campaign
towards the production of gimmicky political broadcasts was
substantially reversed in 1966.[4]

[2] See the remarks of Howard K. Smith and Dean Burch (Republican
National Committee Chairman in 1964), cited in Rubin, Bernard, *Political
Television*, Wadsworth Publishing Company, Inc., Belmont, California,
1967, p. 131.　　　　　　　　　[3] Rubin, Bernard, op. cit., p. 132.
[4] Cf. Butler, D. E. and King, Anthony, *The British General Election of
1966*, op. cit., pp. 140–1. The Conservative Party apparently concluded,
however, that it could make more effective use of its total broadcasting
time if this was divided up into shorter and more numerous spots. The
Conservatives accordingly proposed, without success, that in 1968 the
annual series of party political broadcasts should consist of five-minute

It can also be claimed that the prevailing system upholds a reasonable balance between the rights of access to the ether of both majority and minority political parties. Some of the imperfections associated with a compromise are certainly evident, and in particular the smallest recognized parties–the Communists and the Scottish and Welsh Nationalists–can complain that their five-minute allocations in the 1966 campaign were derisory and that they were scheduled at an unsuitably early hour.[5] But at least the third party in the field has usually been given a substantial quota, and the claims of the other parties have not been entirely ignored. The strongest argument against treating the so-called fringe parties more generously arises from the inroads which would be made on television time by political elements in whose opinions few viewers are likely to be interested. If simultaneous transmission of party broadcasts on all channels was abolished, however, the strength of this argument would be considerably weakened. Minority parties could then be allotted more time in which to present their case, and anyone who did not wish to listen could switch over to another programme.

The system has also progressed in recent years towards the attainment of an acceptable balance between the rights and the obligations of television producers in the political field. Although, in contrast to the restrictions of the 1950s, they have now won a greater measure of freedom to select issues for comment and discussion on the basis of journalistic criteria, they are still governed by an obligation, taking one programme with another, to deal impartially with matters of party controversy and to refrain from editorializing. This is one of the most controversial and sensitive areas of political broadcasting. It has provoked many absurd decisions, and complaints are often voiced about either the alleged one-sidedness of the broadcasters or the petty restrictionism of the politicians. But such friction is an inevitable concomitant of a situation which requires the collaboration of two articulate and determined sets of interests. The value to the viewer of the present balance is that he can profit from the expertise and judgement of

programmes, instead of the usual ten or 15 minutes, to be transmitted on a regional basis. (Cf. *The Times*, November 25. 1967.)

[5] At 6.30 p.m. instead of 9.10 p.m.

professional journalists without worrying about the need to protect himself against the expression of a consistent bias. It is true that some broadcasters deeply resent the anomaly whereby a party can prevent the airing of some issue simply by refusing to allow any of its spokesmen to appear on a programme which was intended to discuss it.[6] Despite the occasional exercise of such a veto, however, there were no important omissions in the range of issues that television managed to cover during the General Elections of 1964 and 1966. Some television journalists have also criticized the reluctance of politicians to appear before live studio audiences of ordinary voters,[7] but it is an exaggeration to imply that such a refusal prevents television from conveying the authentic atmosphere of an election campaign.

The need for a two-fold reform

What, then, is wrong with the organization of election television in Britain? Its fundamental weakness is expressed in the fact that viewers receive at present too much of what interests them least and too little of what they are most keen to see. It is not so much that electors suffer *in toto* from an overdose of politics but that the menu which they are offered within the overall provision is unbalanced. This suggests that the pattern of election television should be reformed along two complementary lines. First, the domination of television campaigning by party broadcasts should be reduced further: in particular their monopoly control of all available channels should be broken, securing thereby the principle of freedom of viewer choice. Second, there should be a planned increase in the provision of what have been called challenging political programmes—and especially of inter-party debates, including some confrontations between the supreme party leaders themselves.

In contemplating reform it is vital to resist the temptation to engage in piecemeal tinkering. In order to avoid the unfortunate consequences that could flow from the isolated adoption of either measure, both changes should be implemented simultaneously. If, for example, party broadcasts were curtailed

---

[6] This complaint was voiced vigorously, for example, in the Granada programme, *Television and the General Election*, which was presented on March 22nd, 1966, during the campaign of that year.   [7] Ibid.

without putting anything in their place, the political literacy of the electorate might be imperilled. But if many challenging programmes were added to the schedules without attacking the privileged status of the party broadcasts, the whole system could become dangerously overloaded. Four main lines of argument have convinced us of the need to follow such a two-pronged approach in reforming the pattern of election television.

The preferences of the consumer

One argument in favour of change along these lines is that most voters would welcome it. Their views were reflected in the 1964 survey by: the majority's dislike of the simultaneous transmission of party broadcasts; the development of a widespread feeling that too many party programmes had been scheduled during the campaign of that year; various expressions of mistrust of unchallenged propaganda; strong support for interviews and debates; and extensive disappointment when the top party leaders declined to meet each other face to face on television. Perhaps the preferences of the consumer should not invariably prevail. But in the end broadcasting exists to serve him, and his wishes should be respected unless some weighty objections, which he has not been in a position to consider properly, can be levelled against what he wants.

Changing the system while retaining its virtues

A second argument for the proposals outlined here is that they would remedy the weaknesses of the existing system without jeopardizing its virtues. One of the achievements of the *status quo* is the exposure of large numbers of viewers to the political parties' opinions about current problems. This study has shown, moreover, that such exposure cannot be dismissed as just a meaningless artifact of simultaneous transmission. Party broadcasts communicate information about party policies successfully to all the different components of the viewing public – including that section of the audience which is moved to keep its set on by little more than a mild spirit of tolerance. It is true that the most deep-seated political attitudes remain impervious to the arts of televised persuasion, but the results of the 1964 survey suggest that party programmes can affect some voters' opinions about the issues that matter at election time and their impressions of the competence of the rival parties to govern. If, therefore, party broadcasts were cut back without the provision of a popular substitute, the flow of political information and ideas from the parties to the electorate–and especially to its least interested elements–would tend to dry up.

From the standpoint of democratic standards of value, another virtue of the present system is the bi-partisan composition of the typical party broadcast audience. Most supporters of one party are exposed through television to at least some of the arguments advanced by their political opponents. This feature probably makes for open-mindedness, tolerance, and political cohesion. But if simultaneous transmission was abolished, the viewing of party programmes would tend to become one-sided, and the audience might eventually consist largely of reinforcement seekers of the originating party.

From the perspective of the broadcasting politician, the television audience must often seem awkwardly heterogeneous. It contains supporters, don't knows, and opponents; and viewers to whom politics is the very essence of life as well as individuals whose exposure arises mainly from their attachment to television itself. Although the politician may find it singularly difficult to appeal in one message to so many diverse elements, it does not follow that the key groups in the audience derive no benefit at all from their exposure to party broadcasts. On the contrary, the average citizen, who, since the previous election, has probably allowed politics to slide to the outermost margin of his concerns, is given an opportunity to bring himself up to date again on political problems. The more active elector is put in touch with the current propaganda themes that his party wishes to project. But the evidence which was presented in Chapter 8, concerning the group of viewers whom we have called vote-guidance seekers, is particularly significant.[8] An important test of a campaign must be how it serves the individual who is uncertain how to vote and who is seeking information and impressions on the basis of which he can make up his mind. In our sample it transpired that the members of this group relied more heavily and distinctively on party

[8] See pp. 144–147.

broadcasts for the materials they wanted than on any other source of the campaign.

It would clearly be irresponsible to attack the party element in a television campaign unless something equally effective from all these points of view could be put in its place. That is why the debate format seems so promising to us. The popularity of confrontations would help to sustain high audience figures for political argument on television. Their two-sided and three-sided character would automatically guarantee the attention of a bi-partisan audience. Vote-guidance seekers would undoubtedly find much material in such programmes for comparing the relative merits of the competing parties and leaders.[9] Even the reinforcement seekers would be able to identify with the standard-bearers of their own party in a visible struggle against the forces of political evil!

Counteracting scepticism and political alienation

A third argument for reducing the flow of unadulterated propaganda on television in favour of more challenging political programmes arises from the need to strengthen the faint disposition of the marginally involved citizen to follow politics. Whereas the typical party broadcast naturally provokes his disbelief and doubt, a debate has a potential, if not for overcoming scepticism, at least for diverting it into constructive channels.

We have already seen that mistrust of campaigning politicians is quite common. A graphic picture has emerged from this survey of the conflicting feelings about political persuasion which buffet many electors. The qualities they look for in politicians highlight the existence of a tension between their desire to be ruled by men of integrity and their fear that such individuals are rather rare birds in the political zoo. Their reasons for watching and avoiding party broadcasts reflect the presence of another tension—between a recognition that political decisions directly affect the circumstances of their everyday lives and sensitivity to the unreliability of politicians'

[9] In fact challenging political television proved more popular among the vote-guidance seekers in our sample than it was in any other motivationally defined group.

promises. Highly educated voters may be able to clear up some of these doubts and uncertainties by consulting specialist sources of information, but the average elector lacks the interest and capacity to follow this course. Other voters may be guided through the shoals of political argument and counter-argument by a devoted partisanship which accepts the complete wisdom of the pronouncements of one party and the utter falsity of its opponents' propaganda. But such an uncritical outlook is of no use to the majority of the electorate, whose party preferences, though stable, are rarely intense. There is a continual danger, then, that uncertainty about the meaning of politics will provoke a disgruntled withdrawal from any further effort to make sense of it. But challenging forms of political television may provide an antidote to such a mood. They have the confidence of the viewer (which party broadcasts evidently lack), and they may encourage the sceptical elector to try to sift the wheat from the chaff of politicians' statements by seeing for himself how they stand up to the questions of an interviewer or the arguments of an opponent. In this way television might help to convert political scepticism from a merely negative grumbling into a somewhat more positive effort to judge politicians and their handling of affairs critically.

The need for such encouragement is probably greatest among those who are most deeply imbued with scepticism. According to some estimates this group may amount to nearly a third of the electorate. For example, 32 per cent of the members of our sample asserted that politicians' arguments usually merited 'little' or 'no' attention.[10] And in the course of a nationwide

---

[10] The following table shows the complete distribution of replies to the question that was asked:

Q: In deciding how to vote in a General Election, how much attention, if any, should a person pay to the arguments that are put forward by the politicians who speak up for the main political parties?

	%
A lot	31
Some	32
A little	21
None	11
Don't know	5
	100
N =	748

survey which was carried out in 1959 (as part of a comparative study of political attitudes in five countries), it was found that 32 per cent of the British voters claimed 'never' to follow 'accounts of political and governmental affairs', while 29 per cent alleged that they paid no attention to 'the campaigning that goes on at the time of a national election'.[11]

Many sociologists would recognize this mentality as a condition which has already been portrayed in the literature of so-called political alienation. This has been defined by one writer as 'the feeling of an individual that he is not a part of the political process'.[12] Various expressions of alienation have been diagnosed, including sensations of powerlessness, normlessness, and social isolation. But the sceptical outlook that we have been examining is closest to what has been called 'meaninglessness', or a feeling that an 'election is without meaning because . . . an intelligent and rational decision is impossible because the information upon which such a decision must be made is lacking'.[13]

Two questions can be raised about this sceptical variant of alienation. First, how grave is it? Second, what, if anything, can be done about it? Is it so serious that deliberate steps to combat sceptical reactions to politics should be taken? If so, is there any evidence to show – as we have tended to imply – that challenging political programmes really could reach the more disaffected elements in the electorate?

The literature about alienation seems at times to sound an exaggerated and uncritical note of alarm about its supposed dangers. Some American writers, for example, regard alienation as a potential breeding ground for totalitarian movements[14] – a prospect which seems rather remote from the realities of

[11] Three alternative responses were offered in the case of both questions: 'regularly', 'from time to time' and 'never' for the first and 'much attention', 'just a little' and 'none at all' for the second. See Almond, Gabriel A., and Verba, Sidney, *The Civic Culture*, Princeton University Press, Princeton, New Jersey, 1963, p. 89.

[12] Levin, Murray B., *The Alienated Voter*, Holt, Rinehart, and Winston, New York, 1962, p. 61.

[13] Ibid, p. 62.

[14] See Abcarian, Gilbert, and Stavage, Sherman M., 'Alienation and the Radical Right', *The Journal of Politics*, Vol. XXVII, No. 4, 1965, pp. 776–96.

political life in this country. Others argue that it undermines the representative character of democratic institutions[15]–a claim which also seems largely theoretical, since, at 76 per cent in the General Election of 1966, the turnout at the polls, though lower than at previous elections, was still encouragingly high. In addition, it is a mitigating fact that political scepticism, as we have measured it, seems to be distributed more or less evenly throughout the population. Table 14.1 shows, for example, that, contrary to what might have been expected, intense scepticism is no more prevalent among unskilled workers than among those who are employed in white-collar jobs–or among the minimally educated than among those who have stayed at school until the age of 16 or later.[16] It appears from this that the availability of a strong Labour Party has helped to integrate

Table 14.1. POLITICAL SCEPTICISM IS NOT RELATED EITHER
TO OCCUPATION OR TO EDUCATION

	Proportions stating that politicians' arguments deserve 'little' or 'no' attention %
Occupation	
Non-manual	31
Skilled manual	34
Semi- and unskilled manual	29
School-leaving age	
14	32
15	31
16 and older	31

[15] According to one American political scientist, for example:
The concept of an enlightened citizenry exercising its franchise in pursuit of its rights and interests is so basic to the theory of the democratic state that the flagrant failure of a sizeable portion of the electorate in Western soceieties even to take the trouble to vote appears to challenge the essential validity of the ideology of popular government.
See Campbell, Angus, 'The Passive Citizen', *Acta Sociologica*, Vol. VI, Fasc. 1–2, 1962, pp. 9–21.

[16] It follows that the tendency (described in Chapter 6) for low-status voters in particular to notice the promises of electioneering politicians was more a sign of their interest in concrete and tangible proposals for social betterment than a reflection of a high degree of political scepticism.

many low-status citizens into the political processes of this country.[17]

Even when all these reassuring points have been assimilated, however, a case for aiming to counteract sceptical attitudes can be developed from two considerations. One is the need to maintain respect for the coinage of political statements so that, when required, a constructive public response to the exercise of government leadership can be expected. As Richard Rose has pointed out in connection with the economic crisis of the 1960s:

> At a time when all parties are pledged to major efforts to alter the economy, every worker and consumer can . . . vote with his feet for or against government pleas for restraint, higher exports, or less spending on luxuries, for there are dozens of economic measures that can be achieved only by the uncoerced co-operation of the population in a nation such as Britain.[18]

[17] In *The Civic Culture* (op. cit., p. 317) figures are presented which show that, in contrast to a tendency in the United States for educational background to be associated positively with degree of involvement in party activity, in Britain education and readiness to work for a political party are not related. An earlier comparative study of political conditions in Norway and the United States also showed that in the former country education had no effect on degree of party activity. The authors of that study argued that the difference between Norway and the United States reflected:

> . . . a major contrast between the two regimes in the character of their party systems: in the one case a highly class-distinct 'status-polarized' party system, in the other much less correspondence between socio-economic cleavage and political conflict. In the highly polarized setting, citizens of little formal education and in lower-status occupations would be under a minimum of cross-pressure and would feel much less discouraged from taking on active roles in the political organizations to which they would give their vote. In a less class-distinct party system, on the other hand, citizens of lower status would be under conflicting pressures and be more likely to be discouraged from active participation in any of the political organizations open to them.

See Rokkan, Stein, and Campbell, Angus, 'Norway and the United States of America', in a special number on 'Citizen Participation in Political Life' of the *International Social Science Journal*, Vol. XVI, No. 1, 1960, pp. 76–99.

[18] Rose, Richard, 'For the People, Not by the People', op. cit.

Second, it is difficult not to be moved, for their own sake, by the plight of those individuals who are exceptionally sensitive to the gulf between the precepts of democratic rhetoric and the realities of its practice. As one writer has said, in commenting upon the results of an empirical study of alienated voters, '. . . the kind of political alienation which Levin describes is incompatible with political happiness whether real or fancied.'[19] There is at least a *prima facie* case for reform if a political order creates distress by projecting a vision of its working which is demonstrably at variance with its actual performance.

But can the involvement in democratic processes of warily sceptical citizens be furthered by the presentation on television of challenging political programmes? Figure 14.1 indicates that the most sceptical members of our sample showed much more interest in a party-leader debate than in ordinary party election broadcasts. The figure contrasts the viewing intentions of the most sceptical and the least sceptical respondents when they were asked in June 1964 (*a*) whether they expected to watch any party broadcasts during the forthcoming campaign and (*b*) whether they would watch a televised confrontation between

Figure 14.1. INTENTIONS TO VIEW PARTY ELECTION
BROADCASTS AND A PARTY-LEADER DEBATE BY
POLITICAL SCEPTICISM

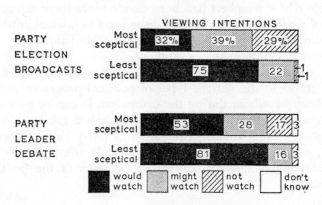

---

[19] Burnham, Walter Dean, 'The Changing Shape of the American Political Universe', *American Political Science Review*, Vol. LIX, No. 1, 1965, pp. 7–29.

THE FUTURE PATTERN

Sir Alec Douglas-Home, Harold Wilson, and Jo Grimond, if one was arranged before the election. It can be seen that there was a wide gap between the professed intentions of the two groups to view party broadcasts; but this narrowed quite considerably when watching a party-leader debate was contemplated.

Viewing intentions need not tally, however, with actual behaviour. In fact we found that the more sceptical viewers watched almost as many party broadcasts during the 1964 campaign as did the respondents who seemed more appreciative of political argument.[20] But the sceptics might virtually drop out of the market for campaign materials altogether if simultaneous transmission of party broadcasts was abolished and no alternative programme form with a special appeal for them was supplied. Figure 14.1 suggests that party-leader debates could provide such an alternative, but no information from British sources can tell us whether the sceptics would actually tune in if any were arranged. The experience of certain other countries, in which televised confrontations are an accepted feature of election campaigning, shows, however, that party-leader debates really do tempt the less politically involved citizen back into the circle of democratic argument. Table 14.2 presents some relevant Swedish data, which were collected during the General Election of 1960 by *Sveriges Radio* from a sample whose members had been divided into three categories according to the degree of their disposition to take an initiative in influencing the political opinions of their fellows: opinion transmitters, intermediates, and indifferents. The table compares the exposure patterns of the opinion transmitters and the indifferents to the various types of political programmes that had been broadcast during the campaign. It can be seen that there was a very wide gap between these two groups in their reception of the Swedish equivalent of party election broadcasts, and that this gap was almost entirely eliminated by the presentation of debates between the leaders of the political parties.[21]

[20] See pp. 147–8.

[21] The data were made available to the authors by the courtesy of Rene Sjoden, Head of Research, *Sveriges, Radio* Stockholm, Sweden, in a letter dated October 27, 1964.

Table 14.2. POLITICAL INVOLVEMENT AND EXPOSURE TO
ELECTION PROGRAMMES IN SWEDEN, 1960

	Opinion transmitters (14% of the sample)	Indifferents* (45% of the sample)
Party presentation programmes (TV)	100	53
Debates (not by party leaders) on economic policy (sound and TV)	100	49
Interviews with party leaders (sound and TV)	100	75
Inter-party debates between party leaders (sound and TV)	100	85

* The exposure of the 'indifferents' is expressed as a percentage of the exposure that had been recorded by the 'opinion transmitters'.

Some practical considerations

Finally, there is a strong practical case for abolishing the simultaneous transmission of party broadcasts and for screening a larger number of challenging programmes. In one word, such a pattern of reform should inject a much-needed *flexibility* into the arrangements for political broadcasting.

As we have already pointed out, such flexibility could favour the creation of more opportunities for the smaller minority parties to present their case on television. Those who fix air time quotas could respond more liberally to the claims of fringe parties, once their acceptance no longer entailed the automatic occupancy of all available channels. In addition, variations in the length and timing of political programmes could be encouraged. The style of party broadcasts at present often seems repetitious and monotonous, probably because they must all be fitted into a standard ten- or 15-minute mould. Under simultaneous transmission a longer treatment is out of the question, since every channel would have to carry it and every viewer would have to put up with it. With the removal of this obstacle, however, it would be possible to tailor the length of a political programme to the needs of its particular subject. One could visualise the scheduling during a campaign of a wide variety of programmes–ranging from short five-minute talks to hour-long

THE FUTURE PATTERN

confrontations and inquisitions in which opportunities for a sustained interchange of views had been deliberately created.

Another refreshing by-product of greater flexibility could be the provision of a stimulus to *innovation* in political programming. The pattern of election television has become altogether too routine and predictable, dominated as it is by thirteen party broadcasts, each almost identical in length with every other, by numerous shots in the news bulletins of the principal party leaders delivering speeches and being heckled on the hustings, and by a series of items prepared by familiar current affairs production teams. Since one of the heavily endorsed reasons for avoiding political broadcasts which emerged from our survey was the statement, 'because they hardly ever have anything new to say', it seems fair to conclude that a reform which shook the conventional provision out of its rather stale rut might help to sharpen the appetite for campaign materials of many viewers.

Despite these advantages, the methods of reform proposed here might also encounter a number of practical objections. Most of the difficulties concern the provision of party-leader debates, and they can be considered under three headings.

First, it may be argued that the transmission of many 'miniconfrontations' in 1966 made very little difference in fact to what proved to be a singularly dull campaign. There is no evidence to show how the viewers themselves felt about these programmes, but our own criticism is that their full potential was insufficiently exploited. In addition to the failure to secure the participation of Messrs. Wilson, Heath, and Grimond, the debates of 1966 suffered from makeshift and *ad hoc* arrangements. They were not part of a coherent sequence, planned as a whole and announced publicly in advance, to which the viewers could then look forward.[22] It should be possible to put this right at the next General Election. Before the official campaign

[22] In 1966 the planning of political items in the nightly *Campaign Report* of *24 Hours* was a more or less daily affair. In the case of *Panorama* there was uncertainty whether the participants in the first confrontation would really agree in the end to face each other or whether they would insist upon being interviewed separately. The efforts which Rediffusion had to make to bring Mr. Callaghan and Mr. MacLeod to the *This Week* studios were only rivaled in laboriousness and exertion by the abortive correspondence concerned with a confrontation of Mr. Wilson and Mr. Heath themselves. Lack of inter-service co-ordination also affected some plans—e.g. when

opens, the political parties and the broadcasting authorities should aim to agree upon the topics and the participants for a series of confrontations, which would be designed to cover the most important issues at the time, and to include the Prime Minister and his opposite numbers, as well as some departmental Ministers and their 'Shadows'. This would not preclude the *ad hoc* scheduling of a few extra debates during the campaign as well, if developments warranted it, and the various parties agreed. The two main advantages of this emphasis on advance planning are first, the ensuring of maximum publicity for those confrontations that are arranged, and second, the encouragement that would be given to the two broadcasting services to co-ordinate their plans for election coverage more closely than has been attempted in the past. Such collaboration is needed to ensure that the various activities which are scheduled do not interfere with each other and do not add up *in toto* to an excessively heavy menu of campaign fare.

A second question-mark which hovers over political debates concerns the *quality* of their contribution to the discussion of election issues. A genuine debate is a demanding occasion, and many politicians may seem unable or unwilling to rise to its requirements. As an American journalist has pointed out:

> ... an illuminating debate must presuppose a willingness on the part of both debaters to explore each other's minds—to probe and to submit to probing in complete good faith—not just fencing, but excavation. It means a deep examination of all the relative views, emotions, and philosophies of the two men.[23]

Stanley Kelley's hope that debates might elevate the tone of campaign argument probably owes something to this vision of their potential, but some of his claims have been criticized for underestimating 'the factor of emotional play that has dominated certain political debates in the past.'[24] In fact we have already had some experience of barren confrontations in this country— e.g. the 1966 meeting on *This Week* between Mr. Callaghan

24 *Hours* felt obliged to cancel a meeting between Mr. Crosland and Sir Edward Boyle because it was learned that they would be appearing earlier in the week on independent television.

23 Coombs, George Hamilton, as cited in the *Final Report* of the Sub-committee on Communications, Committee on Commerce, United States Senate, U.S. Government Printing Office, Washington, D.C., 1962, Part IV, p. 410.   24 Rubin, Bernard, op. cit., p. 31.

and Mr. MacLeod, approximately three-eighths of which was spent in a wrangle over the probable cost of implementing the proposals set out in the Conservative manifesto, and a similar altercation on *24 Hours* between Mr. Crossman and Mr. Boyd-Carpenter, who differed over the exact figures that Labour was entitled to publicize in defence of its housing record. On the other hand, an example of a confrontation at its best was also transmitted during the 1966 campaign, when on *This Week* Mr. Crosland and Sir Edward Boyle deftly exposed and explored their differences of policy and philosophy in the field of education.

The difficulty is that politicians cannot be counted on to realize the full potential of a debate situation and to avoid those lapses of argument and taste to which they seem almost occupationally addicted. Left to themselves, they are more likely to be interested in seeming to win such an encounter than in promoting public enlightenment. Nevertheless, many devices can be used with the aim of involving them in a more constructive debate. From this point of view, the most dangerous programme format is an unguided discussion which is presided over by a chairman who merely keeps time. In a more controlled version of the same format, a TV reporter/chairman assumes a more active responsibility for the debate and poses the detailed questions that the politicians are expected to discuss. This has worked well on occasion, although there is also a danger that the reporter may be tempted to try to provoke a dramatic clash—especially if he assumes that his own superiors would appreciate such an outcome. In the Kennedy–Nixon debates panels of newsmen played a prominent part, putting questions in turn, first to one and then to the other contestant, each having a right to reply to what the other had said. But one observer has complained that:

> . . . the reporters were a problem as they hopped from subject to subject, forcing the candidates into positions where they were not so much debating with one another as competing with one another to give effective answers to the questions. Fewer questions, more carefully considered by their creators and less directed towards the 'hot news' approach, would have been more helpful to the candidates and more constructive for the public.[25]

[25] Ibid, p. 52.

Another technique—which seemed to work well in the 1966 campaign editions of *Panorama*—is the prior presentation of a film report on the issue which is about to be debated. This can give precision and shape to the subsequent discussion, although it also means that one or another participant may complain afterwards that the report was slanted against his own position. On one occasion *Panorama* invited professional experts in the policy field under review to comment afterwards on the problems which the politicians had debated. This helped to extend the discussion beyond the most obvious themes of party controversy into issue areas which the experts deemed important. In another campaign it might be worthwhile to try to mix the experts and the politicians in the same discussion instead of segregating them. In some countries an ambitious format has been adopted, which aims to reproduce in the studio something like the atmosphere of a judicial process. This involves the presentation of a series of programmes, in each of which a spokesman outlines the policies of his party and defends them in a sustained inquisition conducted by the representatives of the other parties. On a subsequent occasion another party's spokesman presents its policies for a similarly searching scrutiny. All these methods are advantageous in certain respects and disadvantageous in others. They show, however, that, with prior thought and care, it should be possible to find some way of curbing the tendency of the politicians to engage in knockabout disputation and of guiding them towards a more relevant clarification of their differences of policy and principle.

A third very real source of practical difficulty in the arrangement of confrontations is the vexed issue of who is entitled to take part in them—and in particular how far the claim of a minority party to do so should be conceded. This was officially cited as one of three factors in the decision not to televise party-leader debates in 1964, and it was apparently the rock on which the many efforts to get Mr. Wilson and Mr. Heath together foundered in 1966. But this difficulty could be overcome if the leaders of the majority parties would consent to the televising of more than one such encounter. Then an agreed proportion of the planned debates could be set aside for two-party and three-party participation, respectively. For example, a Liberal spokesman might be included in three-fifths of all the scheduled debates, at whatever level, and in two out of three of those reserved for the supreme leaders.

These terms might seem too generous in their treatment of a party which has little prospect of ever winning power. There is also a danger that in a three-sided confrontation the Liberal spokesman could afford to be recklessly critical of the other parties, since he would never have to make good on any of his own proposals. In contrast to his freedom, the representatives of the major parties might be cramped by the need to weigh every word carefully in order to avoid embarrassing commitments should they achieve office.[26] These dangers, however, do not seem very substantial to us. There is a precedent for a generous response to Liberal claims, which should continue to be followed in the case of confrontations. The Liberal Party has been given a substantial quota of broadcasting time in the past, and it would be hit particularly hard by a decision to abolish the simultaneous transmission of party broadcasts. In a sense the inclusion of Liberal speakers in a number of confrontations might be regarded as fair compensation for what they would stand to lose on the party broadcasting front. It also does not seem right that the less inhibited voice of a minority party should be virtually stifled merely because it bears a relatively light load of responsibility. A full ventilation of political issues cannot be achieved if only the arguments of the most responsible parties are aired. It is also important to ascertain, through discussion and argument, what opportunities for action are being neglected, and what interests are being ignored, as a consequence of the orthodox notions of governmental responsibility which happen to prevail at a particular time. Finally, we have stressed all along that the appeal of confrontations to viewers arises from their desire to see how the proposals of politicians, who claim to be serving the public good, stand up to a challenge from some independent source. A third-party spokesman should occasionally be in a good position to discharge that function for viewers in relation to both of the major parties.

[26] Rubin, Bernard (ibid. pp. 23–24) discusses this issue in the context of American circumstances.

The power and responsibility of the political parties

So far we have skirted around the most formidable challenge of all to the practicality of establishing a new pattern of election television along the lines proposed here. This is the argument that the political parties themselves would never consent to its introduction. After all, the reforms we have advocated would require a willingness on their part to subordinate at least some short-term advantages to the long-term goal of building an informed democracy. Specifically, they would be expected to give up the monopoly hold of their own broadcasts on all available channels and to accept a further increase in the use of a programme form which is uncontrollable and fraught with risks and uncertainties. They might be tempted to respond to these proposals, therefore, in the spirit of Lewis A. Froman, an American political scientist, who has recently maintained that:

> A campaign is a method of exposure and a mechanism for persuasion. It is not an intellectual exercise in the sense that a high-school debate is. Arguments with the opponent should be avoided, not only because they give him free advertising . . . , but also because he might win the argument. The now famous 'Great Debates' only served to give the lesser-known Senator Kennedy a good deal of free publicity and exposure.[27]

We may hope that such a narrow spirit would not determine the approach of British politicians to the reform of political television, but there is certainly no guarantee that a broader perspective would prevail. The fate in the last two elections of various schemes for arranging a party-leader confrontation even suggests a contrary conclusion. The parties seemed invariably to react according to calculations of their own immediate advantage. Before the 1964 campaign opened, for example, it was in Mr. Wilson's interest to propose a confrontation in order to get on level terms with the incumbent Prime Minister, just as it was in the interest of Sir Alec Douglas-Home to deny him that chance. Similarly in 1966, it was in the interest of Mr. Heath to get to grips with Mr. Wilson, just as it was in Mr.

[27] Froman, Lewis A., 'A Realistic Approach to Campaign Strategies and Tactics', Chapter 1 in Jennings, M. Kent, and Zeigler, L. Harmon, op. cit., p. 16.

Wilson's interest to withhold such an opportunity, except on terms which would equate Mr. Heath's status with that of the Liberal leader. These episodes suggest that considerations of party advantage are bound to dominate the response to any innovation, if it is put forward as a recommendation for a single occasion. It should be stressed, therefore, that we are proposing something quite different: the creation of a new *system* of arrangements for election television, which would apply during all campaigns in the foreseeable future to all the parties, whether they be in or out of office at the time. This means that a party which feared that it stood to lose from the new arrangements on one occasion could at least hope to gain from them at some other time.

Another way of countering the challenge which expects the political parties obstinately to resist reform is to recall that they have not only the power to decide how broadcasting will be used in election campaigns, but also a responsibility for the effects of their decisions on the quality of political life. The present high level of public confidence in television is itself a precious resource, which may be eroded if viewers do not find on the medium the approach to politics that they feel they need. Although the political programmes which viewers prefer may be more exciting and entertaining than typical party broadcasts, they would not transform politicians into performing clowns. On the contrary, the essential strength of what we have called challenging political television is that it offers safeguards to the ordinary elector, reassuring him on points where he might fear being manipulated, taken in, or treated simply as voting fodder. In short, the evidence shows that in the relationship of the public to election television there are some dangers to be avoided and some possibilities to be exploited. The main danger is that the more television is used for short-term party ends, and the more it is treated merely as a vehicle for manipulative propaganda, the more likely it is that electoral cynicism will grow—and justifiably so. The possibility is that through attention to the growing points of public interest in political television—notably confrontations and perhaps the televising of Parliament—a healthier involvement of citizens in the political debate can be nourished.

This issue is connected with the controversial privileges

which the parties enjoy at present in controlling the use of television in politics. Before the opening of each campaign, representatives of the broadcasting authorities and the political parties meet and decide between themselves how the forthcoming election will be covered on radio and television. Even though the legal validity of this machinery is dubious, the outcome is adhered to faithfully. Various arguments for and against the maintenance of this practice have been aired. We have said ourselves that there is a case for making coherent plans for election coverage in advance, and it seems right that they should be influenced by the interests which are affected most directly by a campaign —those of the parties themselves. Some critics complain, however, that the present system gives the parties too much say, extending even to a voice in non-party election programming, and that it is intolerable for decisions which lack any legal basis to be respected as if they were binding. Whatever is felt about the balance of these arguments, one central point is clear: the privileges of the parties can be justified only if their use is governed, not merely by considerations of short-term advantage, but also by a sense of responsibility for meeting the long-term needs of the electorate and of political democracy itself.

APPENDICES

A. FIELDWORK RESULTS AND SAMPLE
REPRESENTATIVENESS

B. THE PREPARATION OF A SCALE OF ATTITUDES
TOWARDS THE POLITICAL PARTIES

C. CONSTRUCTION OF INDICES OF EXPOSURE

D. A COMPARISON OF THREE DIFFERENT MEASURES OF
STRENGTH OF MOTIVATION FOR FOLLOWING ELECTION
TELEVISION

E. CONTENT ANALYSIS OF ISSUES DISCUSSED IN PARTY
ELECTION BROADCASTS ON TELEVISION

F. QUESTIONNAIRES FOR THE MAIN SURVEY

APPENDIX A

FIELDWORK RESULTS AND
SAMPLE REPRESENTATIVENESS

Drawing the sample

A systematic random sample was drawn from the current
electoral registers of the constituencies of Leeds West and
Pudsey. The sampling interval was 107, and the starting point
for each constituency was picked randomly from the first 107
names on its register. This resulted in the drawing of 1,072
names—564 from Leeds West and 508 from Pudsey.

Fieldwork

The fieldwork was carried out by a team of paid and mostly
professional interviewers, who were recruited by public advertisement and by personal recommendation. They were supervised
by a professional Fieldwork Supervisor, Mrs. Pamela Rattee,
who also undertook the training of the less experienced interviewers. A thorough briefing session was held before each
excursion into the field. A draft of each questionnaire was tried
out in pilot interviews on about 20 individuals before being
finalized.

The initial round of interviews

The first round of interviews was held between June 19th
and June 28th, 1964. Nine hundred and eight individuals were
successfully interviewed—of whom 67 were substitutes for those
drawn in the original sample. A name was substituted only if
a listed person was known to have moved from the district. In
that event the substitute taken was the individual listed ten

APPENDIX A

names farther on in the register. Details of the interviewing results follow:

Table A.1. INTERVIEWING RESULTS (INITIAL ROUND)

	N	%
Successfully interviewed	908	85
Refusal	74	7
Not found at home	41	4
Died since completion of register	16	1
Too ill for interview	15	1
Incomplete/erroneous interviews	13	1
Demolition of listed address	5	*
	1072	99

* less than one per cent

The pre-campaign round of interviews

The results of the second round of interviewing, which fell between September 12th and September 20th, 1964, are set out below. The 783 competed interviews amounted to 86 per cent of the reduced sample and 73 per cent of the original sample.

Table A.2. INTERVIEWING RESULTS (PRE-CAMPAIGN ROUND)

	N	%
Successfully interviewed	783	86
Refusal	62	7
Not found at home	30	3
Died since last interview	3	*
Too ill for interview	14	2
Incomplete/erroneous interviews	4	*
Removal since last interview	12	1
	908	99

* less than one per cent.

The post-election round of interviews

The final round of interviews was conducted between October 16th and October 25th, 1964. The 748 completed interviews amounted to 96 per cent of those who had been contacted in the previous round and to 70 per cent of the initially drawn sample. The details were as follows:

APPENDIX A

	N	%
Successfully interviewed	748	96
Refusal	15	2
Not found at home	14	2
Too ill for interview	5	*
Incomplete interview	1	*
	783	100

* less than one per cent.

The characteristics of the drop-outs

One hundred and sixty of those individuals who were interviewed in the initial round did not remain in the panel throughout the survey. They were compared in various respects with the rest of the sample. Table A.4 shows that in demographic characteristics the two groups did not differ greatly from each other. The drop-outs, however, included proportionately more elderly electors, relatively few skilled manual workers, and more people without television in their homes.

Table A.4. Demographic comparison of drop-outs and panel

	Panel %	Drop-outs %		Panel %	Drop-outs %
Sex			*Age*		
Male	47	46	21–29	13	14
Female	53	54	30–44	30	21
	—	—	45–65	42	43
	100	100	66 +	15	22
				100	100
Occupation			*TV ownership*		
Non-manual	29	33	Has TV	91	85
Skilled manual	49	42	No TV	9	15
Non-skilled				—	—
manual	20	21		100	100
Unclassifiable	2	4			
	100	100			
N =	748	160			

APPENDIX A

The next set of comparisons in Table A.5 refers to various indicators of political interest. These reveal only slight differences between the drop-outs and the loyal panel members.[1]

Table A.5. INDICATORS OF POLITICAL INTEREST AMONG THE DROP-OUTS AND PANEL MEMBERS

	Panel %	Drop-outs %		Panel %	Drop-outs %
Degree of interest in following the campaign			Caring about the result of the election		
Very interested	45	41	Great deal	57	59
Somewhat interested	31	33	Somewhat	22	20
Not much interested	23	25	Not much	20	19
Don't know	1	1	Don't know	1	2
	100	100		100	100
Proportions rated strong in motivation for following the campaign on television				41%	38%

When, on the other hand, the voting intentions, elicited in June 1964, were compared (as in Table A.6), it was found that 23 per cent of the drop-outs had failed to support one of the three main parties–in contrast to only 15 per cent of the rest of the sample. It can be seen that Labour supporters in particular had tended to accept their full quota of interviews.

[1] The respondents who were classified as 'reinforcement seekers', however, were exceptionally inclined to remain in the panel, as the following percentages show:

	Panel %	Drop-outs %
Vote-guidance seekers	15	15
Reinforcement seekers	11	4
Both political motives endorsed	23	12
Neither political motive endorsed	51	69
	100	100

(Of those electors who said in June 1964 that they would vote for Labour, only 14 per cent eventually dropped out of the panel—in contrast to a fallout of 19 per cent among the equivalent Conservative supporters, and of 22 per cent among those who did not support either major party at that time.) This helped eventually to over-represent Labour voters in the panel.

Table A.6. Voting intentions (June 1964) of drop-outs and panel members

	Panel %	Drop-outs %
Labour	46	37
Conservative	32	35
Liberal	7	5
Other party	–	1
Won't vote	3	5
Don't know	7	8
No answer	5	9
	100	100

Sample representativeness

To assess the representativeness of the sample we can compare it with the United Kingdom population in terms of age and sex, and compare the reported vote of the panel members with the actual vote in the two constituencies. Those comparisons appear below. It can be seen that our Pudsey respondents reflected the party distribution of the actual vote in their constituency quite faithfully, but that our West Leeds sample members included more than their fair share of Labour supporters. Of those members of our sample who reported having voted in 1964, 49 per cent, in both constituencies combined, supported the Labour Party. This compares with a figure of 43 per cent for Labour's actual share of the total vote in Pudsey and West Leeds.

APPENDIX A

Table A.7. THE REPRESENTATIVENESS OF THE PANEL

	Panel	Whole Population of Great Britain (1961 Census)		Panel	Whole Population of Great Britain
	%	%		%	%
Sex			Age		
Male	46	48	21–29	13	16
Female	54	52	30–44	30	29
	—	—	45–65	42	39
	100	100	66 +	15	16
				100	100

	Panel's Reported Vote	Actual vote in the Constituency
	%	%
Party shares of votes cast		
Pudsey		
Conservative	49·8	46·5
Labour	34·6	34·7
Liberal	15·6	18·8
	100·0	100·0
N =	301	
West Leeds		
Conservative	27·3	34·5
Labour	61·6	50·6
Liberal	11·1	14·9
	100·0	100·0
N =	352	
Combined Constituencies		
Conservative	37·6	40·6
Labour	49·2	42·6
Liberal	13·2	16·9
	100·0	100·1
N =	653	

APPENDIX A

Voting in the two constituencies
West Leeds

1959 General Election
(Population 60,269; turnout 78·3 per cent)
T. C. Pannell (Labour) 25,878; D. L. Crouch (Conservative)
21,285. Labour majority 4,593.

1964 General Election
(Population 60,973; turnout 74·5 per cent)
T. C. Pannell (Labour) 22,968; T. M. Glover (Conservative)
15,697; D. Pedder (Liberal) 6,787. Labour majority 7,271.

1966 General Election
(Population 60,176; turnout 72·0 per cent)
T. C. Pannell (Labour) 24,391; T. M. Glover (Conservative)
13,883; D. Pedder (Liberal) 5,062. Labour majority 10,508.

Pudsey

1959 General Election
(Population 52,285; turnout 86·9 per cent)
J. Hiley (Conservative) 22,752; V. P. Richardson (Labour)
16,241; J. S. Snowden (Liberal) 6,429. Conservative majority
6,511.

1964 General Election
(Population 54,939; turnout 84·5 per cent)
J. Hiley (Conservative) 21,581; B. P. Atha (Labour) 16,100;
J. T. Wilson (Liberal) 8,732. Conservative majority 5,481.

1966 General Election
(Population 55,860; turnout 83·2 per cent)
J. Hiley (Conservative) 20,782; E. Brierley (Labour) 18,410;
R. H. Rhodes (Liberal) 7,353. Conservative majority 2,372.

APPENDIX B

THE PREPARATION OF A SCALE OF ATTITUDES TOWARDS THE POLITICAL PARTIES

One purpose of preparatory work during the early stages of this study was to provide a sensitive device which could be used to record shifts in our respondents' degree of support for each of the three political parties. This appendix outlines the main procedures that were followed and sets out, stage by stage, the decisions which lay behind the final choice of items for the required attitude scale. Since the adopted approach resembled in its essentials that which had been followed by the Television Research Unit in its previous investigation of election television, reference can be made to the report of that study for further details.[1] The objective was to arrive at a relatively short list of descriptive statements which could apply to all three parties, would reflect the most important attitude dimensions along which the electorate was likely to judge them, and would be relevant to the political situation in 1964. To avoid an undue reliance on the subjective judgements of the investigators, the choice of items was guided by a survey of electoral opinions and by the results of a component analysis of their structure.

The initial stages

First, a list of 25 statements which could be made about any party was compiled. Twelve of the 25 items were taken directly from the list that had been drawn up at the equivalent stage in 1959, and the others referred to issues which had subsequently become more prominent in political controversy—e.g. economic

[1] Cf. Trenaman, J. and McQuail, Denis, op. cit., Chapters II and III, and Appendix G.

growth, planning, industrial relations, and Britain's international standing. The wording of the latter was guided by an inspection of spontaneously given opinions about the British political parties which had been collected in 1963 by Professor Donald Stokes and Dr. David Butler from a national sample of electors.

The full list of 25 items was then administered in April 1964 to a sample of 209 local electors, who were asked to indicate which of the statements were true of each of the three parties in turn. (It was made clear that any single statement could apply to any number of parties—from none to all three.) The sample itself was chosen on a quota basis and was representative of the local population in sex, age, and occupational status. But Conservative supporters—who amounted to 51 per cent of the sample, compared with only 34 per cent for the Labour Party—were over-represented, and the resulting bias affected endorsements of many of the individual items. These are set out for the whole sample in Table B.1, where it can be seen that on balance the Conservative Party was judged more favourably on most points. Table B.2 holds party allegiance constant and shows how the Conservative and Labour supporters, respectively, applied the attitude items to the two major parties.

Table B.1. ITEMS APPLIED BY A SAMPLE OF 209 ELECTORS
TO THE THREE MAJOR PARTIES (SECOND EXPLORATORY
SURVEY, APRIL 1964)

	Item true of:		
	Labour Party %	Conservative Party %	Liberal Party %
1. Talks too much	60	48	32
2. Would get the economy moving	35	53	16
3. Just criticizes the others—has no positive policy	33	22	44
4. Out for the nation as a whole	49	58	46
5. Unsound in handling the country's finances	42	22	31
6. Would improve relations between workers and management in industry	50	27	30

315

	Item true of:		
	Labour Party %	Conservative Party %	Liberal Party %
7. Out to raise the standard of living for the ordinary man in the street	69	54	47
8. Has a good team of leaders	37	53	16
9. Would keep prices down	32	26	21
10. Would get things done in a forthright way	40	46	23
11. Too much for controls	65	14	9
12. Has a good set of aims and policies	45	52	33
13. Don't keep their promises	33	44	13
14. Cannot plan for the country's future	26	24	33
15. They have a bad past record	39	27	14
16. Would weaken Britain's voice in world affairs	47	17	34
17. Is disunited and badly organized	26	24	33
18. Would be too free with public money	25	28	13
19. Would try to abolish out-of-date class differences	62	11	35
20. Would make the country more prosperous	28	55	20
21. Not too far to the left or right in politics	22	25	42
22. Too much tied to one class or group	50	49	16
23. Has no clear policy	23	21	47
24. Would know how to run the country well	35	56	18
25. Fair treatment for all races and creeds	65	54	56

N = 209

APPENDIX B

Table B.2. Attitudes of Conservative and Labour Supporters to the Conservative and Labour Parties

	Item true of:			
	Labour Party		*Conservative Party*	
	Labour Supporters	*Conservative Supporters*	*Labour Supporters*	*Conservative Supporters*
	%	%	%	%
1. Talks too much	25	82	68	34
2. Would get the economy moving	78	7	18	80
3. Just criticises the others —has no positive policy	6	52	38	7
4. Out for the nation as a whole	72	37	22	86
5. Unsound in handling the country's finances	6	68	49	4
6. Would improve relations between workers and management in industry	83	31	6	48
7. Out to raise the standard of living for the ordinary man in the street	92	58	18	84
8. Has a good team of leaders	62	23	29	75
9. Would keep prices down	68	10	6	44
10. Would get things done in a forthright way	79	19	21	67
11. Too much for controls	30	84	26	7
12. Has a good set of aims and policies	78	25	19	79
13. Don't keep their promises	15	46	67	27

Table B.2 *(continued)*

	Item true of:			
	Labour Party		*Conservative Party*	
	Labour Supporters	*Conservative Supporters*	*Labour Supporters*	*Conservative Supporters*
	%	%	%	%
14. Cannot plan for the country's future	4	41	49	9
15. They have a bad past record	7	61	54	5
16. Would weaken Britiain's voice in world affairs	7	63	35	5
17. Is disunited and badly organized	8	40	42	8
18. Would be too free with public money	15	21	51	10
19. Would try to abolish out-of-date class differences	79	54	4	17
20. Would make the country more prosperous	62	8	30	76
21. Not too far to the left or right in politics	39	10	29	38
22. Too much tied to one class or group	19	70	79	21
23. Has no clear policy	3	39	37	9
24. Would know how to run the country well	79	11	18	89
25. Fair treatment for all races and creeds	79	59	30	76
N =	72	106		

The principal components analysis

   While providing some insight into the distribution of opinions, these percentages do not reveal the underlying structure of

APPENDIX B

political attitudes. Clarification at that level was sought by means of a series of three principal components analyses (one for each party) on the whole sample endorsements. Such an analysis yields evidence about the inter-relationships between a set of responses given by a group of people, and it suggests the principles on which the correlations may have been based. The separate components which emerge from the analysis (first, second, third, etc.), indicate the distinctive areas of judgement which may be involved in an attitude field and their relative importance. Similarly the relative importance of each item in any component can be gauged from the numerical value of its 'loading' on it. It should be pointed out, however, that the results obtained by this method are sometimes open to more than one interpretation, and that they are affected by the original choice of items for inclusion in the analysis.

In preparing the data for analysis, the responses of sample members were recorded simply as 'Yes–does apply', or not–i.e. any uncertain replies were treated as negative. The correlation matrix was analysed into its principal components according to a method recommended by Thomson,[2] and although ten were obtained, only the first three components were consulted in the process of item selection. Many of the loadings on these components were negative, and, in order to reduce their number, a method of rotation prescribed by Thomson was followed. This required a plotting out of the factor loadings, two at a time, and a re-drawing of axes so as to eliminate as many negative loadings in the re-calculated components as possible. Thus, the first and second components were rotated against each other, and the newly obtained second component was rotated against the third original one. The outcome was a rotated first component (I') ,a twice-rotated second one (II''), and a rotated third component (III'). The full results of the application of these procedures are set out in Table B.3, which lists the loadings on each item for both the unrotated and rotated components–although the interpretation presented below relates only to the latter.

[2] Thomson, G. H., *The Factorial Analysis of Human Ability*, Houghton-Mifflin, Boston, 1948.

Table B.3. RESULTS OF PRINCIPAL COMPONENTS ANALYSIS OF PARTY ATTITUDE ENDORSEMENTS
(SECOND EXPLORATORY SURVEY, APRIL 1964)

(a) *Attitudes to the Labour Party*

	Unrotated loadings			Rotated loadings		
	First Component (I)	Second Component (II)	Third Component (III)	First Component (I')	Second Component (II'')	Third Component (III')
1. Talks too much	·568	·138	−·068	−·067	·581	·055
2. Would get the economy moving	·747	·201	−·145	·492	−·612	·048
3. Just criticizes the others–has no positive policy	−·629	·141	−·218	·015	·679	·045
4. Out for the nation as a whole	·609	·322	·301	·214	·570	·440
5. Unsound in handling the country's finances	−·675	·352	−·014	−·007	·719	·248
6. Would improve relations between workers and management in industry	·582	·078	−·193	·389	·475	−·074
7. Out to raise the standard of living for the ordinary man in the street	·488	·294	·330	·134	·471	·440
8. Has a good team of leaders	·542	·227	−·159	·445	−·411	·059
9. Would keep prices down	·675	·199	−·015	·375	−·580	·136
10. Would get things done in a forthright way	·691	·359	−·045	·503	−·548	·232

	I	II	III	IV	V	VI
11. Too much for controls	− ·592	·228	·288	− ·262	− ·533	·363
12. Has a good set of aims and policies	·642	·372	− ·198	·600	− ·459	·138
13. Don't keep to their promises	− ·444	·360	− ·362	·320	·596	·018
14. Cannot plan for the country's future	− ·550	·330	− ·048	·053	·608	·216
15. They have a bad past record	− ·610	·320	·002	− ·015	647	·236
16. Would weaken Britain's voice in world affairs	− ·698	·244	·021	− 107	·706	·193
17. Is disunited and badly organized	− ·458	·357	− ·405	·342	·620	− ·013
18. Would be too free with public money	− ·555	·384	− ·056	·085	·626	·243
19. Would try to abolish out-of-date class differences	·288	·439	·486	·157	− ·248	·652
20. Would make the country more prosperous	·647	·301	− ·322	·641	− ·449	·002
21. Not too far to the left or the right in politics	·350	·238	− ·148	·377	− ·231	·074
22. Too much tied to one class or group	− ·596	·339	·285	− ·232	− ·550	·443
23. Has no clear policy	− ·469	·349	− ·055	·093	·536	·219
24. Would know how to run the country well	·793	·174	− ·156	·498	− ·659	·022
25. Fair treatment for all races and creeds	·387	·446	·300	·215	− ·333	·531
Mean variance	34·1%	9·1%	5·3%	10·7%	30·5%	7·3%

Table B. 3 (*continued*)

RESULTS OF PRINCIPAL COMPONENTS ANALYSIS OF PARTY ATTITUDE ENDORSEMENTS
(SECOND EXPLORATORY SURVEY, APRIL 1964)

(b) Attitudes to the Conservative Party	Unrotated loadings			Rotated loadings		
	First Component (I)	Second Component (II)	Third Component (III)	First Component (I')	Second Component (II'')	Third Component (III')
1. Talks too much	−·412	·267	·358	−·306	·054	·521
2. Would get the economy moving	·733	·149	·009	·734	·125	−·079
3. Just criticizes the others—has no positive policy	−·445	·374	−·068	−·407	·359	·220
4. Out for the nation as a whole	·763	·086	−·032	·748	·091	−·150
5. Unsound in handling the country's finances	−·636	·187	·150	−·573	·084	·353
6. Would improve relations between workers and management in industry	·511	·319	·174	·566	·190	·193
7. Out to raise the standard of living for the ordinary man in the street	·699	·147	−·098	·680	·177	·163
8. Has a good team of leaders	·613	·098	·278	·660	−·060	·146
9. Would keep prices down	·564	·251	·122	·501	·158	·102

10. Would get things done in a forthright way	·680	·311	·089	·714	·226	·079
11. Too much for controls	−·295	·339	·381	−·180	·105	·551
12. Has a good set of aims and policies	·711	·305	·058	·737	·236	·042
13. Don't keep to their promises	−·495	·164	·366	−·397	·040	·497
14. Cannot plan for the country's future	−·406	·498	−·144	−·370	·503	·207
15. They have a bad past record	−·642	·333	−·229	−·634	·403	−·106
16. Would weaken Britain's voice in world affairs	−·456	·240	−·016	−·422	·216	·201
17. Is disunited and badly organized	−·466	·496	−·245	−·448	·553	·133
18. Would be too free with public money	−·426	·209	·531	−·294	·083	·644
19. Would try to abolish out-of-date class differences	·254	·260	·226	·318	·114	·262
20. Would make the country more prosperous	·771	·153	−·126	·746	·196	·199
21. Not too far to the left or the right in politics	·362	·284	−·281	·331	·385	·178
22. Too much tied to one class or group	·607	·190	−·007	·612	·168	−·045
23. Has no clear policy	·455	·460	−·478	·404	·636	·280
24. Would know how to run the country well	·806	·185	−·025	·802	·173	−·106
25. Fair treatment for all races and creeds	·612	·396	·002	·640	·343	·061
Mean Variance	33·2%	8·1%	5·5%	31·5%	7·7%	7·6%

RESULTS OF PRINCIPAL COMPONENTS ANALYSIS OF PARTY ATTITUDE ENDORSEMENTS
(SECOND EXPLORATORY SURVEY, APRIL 1964)

(c) Attitudes to the Liberal Party	Unrotated loadings			Rotated loadings		
	First Component	Second Component	Third Component	First Component	Second Component	Third Component
1. Talks too much	−·159	·215	·175	·048	·079	·305
2. Would get the economy moving	·644	·009	·034	·582	−·229	−·159
3. Just criticizes the others—has no positive policy	−·200	·651	·012	·108	·509	·439
4. Out for the nation as a whole	·608	·193	−·269	·631	−·108	−·263
5. Unsound in handling the country's finances	−·224	·616	−·131	·070	·573	·337
6. Would improve relations between workers and management in industry	·590	·205	−·135	·620	−·033	−·152
7. Out to raise the standard of living for the ordinary man in the street	·597	·361	−·167	·695	−·156	−·083
8. Has a good team of leaders	·507	−·030	·349	·442	·419	·093
9. Would keep prices down	·658	−·034	·080	·576	−·292	−·154
10. Would get things done in a forthright way	·706	·079	·103	·669	−·248	−·083

11. Too much for controls	·029	·474	·522	·235	−·041	·664
12. Has a good set of aims and policies	·682	·136	−·033	·672	−·111	−·144
13. Don't keep to their promises	·159	·278	·114	−·020	·162	·299
14. Cannot plan for the country's future	−·310	·476	−·203	−·068	·555	·225
15. They have a bad past record	·094	·346	·506	·068	−·077	·611
16. Would weaken Britain's voice in world affairs	−·111	·620	·272	·173	·632	·201
17. Disunited and badly organized	−·240	·586	−·080	−·043	·524	·362
18. Would be too free with public money	−·096	·508	·344	·138	·141	·588
19. Would try to abolish out-of-date class differences	·530	·317	·152	·616	·138	−·080
20. Would make the country more prosperous	·728	·036	·227	·669	−·366	−·024
21. Not too far to the left or the right in politics	·244	·316	·483	·358	·452	·243
22. Too much tied to one class or group	−·142	·498	·564	·092	·004	·760
23. Has no clear policy	−·359	·524	·130	−·091	·555	·322
24. Would know how to run the country well	·744	−·103	·248	·623	−·478	−·095
25. Fair treatment for all races and creeds	·509	·518	·213	·685	·322	·002
Mean Variance	21·2%	14·9%	7·4%	20·0%	12·2%	11·3%

APPENDIX B

Interpretation of the components analysis

First Component (I'). This component brings together high loadings on a group of favourable items for each of the parties concerned in the analysis. An interesting clue to its probable meaning emerges when we pick out those items which were most highly loaded in the case of the Labour Party. They were: would make the country more prosperous; has a good set of aims and policies; would get things done in a forthright way; would know how to run the country well; would get the economy moving; and has a good team of leaders. These statements seem to express a pragmatic emphasis on the provision of competent and efficient government – and especially on the effective management of the nation's economy – as distinct from the social principles with which Labour had traditionally been identified. In addition to the above-mentioned statements, the group of highly loaded items in the Conservative case included: out for the nation as a whole; out to raise the standard of living for the ordinary man in the street; and fair treatment for all races and creeds. The Liberal group of highly loaded items added the following to those which were applied to Labour: out to raise the standard of living for the ordinary man in the street; fair treatment for all races and creeds; would try to abolish out-of-date class differences; and would improve relations between workers and management.

Second Component (II''). This component associates a number of critical items with each of the parties. The most highly loaded items on this component for Labour ranged widely and included such statements as: unsound in handling the country's finances; would weaken Britain's voice in world affairs; just criticizes the others – has no positive policy; they have a bad past record; would be too free with public money; is disunited and badly organized; etc. A similar range of items is highly loaded on this component for the Liberal Party. In the case of the Conservatives, however, the most highly loaded items seemed more selective. They included the following statements: has no clear policy; is disunited and badly organized; cannot plan for the country's future; and they have a bad past record. These are criticisms which might have seemed particularly appropriate to a party which had been long in office and was perceived as passing through an organizational crisis.

Third component (III'). The smaller number of items, which were highly loaded on this component, were again mainly critical, when the Conservative and Liberal Parties were analysed, but it was difficult to find a common core of meaning behind the individual statements. For Labour, however, the items which belonged to the third component seemed to relate in some way to themes of class and equality. The most highly loaded statements were: would try to abolish out-of-date class differences; fair treatment for all races and creeds; too much tied to one class or group; out to raise the standard of living for the ordinary man in the street; and out for the nation as a whole.

The choice of items for inclusion in the attitude scale

The final choice of items was not dominated by any single consideration, but was guided by the following criteria:

1. They should represent at least the first two components.
2. They should be applicable to all three parties.
3. For ease of administration the number of items should not exceed ten.
4. There should be an approximate balance between favourable and critical items.
5. The items as a whole should cover a fairly wide range of specific meanings, and duplication of meaning should be avoided.
6. Very generally worded items should not be included.

In order to apply the first criterion, the 25 original items were listed according to their relative importance (taking all three parties into account) for the first and second components, respectively. First, separate tables were prepared on each component for each party—in which the items were listed in an order which proceeded from high positive loadings through to high negative loadings. Then composite tables were prepared (one for each component) in which the party results were merged. This involved adding together the rank order position which each item had received in the three previous tables for the component concerned. (If, for example, a particular item had the highest loading on the first component for all three parties, it would score three, and if it had the lowest for each party– i.e. it was placed 25th–it would score 75.) By this procedure the first ten items which emerged in each case were as follows:

First component: 20; 12; 24; 10; 2; 4; 25; 7; 8; 6.
Second component: 16; 17; 14; 3; 23; 15; 5; 2; 18; 13.

No item was eligible for inclusion in the final attitude scale if it did not appear on one of these lists. Position in the order also counted, but this was weighed against the other criteria outlined above. For example, similarity of meaning compelled us to choose between item 20 (would make the country more prosperous) and item 2 (would get the economy moving), and the latter was selected, partly because it was expected to be prominent in the election campaign. Another similar pair of eligible statements comprised items 24 (would know how to run the country well) and 10 (would get things done in a forthright way), and this was settled in favour of the former. The wording of item 23 (has no clear policy) seemed preferable to that of item 3 (just criticizes the others–has no positive policy). The inclusion of items 4, 7, 8, 13, and 16 helped to satisfy our fifth criterion of choice (see above). The attitude scale was composed, then, of the following items:

2. Would get the economy moving.
4. Out for the nation as a whole.
7. Out to raise the standard of living of the ordinary man in the street.
8. Has a good team of leaders.
13. Don't keep to their promises.
16. Would weaken Britain's voice in world affairs.
17. Is disunited and badly organized.
23. Has no clear policy.
24. Would know how to run the country well.

Four of these nine items (4, 7, 13, and 23) had also formed part of the party attitude scale used in the 1959 study.

APPENDIX C

CONSTRUCTION OF INDICES
OF EXPOSURE

This study made use of a number of indices of exposure to different sources of information and persuasion during the election campaign. The method involved weighting the degree to which respondents were open to possible influence. In addition, an index of their customary usage of television generally was prepared.

1. *Weight of viewing*

This index applied only to the owners of television sets and was based on a combination of their answers to two questions.

		No. of nights per week devoted to viewing			
		Less than 1	*1–2*	*3–4*	*Most*
Average number of hours of viewing when set is in use	— 1	L	L	L	L
	1 +	L	L	L	M
	2 +	L	L	M	M
	3 +	L	L	M	H
	4 +	L	L	M	H
	5 +	L	L	H	H

APPENDIX C

One requested an estimate of the number of nights per week during which they watched anything on television (the replies to which were coded as follows: most, three or four, one or two, and less than one). The other sought an estimate of the number of hours they viewed on an average evening when the set was in use (with answers coded as follows: under an hour, one hour or more, two hours or more, three hours or more, four hours or more, and five hours or more). The lines of demarcation which were drawn to distinguish the 'light', 'medium', and 'heavy' viewers in the sample are shown in the table on page 329.

2. *Viewing of party election broadcasts*

Respondents were asked which of the 13 broadcasts they had seen, and they were reminded of the content of each one. A score of one was given for each broadcast seen, so the scoring range was 0–13.

3. *Exposure to television news*

Respondents were asked how often they had watched (*a*) the main evening news during the campaign, and (*b*) the special late election news programmes (*Election News Extra* on BBC and *Election '64* on ITV). A composite score (with a range of 0–9) was then compiled on the following basis:

	Number of times seen per week	Score
MAIN NEWS	1–2	1
	3–4	2
	Most	3
LATE NIGHT ELECTION NEWS	1–2	2
	3–4	4
	Most	6

4. *Viewing of other political programmes on television*

A total score for seeing other programmes which contained material about the election was given to each respondent. Its range of 0–14 was made up as follows:

APPENDIX C

	Number of times seen	Score
THIS WEEK	1	1
	2	2
	3	3
ELECTION GALLERY	One to three	2
	Four or more	4
QUESTION TIME	1	1
	2	2
	3	3
ELECTION MARATHON	1	1
	2	2
	Three or more	3
LOOK NORTH	Regularly	1

5. *Listening to political programmes on the radio*

A total score for listening to radio programmes which contained material about the election was given to each respondent. Its range of 0–12 was made up as follows:

	Number of times heard	Score
PARTY ELECTION BROADCASTS	1–2	2
	About 4–5	4
	Most	5
MAIN EVENING NEWS	Occasionally	1
	2–3 per week	2
	Regularly	3
LATE ELECTION NEWS	Occasionally	1
	2–3 per week	2
	Regularly	3
QUESTION TIME	Heard any	1

6. *Newspaper reading of election news*

The respondents were asked if they had read reports of election speeches in a newspaper, and how often, and how much of the reports they had read. The constituents of this score (the range of which was 0–5) were:

APPENDIX C

FOR READING REPORTS

Only occasionally	1
About 2 or 3 times per week	3
Fairly regularly	3

FOR AMOUNTS OF THE REPORTS READ

Just a little	–
About half	1
Nearly all	2

7. *Participation in the local campaign*

The respondents were asked about the extent to which they had been canvassed, had seen local candidates, had heard them speak at a meeting, had read their electoral addresses, and could recall their names. The scoring range of 0–5 was made up as follows:

	Score
Talked to a canvasser	1
Saw any local candidate	1
Correctly named one candidate	1
Heard a local candidate speak at at a meeting	1
Read an electoral address	1

8. *Special indices for leader appearances on television*

It is normally very difficult to distinguish material about a political leader in any medium from material about his party. There seemed to be two exceptions, however, in the television campaign of 1964: the BBC's *Election Forums*, each of which had been devoted to a single party leader (20 minutes for Mr. Grimond and 30 minutes each for Sir Alec Douglas-Home and Mr. Wilson); and those party broadcasts in which the leaders themselves addressed the electorate (occupying a part or the whole of the programme concerned, as the case might be).

An attempt was made to take these appearances into account when assessing the influence of exposure to the campaign on the changing public images of the three party leaders. For

APPENDIX C

Election Forum a seen/not seen distinction applied to a particular leader's edition, but a total score was also given to each respondent according to the number of these programmes that he had seen (range: 0–3). In scoring for exposure to a leader in party broadcasts, account was taken of the total amount of time devoted to his appearances in those programmes in which he figured. Scoring details follow:

		Score
MR. WILSON	*Range 0–5*	
	Seen September 28, 1964	2
	Seen September 12, 1964	3
SIR ALEC DOUGLAS-HOME	*Range 0–4*	
	Seen September 26th, 1964	1
	Seen September 13, 1964	3
MR. GRIMOND	*Range 0–3*	
	Seen September 10, 1964	3

Appendix D. A Comparison of Three Different Measures of Strength of Motivation for Following Election Television

	June ratio scores			September ratio scores			Reactions to Sept.* broadcast		
	Strong	Medium	Weak	Strong	Medium	Weak	Strong	Medium	Weak
	%	%	%	%	%	%	%	%	%
I. Q.: Would you like to see less, more, or about the same time given to politics on TV as there is now?									
More	21	8	6	17	12	7	21	13	9
Same	61	56	34	56	57	38	58	65	47
Less	14	24	41	19	19	36	17	15	29
Don't know	4	13	20	7	12	19	4	7	15
	100	101	101	99	100	100	100	100	100
II. Reactions to simultaneous transmission of party broadcasts on all channels.									
Like	51	31	17	42	31	25	41	39	34
Dislike	36	51	62	43	50	54	42	46	49
Don't know	12	17	21	14	19	21	17	14	17
	99	99	100	99	100	100	100	99	100
III. Intentions (June 1964) to view party broadcasts during the campaign.									
Definitely will	74	53	25	69	47	28	80	67	44
Might	24	39	50	27	47	47	17	27	44
Definitely will not	2	8	22	4	5	22	2	4	12
Don't know	–	–	3	1	–	2	1	1	1
	100	100	100	101	99	99	100	99	101
IV. Q.: Do you care who wins the election a great deal, somewhat, or not very much?									
Great deal	67	60	39	66	51	45	74	62	51
Somewhat	20	20	27	19	27	24	16	25	23
Not very much	11	20	34	14	20	30	10	11	25
Don't know	1	–	1	–	2	–	–	1	1
	100	100	101	99	100	99	100	99	101

	C1	C2	C3	C4	C5	C6	C7	C8	C9
V. Opinions about the amount of attention deserved by campaigning politicians.									
A lot	40	27	17	37	29	19	45	34	24
Some	40	30	29	34	35	29	28	35	35
A little/none	20	38	46	26	29	46	23	30	36
Don't know	–	5	8	3	6	6	3	1	5
	100	100	101	99	100	99	100	99	100
VI. Number of party election broadcasts seen during the campaign.									
8–13	32	20	16	32	18	15	41	34	18
5–7	29	31	20	31	32	17	32	25	26
1–4	22	33	35	23	35	35	17	30	31
None	17	15	29	14	15	33	10	11	24
	100	99	100	100	99	100	99	100	100
VII. Reactions (Oct. 1964) to TV coverage of the campaign.									
About right or too few programmes	53	38	27	46	17	52	55	38	37
Too many programmes	46	56	70	50	78	47	41	60	60
Don't know	1	6	4	4	6	2	3	1	4
	100	100	101	100	101	101	99	99	101

* See Chapter 7 (and particularly Tables 7.1 and 7.2) for details about how viewers were classified according to these different measures of motivation.

CONTENT ANALYSIS OF ISSUES DISCUSSED IN PARTY ELECTION BROADCASTS ON TELEVISION

In preparing the figures set out in the tables below, the number of lines devoted in the party broadcast transcripts to each issue was calculated as a percentage of the total number of lines of verbal speech found in the scripts. They do not add up to 100 per cent because (a) certain lines were not classifiable in terms of issue categories and (b) other lines were classified under more than one issue category.

The content categories were derived from the list of 16 issues which sample members had been asked to endorse in the pre-campaign and post-election interviewing rounds. But the analysis also takes account of material which was devoted to issues not mentioned in that list (e.g. regional development, and the costing of rival party programmes). The latter are marked with an asterisk in the tables.

Labour Party Election Broadcasts	%
Economic growth and stability	15·7
Housing and rents	14·1
Education	9·5
Pensions	8·7
Cost of living*	5·9
Nuclear deterrent	5·9
Standard of living	5·9
Regional development*	4·4
Full employment	4·2
Costing of rival party programmes*	3·0

APPENDIX E

Labour Party Election Broadcasts (continued)

	%
Incomes policy	2·8
Immigration and race relations*	2·2
Automation and the scientific age	1·5
Industrial modernization	1·3
Britain's standing in the world	1·3
Health and hospital services	1·0
Road and traffic problems	0·6
Other transport*	0·5
Nationalization	–
Government restrictions	–
Unemployment and sickness benefits	–

N = 862·5 lines, 177·5 of which did not refer to issue themes.

Conservative Party Election Broadcasts

	%
Standard of living	14·5
Nationalization	13·0
Housing and rents	12·7
Nuclear deterrent	12·4
Regional development*	9·0
Economic growth and stability	8·3
Education	8·1
Britain's standing in the world	8·0
Pensions	6·6
Government restrictions	6·3
Industrial modernization	5·4
Costing of rival party programmes*	2·1
Aid to developing countries*	2·1
Full employment	1·8
Road and traffic problems	1·6
Cost of living*	1·6
Automation and the scientific age	1·5
Health and hospital services	0·7
Agricultural conditions*	0·6
Unemployment and sickness benefits	0·3
Incomes policy	0·3

N = 791·5 lines, 55 of which did not refer to issue themes.

APPENDIX E

Liberal Party Election Broadcasts   %

The point of voting Liberal*
(not a wasted vote, need for more Liberal MPs,
need for Liberal-minded electors to vote for their
convictions, etc.)   32·5
Pensions   13·7
Regional development*   8·7
Industrial modernization   8·0
Education   7·8
Costing of rival party programmes*   6·4
Housing and rents   5·5
Economic growth and stability   3·5
Nationalization   1·2
Cost of living*   1·2
Road and traffic problems   1·1
Incomes policy   0·9
Other transport*   0·9
Unemployment and sickness benefits   0·8
Full employment   0·6
Aid to developing countries*   0·5
Nuclear deterrent   0·4
Standard of living   0·4
Agricultural conditions*   0·3
Britain's standing in the world   –
Automation and the scientific age   –
Health and hospital services   –
Government restrictions   –

N = 564 lines, 77·5 of which did not refer to issue themes.

338

APPENDIX F

QUESTIONNAIRES FOR THE MAIN SURVEY

---

1. Initial Round–June 1964

1. (*a*) Do you read any daily newspapers regularly?   Yes
By regularly I mean about three out of every   No
four issues.

    (*b*) If so, which ones?

Bradford Telegraph and Argus
Daily Express
Daily Herald
Daily Mail
Daily Mirror
Daily Sketch
Daily Telegraph
Daily Worker
The Guardian
The Times
Yorkshire Post
Yorkshire Evening Post
Others (write in)

2. Have you a radio set?   Yes
    No

3. (*a*) Have you a television set in your home?   Yes
    No

(IF INFORMANT ONLY HAS RADIO,
PROCEED TO QUESTION 5. IF HE
HAS NEITHER RADIO NOR TELE-
VISION, PROCEED TO QUESTION 8.)

APPENDIX F

(b) Would you say that, in general, you watch ITV more often than BBC, BBC more often than ITV, or both equally?

> ITV-inclined
> Both equally
> BBC-inclined

(c) Roughly how many nights a week do you watch anything on television?

> Most
> 3 or 4
> 1 or 2
> Less than 1

(d) And roughly how long, on the average, do you watch when your television set is on in the evenings?

> Under an hour
> 1 +
> 2 +
> 3 +
> 4 +
> 5 +

4. (a) Now I want to ask you a few questions about the coverage of politics on television. Would you like to see less, more, or about the same time given to politics on television as there is now?

> Less
> Same
> More
> Don't know

(b) Why do you say that?

(c) It has been suggested recently that the proceedings of Parliament should be televised, although some people don't like the idea very much. What do you think? Do you like this idea very much, like it somewhat, or doesn't it matter to you one way or the other?

> Very much
> Somewhat
> Indifferent
> Don't know

(d) Why do you say that?

5. (a) From time to time party political broadcasts are put out on television and radio. I should like to know who you feel they are mainly aimed at. Would you say that they are, or are not, meant for you and people like yourself?

> Meant for me
> Only sometimes
> Not meant for me
> Don't know

(b) (IF 'NOT MEANT FOR ME') Who would you say they are meant for?

340

APPENDIX F

6. (ONLY FOR THOSE WITH TV). | Like
And when party political broadcasts | Dislike
are televised, they go out on both BBC | Don't know
and ITV at the same time. Do you like
or dislike that arrangement?

7. (*a*) Have you ever seen a party political | Yes
broadcast on television or heard one | No
on the radio? | Don't know
(PUT QUESTION 7(*b*) TO THOSE
WHO SAY 'YES'. PUT QUESTION
7(*c*) BELOW TO EVERYONE.)

(*b*) Here is a list of statements that different
people have made when asked why
they watch party political broadcasts.
(HAND CARD A TO INFOR-
MANT.) Please look them through.
Now just give me the numbers of any
reasons which have ever applied to
you when you watched party political
broadcasts.
1. To use as ammunition in arguments with others
2. To judge what political leaders are like
3. To see what some party would do if it got into power
4. To help make up my mind how to vote in an election
5. To remind me of my party's strong points
6. To judge who is likely to win an election
7. To keep up with the main issues of the day
8. To enjoy the excitement of an election race
(PUT TO ALL)

(*c*) And here is a list of reasons that
different people have given for avoiding party political broadcasts. (HAND
CARD B TO INFORMANT.)
Please look them through. Now just
give me the numbers of any reasons
for not watching party political broadcasts that have ever applied to you.

341

1. Because I am not much interested in politics
2. Because I prefer to relax when watching television
3. Because you can't always trust what politicians tell you on television
4. Because some speakers talk down to the audience
5. Because my mind was already made up
6. Because some speakers talk over one's head
7. Because politics should not intrude into the home and family affairs
8. Because they hardly ever have anything new to say
9. Because I dislike being 'got at' by politicians

8. (a) In deciding how to vote in a General Election how much attention, if any, should a person pay to the arguments that are put forward by the politicians who speak up for the main political parties? ... Why do you say that? ... Would you say any more about that?

(b) Summing it up then: Would you say that a voter should normally pay a a lot, some, a little, or no attention to the arguments of campaigning politicians?

A lot
Some
A little
None
Don't know

9. (a) As you know, a General Election will be held sometime this autumn. Do you care who wins the election a great deal, somewhat, or not very much?

Great deal
Somewhat
Not much
Don't know

(b) When the campaign starts, do you think you will probably be very interested, somewhat interested, or not much interested in following it?

Very
Somewhat
Not much
Don't know

(c) (ONLY FOR THOSE WITH TV AND/OR RADIO)
Do you think that you will definitely watch, might watch, or will definitely *not* watch any party political broadcasts on television (IF ONLY HAS RADIO: Listen to any on radio) during the campaign?

Definitely will
Might
Definitely not
Don't know

APPENDIX F

10. Different people notice different things about the politicians who take part in an election campaign. Here is a list of some of the things that a person following a campaign might be aware of. (HAND CARD C TO INFORMANT.) Please look them through and give me the letters of the two things you notice most often about the politicians taking part in an election campaign ... And which of *those* do you notice most often?

   (*a*) The opinions which politicians express on current issues
   (*b*) The principles which politicians say that they stand for
   (*c*) The promises which politicians make
   (*d*) The personalities of politicians
   (*e*) Don't know

11. (*a*) During an election campaign politicians often make pledges and promises. Do you ever feel that they cannot be relied on to be kept?

   Yes
   No
   Don't know

   (*b*) (IF YES.) Do you feel that way usually, occasionally, or rarely?

   Usually
   Occasionally
   Rarely

12. (*a*) In addition, politicians often quote various facts and figures during an election. Do you ever think that they might be misleading?

   Yes
   No
   Don't know

   (*b*) (IF YES.) Do you feel that way usually, occasionally, or rarely?

   Usually
   Occasionally
   Rarely

13. And thinking now of the attacks which politicians make on the opposing party and its policies, do you find that you usually object, occasionally object, or rarely object to such attacks?

   Usually
   Occasionally
   Rarely
   Don't know

14. Next I want to ask you some questions about political *news*. The newspapers, radio, and television all provide news about political affairs. In your opinion

343

APPENDIX F

which of them – newspapers, radio, or television – are best for the following things:

(a)	For giving you the most *up-to-date* news about political events?	Newspapers Radio Television Don't know
(b)	For providing the most *impartial* treatment of political issues?	Newspapers Radio Television Don't know
(c)	For giving the *most full account* of some political event?	Newspapers Radio Television Don't know
(d)	For being the most *trustworthy* source of news?	Newspapers Radio Television Don't know
(e)	For helping you to understand political issues best?	Newspapers Radio Television Don't know
(f)	For helping you to weigh up the qualities of our political leaders best?	Newspapers Radio Television Don't know

15. If you wanted to weigh up the qualities of some political leader who was appearing on television, which of the following kinds of programme do you feel would help you most? (READ OUT LIST BELOW) ... And which next?

His delivery of a *talk*
His being *interviewed* by a reporter
like Robin Day or Ian Trethowan
A *debate* between him and a political opponent
Don't know

16. Suppose that a television debate was arranged between Alec Douglas-

Definitely
would

Home, Harold Wilson, and Jo Grimond during the forthcoming campaign. Do you think that you would definitely try to watch it, might watch it, or would definitely *not* try to watch it?

Might
Definitely not
Don't know

17. Now I want to find out what you think television is able to show us about politicians. Here is a list of qualities that television might bring out in a politician. (HAND CARD D TO INFORMANT.) Please look them through. Now at the bottom of the card you will find an unfinished sentence. Please complete it by choosing the three qualities from the list that television is most able to reveal. Television is most able to show us whether a politician is ————, ————, and ————.

Persuasive
Strong
Likeable
Inspiring
Kindly
Confident
Able
Sincere
Unassuming
Fair-minded
Hard-working
Straight-forward

18. Now I want you to consider the qualities that a politician needs to have if he is going to help in running the country well. If you will turn over the card you will find the same list of qualities as before but a different sentence at the bottom. Please finish that sentence by choosing the three qualities that it is most important for a politican to have if he is to help in running the country well.
It is most important for a politician who is going to help in running the country to be ————, ———— and ————.

19. Summing it all up: some people say that it is pretty easy to get a true picture of what a politician is like from his appearances on television; but others say that it is difficult to judge a politician by his television appearances. What do you think? Is it usually easy or difficult?

Easy
It depends
Difficult
Don't know

20.   Now I want you to rate the leaders of the three main political parties of this country in terms of certain qualities. Here is an example of the way it is to be done. (SHOW THIS PAGE TO THE INFORMANT.) Suppose that we wanted you to rate Sir Winston Churchill. Then here is the way the scale you would be given would start out.

CHURCHILL

Good   — — — — — — — Bad
Weak   — — — — — — — Strong

Taking the first of these lines, if you felt that Churchill was *very* good, you would mark it this way:

Good   √ — — — — — — Bad

If you thought he was *fairly* good, you would mark it this way

Good   — √ — — — — — Bad

If you thought he was only *slightly* good, you would mark it this way:

Good   — — √ — — — — Bad

If you felt he was neither good nor bad (you felt neutral about him), you would tick the middle space. If you felt he was very bad you would mark the space at the far right, and so on. Now just try the second line above: rate Churchill on the weak/strong scale.

Have you any questions? . . . Now we can do the ratings that we are really interested in. In general it is best to work fairly quickly.

(TURN TO THE NEXT PAGE AND HAND THE QUEST-IONNAIRE TO THE INFORMANT SO THAT HE CAN RATE SIR ALEC DOUGLAS-HOME, HAROLD WILSON, AND JO GRIMOND)

SIR ALEC DOUGLAS-HOME

Persuasive Speaker	— — — — — — —	Unpersuasive Speaker
Weak	— — — — — — —	Strong
Likeable	— — — — — — —	Disagreeable
Inspiring Leader	— — — — — — —	Uninspiring Leader

APPENDIX F

Unsure of Himself	—	—	—	—	—	—	—	Confident
Able	—	—	—	—	—	—	—	Incompetent
Insincere	—	—	—	—	—	—	—	Sincere
Conceited	—	—	—	—	—	—	—	Unassuming
Fair	—	—	—	—	—	—	—	Unfair
Hard-working	—	—	—	—	—	—	—	Lazy
Straight-forward	—	—	—	—	—	—	—	Two-faced
Kindly	—	—	—	—	—	—	—	Inhumane

HAROLD WILSON
(Scales as for Sir Alec Douglas-Home)

JO GRIMOND
(Scales as for Sir Alec Douglas-Home)

21. (a) If the General Election were held to-morrow, which Party would you vote for?

Conservative
Labour
Liberal
Other
Would not vote
Don't know
No answer

(TO ALL EXCEPT NON-VOTERS, 'DON'T KNOW'S', AND 'NO ANSWER'S')

(b) Does this mean that you have definitely made up your mind to vote that way in October?

Yes
No

(TO NON-VOTERS, 'DON'T KNOW'S', AND 'NO ANSWER'S')

(c) Well, which way do you lean?

Conservative
Labour
Liberal
Other
None
Don't know
No answer

347

APPENDIX F

(PUT QUESTION 22 TO ALL CONSERVATIVE, LABOUR, AND LIBERAL SUPPORTERS AND LEANERS WITH TELEVISION OR RADIO. ASK IT ABOUT A PARTY POLITICAL BROAD-CAST OF A PARTY THEY *OPPOSE:* TO CONSERVATIVES AND LIBERALS ABOUT A LABOUR BROADCAST; TO LABOUR SUPPORTERS AND LEANERS ABOUT A CONSERVATIVE BROADCAST)

22. (*a*) You say that you support (lean to) the   Yes
Conservative (Liberal, Labour) Party.   No
Now suppose that a Labour (Con-   Don't know
servative) Party political broadcast
was being put on over television (the
radio) next week. Do you think that
you might watch it (listen to it)?

(*b*) (IF YES.) Now I want to find out why you might
watch a party political broadcast put out by a party
that you do *not* support. Here is a list of reasons that
people have given us for doing that. (HAND CARD
E TO INFORMANT.) Please look them through.
Now tell me which ones explain why you might watch
a Labour (Conservative) Party political broadcast.
Just give me the numbers of any that apply.
1. Would help me decide finally how to vote
2. Would help me see why I disagree with them
3. To learn about some of their good points
4. To find out what they would do if they got in power
5. Because it's only fair to hear both sides
6. Would help me when arguing with people who
support them

23. (*a*) How did you vote in 1959, when   Conservative
Macmillan led the Conservatives,   Labour
Gaitskell the Labour Party, and   Liberal
Grimond the Liberals?   Other
                                 Abstained
                              Under age
                            Don't know
                            No answer

(b) Did you live in this constituency at   Yes
that time or not?   No
                                     Don't know

24. The people of this country are sometimes put into these classes. (HAND CARD F TO INFORMANT.) Which one would you say you belong to?

                           Labouring working class
                               Skilled working class
                               Lower middle class
                               Middle class
                               Upper middle class
                               Don't know

25. Would you mind telling me a few particulars about yourself so that we will know how far we have a fair sample of the people in this area?

(a) Are you married?   Single
                               Married
                               Separated,
                               widowed,
                               or divorced

(b) How old were you at your last   21–29
birthday?   30–44
         (EXACT AGE)........   45–65
                               66 +

(c) How old were you when you left   14 or before
school?   15
                               16
                               17
                               18 or over

(d) What kind of school was that?   Elementary
                          Secondary Modern
                               Grammar
           Public or other private
                      Other (write in)

(e) Did you have any full-time or part-   Yes
time education after leaving school?   No

APPENDIX F

(f) (IF YES.) What was that?

University
Technical College
College of Art
Commercial College
Secretarial College
Teachers' Training College
Other (write in)

(g) What is your occupation?

(h) Sex of informant

Male
Female

2. PRE-CAMPAIGN ROUND–SEPTEMBER 1964

1. First, I want to know whether you saw anything on television on Friday, September 11th, either at home or elsewhere. Here are the programme lists for that evening. (SHOW *RADIO TIMES* AND *TV TIMES* TO INFORMANTS.) I am interested only in the programmes between about 8.00 and 10.30 p.m.

   (GO THROUGH THE LISTS WITH THE IN-FORMANT, ASKING IF HE SAW *ANY PART* OF EACH PROGRAMME AND CIRCLING THE APPROPRIATE CODES)

   Stage Coach West
   ITV News
   Horn Meets Blues
   A World of His Own–Roy Kinnear
   BBC News
   Labour Party Broadcast
   It's a Woman's World–Laura
   Saints and Sinners

2. (TO THOSE WHO *SAW* THE LABOUR PARTY BROADCAST)

   Thinking of the Labour Party political broadcast, how did it come about that you watched that programme? ... Did anything else encourage you to watch it? ... Anything else?

350

APPENDIX F

3. (TO THOSE WHO *DID NOT SEE* THE LABOUR PARTY BROADCAST)

  (*a*) Thinking of the Labour Party political broadcast, why didn't you watch that programme? ... Were there any other reasons?

  (*b*) Did you mind not watching it? ... Why was that? (IF INFORMANT DID NOT SEE BROADCAST BECAUSE HAD NO TV JUST WRITE THIS IN UNDER 3(*a*) AND PROCEED TO QUESTION 4)

4. Here on this card are some questions that matter to everybody. Please read them through and tell me which *five* questions are the most important for the next government to tackle.

(HAND CARD I TO INFORMANT AND RING CODES BESIDE ISSUES CHOSEN)

    Raise Britain's standing in the world
    Meet the challenge of automation and the scientific age
    Settle the future of Britain's nuclear deterrent
    Get fast and steady growth of the economy
    Give old people better pensions
    Decide the future of nationalization
    Provide more houses at reasonable prices and fair rents
    Improve the health and hospital services
    Maintain and raise the general standard of living
    Avoid unnecessary government restrictions
    Work out an incomes policy with the unions and employers
    See there is no return of unemployment
    Modernize British industry
    Provide a better education for all children
    Deal with road and traffic problems
    Make a new approach to unemployment and sickness benefits

5. Here are some statements that have been made about the three main political parties. (HAND CARD II TO INFORMANT)

APPENDIX F

(a) As I go through them with you please tell me which in your opinion are true of the .... Party.

(b) Now which are true of the .... Party?

(c) And which are true of the .... Party? (GO THROUGH ENTIRE LIST FOR *EACH* PARTY. ROTATE ORDER OF PARTIES)

Out for the nation as a whole

Out to raise the standard of living for the ordinary man in the street

Is disunited and badly organized

Would weaken Britain's voice in world affairs

Would get the economy moving

Has a good team of leaders

Has no clear policy

Would know how to run the country well

Don't keep to their promises

6. Repeat of Question 20 of initial round questionnaire.

7. Here are some policies that the three main parties have suggested for dealing with the issues of the day. (HAND CARD III TO INFORMANT.) As I go through them with you, please tell me which party— Conservative, Labour, or Liberal—you think has put forward each policy.

1. Which party proposes to keep Britain's independent nuclear deterrent?

2. Which party proposes public ownership of most building land?

3. Which party stresses variety in secondary education and does not insist on abolition of the 11-plus examination?

4. Which party wants to set up elected regional councils with powers to plan and spend for local needs?

5. Which party suggests the setting up of new government Ministries of Economic Affairs and of Overseas Development?

6. Which party recommends compulsory consultation and negotiation between management and workers in large firms?

352

APPENDIX F

7. Which party stands for private ownership of steel and no increase in the state's share of the steel industry?
8. Which party proposes to fix rates according to the value of sites?
9. Which party proposes half pay for the unemployed, the sick, and old people through the state insurance scheme?

8. During the coming General Election campaign, will you:

(a) Find out who all your local candidates are?   Yes
       No
       Don't know

(b) Read their election addresses?   Yes
       No
       Don't know
       Those of the candidate I support

(c) Go to any of their meetings?   Yes
       No
       Don't know

9. (a) Do you think you might watch any party election broadcasts on television or listen to any on the radio during the coming election campaign?   Yes   No   Don't know
(PUT QUESTION 9(b) BELOW TO THOSE WHO SAY 'YES'. PUT QUESTION 9(c) BELOW TO EVERYONE)

(b) Here are some statements that different people have made when asked why they watch (listen to) party election broadcasts. (HAND CARD IV TO INFORMANT.) Please look them through. Now just give me the numbers of any reasons that explain why you might watch (listen to) party election broadcasts during the campaign.
1. To use as ammunition in arguments with others
2. To judge what political leaders are like
3. To see what some party will do if it gets into power

353

4. To help make up my mind how to vote in the election
5. To remind me of my party's strong points
6. To judge who is likely to win the election
7. To keep up with the main issues of the day
8. To enjoy the excitement of the election race

(c) And here are some reasons that different people have given for avoiding party election broadcasts. (HAND CARD V TO INFORMANT.) Please look them through. Now just give me the numbers of any reasons that might occasionally put you off watching party election broadcasts during the campaign.

1. Because I am not much interested in politics
2. Because I prefer to relax when watching television
3. Because you can't always trust what politicians tell you on television
4. Because some speakers talk down to the audience
5. Because my mind is already made up
6. Because some speakers talk over one's head
7. Because politics should not intrude into the home and family affairs
8. Because they hardly ever have anything new to say
9. Because I dislike being 'got at' by politicians

10. (a) If Polling Day were tomorrow, which party would you vote for?

Conservative
Labour
Liberal
Other
Would not vote
Don't know
No answer

(TO ALL EXCEPT NON-VOTERS, 'DON'T KNOW'S, AND 'NO ANSWER'S)

(b) Does this mean that you have definitely made up your mind to vote that way in October?

Yes
No

(TO NON-VOTERS, 'DON'T KNOWS', AND 'NO ANSWER'S')

354

APPENDIX F

(c) Well, which way do you lean?

Conservative
Labour
Liberal
Other
None
Don't know
No answer

3. POST-ELECTION ROUND—OCTOBER 1964

1. Have you seen any television programmes anywhere during the past
four weeks since we last called?
(IF YES, GO ON TO Q.2)
(IF NO, GO ON TO Q.14)

Yes
No

2. (a) We are interested in your impression
of how TV covered the election campaign. First, do you think the amount
of time spent on politics during the
campaign was about right? Or were
there too few or too many political
programmes?

About right
Too few
Too many
Don't know

(b) (IF TOO MANY OR ABOUT RIGHT) Do you
thank that any of these steps should have been taken?
(HAND CARD I TO INFORMANT)

Have less campaign news in the TV news bulletins
Cut down the number of party election broadcasts
Have party election broadcasts on one channel only
Keep special political programmes—like GALLERY
and THIS WEEK—off the air during the campaign

(c) (IF TOO FEW) What exactly did you miss—or
wish there had been more of?

3. (a) Now I want to find out what programmes, if any, you watched during
the campaign. Right at the beginning
of the campaign, the BBC put on three
ELECTION FORUMS in which the
party leaders answered questions sent

Yes
No
Don't know

355

in by viewers. Did you happen to see
any of those programmes?

(IF YES)

(b) Which ones did you see? The one   Grimond
with Grimond? With Wilson? With   Wilson
Sir Alec Douglas-Home?   Home

(c) Do you think that kind of programme   Good idea
was a good idea or a bad idea?   Bad idea
    Don't know

4. (a) Did you happen to see any of the   Yes
television broadcasts put on by the   No
political parties at 9.30 p.m. nearly   Don't know
every evening?

(IF YES OR DON'T KNOW, ASK Q. 4(b))
(IF NO, GO ON TO Q.5)

(b) I have a list of all these party broadcasts here. As I go
through it, please say which ones you remember
seeing.

(READ OUT DETAILS OF PROGRAMMES
FROM YOUR LIST)

5. (a) Did you see any TV news bulletins at   Yes
around 6 or 9 in the evenings during   No
the campaign?

(b) (IF YES.) On roughly how many Most evenings
evenings a week did you watch them? About 3 or
    4 a week
    1 or 2 a week
   Less than 1 a week

6. (a) Special election news programmes   Yes
were broadcast late at night on both   No
channels during the campaign. ITV's
was called ELECTION '64, and
BBC's was called ELECTION NEWS
EXTRA. Did you happen to see any
of those programmes?

(b) (IF YES). Roughly how many nights a week did you see any of them?   Most evenings
About 3 or
4 a week
1 or 2 a week
Less than 1 a week

7. Did you regularly watch the BBC northern news magazine, called LOOK NORTH, at five past six during the campaign?   Yes
No

8. (a) Granada put on an ELECTION MARATHON in which Northern candidates spoke briefly. The programmes were broadcast at 3.00 in the afternoons. Did you happen to see any of them?   Yes
No

(b) (IF YES.) Roughly how many MARATHON programmes did you see?   3 +
2
1

9. (a) On Thursday evenings, THIS WEEK, an ITV programme, covered different election issues. Did you happen to see THIS WEEK at all during the campaign?   Yes
No

(b) (IF YES.) Roughly how many did you see?   3
2
1

10. (a) Did you happen to see any of the six BBC ELECTION GALLERY programmes? In them Robin Day, Ian Trethowan, and Robert McKenzie commented on the campaign at five minutes to seven.   Yes
No

(b) (IF YES.) About how many did you watch?   Most (4 +)
A few (3 −)

11. Is it a good idea or a bad idea for programmes like GALLERY and   Good idea
Bad idea

357

	THIS WEEK to comment on the issues during an election campaign?		Don't know
12.	Would you have liked to see some TV debates between leading figures of the different parties?		Yes No Don't know
13. (a)	Some other BBC programmes at five minutes to 7 were called QUESTION TIME. In them candidates answered questions put by newspapermen. Did you happen to see any?		Yes No
(b)	(IF YES.) Roughly how many did you see?		3 2 1
14.	QUESTION TIME was also broadcast over the radio. Did you happen to hear any of these programmes on the radio? (IF INFORMANT HAS SEEN NO TV, ADAPT Q.13(a))		Yes No
15. (a)	Most evenings there were party election broadcasts on the radio–on the Home Service at ten past ten and on Light at 7.00. Did you hear any of them?		Yes No
(b)	(IF YES). Roughly how many did you hear?		Most of them About 4 or 5 Only 1 or 2
16. (a)	Have you heard any of the full evening news bulletins on sound radio during the campaign (10 o'clock in the Home Service and 7 o'clock in the Light)? (IF YES, ASK (b), (c) AND (d))		Yes No
(b)	Roughly how often did you listen to them?		Fairly regularly About 2 or 3 a week Only occasionally

(c) Most evenings there was a round-up of election events after the 10 o'clock news on the Home Service. Did you hear any of them? — Yes / No

(d) (IF YES). Roughly how often did you listen to them? — Fairly regularly / About 2 or 3 a week / Only occasionally

17. (a) Have you been reading the reports of the election speeches in the newspaper–if you happen to take one? — Yes / No
(IF YES, ASK (b) AND (c))

(b) About how often would you have looked at them? — Fairly regularly / About 2 or 3 times a week / Only occasionally

(c) Roughly how much of these election reports have you usually read? — Nearly all / About half / Just a little

18. (a) During the election campaign did any canvassers call at your house? — Yes / No

(b) (IF YES.) Did you have a chance of talking about any political questions with them? — Yes / No

19. Did you discuss the issues of this election with anyone other than a canvasser during the campaign? — Yes / No

20. Did you see any of the local candidates anywhere during the campaign? — Yes / No

21. Do you happen to remember the names of your candidates? — No
(WRITE ALL NAMES GIVEN)

22. (a) Have you heard any of the local candidates speaking? — Yes / No

(b) (IF YES.) Where was that? — Indoor meeting / Open-air meeting / On TV

23.   Have you read any of the election   Yes
       addresses sent round by the local can-   No
       didates?

24.   Now that the election campaign is over, what is your
       final impression of the Labour, Conservative, and
       Liberal Parties?

    (a)   Will you please go through the opinions on this card
       with me (HAND CARD II TO INFORMANT) and
       say which you think are true, first, of the ....
       Party?

    (b)   Now which are true of the .... Party?

    (c)   And which are true of the .... Party?
       (GO THROUGH ENTIRE LIST FOR *EACH*
       PARTY. ROTATE ORDER OF PARTIES)
       Repeat of statements in Question 5 of pre-campaign
       round questionnaire.

25.   Here are the questions that face the politicians in the
       new Government. Would you look them through
       again and say which *five* you think are the most
       important?
       (HAND CARD III TO INFORMANT AND
       RING CODES BESIDE ISSUES CHOSEN)
       Repeat of statements in Question 4 of pre-campaign
       round questionnaire.

26.   Here are some of the policies put forward by the
       parties during the election campaign. (HAND CARD
       IV TO INFORMANT.) As I go through them with
       you, please tell me which party–Conservative,
       Labour, or Liberal–you think put forward each
       policy.
       Repeat of statements 1, 2, 3, 4, 5, and 8, in Question
       7 of pre-campaign round questionnaire.

27.   Repeat of Question 20 of initial round questionnaire.

28.   Compared with most of the people   More
       you know, are you more likely or less   Same
       likely to be asked your views about   Less
       politics?   Don't know

APPENDIX F

29. (a) Did you yourself happen to vote on Polling Day?

Yes
No

(b) (IF YES.) Which party did you yourself vote for?

Conservative
Labour
Liberal

30. Did you find during the election that most of your friends supported the Conservatives, the Labour Party, or the Liberals? Or were they pretty evenly divided?

Conservative
Labour
Liberal
Divided
Don't know

31. (IF EMPLOYED.) How about most of the people you work with? Did you find that they supported the Conservatives, the Labour Party, or the Liberals?

Conservative
Labour
Liberal
Divided
Don't know
Not employed

32. What party did your father support in this election?

Conservative
Labour
Liberal
None
Don't know
Not living

33. (IF MARRIED.) What party did your wife/husband support in this election?

Conservative
Labour
Liberal
None
Don't know
Not married

BIBLIOGRAPHY OF MATERIALS
ON POLITICAL COMMUNICATIONS

Alexander, Herbert E., 'Broadcasting and Politics', Ch. 5 in Jennings, M. Kent, and Ziegler, L. Harmon (Eds.), *The Electoral Process*, Prentice-Hall, Inc., Englewood Cliffs, N.J., 1966.

Becker, Samuel L., 'Broadcasting and Politics in Great Britain', *Quarterly Journal of Speech*, Vol. LIII, No. 1, 1967, pp. 34–43.

Becker, Samuel L., 'Presidential Power: The Influence of Broadcasting', *Quarterly Journal of Speech*, Vol. XLVII, No. 1, 1961, pp. 10–18.

Berelson, Bernard, Lazarsfeld, Paul F. and McPhee, William N., *Voting: A Study of Opinion Formation in a Presidential Campaign*, The University of Chicago Press, Chicago, 1954.

Blumler, Jay G., 'Parliament and Political TV', *Encounter*, March 1967, pp. 52–6.

Blumler, Jay G. and Madge, John, *Citizenship and Television*, PEP Report, Political and Economic Planning, London, 1967.

Butler, D. E., 'Political Television', Seventh Annual Lecture, Research Students' Association, The Australian National University, Canberra, 1967.

Campbell, Angus, Gurin, Gerald, and Miller, Warren E., 'Television and the Election', *Scientific American*, Vol. CLXXXVIII, No. 5, 1953, pp. 46–8.

Carter, Richard F., 'Stereotyping as a Process', *Public Opinion Quarterly*, Vol. XXVI, No. 1, pp. 77–91.

Clausse, Roger, 'Presse, Radio, et Télévision Belges dans la Campagne Électorale de Mars 1961', *Res Publica*, Vol. III, No. 4, 1961, pp. 369–87.

BIBLIOGRAPHY

Clausse, Roger, 'Presse, Radio et Télévision Belges dans la Campagne Électorale de Mai 1965', *Res Publica*, Vol. VIII, No. 1, 1966, pp. 24–66.

Converse, Philip E., 'Information Flow and the Stability of Partisan Attitudes', Ch. 8 in Campbell, Angus, Converse, Philip E., Miller, Warren E., and Stokes, Donald E., *Elections and the Political Order*, John Wiley and Sons, Inc., New York, 1966.

Converse, Philip E., 'The Nature of Belief Systems in Mass Publics', Ch. VI in Apter, David E. (Ed.), *Ideology and Discontent*, The Free Press, Glencoe, Illinois, 1964.

Cranston, Pat, 'Political Convention Broadcasts: Their History and Influence', *Journalism Quarterly*, Vol. XXXVII, No. 2, 1960, pp. 186–94.

Doig, Ivan, 'Kefauver vs. Crime: TV Boosts a Senator', *Journalism Quarterly*, Vol. XXXIX, No. 4, 1962, pp. 483–90.

van Eerde, H. and van Gent, B., 'Politieke televisie in Engeland, 1964', *Communicatie*, No. 6, 1965, pp. 33–51.

'First Report on Constituency Television in a General Election', Granada TV Network, Manchester, 1960.

First Report from the Select Committee on Broadcasting etc. of Proceedings in the House of Commons, Her Majesty's Stationery Office, London, 1966.

Glaser, William A., 'Television and Voting Turnout', *Public Opinion Quarterly*, Vol. XXIX, No. 1, 1965, pp. 71–86.

Greenberg, Bradley S. and Parker, Edwin B. (Eds.), *The Kennedy Assassination and the American Public*, Stanford University Press, Stanford, California, 1965.

Harrison, Martin, 'Television and Radio', Ch. X in Butler, D. E. and King, Anthony, *The British General Election of 1964*, Macmillan and Co., Ltd., 1965.

Harrison, Martin, 'Television and Radio', Ch. VII in Butler, D. E. and King, Anthony, *The British General Election of 1966*, Macmillan and Co., Ltd., 1966.

Hughes, Colin A. and Western, John S., *The Prime Minister's Policy Speech: A Case Study in Televised Politics*, Australian National University Press, Canberra, 1966.

Janowitz, Morris, and Marvick, Dwaine, *Competitive Pressure and Democratic Consent*, Institute of Public Administration, University of Michigan, Ann Arbor, Michigan, 1956.

BIBLIOGRAPHY

Katz, Elihu and Lazarsfeld, Paul F., *Personal Influence: The Part Played by People in the Flow of Mass Communications*, The Free Press, Glencoe, Illinois, 1955.

Kelley, Stanley, Jr., 'Campaign Debates: Some Facts and Issues', *Public Opinion Quarterly*, Vol. XXVI, No. 3, 1962, pp. 329–34.

Kelley, Stanley, Jr., *Political Campaigning: Problems in Creating an Informed Electorate*, The Brookings Institution, Washington, D.C., 1960.

Key, Jr., V. O., *Public Opinion and American Democracy*, Alfred A. Knopf, New York, 1964.

Kraus, Sidney (Ed.), *The Great Debates*, Indiana University Press, Bloomington, Indiana, 1962.

Kraus, Sidney, 'Presidential Debates in 1964', *Quarterly Journal of Speech*, Vol. L., No. 1, 1964, pp. 19–23.

Lang, Gladys Engel and Lang, Kurt, 'The Influential Structure of Political Communications: A Study in Unwitting Bias', *Public Opinion Quarterly*, Vol. XIX, No. 2, 1955, pp. 168–84.

Lang, Kurt and Lang, Gladys Engel, 'The Mass Media and Voting', Ch. 12 in Burdick, Eugene J. and Brodbeck, Anthony J. (Eds.), *American Voting Behavior*, The Free Press, Glencoe, Illinois, 1959.

Lang, Kurt, and Lang, Gladys Engel, 'The Unique Perspective of Television', *American Sociological Review*, Vol. XVIII, No. 1, 1953, pp. 103–12.

Lazarsfeld, Paul F., Berelson, Bernard, and Gaudet, Hazel, *The People's Choice: How the Voter Makes up his Mind in a Presidential Campaign*, Columbia University Press, New York, 1944.

McGrath, Joseph E. and McGrath, Marion F., 'Effects of Partisanship on Perceptions of Political Figures', *Public Opinion Quarterly*, Vol. XXVI, No. 2, 1962, pp. 236–48.

Merton, Robert K., *Mass Persuasion*, Harpers, New York, 1946.

Michelat, Guy, 'Télévision, Moyens d'Information et Comportement Electoral', *Revue Française de Science Politique*, Vol. XIV, No. 5, 1964, pp. 877–905.

Pickles, William, 'Political Attitudes in the Television Age', *Political Quarterly*, Vol. XXX, No. 1, 1959, pp. 54–66.

Pye, Lucian (Ed.), *Communication and Political Development*, Princeton University Press, Princeton, N.J., 1963.

BIBLIOGRAPHY

Remond, Réné, and Neuschwander, Claude, 'Télévision et Comportement Politique', *Revue Française de Science Politique*, Vol. XIII, No. 2, 1963, pp. 325–47.

Rokkan, S., *Readers, Viewers, Voters*, Guildhall Lectures, Granada TV Network, Manchester, 1964.

Roper, Elmo, and Associates, 'The Public's View of Television and Other Media, 1959–1964', Television Information Office, New York, N.Y., 1965.

Rose, Richard, *Influencing Voters: A Study of Campaign Rationality*, Faber and Faber, London, 1967.

Rose, Richard, *Politics in England: An Interpretation*, Faber and Faber, London, 1965, Ch. VIII.

Rose, Richard (Ed.), *Studies in British Politics*, Macmillan, London, 1966, Ch. III.

Roucek, Joseph S., 'The Influence of Television on American Politics', *Il Politico*, Vol. XXVIII, No. 1, 1963, pp. 124–34.

Rubin, Bernard, *Political Television*, Wadsworth Publishing Company, Inc., Belmont, California, 1967.

Salant, Richard S., 'The Television Debates: A Revolution that Deserves a Future', *Public Opinion Quarterly*, Vol. XXVI, No. 3, 1962, pp. 335–50.

Schramm, Wilbur, and Carter, Richard F., 'The Effectiveness of a Political Telethon', *Public Opinion Quarterly*, Vol. XXIII, No. 1, 1959, pp. 121–7.

Sears, David O., and Freedman, Jonathan L., 'Selective Exposure to Information: A Critical Review', *Public Opinion Quarterly*, Vol. XXXI, No. 2, 1967, pp. 194–213.

Sigel, Roberta S., 'Effect of Partisanship on the Perception of Political Candidates', *Public Opinion Quarterly*, Vol. XXVIII, No. 3, 1964, pp. 488–96.

Simon, Herbert A., and Stern, Frederick, 'The Effect of Television upon Voting Behavior in the 1952 Presidential Election', *American Political Science Review*, Vol. IL, No. 2, 1955, pp. 470–7.

Tannenbaum, Percy H., 'What Effect When TV Covers a Congressional Hearing?', *Journalism Quarterly*, Vol. XXXII, No. 3, 1955, pp. 434–40.

'Television and Politics', *Journal of the Society of Film and Television Arts*, No. 19, Spring 1965.

BIBLIOGRAPHY

Thomson, Charles A. H., *Television and Presidential Politics*, The Brookings Institution, Washington, D.C., 1956.

Trenaman, J. and McQuail, Denis, *Television and the Political Image*, Methuen and Co., Ltd., London, 1961.

Trenaman, Joseph, 'La Televisione come Mezzo di Persuasione Politica', *Lo Spettacolo*, Vol. XI, No. 2, 1961, pp. 103–9.

Waltzer, Herbert, 'In the Magic Lantern: Television Coverage of the 1964 National Conventions', *Public Opinion Quarterly*, Vol. XXX, No. 1, 1966, pp. 33–53.

Wiebe, Gerhart D., 'Merchandising Commodities and Citizenship on Television', *Public Opinion Quarterly*, Vol. XV, No. 4, 1951–2, pp. 679–91.

Wiebe, Gerhart D., 'Responses to the Televised Kefauver Hearings: Some Social Psychological Implications', *Public Opinion Quarterly*, Vol. XVI, No. 2, 1952, pp. 179–200.

Lord Windlesham, *Communication and Political Power*, Jonathan Cape, London, 1966.

INDEX OF SOURCES CITED

367

INDEX OF SOURCES CITED

INDEX OF SUBJECTS

369

INDEX OF SUBJECTS

moral test not posed in, 239

perceptions of, 14, 29, 89–92, 107–114, 233, 289, 291 n.

politicians' attacks as feature of, 81, 105, 108

Campaign Report, 41 n., 296 n.

Challenging forms of political TV (*see also* Debates and Interviews):

as antidote to scepticism, 289, 293–5

appeal of, 104–6, 114, 300, 302

need for more, 285, 295

preferences for, by difficulty of judging leaders, 119–20

preferences for, 102, 104

preferred by vote-guidance seekers, 146–7, 288 n.

as substitute for challenge of events, 120–1

Confrontations (*see* Debates)

Conservative Party (*see also* Attitudes to):

broadcasts' style, 42

campaign and inter-election losses compared, 186–7

deterrent policy understood, 159–160

election strategy, 7, 60–1, 157, 172–3

issues stressed by, 170, 172, 212, App. E

national party, rating as, 190–1, 194

supporters' invulnerability to propaganda, 193–4

Constituencies:

choice of, 19–21

voting in, App. A

Credibility (*see* Scepticism)

Critical elections, 279, 281

Crosland, Antony, 297 n., 298

Crossman, R. H. S., 298

Customary TV use:

and campaign exposure, 140–1, 143–4, 165–6

measurement, 46 n., 140, App. C

and media ratings, 45–7

role in information gain, 165–6

and scepticism, 148

and strength of motivation to follow election TV, 141–2, 143–4

Debates on TV (*see also* Kennedy-Nixon debates):

advantages of, 285, 288, 293–5, 302

case for Liberal participation in, 299–300

need to plan, 296–7

objections to examined, 296–303

and reinforcement seekers, 288

reluctance of parties to engage in, 41, 87, 301–2

use in 1966, 41 n.

use in Sweden, 294–5

and vote-guidance seekers, 147, 288

Douglas-Home, Sir Alec (*see also* Attitudes to):

appearance in party broadcasts, 61, 251

attitude to confrontations, 87 n., 301

campaign difficulties of, 258

Economic growth issue:

changes in salience, 170–1

changing salience and campaign exposure, 178–80, 212–13

c. salience and demographic characteristics, 176

c. salience among 'new Liberals', 267 n.

c. salience and occupation, 175–7, 197

c. salience and occupation by vote, 177, 197

c. salience and partisanship of highly motivated, 210–12

c. salience and party attitude change, 173–4

c. salience and vote change, 173

in Labour broadcasts, 172, App. E

role in party conflict, 172–3, 176

Education:

and age, 44–5

and leader qualities valued, 116–117

and media ratings, 44–7

and noticing campaign promises, 111–12

and opinion leadership, 150

and political activity, 292 n.

and reasons for watching party broadcasts, 77–8